OREGON HIKING

OREGON HIKING

The Complete Guide to More Than 280 Hikes

FIRST EDITION

Megan McMorris

AVALON
TRAVEL

FOGHORN OUTDOORS
OREGON HIKING
The Complete Guide to
More Than 280 Hikes

First Edition

Megan McMorris

Text © 2004 by Megan McMorris.
All rights reserved.
Illustrations and maps © 2004
by Avalon Travel Publishing.
All rights reserved.

Avalon Travel Publishing is a division
of Avalon Publishing Group, Inc.

Some photos and illustrations are used by permission
and are the property of the original copyright owners.

ISBN: 1-56691-670-4
ISSN: 1547-2949

Please send all feedback about this book to:

ⒻOGHORN OUTDOORS®
Oregon Hiking
Avalon Travel Publishing
1400 65th Street, Suite 250
Emeryville, CA 94608, USA
atpfeedback@avalonpub.com
www.foghorn.com

Printing History
1st edition—April 2004
5 4 3 2 1

Editor: Marisa Solís
Series Manager: Marisa Solís
Copy Editor: Elizabeth Wolf
Proofreader: Wendy Taylor
Graphics Coordinator: Deb Dutcher
Illustrator: Bob Race
Production Coordinator: Darren Alessi
Cover and Interior Designer: Darren Alessi
Map Editor: Olivia Solís
Cartographers: Kat Kalamaras, Suzanne Service, Mike Morgenfeld
Indexer: Matt Kaye

Front cover photo: Cabin Creek Falls, Mount Defiance/Starvation Ridge Trail,
Columbia River Gorge © David Schiefelbein

Printed in the United States of America by Malloy Inc.

Contents

SPECIAL TOPICS

Emergency Kit 5 • *Leave No Trace 8* • *Can I Hike Through? A Guide to the
Oregon Coast and Pacific Crest Trails 12*

Including:
- Cape Blanco State Park
- Cape Meares State Park
- Cape Perpetua Scenic Area
- Cascade Head Scenic Area
- Ecola State Park
- Fort Stevens State Park
- Hagg Lake
- Kalmiopsis Wilderness

- Oregon Coastal Range
- Oregon Dunes National
  Recreation Area
- Saddle Mountain State
  Natural Area
- Siskiyou National Forest
- Siuslaw National Forest
- Sunset Bay State Park
- Tillamook State Forest

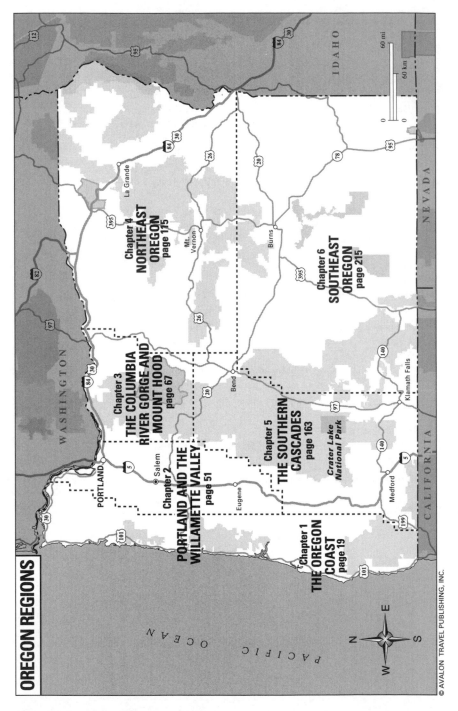

OREGON REGIONS

© AVALON TRAVEL PUBLISHING, INC.

Our Commitment

We are committed to making *Foghorn Outdoors Oregon Hiking* the most accurate, thorough, and enjoyable hiking guide to the state. Every hiking trail in this book has been carefully reviewed and presented with the most up-to-date information. Be aware that with the passing of time some of the fees listed herein may have changed, and trails may have closed unexpectedly. If you have a specific need or concern, it's best to call the location ahead of time.

If you would like to comment on the book, whether it's to suggest a hike we overlooked, or to let us know about any noteworthy experience—good or bad—that occurred while using *Foghorn Outdoors Oregon Hiking* as your guide, we would appreciate hearing from you. Please address correspondence to:

Foghorn Outdoors Oregon Hiking, first edition
Avalon Travel Publishing
1400 65th Street, Suite 250
Emeryville, CA 94608

email: atpfeedback@avalonpub.com
If you send us an email, please put "Oregon Hiking" in the subject line.

How to Use This Book

Foghorn Outdoors Oregon Hiking is divided into six chapters based on major regional areas in the state. Each chapter begins with a map of the area, which is further broken down into detail maps. These detail maps show the location of all the hikes in that chapter.

This guide can be navigated easily in two ways:

1. If you know the name of the specific trail you want to hike, or the name of the surrounding geographical area or nearby feature (town, national or state park, forest, mountain, lake, river, etc.), look it up in the index and turn to the corresponding page.

2. If you know the general area you want to visit, turn to the map at the beginning of the chapter that covers the area. Each chapter map is broken down into detail maps, which show by number all the hikes in that chapter. You can then determine which trails are in or near your destination by their corresponding numbers. Hikes are listed sequentially in each chapter so you can turn to the page with the corresponding map number for the hike you're interested in.

About the Trail Profiles

Each hike in this book is listed in a consistent, easy-to-read format to help you choose the ideal hike. From a general overview of the setting to detailed driving directions, the profile will provide all the information you need. Here is an example:

Map number and hike number

Round-trip mileage (unless otherwise noted) and the approximate amount of time needed to complete the hike (actual times can vary widely, especially on longer hikes)

Map on which the trailhead can be found and page number on which the map can be found

The difficulty rating (boot—rated 1–5) is based on the steepness of the trail and how difficult it is to traverse; the quality rating (mountain—rated 1–10) is based largely on scenic beauty, but it also takes into account how crowded the trail is and whether noise of nearby civilization is audible

General location of the trail, named by its proximity to the nearest major town or landmark

1 SOMEWHERE USA HIKE
9.0 mi/5.0 hrs
At the mouth of the Somewhere River on Lake Someplace

Map 1.2, page 24

Each hike in this book begins with a brief overview of its setting. The description typically covers what kind of terrain to expect, what might be seen, and any conditions that may make the hike difficult to navigate. Side trips, such as to waterfalls or panoramic vistas, in addition to ways to combine the trail with others nearby for a longer outing, are also noted here. In many cases, mile-by-mile trail directions are included.

User Groups: This section notes the types of users that are permitted on the trail, including hikers, mountain bikers, horseback riders, and dogs. Wheelchair access is also noted here.

Permits: This section notes whether a permit is required for hiking, or, if the hike spans more than one day, whether one is required for camping. Any fees, such as for parking, day use, or entrance, are also noted here.

Maps: This section provides information on how to obtain detailed trail maps of the hike and its environs. Whenever applicable, names of U.S. Geologic Survey (USGS) topographic maps and national forest maps are also included; contact information for these and other map sources are noted in the Resources section at the back of this book.

Directions: This section provides mile-by-mile driving directions to the trailhead from the nearest major town.

Contact: This section provides an address and phone number for each hike. The contact is usually the agency maintaining the trail but may also be a trail club or other organization.

About the Maps

This book is divided into chapters based on regions; an overview map of these regions follows
the table of contents and is printed on the inside of the back cover. At the start of each chapter,
you'll find a map of the entire region, enhanced by a grid that divides the region into smaller sections. These sections are then enlarged into individual detail maps. Trailheads are noted on the
detail maps by number.

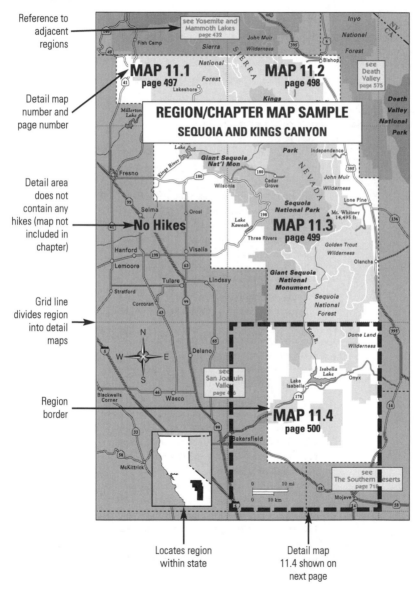

Reference to adjacent regions

Detail map number and page number

Detail area does not contain any hikes (map not included in chapter)

Grid line divides region into detail maps

Region border

Locates region within state

Detail map 11.4 shown on next page

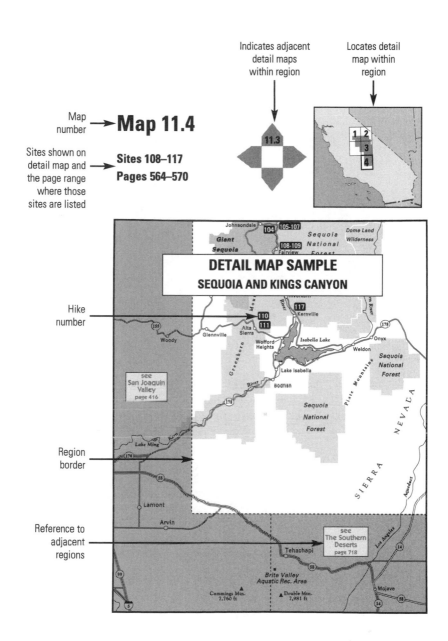

Map number → **Map 11.4**

Indicates adjacent detail maps within region

Locates detail map within region

Sites shown on detail map and the page range where those sites are listed → **Sites 108–117**
Pages 564–570

DETAIL MAP SAMPLE
SEQUOIA AND KINGS CANYON

Hike number

Region border

Reference to adjacent regions

Introduction

Introduction

Hey, your time is precious. You don't want to waste it by wandering aimlessly in search of a trailhead, or by spending hours driving to a trail only to discover it's snowed in or is too rough of a road for your dainty car.

Well, this book takes away all of those miseries. In order to bring you this book, my research team and I have literally hit upon more than 280 trails. I experienced the A–Z spectrum of hiking and made nearly every mistake in the book so you wouldn't do it. As they say, it was a dirty job, but someone had to do it, right? Well, I did.

These are a few of the highlights: I've been stuck in the dark without a headlamp. I've backed my car down a ditch. I've been the recipient of roughly 1,543 mosquito bites—and my dog found she was particularly popular with ticks. I've driven miles into the wilderness only to discover a snowed-in road or a nonexistent trail. I've come face-to-face with a bear (well, okay, it was about 100 feet away, but still). I've sat out lightning storms in my tent. I've literally hiked through snow, hail, wind, *and* rain to bring you this book. And I've enjoyed every step of the way.

The result? The most comprehensive, accurate, fun-to-read guide to the entire state of Oregon that you will find in the cozy confines of one book. For each listing, I include not only detailed driving directions, but whether the road is rough-going on the way in, as well as when the snow tends to clear from higher-elevation hikes. I note areas where trails tend to be not well marked so you can arm yourself with a map before you go. My aim is to give you as many details in each listing as are practical so you can choose whether it's the right hike for you *before* you go. If you like adventure, there are plenty of remote areas to explore. If you like everything marked for you and want to just soak up the scenery, I have you covered too. From short, paved hikes to multiday backpacking trips in wilderness areas, and everything in between, there is something for everyone in this book.

So now that I've done the research for you, it's up to you to get out there and experience Oregon for what it is: a state like no other, with 13 national forests, 115 state parks, 38 wilderness areas, five state forests, four national monuments, and one national scenic area. Within its borders, Oregon holds the record for the deepest lake in the country, one of the clearest lakes in the world, one of the highest waterfalls in the country, the deepest gorge in the country, and the second-most climbed summit in the world.

But enough of my yakking. See it all for yourself, and let this book be your guide. Thanks for letting me do the dirty work for you.

Hiking Tips

Don't Leave Home Without . . .

When it's a sunny day, it can be tempting to just head out with nothing but lightweight clothes and a Snickers bar. Hey, you're only going four miles; what's the big deal, right? Not so fast: Plenty of people have made just that mistake and have been lucky to live to tell about it. This checklist hits upon all the must-brings.

Map and Compass/Altimeter or GPS

Let's start with the obvious, shall we? A map is essential for those "am I supposed to take a left here?" moments. Even the seemingly obvious trails can become confusing when you're actually hiking them. Consider a map to be your security blanket, just to make sure you're on the right trail. Although this book provides many details of major trail junctions you'll come across, keep in mind that some areas can be a trail jungle out there, with many intersecting paths just begging to lead you astray. Not to mention the fact that some trails are not well marked due to fire damage, wind, or, depending on the area, the locals getting a little crazy with their BB guns. Get a map from the trail's managing agency (many can be easily purchased online; sources are provided with each trail featured in this book, and their contact information is listed in the Resources section at the back of the book). You'll be glad you have it.

Of course, a compass and an altimeter are useful, as is a GPS navigational device, but only if you know how to use them. If you haven't checked out GPS devices lately, some of them are truly amazing, tracking your exact route and letting you download it to your computer. They also can be useful for figuring out elevation: If you know you're supposed to climb to 4,000 feet and then turn right, and you suddenly discover you're at 6,000 feet, you've probably missed your turn.

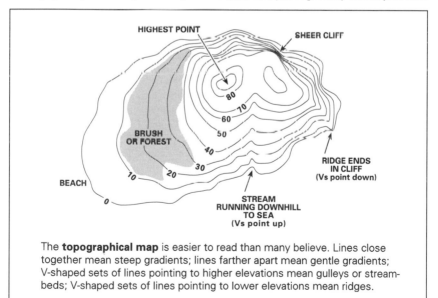

The **topographical map** is easier to read than many believe. Lines close together mean steep gradients; lines farther apart mean gentle gradients; V-shaped sets of lines pointing to higher elevations mean gulleys or streambeds; V-shaped sets of lines pointing to lower elevations mean ridges.

(Let's just say a GPS came in handy for this writer a time or two. Enough said.) The only problem is, GPS devices often don't work in remote areas, so it's a Catch-22: The more remote the area you're in—and therefore the more likely you'll get disoriented—the least likely you are to get a satellite signal. It's a good idea not to get too hooked on technology; if you're planning on traveling in the backcountry, you should back up a GPS with a compass and an altimeter.

Food and Water

Isn't hiking great? What other sport allows you to exercise and eat at the same time? It's like a buffet with a view! Of course, there are other reasons to pack food other than munching on tasty morsels while you check out the scenery, the main one being this: The unexpected can happen out on the trail. You could get turned around or linger longer than you planned at a viewpoint, when suddenly your blood sugar dips to dangerous levels. Even if you gorged on an all-you-can-eat buffet before you hit the trail-head, you'd be surprised at how quickly your stomach will be crying for more once you've trekked up 2,000 feet. The best foods are those that have a little combination platter packed inside them: a mixture of salt (to replenish sodium you're losing to sweat), sugar (to boost your blood sugar levels), and carbs and/or protein (to give you sustained energy and fill you up). Trail mix has all those delicious features and more. Take it from someone who's been there: It's best to leave the chocolate for after the hike, because that nice Snickers bar can be reduced to a soggy mess in your trail pack, which is a crime.

Water filters are a wise investment since all wilderness water should be considered contaminated. Make sure the filter can be easily cleaned or has a replaceable cartridge. The filter pores must be 0.4 microns or less to remove bacteria.

More important than food, though, is water. Dehydration can creep up on you. You may not even feel thirsty, when suddenly you become a little dizzy. Another mile of walking, and suddenly you feel as if you've just caught a bad case of the flu. Even if you're hiking just a few miles, it's better to be prepared in case you're out on the trail longer than you planned. (It happens.) You don't have to lug a water bottle along, either; many hydration packs available these days do double-duty as a pack and water carrier, without the extra weight of a bottle (and you don't have to carry anything in your hands). The whole hydration-pack concept is quite the rage now, which means that many manufacturers have leapt onto the bandwagon. Having tried many different brands, my personal favorite remains CamelBak, the company that first created the concept. The CamelBak Cloud is as big as a daypack to accommodate all your gear, carries 70 ounces of

Emergency Kit

Have you ever seen the finish line of a marathon, where the runners walk around looking like big baked potatoes under those Mylar space blankets? You wouldn't think this flimsy fabric would do much, but Mylar holds in body heat and protects from chilling wind. A space blanket is lightweight and cheap (a good one will set you back just $5), and has many functions: You can use it as a ground cover, impromptu shelter, fashionable sarong—whatever your pleasure.

But there's a reason I'm going on about space blankets: There's a chance you may run into some hazards on the trail. Whether it's as simple (but annoying) as a flock of mosquitoes or as dangerous as getting lost overnight, you should always expect the unexpected out on the trail and tote along an emergency kit. At a minimum it should contain:
- bandages
- insect repellent
- pocketknife
- space blanket
- waterproof matches
- whistle

water, and looks cool, to boot. However you carry water, though, just do it. If you're traveling on an overnight trip, you'll want to add a water filter to this list. Filtering water is a must if you're going to access water in the backcountry, unless you want to swallow a couple of microorganisms. Not only are they not very tasty, they also wreak havoc on your intestines. As with hydration packs, the water filters available now are lighter and easier to use than ever.

Extra Clothing

Just as you can't judge a book by its cover, you can't judge the weather by the trailhead. Rain, snow, and the occasional hailstorm are only the tip of the iceberg—even on a sunny day, you can reach a gusty ridge top that will cause your body temperature to plummet. At the very least, bring along something warm and cozy, like a fleece vest or pullover, and add a lightweight waterproof jacket with a hood. Speaking of your head, throw a hat in there while you're at it, and not your Yankees baseball cap. A warm, fuzzy hat will turn a miserable, cold hike into a fun jaunt through the Oregon wilds, as will a pair of gloves.

As for what to wear on a hike, I have two words for you: Cotton kills. Cotton laps up moisture like nobody's business, be it from your body (from sweat) or from the elements. Add a pair of denim jeans to that ensemble and you'll be one unhappy camper by the time you get back to the trailhead. Think light. Think breathable. Think fabrics like CoolMax or PolarTec, which wick moisture from your body and keep you toasty. Pull on a fleece over that to insulate you, top it off with a water-resistant and breathable or waterproof layer, and you're good to go. And don't forget about the drive home: Leave in your car an extra towel, a pair of socks, and comfy slip-in sandals for your trip home. Changing into a clean, dry pair of socks (and getting out of those shoes that may be hurting your feet by now) makes a big difference, as does the towel for wiping the sweat or rain from your brow.

Watch

You won't find a watch on any 10 Essentials list that I've ever seen. Yeah, yeah, you're supposed to be out enjoying nature and not worrying about what time it is, but a watch can be handy out on the trail. Time marches to the beat of a different drummer in the wilderness—what seems like two hours may really be only one (or vice versa). Why does it matter what time it is? For starters, if you're planning an out-and-back hike, it's a good way to gauge your turnaround point. If you're planning to hike a loop with several junctions, it can help you figure out how far you've hiked. Using the general rule that the average person hikes a mile in a half-hour (most experienced hikers will be much faster), you'll have a sense of when you should start looking for a turn, or if you may have missed it altogether. Of course, a watch is also good for bragging purposes ("Dude, I hiked, like, seven hours and 42 minutes today!"). But you're way too mature for that nonsense, right?

Sunscreen and Sunglasses

Just like a sunny day can turn into a sogfest, a rainy, cloudy one can suddenly turn into a brilliant, sunshiny day. And then there you are, on the peak enjoying a view, perhaps enjoying an impromptu picnic, getting sizzled without realizing it. On the way home, you fill your tank at the gas station and notice the attendant peering at you with interest. "He must not see many true outdoors people like me," you think to yourself, feeling pretty cool. And then you arrive home to hit the shower and see yourself in the bathroom mirror: Your sun-glazed eyes peek back at you from a lobster-hued face. You're burned. Really burned. Don't let it happen to you. Bring sunscreen and sunglasses, even if it's not sunny; those pesky UV rays can filter through the clouds too.

Light Source

Time can fly when you're having fun, and so can light. You may have planned for a simple five-mile jaunt, but once you're out there, you realize that hey, you're feeling good, why not try to make it to that scenic waterfall you've been hearing so much about just two miles up the trail? And while you're at it, what's that viewpoint up there? You know the story: Before you know it, the light grows dim, and darkness creeps up on you. Trust me, it's no fun hiking in the forest by yourself in the pitch dark. You don't need to lug along a heavy flashlight, either: Headlamps are light and add the extra bonus of keeping your hands free as you negotiate the dark shadows of night. You'll be glad you have it.

Footwear

Just like you want to stand arm's length away from two bikers talking bikes, nothing stirs up a frenzy more than two hikers comparing boots. That's because there are so many styles to choose from.

The type of boot you choose depends on what type of hike you're planning. For day hikes where you don't have to carry everything but the kitchen stove on your back, you can go with a lightweight trail-running shoe. They're light, they know their way around rocks, and they also have the extra bonus of flexibility (read: fewer blisters). Think about it: If these guys were made to run up, over, and through obstacles, they'll be just as good for walking. I've tried almost every brand out there, and once I hit upon Asics Gel there was no going back. They're the least clunky of the bunch and have great traction, to boot. Another popular brand is Montrail. The average price for a good trail-running shoe is about $80.

Of course, there's a downside to trail runners. They don't offer much in the way of ankle support, so you'll want to get a lightweight hiking boot if you're planning a longer day hike or a short backpacking trip. The good thing about lightweight hikers compared to trail runners is not only the extra ankle support but the superior traction to power through mud and snow. They're also relatively flexible, requiring less breaking in than heavier boots. A good pair of light hiking boots will set you back about $100.

For extended backpacking trips, you'll want to take things up a notch with a true backpacking boot. A midweight or heavy backpacking boot is the full tamale in the hiking boot world. They extend above your ankle to provide even more support when you're carrying a heavy backpack. As a result, they tend to be stiffer, so you'll want to break them in before setting out. Unless you're planning to through-hike the Pacific Crest Trail, you'll be better off with a midweight hiking boot for weekend or weeklong backpacking trips. A pair of midweight hiking boots ranges in price from $125 to over $200.

To throw a wrench into everything, there really are no hard-and-fast rules when it comes to shoes. Everyone has their little quirks about shoes and I've seen it all on the trail. The most important thing: While it's oh-so handy to click and pick online, you should definitely try on a few pairs before you sign the dotted line; something that looks pretty cool on the Internet may become the bane of your existence on the trail. A good fit is everything, and stores like REI are excellent sources for trying on a range of styles and brands (plus the store employees are at the top of their game, knowledge-wise).

Finally, a good pair of shoes is nothing without the right kind of socks. The best route to a blister-free hike is a sock that wicks moisture away from your feet. Again, the type of socks you pick depends on what type of hike you're planning. For shorter hikes, you're fine with a lightweight sock that gives you a little cushioning and wicks sweat away. Longer trips call for heavier socks with a liner underneath. SmartWool is the go-to brand for the full range of socks made from breathable yet sturdy Merino wool. You may look at the price tag and balk (about $15 per pair), but believe me, they're worth it.

Trail Etiquette

You're out in the middle of the trail, free from the pressures of life and all the rules that go along with it. Right? Kinda. There are a few finer points on trail etiquette that will make for smoother sailing for yourself and fellow hikers. (Don't worry, you can still talk with your mouth full and slurp your water all you like.)

Horses, Mountain Bikers, and Fellow Hikers

Just as there are highway traffic rules (which you always follow, right?), there are rules of the "road" for dealing with other people on the trail. Here's a Trail Manners 101 checklist.

Horses: Probably the most confusing fellow trail users are the four-legged types. They can spook easily, so you'll want to take care not to cause a horse heart attack. You may have all the right intentions, but sometimes the smallest things can set off these sensitive creatures. While hikers should always yield to horses, make sure the horse has seen you before you go diving behind a tree—you don't want to startle the poor beast. Also, some horses are frightened by big backpacks; keep your distance, and never go up to pet the creature, no matter how tempting its pretty eyes are. Horseback riders usually let hikers know the quirks of their animals, but nevertheless, always yield, and make your presence known to horses. Luckily, many trails open to horses are wide enough for you to safely keep your distance and let them pass with ease.

Leave No Trace

If you want trails to stick around for a while, there are a few simple rules to follow. Number one is to stay on the trail and don't cut switchbacks. It can be tempting to hike around a muddy or wet area, but if everyone did this, the trail would eventually widen and make the problem even worse. Second, the phrase "leave only footprints, take only pictures" says it all. If you're camping, pack out everything you brought (it's handy to carry Ziploc or garbage bags to separate your trash, and don't be shy about picking up others' "misplaced" trash while you're at it). Bury human waste at least 200 feet away from campsites, trails, or water sources. For more tips on responsible hiking visit the Leave No Trace website at visit www.lnt.org.

Mountain bikers: Bikers are supposed to yield to hikers and restrain the screaming pace of descent. Why the chuckling? Well, nothing against bikers, but sometimes this doesn't happen. I don't want to get into trouble with the trail police or anything, but this is a rule that personally just doesn't make sense to me. After all, it's much easier for hikers to step aside than it is for bikers to slow down, stop, and move aside (without falling off said bike, no less), especially when they're going up or down hills. To avoid getting into an all-out rumble about it, what's the big deal about a quick sidestep to let a biker cruise right on through? They'll appreciate it, you'll feel cool about being such a great guy/chick, and everyone wins.

Fellow hikers: Horses aren't the only creatures who can spook easily on a trail. When you're lost in thought, feeling like you're alone in the world, having someone creep up on you from behind can give the nerves quite a jolt. Whenever you come across another hiker who is headed in the same direction (i.e., their back is turned toward you), before you pass them, say "hi," "hello," "yo"—whatever your salutation of choice (don't be shy!). When you're hiking up or down a hill and you come across a fellow hiker, the uphill hiker gets the right of way.

Hiking with Dogs

Dogs are perfect hiking companions. They keep you company but don't talk your ear off about their troubles, they never say "I told you so" when you turn the wrong way, and they're cute, to boot. But please keep one thing in mind: Not everyone shares your enthusiasm for the canine species. Your friendly doggie may be running toward a fellow hiker hoping for a little pat on the head, but someone who is afraid of dogs (or maybe just isn't in a "dog mood" that day) may misread your dog's eager demeanor as an appetite for a healthy chunk out of their leg. I really can't resist going on a bit about this topic, because it is my only pet peeve (yeah, yeah, no pun intended) on the trail. I cannot count how many times I've encountered an unleashed dog who comes charging at me and my (leashed) dog, and the owner just smiles and says, "Oh, he's friendly"—if they say anything. Not only is this dangerous—not all dogs know how to play well with others—but it's simply inconsiderate to other people. You can let your furry friend romp all she wants when there's no one else around, although your dog should always be under voice control, stay on the trail, and leave wildlife in peace. But if the trail is the least bit crowded, please do us all a big favor: Acquaint yourself with the handy gadget known as a leash, and use it. Now I shall step away from the microphone and off the podium. Thanks for listening.

Dealing with the Great Outdoors

You may have some unexpected visitors on the trail. Use these tips to keep you safe (and sane) when you happen across the following Oregon creatures and plants.

Rattlesnakes, Bears, and Cougars

While some forest natives like deer are a joy to see when you're out on the trail, these three guys can make your heart skip a beat. Be prepared before you go, so you can keep your cool and avoid confrontations.

Rattlesnakes: There are 15 species of snakes in Oregon, but the only poisonous one is the Western rattler. They're more active in spring, summer, and early fall, and are mostly found in the southern and eastern regions of the state. You don't need to be a snake expert in order to identify these slithery guys, because you'll most likely hear them before you see them: The unmistakable rattle sound will instantly freeze you in your tracks. This is actually a good thing, because rattlesnakes rarely attack a nonmoving object. Once the snake realizes you're not a threat, it will retreat. In the unlikely event you are bitten—and keep in mind that many bites are "dry bites" with no venom, and that overall the bites are rarely lethal—you need to be treated within 18 hours. The most important thing to remember—and probably the hardest thing to do—is to remain calm and move slowly so your blood isn't racing through your body. Remove any restrictive clothing, don't attempt to apply a tourniquet, and don't ice the bite. Just walk, calm, cool, and collected, back to your car and drive yourself to a hospital.

Bears: You may have aced the bear question on the Worst-Case Scenario Survival Guide game at your family holiday gathering, but when you actually see a bear in the forest, it's amazing how all that handy knowledge can fly out of your head when adrenaline takes charge. The good news is that Oregon has only black bears—which actually are sometimes brown—so there's no need to identify which type of bear it is if you encounter one. There are 25,000 black bears in the state, mainly in mountainous and forested areas like Mount Hood, Mount Jefferson, and the Wallowa Mountains.

The most important thing to remember when you see a bear is to do the opposite of what your body tells you to do: Don't run. Bears can clock speeds of 35 mph and are more likely to go after you if you're running away. Usually bears want nothing to do with humans; they often hear you before you even see them and will leave the area undetected. If you and a bear do spot each other, back away slowly but surely while facing the bear, reassuring it with such niceties as "nice bear, yes, aren't you sweet." It will likely move away from you. If you come across a bear who got out on the wrong side of its bear bed and decides to charge you, try to stay calm (yeah, right) and be prepared to fight back. Never look a bear in the eyes, because it will view this as aggression, but do make yourself look as big as possible by waving your arms over your head or opening your coat. If it comes close enough to attack, now is not the time to drop and play dead (that's for Grizzlies). Fight back with anything you have—sticks, rocks, your hiking guidebook. Give it what you got. If you have a backpack filled with food, throw it at the beast—a hungry bear will most likely be more interested in your trail mix than in you as an appetizer.

While all this is tidy advice, everyone has a dramatically different bear story. Black bears can be unpredictable, so the best rule is to make noise when you're out alone so you don't surprise a bear, and try to remain calm if you do encounter one. If you have a dog, make sure it's leashed so it doesn't run after the bear, because that will provoke it to come after both of you. A personal story: Once when I was hiking through a remote area with my dog, we encountered a bear. Thankfully, my dog was remarkably calm (although her little heart was probably beating just as fast as mine was). She didn't go after the bear or bark, like she would normally do with smaller creatures. Dogs are smart; they will most likely stick by you to protect you, and will be aggressive only if the bear charges. No matter what, though, you should always bring a leash to protect both of you.

If you're camping, never leave food in your tent. Leave your food in the car or secure it in a bear canister at the campsite; if backpacking, hang your food from a tree. If a bear saunters into your campsite, the main rule is to cause a scene: Bang pots and pans, blow a whistle, throw rocks. Most likely the creature will scamper away, figuring you're not worth the trouble.

Finally, on the trail is not the place to try out that new cologne or perfume. Bears are attracted to fragrances just like we are.

Cougars: Also called mountain lions, panthers, and pumas, cougars are the largest member of the cat family in Oregon. Their habitats are as varied as their names. These highly adaptable creatures can be seen in zones ranging from high alpine areas to desert regions. Most of the mountain lions in Oregon live in the southern coastal region and in the northeastern corner of the state, but they pretty much dwell anywhere in between—you may have hiked through mountain lion territory without knowing it. And you probably wouldn't know it, because these big cats are notoriously secretive and will usually run away at the first sign of humans. The risk of being attacked by a mountain lion is smaller than that of being hurt by a dog, bee, or even a deer. Of course, there is always the slightest chance that a cougar will attack, so it's best to be prepared.

The rules are similar to the above bear rules: Don't run, make yourself appear as large as possible, and fight back if attacked. If you're hiking with children, pick them up—but this time ignore that "bend at the knees when lifting heavy objects" tip, because you don't ever want to crouch in front of a cougar. Face the animal, speak in a loud voice, and give it your best beady-eyed stare right in the eyes. It will likely run away with its tail between its legs.

Poison Oak, Poison Ivy, Stinging Nettles, and Ticks

They may not be as scary as the above creatures, but you're much more likely to come across poison oak and ivy, stinging nettles, and ticks on your hike. With some simple tips, you can learn to avoid these nuisances and keep them from taking all the fun out of hiking.

Poison Oak and Ivy: The best way to avoid encounters with poison oak and ivy is to wear long pants when you hike. Poison oak thrives more in the western area of the state, while its counterpart, poison ivy, takes over the eastern region. Learn to identify these plants: They have the infamous "leaves of three" and constantly change colors throughout the year (hoping to fool you into touching them, most likely). In the spring, the leaves are reddish; then they turn green in the summer, bursting into yellow, orange, or red in the fall. The berries don't change, though, so if you see the duo of three leaves with white berries, don't touch it. If you accidentally come into contact, wash with hot water and soap

Avoiding Poison Oak: Remember the old Boy Scout saying: "Leaves of three, let them be."

as soon as possible (or, if near a water source, rinse off right away); when you get home, make sure that everything that came into contact with these pesky plants is thoroughly washed, including your dog. If the oil got on your dog's fur, it can easily get on you, so treat your canine friend to a post-hike bath. Along with learning to identify and keeping away from these plants, slather on a cream with bentoquatum, like Ivy Block, before you head out, and bring along some wipes, like Tecnu, to use after you've been exposed.

Stinging Nettles: Brush up against a stinging nettle and you'll know it immediately—it causes an intense sting and white bumps as the acid (the same substance that acid ants produce) is released onto your skin . Nettles thrive in the coastal range of the state in forested areas and have heart-shaped leaves with razorlike edges. The good news is, unlike poison oak or ivy, the itch lasts only 24 hours at the most, and then you'll be good as new. To soothe the itch, spit on the site. When you get home, apply a baking soda poultice or hydrocortisone lotion, and just be thankful you're not a monk: In the Middle Ages, the brothers thrashed themselves with the sharp-toothed leaves for penance!

Ticks: There are four types of ticks in Oregon, but only one of them carries the dreaded Lyme disease: the Western black-legged tick. Generally, ticks are more active in the spring and summer. They thrive in tall grasses and low shrubs. Dogs are much more likely to come across a tick, so make sure to check your little guy or gal out, especially on the head, behind the ears, and on the stomach, where the fur is shorter. For humans, the best way to deter these stubborn creatures is to wear long pants and a long-sleeved shirt. Check yourself thoroughly after hiking, and if you find one burrowed in your skin, pull it out carefully with tweezers. Keep in mind that you need to remove the entire body and head, so grasp it firmly from the skin surface. Although only a small percentage of the Western black-legged ticks actually carry Lyme disease, have a doctor examine the tick if it's black; the brown types are harmless, but you may want to get it checked out just in case. See a doctor immediately if you begin to experience flu-like symptoms. Since dogs are more susceptible, you can also get a tick-prevention prescription, like FrontLine, for your four-legged friend.

Permits and Land Use

Oregon has 115 state parks, 13 national forests, and five state forests. What's the diff? Here's a quick guide to the different types of forests and parks, plus what permits you'll need (and information on where your hard-earned money is going).

Parks, Forests, and Wilderness Areas

Oregon is filled to capacity with parks, forests, and wilderness areas, all with different rules and managing agencies. Here's what you need to know: First of all, the National Forest Service (a division of the U.S. Department of Agriculture) manages the 13 national forests in Oregon. The national forests in Oregon include Deschutes, Fremont, Malheur, Mount Hood, Ochoco, Rogue River, Siskiyou, Siuslaw, Umatilla, Umpqua, Wallowa-Whitman, Willamette, and Winema. Some forests require a Northwest Forest Service pass at most trailheads, while others, like Fremont, Malheur, and Ochoco, are free.

Then you have your state forests, which are managed by the Oregon Department of Forestry. These include Clatsop, Elliott, Santiam, Tillamook, and Sun Pass.

Moving on down the line are the state parks, which are managed by the Oregon State Parks and Recreation Department. There are 115 state parks, 26 of which require a parking fee or pass. Still with me? Good.

Can I Hike Through?
A Guide to the Oregon Coast and Pacific Crest Trails

There are two major long-distance trails in Oregon: the 360-mile Oregon Coast Trail, which extends from Astoria to Brookings, and the Pacific Crest Trail (PCT), which extends 2,650 miles from Mexico to Canada, about 450 miles of which fall within Oregon state lines. Both of these trails hit many other trails along the way.

On the Oregon Coast Trail, you'll cross rivers, go through towns, and even ferry across a bay before all is said and done. Most people access the trail during shorter day hikes, all of which are covered in this book. If you really want to do the entire length, it's strongly suggested that you get a point-to-point guide, one of which is available for free through the Oregon State Parks and Recreation Department at 800/551-6949 (you can also download it from www.oregonstateparks.org).

The Pacific Crest Trail is a more popular through-hiking adventure because it sticks to the trail at all times, entering Oregon at Rogue River National Forest, hitting Umpqua and Deschutes National Forests, Crater Lake National Park, and Willamette and Mount Hood National Forests before entering the Columbia River Gorge National Scenic Area and crossing the Bridge of the Gods near Cascade Locks over to Washington. The most popular day hikes that access the mighty PCT are also listed in this book. If you plan to hike a sizable portion or all of the PCT, you should get a point-by-point guide. One worthy resource is *The Pacific Crest Trail: Oregon–Washington,* by Jeffrey Schaffer and Andy Selters (Wilderness Press, 2003).

Then there are the 38 designated wilderness areas, managed by the Forest Service or the Bureau of Land Management and set aside as protected areas. Typically, you'll need a wilderness permit to enter these areas.

Add in the four national monuments (Newberry Crater, Oregon Caves, John Day Fossil Beds, and Cascade-Siskiyou), one national park (Crater Lake), and one national scenic area (Columbia River Gorge)—all governed by the Bureau of Land Management, the Forest Service, the National Park Service, or other agencies—and there you have it. (Don't worry, you won't be quizzed on this.)

Where is Your Money Going?
The most widely used permit in the state is the Northwest Forest Service Pass. Each featured trail in this book provides information on whether you need this pass or not. You can buy an annual pass ($30) with a quick and painless online transaction through Nature of the Northwest (www.naturenw.org). They're mysteriously speedy about shipping anything you order, and you can just put 'er in your windshield and never worry about it again. Before you start your grumbling, realize that the money goes toward maintaining the trails and keeping them around, which is what you want, right? Consider this: In 2002, $3.6 million was raised from pass sales, resulting in 7,000 miles of trail maintenance. Some state parks also have entry fees of $3; you can buy an annual pass ($25) by calling the Oregon State Parks and Recreation Department at 800/551-6949.

Best Hikes in Oregon

So many trails, so little time. Here's a guide to the best of the bunch in nine categories, listed in alphabetical order.

Top 10 Waterfall Hikes

1. **Drift Creek Falls,** The Oregon Coast, page 37
2. **Eagle Creek to Tunnel Falls,** The Columbia River Gorge and Mount Hood, page 80
3. **Multnomah Falls,** The Columbia River Gorge and Mount Hood, page 75
4. **Oneonta/Horsetail Falls Loop,** The Columbia River Gorge and Mount Hood, page 76
5. **Paulina Creek/Paulina Falls,** Southeast Oregon, page 221
6. **Ramona Falls,** The Columbia River Gorge and Mount Hood, page 87
7. **Tamanawas Falls,** The Columbia River Gorge and Mount Hood, page 90
8. **Trail of Ten Falls/Canyon Trail,** Portland and the Willamette Valley, page 60
9. **Vivian Lake/Salt Creek Falls,** The Southern Cascades, page 190
10. **Wahkeena Falls Loop,** The Columbia River Gorge and Mount Hood, page 74

Salt Creek Falls

© KEVIN FOREMAN

Top 10 Lung-Busting Hikes

1. **Eagle Creek to Diamond Lake,** Northeast Oregon, page 138
2. **Eagle Creek to Echo/Traverse Lakes,** Northeast Oregon, page 138
3. **Elk Mountain,** The Oregon Coast, page 29
4. **Hawkins Pass,** Northeast Oregon, page 137
5. **Kings Mountain,** The Oregon Coast, page 29
6. **Lakes Basin Loop,** Northeast Oregon, page 136
7. **Mount Defiance/Starvation Ridge,** The Columbia River Gorge and Mount Hood, page 81
8. **Onion Creek to Strawberry Mountain,** Northeast Oregon, page 156
9. **Paulina Peak,** Southeast Oregon, page 222
10. **South Sister Summit,** The Southern Cascades, page 182

Top 10 Hikes with Children

1. **Big Obsidian Flow Trail,** Southeast Oregon, page 222
2. **Big Pine Interpretive Loop Trail,** The Oregon Coast, page 47
3. **Cape Meares,** The Oregon Coast, page 31

Flood of Fire, John Day Fossil Beds National Monument

Top 10 Wildflower Hikes

Top 10 Backpacking Hikes

Top 10 Lake Day Hikes

Top 10 River Hikes

South Fork Walla Walla

Top 10 Wildlife-Viewing Hikes

1. **Bearwallow to Standley Cabin,** Northeast Oregon, page 131
2. **Black Canyon,** Northeast Oregon, page 145
3. **Gearhart Mountain,** Southeast Oregon, page 224
4. **Nine Mile Ridge,** Northeast Oregon, page 129
5. **North Fork John Day River,** Northeast Oregon, page 147
6. **North Fork Malheur,** Northeast Oregon, page 158
7. **Pine Creek,** Northeast Oregon, page 155
8. **Sunset Bay to Cape Arago,** The Oregon Coast, page 39
9. **Tillamook Head,** The Oregon Coast, page 27
10. **Yaquina Head Lighthouse,** The Oregon Coast, page 34

Top 10 Viewpoints

1. **Cape Lookout,** The Oregon Coast, page 32
2. **Discovery Point,** The Southern Cascades, page 205
3. **Lakes Lookout,** Northeast Oregon, page 149
4. **Mountaineer Trail to Silcox Hut,** The Columbia River Gorge and Mount Hood, page 96
5. **Pacific Crest Trail Bypass/Rim Trail,** The Southern Cascades, page 203
6. **Paulina Peak,** Southeast Oregon, page 222
7. **Saddle Mountain,** The Oregon Coast, page 28
8. **South Sister Summit,** The Southern Cascades, page 182
9. **Timberline Trail,** The Columbia River Gorge and Mount Hood, page 97
10. **Wygant Point,** The Columbia River Gorge and Mount Hood, page 82

© MEGAN McMORRIS

Chapter 1

The Oregon Coast

Chapter 1—The Oregon Coast

L et's face it: Oregon isn't about to be nicknamed "the Sunshine State" anytime soon. You won't find MTV filming a spring-break beach party here, and you'd be hard-pressed to find a bikini anywhere. That is precisely its appeal. Instead, you'll find windswept beaches, majestic rocky bluffs, lighthouses, and the Oregon Dunes along famous U.S. 101. We know, it all sounds clichéd—and it is, in a way. Don't be surprised if you feel a weird sense of déjà vu when you explore the coast—it's just because of the many postcards and ads that have been shot here.

The entire Oregon coast is public property, which means you can hike from one end to the other—literally. The 360-mile Oregon Coast Trail (OCT) extends from the northern tip in Astoria to the California border at Brookings-Harbor; many of the hikes in this chapter join the OCT. The coast is broken up by locals into three categories: the north coast (including the towns of Astoria, Seaside, Cannon Beach, and Tillamook), the central coast (including Lincoln City, Depoe Bay, Newport, Waldport, Yachats, and Florence), and the south coast (including Coos Bay, North Bend, Port Orford, Bandon, Gold Beach, and Brookings-Harbor).

But the ocean isn't the only hot spot in the coastal region: The Tillamook State Forest in the north coast, the Siuslaw National Forest in the north and central coast, and the Siskiyou National Forest in the south coast round out the area and offer some of the tougher hikes and peaks for great views of the coast. One side note: The Biscuit Fire in 2002, estimated to be one of Oregon's largest wildfires in recorded history, burned 499,965 acres in southern Oregon and northern California. It swept through most of the Kalmiopsis Wilderness in the Siskiyou National Forest, which means that many trails at this writing have not bounced back enough to travel through (although many have been maintained and are included in this chapter).

Unlike some of the higher-elevation trails in other regions of the state, which are covered by snow sometimes through July, the coast is hikeable year-round. In fact, it's a popular destination in the winter months, as it's a top whale-watching spot from December to February and from March to May. During whale-watching weeks in December and March, trained volunteers will help you spot the spouts at 29 locations along the coast.

There are more short hikes in this chapter than in others, and there's a reason for that. We just couldn't leave out some of the gorgeous lighthouse jaunts. One idea is to plan several hikes in one day as you drive down the coast—a perfect way to gently introduce kids to hiking.

Of course, you'll want to check out the local flavors while you're here: Moe's Clam Chowder is famous; it originated in Newport and has five locations along the coast. The entire coast is lined with fishing villages and cute coastal towns—Cannon Beach in particular (in the north coast) is popular with bed-and-breakfast types. If you're more of a tent person, there are plenty of year-round sites all along the coast. Just hit the road down U.S. 101 and see all the signs lined up pointing you to beachside camping.

Whether you decide to hit a few small hikes in a day or want a lung-busting peak, you'll find it all here. In fact, the only thing you won't find is a teeny-weeny bikini.

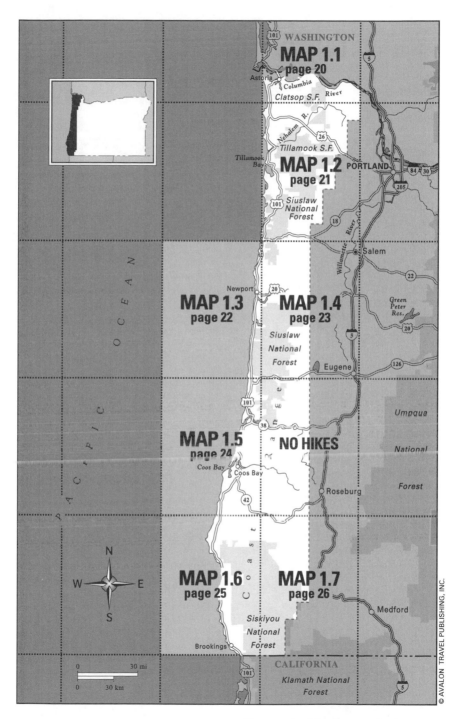

Map 1.1

Hike 1
Page 27

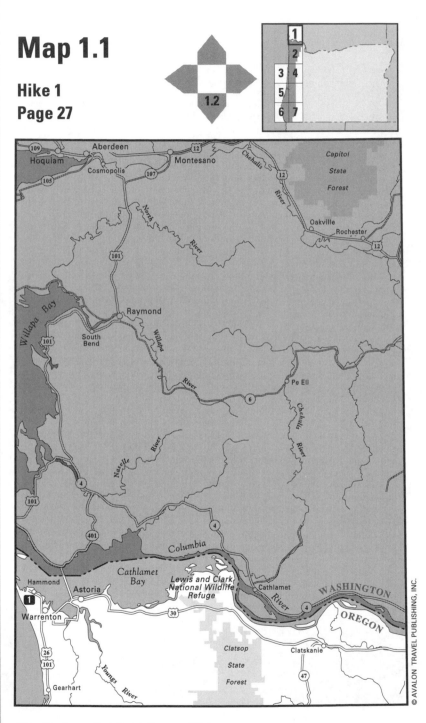

Map 1.2

Hikes 2–14
Pages 27–34

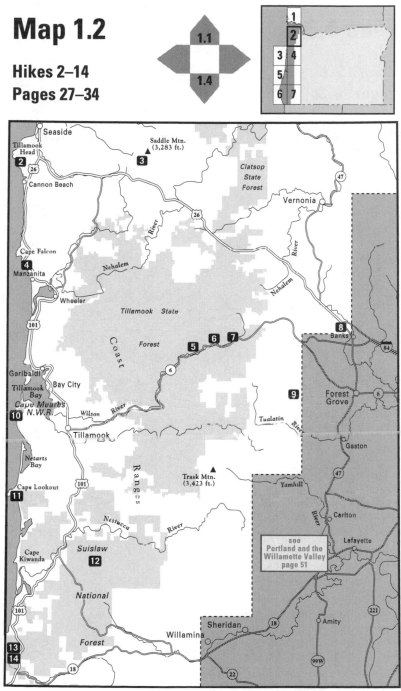

Map 1.3

Hikes 15–19
Pages 34–36

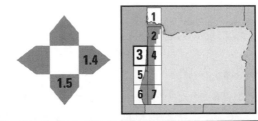

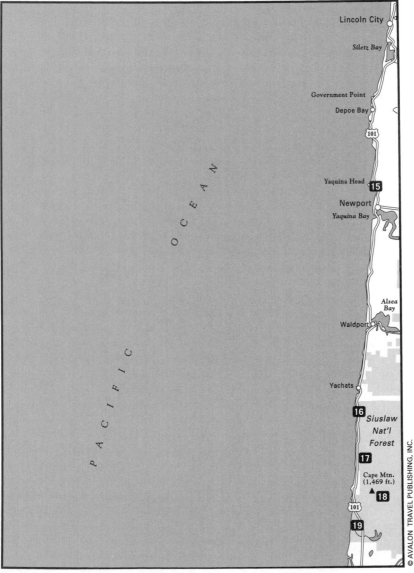

Lincoln City

Siletz Bay

Government Point

Depoe Bay

101

O C E A N

Yaquina Head 15

Newport
Yaquina Bay

Alsea Bay

Waldport

P A C I F I C

Yachats

16 *Siuslaw Nat'l Forest*

17

Cape Mtn.
(1,469 ft.)
▲ 18

101

19

© AVALON TRAVEL PUBLISHING, INC.

Map 1.4

Hikes 20–21
Page 37

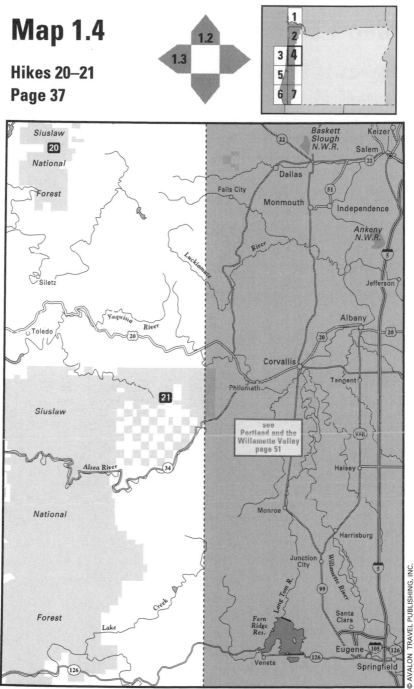

Map 1.5

Hikes 22–25
Pages 38–39

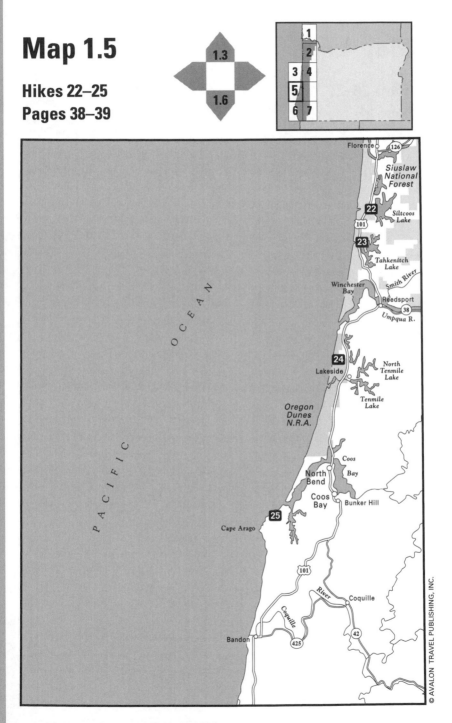

Map 1.6

Hikes 26–37
Pages 40–45

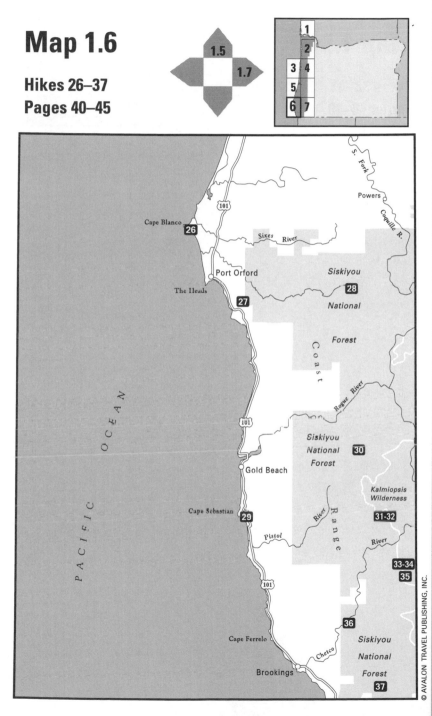

Map 1.7

Hikes 38–43
Pages 46–48

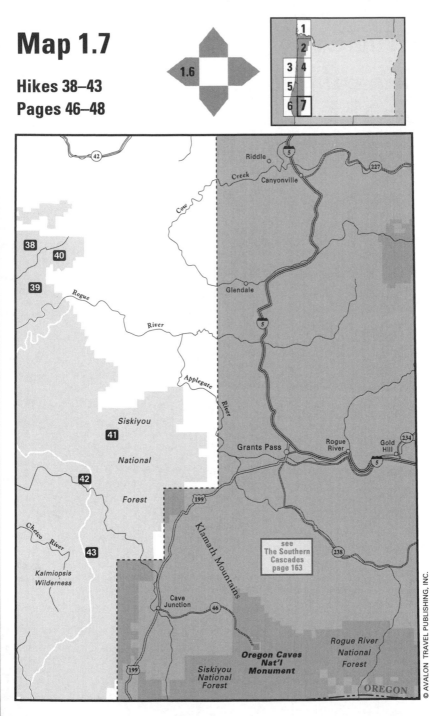

■ FORT STEVENS STATE PARK
1.0–9.0 mi/5.0 hrs

west of Astoria on the northwestern point of Oregon

Map 1.1, page 20

This state park has an interesting set of claims to fame within its 3,700 acres. The site originally served as the primary military defense installation in the Harbor Defense System, at the mouth of the Columbia River. There it stood for 84 years, from the Civil War until the end of World War II. Although some relics remain—you can explore the abandoned gun batteries, climb to the commander's station for a view, and visit the military museum on the property—it now primarily serves more civilian needs. The Oregon Coast Trail starts here, and in addition to the historical artifacts, there are also six miles of hiking trails and nine miles of paved biking paths. Swing by the information kiosk at the park entrance before planning your attack, because there's plenty to choose from. An easy-to-follow 2.4-mile path around Coffenbury Lake is a good way to start your day. Then hit the Peter Iredale shipwreck and follow the two-mile beachside bike path for great ocean views. No matter how you decide to spend your day, you can't really go wrong in this jam-packed park.

User groups: Hikers, dogs, and mountain bikes. No horses are allowed. Wheelchair access is available on paved portions of trails.

Permits: Permits are not required. A $3 day-use fee is collected at the park entrance, or you can get an annual Oregon Parks and Recreation pass for $25; contact Oregon Parks and Recreation, 800/551-6949. Another option is to buy the Oregon Pacific Coast Passport, which is valid at 17 locations along the coast; it costs $35 for a year or $10 for a five-day pass and is available at local vendors and through the Oregon Parks and Recreation Department.

Maps: For a free park brochure and map, contact Oregon Parks and Recreation Department, 800/551-6949, www.oregonstateparks.org.

For a topographic map, ask the USGS for Warrenton.

Directions: From Astoria, drive four miles south on U.S. 101 to Fort Stevens State Park. (From Seaside, drive nine miles north.) Follow signs for 4.5 miles into the park and continue to the campground entrance and picnic area A, where Coffenbury Lake is located.

Contact: Oregon Parks and Recreation Department, 1115 Commercial Street Northeast, Salem, OR 97301, 800/551-6949, www.oregonstate parks.org.

■ TILLAMOOK HEAD
4.0 mi/2.0 hrs

two miles north of Cannon Beach on the Oregon Coast

Map 1.2, page 21

This is quintessential Oregon coast—you've got massive jutting rocks, a distant lighthouse, and scenic viewpoints. What else do you need? A camera and binoculars, to capture the beauty and to watch out for whale spouts. This is a popular whale-watching spot in the months of December and March. In fact, Ecola State Park, where the trail is located, takes it name from the Chinook word for "whale." While Tillamook Head Trail extends for eight miles point to point—which is part of the Oregon Coast Trail, not to mention the trail of choice for Lewis and Clark explorers—a great loop option starts from the Indian Creek parking lot. Look for the outhouse in the parking lot; the trailhead begins there with a handy map to show you what's in store. This well-marked and well-mapped trail leads to mind-blowing viewpoints, including an old military bunker viewpoint (great news for view-lovers, but not for height-haters) where you can see the Tillamook Rock Lighthouse, nicknamed "Terrible Tilly" for its exposure to harsh winds and storms. The breeze and white noise from the ocean provide a refreshing backdrop for this scenic trail.

User groups: Hikers and dogs. No mountain bikes or horses are allowed. No wheelchair facilities.

Permits: Permits are not required. A $3 day-use fee is collected at the park entrance, or you can get an annual Oregon Parks and Recreation pass for $25; contact Oregon Parks and Recreation, 800/551-6949. Another option is to buy the Oregon Pacific Coast Passport, which is valid at 17 locations along the coast; it costs $35 for a year or $10 for a five-day pass and is available at local vendors or through the Oregon Parks and Recreation Department.

Maps: For a free park brochure and map, contact Oregon Parks and Recreation Department, 800/551-6949, www.oregonstateparks.org. For a topographic map, ask the USGS for Tillamook Head.

Directions: At the north end of Cannon Beach, follow signs for two miles to the park entrance. Drive through the park to the Indian Creek picnic area (closed in winter).

Contact: Oregon Parks and Recreation Department, 1115 Commercial Street Northeast, Salem, OR 97301, 800/551-6949, www.oregonstate parks.org.

❸ SADDLE MOUNTAIN
5.0 mi/4.0 hrs

east of Seaside in Saddle Mountain State Natural Area

Map 1.2, page 21

When you're driving in on the windy road, you may wonder if you're headed directly to the summit, since it's such a long road—seven miles, to be exact. Suddenly, you'll round a bend and see it looming before you, a great craggy peak towering over the parking lot. It's an impressive sight, as are the many viewpoints along the way. The well-marked trailhead starts off with gentle switchbacks, but the final mile can be a little treacherous, with rocky crossings, so make sure your soles have traction—and your nerves are height-proof. There's just one, easy-to-navigate trail to the top of this 3,283-foot mountain, which is shaped like a saddle, hence the name. The trail can still be covered in snow through May, so it's best to check the weather beforehand. On a clear, sunny day, it offers one of the best views around of the Tillamook Forest and the coastal range.

User groups: Hikers and dogs. No mountain bikes or horses are allowed. No wheelchair facilities.

Permits: Permits are not required. Parking and access are free.

Maps: For a free brochure and map, contact Oregon State Parks, 800/551-6949, www.oregonstateparks.org. For a topographic map, ask the USGS for Saddle Mountain.

Directions: From Portland, drive about 65 miles west on U.S. 26 (or 10 miles east from Seaside) and turn north at the Saddle Mountain State Park road sign. Drive seven miles to the trailhead.

Contact: Oregon Parks and Recreation Department, 1115 Commercial Street Northeast, Salem, OR 97301, 800/551-6949, www.oregonstate parks.org.

❹ NEAHKAHNIE MOUNTAIN
2.8 mi/1.5 hrs

in Oswald West State Park on the north coast

Map 1.2, page 21

If you're hiking with a canine companion who stops to paw and sniff at the ground, take a closer look: You may have happened upon the buried treasure that local legend claims is hidden on this mountain (just make sure to reward your buddy with a nice jeweled collar or something). But be careful, because it's also rumored to be haunted by the ghosts of shipwrecked Spanish pirates who guard their lost treasure, and you know how testy Spanish pirates can get! The name of this popular mountain means "home of the Gods," and on your hike you'll wonder whether you're going straight to the heavens—not only because of the steep ascent, but because of the ocean views that await you at the top. Return the way you came once you bag the peak—and if you find yourself sans treasure, pick a few treasures of your own: Thimbleberries, tasty morsels when they're in season (mid-July to late August), line the route.

Stick around for some excellent beachside walks as well (before you go pick up a brochure for trail maps).

User groups: Hikers and dogs. No horses or mountain bikes are allowed. No wheelchair access.

Permits: Permits are not required. Parking and access are free.

Maps: For a free Oswald West State Park brochure and trail map, contact Oregon Parks and Recreation Department, 800/551-6949, www.oregonstateparks.org. For a topographic map, ask the USGS for Arch Cape and Nehalem.

Directions: From Cannon Beach, drive 10 miles south on U.S. 101 to Oswald West State Park. Between mile markers 41 and 42, turn left (east) onto gravel Road 38555 and drive .6 mile to the trailhead. Park on the side of the road, and look for the brown trail sign on the left side of the road.

Contact: Oregon Parks and Recreation Department, 1115 Commercial Street Northeast, Salem, OR 97301, 800/551-6949, www.oregonstate parks.org.

5 KINGS MOUNTAIN
5.0 mi/3.5 hrs

in Tillamook State Forest north of Highway 6

Map 1.2, page 21

Like neighboring Elk Mountain, this 3,226-foot peak is a rocky adventure. You'll gain 2,700 feet on your way up to a great scenic view of the coastal range (and even Mount Hood on a clear day), but you have to work to get there. Be careful on your way up, as the route is rocky and steep, and can be snow-covered through May. If you think you have it bad, here are some facts to ponder to take your mind off your aching legs: The Tillamook Forest went through a run of bad luck from the 1930s through the 1950s, when a series of logging fires decimated trees withing a combined total area of 355,000 acres, enough timber to build one million five-room homes. Today, the second-growth forest shows barely any signs of the destruction, thanks to

the determined efforts of the locals, who went on a planting frenzy, armed with 72 million seedlings (don't mess with Oregonians and their trees!). If the climb isn't enough of a challenge for you, you can combine this trail with Elk Mountain summit for a loop hike (see the Elk Mountain listing for directions).

User groups: Hikers and dogs. No mountain bikes or horses are allowed. No wheelchair access.

Permits: Permits are not required. Parking and access are free.

Maps: For a Tillamook Forest Visitor Map & Guide, contact the Forest Grove District Office, 503/357-2191, www.odf.state.or.us/tsf. For a topographic map, ask the USGS for Rogers Peak.

Directions: From Portland, drive 42 miles west on U.S. 26 and Highway 6 to the trailhead and parking area near milepost 25, on the right (north) side of the road.

Contact: Tillamook State Forest, Forest Grove District Office, 801 Gales Creek Road, Forest Grove, OR 97116, 503/357-2191, www.odf .state.or.us/tsf.

6 ELK MOUNTAIN
3.0 mi/2.5 hrs

in Tillamook State Forest north of Highway 6

Map 1.2, page 21

Why trudge up miles and miles of switchbacks slowly inching their way up to the summit? This trail doesn't mess around; instead, it cuts a path 1.5 miles directly up to the 2,788-foot peak. Or at least it will feel this way when you're climbing it. Bring along some gloves for this one, as you'll be scrambling up plenty of rocks on the steep ascent. It's not for the faint of heart—or of leg muscle—but at least it gets you to your destination faster, with plenty of gorgeous views of the Tillamook Forest and surrounding coastal mountains. Head back the way you came for a steep but relatively short descent. This trail can also be combined with Kings Mountain for a tough

11.5-mile loop by continuing past the summit of Elk Mountain to the junction with Kings Mountain Trail (take a left at the junction). Descend Kings Mountain, continuing until you nearly reach the trailhead, and take a left onto the 3.5-mile Wilson River Trail back to the Elk Mountain trailhead.

User groups: Hikers and dogs. Mountain bikes and horses are not allowed. No wheelchair facilities.

Permits: Permits are not required. Parking and access are free.

Maps: For a Tillamook Forest Visitor Map & Guide, contact the Forest Grove District Office, 503/357-2191, www.odf.state.or.us/tsf. For a topographic map, ask the USGS for Cochran.

Directions: From Portland, drive 44 miles west on U.S. 26 and Highway 6 to the Elk Creek Campground, near milepost 28. Parking and the trailhead are on the right (north) side of the road.

Contact: Tillamook State Forest, Forest Grove District Office, 801 Gales Creek Road, Forest Grove, OR 97116, 503/357-2191, www.odf .state.or.us/tsf.

7 GALES CREEK
4.0 mi/2.0 hrs

in Tillamook State Forest north of Highway 6

Map 1.2, page 21

The initial descent isn't exactly knee-friendly, but Gales Creek makes up for it by being convenient and straightforward (read: no heavy-duty navigation is required). After the short but steep downhill trek to the creek bed, it's a pleasant stroll through a surreal mixture of ferns and tall Douglas firs, making you feel as if you've just stepped onto a movie set. You might share the trail with mountain bikers, who like the screaming descent and twisty trail, so keep your head up. Pack a lunch to enjoy when you hit the campground, where picnic tables line the creek. Head back the way you came for a pleasant but heart rate–raising hike back up to your car. To make a loop (6.5 miles total from the trailhead), continue past the campground

for almost a mile, turn left on Storey Burn Trail at the T-junction, and continue to the Storey Burn Road, turning left to hike two miles back to the car on the gravel road.

User groups: Hikers, dogs, and mountain bikes. Horses allowed only on Storey Burn Trail. No wheelchair facilities.

Permits: Permits are not required. Parking and access are free.

Maps: For a Tillamook Forest Visitor Map & Guide, contact the Forest Grove District Office, 503/357-2191, www.odf.state.or.us/tsf. For a topographic map, ask the USGS for Timber and Cochran.

Directions: From Portland, drive 39 miles west on U.S. 26 and Highway 6 to the Gales Creek trailhead signpost and parking area near milepost 33, on the right (north) side of the highway.

Contact: Tillamook State Forest, Forest Grove District Office, 801 Gales Creek Road, Forest Grove, OR 97116, 503/357-2191, www.odf .state.or.us/tsf.

8 BANKS-VERNONIA STATE TRAIL
2.0–21.0 mi one-way/
1.0 hr–1.0 day

between the towns of Banks and Vernonia off Highway 47

Map 1.2, page 21

If you're tired of the old switchback routine up a never-ending slope and just want to lose yourself in nature without, well, getting *lost,* this old Rails to Trails hike is calling your name (well, not literally—that would be creepy, but you know what I mean). The old railway trail was the first linear state park in Oregon, and what it may lack in scenery it makes up for in a feeling of Serenity Now, as you pass through meadows, past streams, and over bridges. Although it starts in Vernonia, where the path offers a paved portion for hikers and cyclists, and a separate gravel path for horses, another popular setting-off point is Buxton, where you can walk over the train trestle. There are also three other parking spots along the way, so pick your pleasure. Wherever you start, you can be sure of a peaceful stroll; even when others are around, the wide path makes room for everyone, so you're not bumping elbows with other peace-seekers.

User groups: Hikers, mountain bikes, horses, and dogs. Wheelchair facilities at the paved portions and parks.

Permits: Permits are not required. Parking and access are free.

Maps: For a free trail map and brochure, contact Oregon State Parks, 800/551-6949. For a topographic map, ask the USGS for Vernonia and Buxton.

Directions: From Portland, drive approximately 28 miles west on U.S. 26 to Banks and turn right on Highway 47. Several trailheads line this route, all directly off Highway 47: Banks, Manning (4 miles from Banks), Buxton (6 miles from Banks), Top Hill (12 miles from Banks), and Beaver Creek (16 miles from Banks). The northern section is located at Anderson Park in Vernonia, 20 miles from Banks, off Highway 47.

Contact: Oregon Parks and Recreation Department, 1115 Commercial Street Northeast, Salem, OR 97301, 800/551-6949, www.oregonstate parks.org.

9 HAGG LAKE LOOP
15.4 mi/7.5 hrs

south of Forest Grove off Highway 47

Map 1.2, page 21

This lakeside trail is popular with Portland-area triathletes, who take advantage of the three types of training terrain: swimming in the lake, running on the trail, and biking the paved bike route surrounding the lake. In fact, many running, biking, and triathlon races are held at this lake, so it's a good idea to check ahead of time to make sure the schedule is clear (unless spectating sweaty bodies is your thing). The 15.4-mile loop is popular with mountain bikers, so keep your eye out for two-wheeled types, and keep your pets on a leash. Throughout the lake loop, you get a change of scenery almost every time you round a bend—from

open wildflower meadows to old-growth forest. For those who don't like to navigate much on their hike, you'll like this one because it's practically impossible to get lost since it parallels the surrounding paved road the whole time. Although it's a quick getaway for those who live nearby, it can get a bit crowded with all the different types of users (it's also popular for fishing and boating). Also, steer clear on a day after a big rain, when it can be a sogfest here, especially in the spring and fall. Occasional washouts on the path mean you'll have to sometimes walk on the road.

User groups: Hikers, dogs, and mountain bikes. Horses are not allowed. There is wheelchair access at the boat ramps and picnic areas.

Permits: Permits are not required. A $5 day-use fee is collected at the park entrance.

Maps: For a map, contact Washington County Facilities Management, 169 North 1st Avenue, MS 42, Hillsboro, OR 97124. For a topographic map, ask the USGS for Gaston.

Directions: From Portland, drive about 20 miles west on Highway 26 to Forest Grove Exit/Glencoe Road, following Glencoe Road/Highway 8 for five miles into Hillsboro. From Hillsboro, turn left (south) onto Highway 47, and drive 5.9 miles to the yellow flashing light and signs for Hagg Lake/Scoggins Valley Park. Turn right and drive 3.7 miles to the park entrance. There is no official trailhead, so you can park at any of the three boat ramps or two picnic areas surrounding the lake.

Contact: Washington County Facilities Management, 169 North 1st Avenue, MS 42, Hillsboro, OR 97123, 503/359-5732 (for trail and weather conditions) or 503/846-8715 (for all other questions).

10 CAPE MEARES
0.5–4.0 mi/0.5–2.0 hrs

northwest of Tillamook in Cape Meares State Park

Map 1.2, page 21

This area's trails offer a taste of everything—a lighthouse, a giant tree, tidbits on local wildlife, and great views. Plaques line the route, helping hikers spot different seabirds on the nearby Three Arches Rocks, where common murres and tufted puffins like to rest their little feet. The area is a conglomeration of mini-hikes, so here's a guide: At the park entrance, you can pick up a short trail to a big spruce—you'll know it when you come across, well, a big spruce—and the beach. Then drive into the parking area, where you can visit the lighthouse. On your way back up the path, pick up Octopus Tree Trail, where you'll find a giant Sitka spruce appropriately called the "Octopus Tree" because its limbs extend out to form multiple trunks. Strong coastal winds sculpted its unusual shape. The Octopus Tree's base has a circumference of about 50 feet. If you want to walk farther, continue on the trail until you hit the road, then turn back the way you came.

User groups: Hikers and dogs. No mountain bikes or horses are allowed. Parts of the paved trail are wheelchair accessible.

Permits: Permits are not required. Parking and access are free.

Maps: For a free park brochure, contact the Oregon Parks and Recreation Department, 800/551-6949, www.oregonstateparks.org. For a topographic map, ask the USGS for Netarts.

Directions: From U.S. 101 at Tillamook, drive 10 miles west on the Three Capes Scenic Highway to the park entrance, on the right side of the road. The first trailhead is at the front entrance, while the lighthouse and other trails are at the end of the road.

Contact: Oregon Parks and Recreation Department, 1115 Commercial Street Northeast, Salem, OR 97301, 800/551-6949, www.oregonstate parks.org.

⓫ CAPE LOOKOUT
5.0 mi/3.0 hrs

southwest of Tillamook off U.S. 101

Map 1.2, page 21

On a scenic coast with views, views, and more views, it's hard to stand out from the crowd— and yet Cape Lookout does it well. You gotta admire a trail that doesn't mince words—Lookout Trail just says it like it is, plain and simple. The 2.4-mile trail travels through the forest down the length of the peninsula, where you'll be hit with a hard-to-beat southern view of the sea 400 feet below, and maybe even a whale or two. Along the way, you'll find a plaque that memorializes a plane crash site from the '40s. At the tip of the cape, you can rest on a bench that looks out over the sea—that is, if you get there on a not-so-crowded day, as it can get a smidge packed on a sunny weekend. And you'll be lucky if you see some rays, as Cape Lookout is the proud recipient of 100 inches of rain a year. Two other trails also take off from the parking area; one heads down to a secluded beach, the other to a campground, so if you have extra energy to burn, you can make a day out of it.

User groups: Hikers and dogs. No mountain bikes or horses are allowed. No wheelchair facilities.

Permits: Permits are not required. A $3 day-use fee is collected at the park entrance, or you can get an annual Oregon Parks and Recreation pass for $25; contact Oregon Parks and Recreation, 800/551-6949. Another option is to buy the Oregon Pacific Coast Passport, which is valid at 17 locations along the coast; the cost is $35 for a year or $10 for a five-day pass. It is available at local vendors or through the Oregon Parks and Recreation Department.

Maps: For a free brochure, contact the Oregon Parks and Recreation Department, 800/551-6949, www.oregonstateparks.org. For a topographic map, ask the USGS for Sand Lake.

Directions: From Tillamook, drive west on Three Capes Scenic Highway for 13 miles. The trailhead is on the right side of the road (2.5 miles past the campground).

Contact: Oregon Parks and Recreation Department, 1115 Commercial Street Northeast, Salem, OR 97301, 800/551-6949, www.oregon-stateparks.org.

12 PIONEER-INDIAN TRAIL TO MOUNT HEBO
6.5 mi/4.0 hrs

between Tillamook and Lincoln City in Siuslaw National Forest

Map 1.2, page 21

This trail was the first developed transportation route between the Willamette and Tillamook Valleys. It travels through Sitka spruce (second-growth, courtesy of the infamous Tillamook Burn, which destroyed 355,000 acres of forest from the '30s through the '50s) and operates like a little nature museum, with plaques along the trail detailing fun facts about the area's plant life. Here's one: Did you know that braken fern, which lines the trail and can grow to five feet tall, is edible when it first sprouts in spring? Now you do. The trail markings are somewhat sporadic because new loop trails are currently under construction, so keep to the main trail. When you hit Road 14, turn right to take the side trip to the summit of 3,164-foot Mount Hebo. When you've had your fill of the view, head back the way you came for a 6.5-mile round-trip. (The full length of Pioneer-Indian Trail is eight miles one-way, so shoot for a turning-around point when you've had enough history and nature lessons.)

User groups: Hikers, dogs, and horses. Mountain bikes are not allowed. No wheelchair facilities.

Permits: A federal Northwest Forest pass is required to park here; the cost is $5 for a day pass or $30 for an annual pass. You can buy a day pass at the trailhead, at ranger stations, through private vendors, or through Nature of the Northwest Information Center. Another option is to buy the Oregon Pacific Coast Passport, which is valid at 17 locations along the coast; the cost is $35 for a year or $10 for a five-day pass. It is available at local vendors or through the Oregon Parks and Recreation Department.

Maps: For a map of the Siuslaw National Forest, contact the Nature of the Northwest Information Center. For a topographic map, ask the USGS for Hebo and Niagara Creek.

Directions: From Tillamook, travel 20 miles south on Highway 101 to Hebo, and turn left (east) on Highway 22. Following signs to Hebo Lake, turn left on Highway 14 and continue four miles to the Hebo Lake Campground and the trailhead.

Contact: Siuslaw National Forest, Hebo Ranger District, 31525 Highway 22, Hebo, OR 97122, 503/392-3161.

13 HART'S COVE
5.4 mi/2.5 hrs

north of Lincoln City in Cascade Head Scenic Area

Map 1.2, page 21

Hart's Cove stands out from the crowd in many ways. Whereas most trails like to climb to a viewpoint, this spectacular cove isn't content to conform to the normal trail format. Instead, you'll encounter an original steep descent on the 2.7-mile journey down to the scenic spot. Rest up and take in the sweeping views of the ocean, a waterfall, and surrounding capes before climbing back through the spruce forest where you came from. Note: This trail is closed from January 1 to July 15.

User groups: Hikers and dogs. No mountain bikes or horses are allowed.

Permits: Permits are not required. Parking and access are free.

Maps: For a map of the Siuslaw National Forest, contact the Nature of the Northwest Information Center. For a topographic map, ask the USGS for Neskowin.

Directions: From Lincoln City, drive north on U.S. 101 for six miles to Forest Service Road 1861. Turn left and drive four miles to the end of the road and the trailhead, on the left side of the road.

Contact: Siuslaw National Forest, Hebo Ranger District, 31525 Highway 22, Hebo, OR 97122, 503/392-3161.

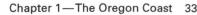

14 CASCADE HEAD NATURE CONSERVANCY TRAIL
4.5–6.0 mi/2.0–4.0 hrs 🥾 ◀8

North of Lincoln City in Cascade Head Scenic Area

Map 1.2, page 21

The Cascade Head Scenic Area is home to my favorite rare plant name: the hairy checkermallow. The "mallow," as we've nicknamed it, also shares digs with other rare species, like the Cascade Head catchfly and the Oregon silverspot butterfly. No wonder the Nature Conservancy has gotten their hands on this treasure trove of plants and wildlife; they like to gently remind hikers to keep their feet on the trail and their furry friends at home. Don't let the term "nature trail" mislead you into thinking this trail is a snap—you'll climb 1,200 feet on the 4.5-mile round-trip. The views are worth it as you wind your way along the grasslands to the top of the headland. Turn back at the unmarked upper viewpoint (you can also drive from the other side to hit the upper view for a one-mile level hike, but that's not as much fun, right?). Along with the good news comes the bad, though: While the lack of tree coverage means stellar views, this trail is best enjoyed on a day that is light in the wind category. Trust me.

Two other trails lead from this area: Hart's Cove (see listing in this chapter) and Cascade Head Trail, which runs six miles through rainforest from Falls Creek to Three Rocks Road.

User groups: Hikers and horses. Dogs and mountain bikes are not allowed. No wheelchair facilities.

Permits: Permits are not required. Parking and access are free.

Maps: For a map of the Siuslaw National Forest, contact the Nature of the Northwest Information Center. For a topographic map, ask the USGS for Neskowin.

Directions: From Lincoln City, drive three miles north on U.S. 101 to Three Rocks Road. Turn left, drive two miles, and park at Knight Park. To reach Cascade Head Trail, turn right to a parking area and trailhead immediately after turning onto Three Rocks Road.

Contact: Siuslaw National Forest, Hebo Ranger District, 31525 Highway 22, Hebo, OR 97122, 503/392-3161.

15 YAQUINA HEAD LIGHTHOUSE
0.5–4.0 mi/0.5–2.0 hrs 🥾 ◀7

north of Newport off U.S. 101

Map 1.3, page 22

Don't you hate it when you get to your hard-earned destination hoping to find a shiny plaque declaring that you've arrived, with maybe a few bits of trivia thrown in for good measure, and you find nothing? Well, you'll be in plaque heaven at Yaquina Head Lighthouse, and you won't have to hike far to reach one. This area includes a variety of trails. Choose among the tallest lighthouse in Oregon (complete with a 93-foot spiral staircase), a half-mile jaunt up to Salal Hill ("the big hill"), a stroll down to Cobble Beach (which, as the name suggests, is filled with naturally formed basalt cobbles), or Quarry Cove Trail to view the tidepools. With any destination you choose, you're guaranteed a good view and some facts to fill your head. This is also a hot spot for watching migrating whales. Harbor seals and common murres (which look like a beach version of penguins) take up residence on the rocks nearby.

User groups: Hikers and mountain bikes. No dogs or horses are allowed. There is wheelchair access.

Permits: Permits are not required. There is a $5 parking fee collected at the park entrance, or you can get an annual Oregon Parks and Recreation pass for $25; contact Oregon Parks and Recreation, 800/551-6949. Another option is to buy the Oregon Pacific Coast Passport, which is valid at 17 locations along the coast; the cost is $35 for a year or $10 for a five-day pass. It is available at local vendors or through the Oregon Parks and Recreation Department.

Maps: For a brochure and map, contact the Bureau of Land Management, 541/574-3100.

For a topographic map, ask the USGS for Newport North.

Directions: From Newport, drive two miles north on U.S. 101 to the park entrance. All the trailheads start from the parking area and are well marked and easy to find.

Contact: Bureau of Land Management, 1717 Fabry Road Southeast, Salem OR, 541/574-3100.

16 CAPE PERPETUA
1.0–6.25 mi/0.5–3.5 hrs

south of Yachats off U.S. 101

Map 1.3, page 22

Ten trails lead from Cape Perpetua Scenic Area, and the trail names don't mess around—they tell it like it is here. My favorite trail name is Trail of the Restless Waters, which leads to Devil's Churn, where waves crash across the rocks. Check the map (available at the visitors center) and take your pick. If you feel like a climb, try Cape Perpetua Trail to the summit—worth the 1.3-mile push. Once you're up there, wind your way around .25-mile Whispering Spruce Trail, which encircles the summit and offers great views from all sides of the neighboring capes and Heceta Head Lighthouse below. Once you head back down, a mile on Giant Spruce Trail leads to a hefty member of the spruce family (what did you expect, a giant fern?). Not enough? There's more, including the 6.25-mile Cummins Creek Loop and the one-mile Discovery Loop Trail.

User groups: Hikers and dogs. No mountain bikes or horses are allowed. Part of Whispering Spruce Trail is wheelchair accessible.

Permits: A federal Northwest Forest pass is required to park here. The cost is $5 for a day pass or $30 for an annual pass. You can buy a day pass at the trailhead, at ranger stations, from private vendors, or through Nature of the Northwest Information Center. Another option is to buy the Oregon Pacific Coast Passport, which is valid at 17 locations along the coast; the cost is $35 for a year or $10 for a

five-day pass and is available at local vendors or through the Oregon Parks and Recreation Department.

Maps: For a map of the Siuslaw National Forest, contact the Nature of the Northwest Information Center. For a topographic map, ask the USGS for Yachats.

Directions: From Waldport, drive 11 miles south on U.S. 101 to the Cape Perpetua Visitors Center parking area on the left (east) side of the road. All the well-marked trailheads start from this parking area.

Contact: Siuslaw National Forest, Waldport Ranger District, 1094 Southwest Pacific Highway, Waldport, OR 97394, 541/563-3211.

17 CARL WASHBURNE STATE PARK TO HECETA HEAD LIGHTHOUSE
6.0 mi/3.0 hrs

between Florence and Yachats off U.S. 101

Map 1.3, page 22

Washburne State Park is more of a jumping-off point than a destination in and of itself (no offense, Carl). One option is to start from the campground and head to the scenic lighthouse. First, park at the day-use area and then scurry across the road to the trailhead, on the right side of the campground entrance road. Take Valley Trail, a shady forested path, south along China Creek for a good change of pace from the windblown coast. Hikers can either do an out-and-back, or if you're someone who likes a destination hike, keep on keepin' on until the trail reaches the highway (just under two miles down), cross the highway, and take the steep climb on Heceta Head Trail to the lighthouse. Heceta Head, shining proudly since 1894, boasts the brightest light on the coast. You can also drive directly to the lighthouse, but hey, this book is all about hiking, right? After checking out the view, you can head back the way you came or turn left on the interesting Hobbit Trail and walk down to the beach for scenery and an easy 1.5-mile stroll along the beach back to the day-use parking lot.

User groups: Hikers, dogs, and horses. No mountain bikes are allowed. No wheelchair facilities.

Permits: Permits are not required. Parking and access are free.

Maps: For a free park brochure, contact Oregon State Parks, 800/551-6949, www.oregonstateparks.org. For a topographic map, ask the USGS for Heceta Head.

Directions: From Florence, drive 14 miles north on U.S. 101 to the day-use area of Washburne State Park, on the west side of the highway. Park here and cross the highway to the campground entrance. The Valley Trail trailhead is on the right side of the campground entrance road.

Contact: Oregon Parks and Recreation Department, 1115 Commercial Street Northeast, Salem, OR 97301, 800/551-6949.

18 CAPE MOUNTAIN
2.0 mi/1.0 hr

north of Florence in the Siuslaw National Forest

Map 1.3, page 22

History lovers, rejoice—Cape Mountain is the site of an old fire lookout built in 1932, and photos of what it used to look like await you on the summit. The vista is rarely crowded, so you'll probably get to enjoy the view of the ocean below all by yourself. Hikers who are directionally challenged will appreciate this trail, as it's got to be the best-marked trail in the entire state. However, first you have to find the trailhead, which, ironically, is hard to find. From the parking lot, look to the left of the restrooms, where a posted map will help you get your bearings. You'll start off on the Princess Tasha trail, and then fork left to reach the summit, returning the way you came (all junctions are ridiculously well marked). This trail is actually made for horses, so keep an eye out for hooved creatures.

User groups: Hikers, dogs, mountain bikes, and horses. No wheelchair facilities.

Permits: None required. Parking and access are free.

Maps: For a map of the Siuslaw National Forest, contact the Nature of the Northwest Information Center. For a topographic map, ask the USGS for Mercer Lake.

Directions: From Florence, drive seven miles north on U.S. 101 and turn right on Herman Peak Road. Drive three miles to Dry Lake parking area.

Contact: Siuslaw National Forest, Mapleton Ranger District, 4480 Highway 101, Building G, Florence, OR 97439, 541/902-8526.

19 SUTTON CREEK DUNES
5.0 mi/2.5 hrs

south of Florence off U.S. 101

Map 1.3, page 22

If you want to get some sand—and water—in your shoes, try the hike to Sutton Creek dunes. Choose from three loops along and in the dunes, for five miles total. Our suggestion: First, head up to the Holman Vista viewing deck (right by the parking area) to get your bearings, then try the longer three-mile loop, which starts at the parking area and follows Sutton Creek. Once you hit the campground, you'll have to ford the creek, so take your sandals along. The trail then enters the dunes, so prepare to add some sand to your wet shoes. If you're ready for more after you get back to your car, try one of the smaller one-mile loops or head to the beach to frolic in the sand (you'll have to ford the creek again, but by now you're a creek-crossing pro).

User groups: Hikers, dogs, and horses. No mountain bikes allowed. The Holman Vista viewing deck is wheelchair accessible.

Permits: A federal Northwest Forest pass is required to park here. The cost is $5 for a day pass or $30 for an annual pass. You can buy a day pass at the trailhead, at ranger stations, from private vendors, or through Nature of the Northwest Information Center. Another option is to buy the Oregon Pacific Coast Passport, which is valid at 17 locations along the coast; the cost is $35 for a year or $10 for a five-day pass, and it is available at local vendors or through the Oregon Parks and Recreation Department.

Maps: For a map of the Siuslaw National Forest, contact the Nature of the Northwest Information Center. For a topographic map, ask the USGS for Mercer Lake.

Directions: From Florence, drive five miles north on U.S. 101 to Sutton Road. Turn left (west) and drive two miles to the end of the road. Park in the Holman Vista day-use area to find the well-marked trailheads.

Contact: Siuslaw National Forest, Mapleton Ranger District, 4480 Highway 101, Building G, Florence, OR 97439, 541/902-8526.

20 DRIFT CREEK FALLS
3.0 mi/1.5 hrs

south of Lincoln City in the Siuslaw National Forest

Map 1.4, page 23

As you drive on the 10-mile stretch of twisting road you may be muttering to yourself, "This better be worth it!" It is. Perhaps the most awe-inspiring part of Drift Creek Falls Trail is not the beautiful 75-foot waterfall, but the suspension bridge that hovers 100 feet over the creek (acrophobes would be wise to look straight ahead while crossing the 240-foot-long bridge). It is an exhilarating walk to the other side, where a tree trunk/picnic bench awaits. Have a seat for a stellar view of the waterfall and bridge.

User groups: Hikers and dogs. No horses or mountain bikes allowed. No wheelchair facilities.

Permits: A federal Northwest Forest pass is required to park here. The cost is $5 for a day pass or $30 for an annual pass. You can buy a day pass at the trailhead, at ranger stations, from private vendors, or through Nature of the Northwest Information Center. Another option is to buy the Oregon Pacific Coast Passport, which is valid at 17 locations along the

coast; the cost is $35 for a year or $10 for a five-day pass, and it is available at local vendors or through the Oregon Parks and Recreation Department.

Maps: For a map of the Siuslaw National Forest, contact the Nature of the Northwest Information Center. For a topographic map, ask the USGS for Stott Mountain.

Directions: From Lincoln City, drive on U.S. 101 to the south edge of town and turn east onto Drift Creek Road (Road 17) for 10 miles to the small parking area and the well-marked trailhead.

Contact: Siuslaw National Forest, Hebo Ranger District, 31525 Highway 22, Hebo, OR 97122, 503/392-3161.

21 MARY'S PEAK
5.8–11.0 mi/3.0–6.0 hrs

west of Philomath in the Oregon Coastal Range

Map 1.4, page 23

There are two ways to get to the highest peak in the Coastal Range: East Ridge Trail (5.8 miles round-trip, gaining 1,500 feet in elevation) and North Ridge Trail (11 miles round-trip, gaining 2,300 feet). Okay, actually there's a third route to the summit—you can drive directly to it—but that's not much fun, now is it? Whatever route you choose, you end up at the top of the 4,097-foot peak with great views of Mount Hood, Mount Adams, Mount St. Helens, Mount Rainier, Sisters, and the college town of Corvallis (home of Oregon State University). You'll be sharing the view with many softer souls who have driven to the top, but you'll know you earned the view. Bask in the glory of a job well done—or try the two-mile Meadow Edge loop up top—before you head back down the route you came from.

User groups: Hikers, dogs, mountain bikes, and horses. The top of the summit is wheelchair accessible.

Permits: A federal Northwest Forest pass is required to park here. The cost is $5 for a day pass or $30 for an annual pass. You can buy a day pass at the trailhead, at ranger stations, from private vendors, or through Nature of the Northwest Information Center. Another option is to buy the Oregon Pacific Coast Passport, which is valid at 17 locations along the coast; the cost is $35 for a year or $10 for a five-day pass, and it is available at local vendors or through the Oregon Parks and Recreation Department.

Maps: For a map of the Siuslaw National Forest, contact the Nature of the Northwest Information Center. For a topographic map, ask the USGS for Mary's Peak and Alsea.

Directions: From Corvallis to the North Ridge trailhead, drive west on U.S. 20 through Philomath to the U.S. 34 junction. Continue on U.S. 20 about two miles to Woods Creek Road, drive six miles to the trailhead, and park at the side of the road. From Corvallis to the East Ridge trailhead, drive west on U.S. 20 through Philomath to the U.S. 34 junction. Drive west on U.S. 34 for nine miles, and turn right on Mary's Peak Road. The trailhead and small parking area are 5.5 miles in, on the right.

Contact: Siuslaw National Forest, Waldport Ranger District, 1094 Southwest Pacific Highway, Waldport, OR 97394, 541/563-3211.

22 SILTCOOS LAKE
4.0 mi/2.0 hrs

south of Florence in the Oregon Dunes National Recreation Area

Map 1.5, page 24

If you're one of those goal-oriented people who likes to have a destination when hiking, try this relatively easy stroll through the forest. Enjoy the trip out to the lake, because the lake itself is not the most scenic in the state. It's a shady trail through second-growth Sitka spruce and Douglas fir forest, and is refreshing on a hot day. About one mile in, the trail splits into north and south routes, appropriately named North and South Trails, both of which end at the lake. Once you reach the lake, head back on the other trail to complete the loop. At the lake, there are five campsites where you can hang out for a picnic or simply rest your soles (the lake is also renowned for fishing).

User groups: Hikers, dogs, and mountain bikes. No horses are allowed. No wheelchair facilities.

Permits: A federal Northwest Forest pass is required to park here. The cost is $5 for a day pass or $30 for an annual pass. You can buy a day pass at the trailhead, at ranger stations, from private vendors, or through Nature of the Northwest Information Center. Another option is to buy the Oregon Pacific Coast Passport, which is valid at 17 locations along the coast; the cost is $35 for a year or $10 for a five-day pass, and it is available at local vendors or through the Oregon Parks and Recreation Department.

Maps: For a map of the Siuslaw National Forest, contact the Nature of the Northwest Information Center. For a topographic map, ask the USGS for Goose Pasture, Florence, Tahkenitch Creek, and Fivemile Creek.

Directions: From Florence, drive seven miles south on U.S. 101 to the Siltcoos Lake sign on your left, and turn into the parking area and trailhead.

Contact: Oregon Dunes National Recreation Area, 855 Highway 101, Reedsport, OR 97467, 541/271-3611.

23 TAHKENITCH DUNES
6.0 mi/3.0 hrs

south of Florence in the Oregon Dunes National Recreation Area

Map 1.5, page 24

If you like a change of scenery while you hike, try this interesting loop: The first .5 mile is through a forest before you reach the sand, then it's another 1.5 mile through dunes to the water. Hang a left when you reach the ocean, and walk along the water for about a mile until you hit Threemile Lake Trail, which handily suggests its length: three miles. This trail travels past the freshwater Threemile Lake and offers up a few good vistas of the sea before slipping into a second-growth forest with spruce and ferns and heading back to the parking lot.

User groups: Hikers, dogs, and horses. No mountain bikes allowed. No wheelchair facilities.

Permits: A federal Northwest Forest pass is required to park here. The cost is $5 for a day pass or $30 for an annual pass. You can buy a day pass at the trailhead, at ranger stations, from private vendors, or through Nature of the Northwest Information Center. Another option is to buy the Oregon Pacific Coast Passport, which is valid at 17 locations along the coast; the cost is $35 for a year or $10 for a five-day pass, and it is available at local vendors or through the Oregon Parks and Recreation Department.

Maps: For a map of the Oregon Dunes National Recreation Area, contact the Nature of the Northwest Information Center. For a topographic map, ask the USGS for Tahkenitch Creek.

Directions: From Reedsport, drive 7.5 miles north (or 12.5 miles south from Florence) on U.S. 101 to the Tahkenitch Lake Campground. Park in the day-use area and walk to the well-marked trailhead.

Contact: Oregon Dunes National Recreation Area, 855 Highway 101, Reedsport, OR 97467, 541/271 3611.

24 UMPQUA DUNES
5.0 mi/3.0 hrs

south of Reedsport in the Umpqua Dunes Scenic Area

Map 1.5, page 24

Have you ever wanted to get a picture of yourself in the middle of the desert, crawling on hands and knees with nothing in sight, but don't have the time or resources to high-tail it to the Sahara? Here's your chance (not that I've ever participated in such a silly display, you understand). The Oregon Dunes are a must-see area of the coastal region, and Umpqua Dunes is perhaps the most impressive of them all. Be prepared for sand in your shoes, because most of the six-mile trail is actually in the dunes. You'll start off on a well-marked, .5-mile interpretive trail before you hit the sandy stuff. Now

the fun begins. Using the ocean as your beacon, either climb up on the large dune to your left (you can't miss it) or keep just to the right of it, looking for the blue trail blazes in the distance. It's like a beach treasure hunt to find the next blue marker in the middle of what seems like a never-ending desert (now's your chance to snap the aforementioned picture). The trail leads to the beach and then returns the way it came.

User groups: Hikers, dogs, and horses. Mountain bikes are not allowed. No wheelchair facilities.

Permits: A federal Northwest Forest pass is required to park here. The cost is $5 for a day pass or $30 for an annual pass. You can buy a day pass at the trailhead, at ranger stations, from private vendors, or through Nature of the Northwest Information Center. Another option is to buy the Oregon Pacific Coast Passport, which is valid at 17 locations along the coast; the cost is $35 for a year or $10 for a five-day pass, and it is available at local vendors or through the Oregon Parks and Recreation Department.

Maps: For a map of the Oregon Dunes National Recreation Area, contact the Nature of the Northwest Information Center. For a topographic map, ask the USGS for Lakeside.

Directions: From Reedsport, drive 10.5 miles south on U.S. 101 to the Umpqua Dunes Trail signpost. Turn west (right) into the parking area and the trailhead.

Contact: Oregon Dunes National Recreation Area, 855 Highway 101, Reedsport, OR 97467, 541/271-3611.

25 SUNSET BAY TO CAPE ARAGO
8.0 mi/4.0 hrs

west of Coos Bay between Sunset Bay State Park and Cape Arago

Map 1.5, page 24

You'll be kicking yourself if you didn't bring your camera on this hike. A four-mile stretch of the Oregon Coast Trail, this unique trail is a prime whale-watching spot. Sir Francis Drake first spotted this cape in the 1500s, and modern visitors have been flocking ever since. A fun fact: On October 4, 1973, the first transcontinental hot-air balloon crossing started from this spot. The balloonist landed a month later on Chesapeake Bay, on the East Coast. You don't need to reach magical heights to glimpse some great views of the water below, though—the cliffside path is filled with views the whole way. Starting from Sunset Bay, stroll for two miles to an observation deck, then continue south along the coast for stellar views of the cape, plus a sea lion viewpoint (you can hear their calls from the water below). You need to walk along the road for .5 mile at the southern end to reach Cape Arago, but it's well worth it, as another observation deck awaits. (For a shuttle hike, you can leave one car at the cape itself and another at Sunset Bay.)

User groups: Hikers and dogs. No horses or mountain bikes are allowed.

Permits: Permits are not required. Parking and access are free.

Maps: For a free brochure, contact the Oregon Parks and Recreation Department at 800/551-6949. For a topographic map, ask the USGS for Charleston and Cape Arago.

Directions: From Coos Bay, drive south 12 miles on Cape Arago Highway, following signs to Sunset Bay State Park. Park in the day-use picnic area to the right; the trailhead is located to the right of the restrooms and is marked as the Oregon Coast Trail.

Contact: Oregon Parks and Recreation Department, 1115 Commercial Street Northeast, Salem, OR 97301, 800/551-6949, www.oregonstateparks.org.

Park. Cape Blanco is the westernmost point of Oregon, and its lighthouse has a few claims to fame: The oldest continuously operating lighthouse, it stands taller than any others on the coast, at 245 feet. There are a few short trails (less than .5 mile) that take you to the lighthouse or along the beach, but we've chosen to spotlight the Hughes House trail. This 2.6-mile round-trip leads to an 11-room historic house built in 1898 that you can tour. (Visitors can also drive directly to the house, open Thursday through Monday, 10 A.M. to 3:30 P.M. from April to October). After touring the house, return the way you came and explore the great views of the beach, or head to the lighthouse.

User groups: Hikers and dogs. Mountain bikes are allowed only on roads. Horses are allowed only on designated horse trails. There is wheelchair access on paved portions.

Permits: Permits are not required. Parking and access are free.

Maps: For a free map, contact Oregon Parks and Recreation Department, 800/551-6949, www.oregonstateparks.org. For a topographic map, ask the USGS for Cape Blanco.

Directions: From Port Orford, drive four miles north on U.S. 101 and turn left (west) onto Cape Blanco Highway. Drive five miles and park at the lighthouse entrance parking area, where the trails start. For the Hughes House Trail, backtrack along the road; the trailhead is on the left (north) side of the road, roughly .2 mile down.

Contact: Oregon Parks and Recreation Department, 1115 Commercial Street Northeast, Salem, OR 97301, 800/551-6949, www.oregonstateparks.org.

26 CAPE BLANCO
2.6 mi/1.5 hrs

northwest of Port Orford in Cape Blanco State Park

Map 1.6, page 25

With a campground on the premises, including four beachside log cabins, you can while away an entire weekend at Cape Blanco State

27 HUMBUG MOUNTAIN
5.5 mi/2.5 hrs

south of Port Orford off U.S. 101

Map 1.6, page 25

If you want to enjoy this trail with elbow room, get there early, as the parking lot quickly fills up on a sunny weekend day—especially since there's a campground nearby. From the conveniently located trailhead right off Highway 101, you'll quickly leave the traffic noise behind as you start your ascent; suddenly you'll round a bend and find yourself in the middle of the fern and Douglas fir forest, serenaded by birdsong and the rushing creek below. Although we like the fact that every .5 mile is marked, it can also evoke feelings of "what, we've only gone a half mile?" because the trail gains over 1,700 feet in elevation. Catch your breath at a bench and look out over at Cape Blanco to the north. After a mile, the trail splits: The steeper West Trail tops out at the summit in 1.5 miles, while East Trail takes its time, reaching the top in 2 miles. Take your pick, then choose the other trail for the return trip. At the top, a short trail leads to a bench facing south, a prime place to enjoy a picnic. Although there's a clearing where you can view the ocean in the distance, trees partially block the full view.

User groups: Hikers and dogs. No mountain bikes or horses are allowed. No wheelchair access.

Permits: Permits are not required. Parking and access are free.

Maps: For a free map, contact Oregon Parks and Recreation Department, 800/551-6949, www.oregonstateparks.org. For a topographic map, ask the USGS for Port Orford.

Directions: From Port Orford, drive six miles south on U.S. 101. The parking area and trailhead are on the right side of the highway.

Contact: Oregon Parks and Recreation Department, 1115 Commercial Street Northeast, Salem, OR 97301, 800/551-6949, www.oregonstateparks.org.

28 BARKLOW MOUNTAIN TRAIL
2.0 mi/1.0 hr

northeast of Gold Beach in the Siskiyou National Forest

Map 1.6, page 25

Attention to those of you who love off-road adventuring: Here's your chance to test your tires, brakes, obstacle-maneuvering skills—and

your new paint job. If you're the type who winces at each and every bump in the road ("Ack, did I just lose my muffler?"), you may want to skip this trail. But once you've reached your destination, you'll most likely be able to enjoy the scenery solo. After you've unclenched your fingers from the steering wheel and done a quick once-over to make sure your car is still intact, start on the trailhead. You can choose between a lookout site to the right or travel to the left toward a deserted Forest Service shelter. Try the old fire lookout first, which takes you to the highest point on 3,579-foot Barklow Mountain for views of the Siskiyou mountain range. Then return back to the junction and head across a slope, where you can revel in more peaceful views before heading into the forest to the shelter, where old relics remain. The trail is short and sweet, but it's perfect if you like peace and quiet and believe that "part of the fun is getting there."

User groups: Hikers and dogs. No mountain bikes or horses are allowed. No wheelchair facilities.

Permits: Permits are not required. Parking and access are free.

Maps: For a map of the Siskiyou National Forest, contact the Nature of the Northwest Information Center. For a topographic map, ask the USGS for Barklow Mountain.

Directions: From Port Orford, turn right (east) onto Elk River Road. Drive on Highway 208 for 18.8 miles, then turn right onto Forest Service Road 5325. Continue nine miles and turn left onto Forest Service Road 3353. After 9.5 miles, turn left on bumpy, dirt Spur Road 220 and go one mile to the end of the road and the trailhead.

Contact: Siskiyou National Forest, Powers Ranger District, Powers, OR 97466, 541/439-3011.

29 CAPE SEBASTIAN
3.0 mi/1.0 hr

south of Gold Beach off U.S. 101

Map 1.6, page 25

You don't even need to get out of your car to

witness the picture-perfect scenery of Cape Sebastian, since the parking lot sits 200 feet above sea level. The 1.5-mile trail starts from the south parking lot, turning from a paved walkway into a path through Sitka spruce forest, ending at the cape's edge. You'll want to linger here, and the Oregon State Parks Department has read your mind: Plenty of benches line the path, so you can take your time strolling the area and lining up that perfect shot. Bring warm clothes, because the wind can take the temperature down several notches, even on a sunny day. Another packing must: binoculars. The views extend 50 miles north to Humbug Mountain and 50 miles south to Crescent City, California and the Point Saint George lighthouse.

User groups: Hikers, dogs, and mountain bikes. No horses are allowed. The first section of the trail is paved for wheelchair access.

Permits: Permits are not required. Parking and access are free.

Maps: For a topographic map, ask the USGS for Cape Sebastian.

Directions: From Gold Beach, drive 4.5 miles south on U.S. 101 to the park entrance on the right (west) side of the highway. Drive .5 mile to the south parking lot.

Contact: Oregon Parks and Recreation Department, 1115 Commercial Street Northeast, Salem, OR 97301, 800/551-6949, www.oregonstate parks.org.

30 SNOW CAMP LOOKOUT
7.0 mi/3.5 hrs

northeast of Brookings in the Kalmiopsis Wilderness of Siskiyou National Forest

Map 1.6, page 25

This popular lookout cabin, perched 4,223 feet on Snow Camp Mountain, was unfortunately destroyed in the 2002 Biscuit Fire (plans are currently under way to rebuild it as a rental cabin). The good news is, the views remain, as does the steep climb to get here. The trail first gives you a break by descending into the Windy Valley meadow, where you cross the stream. Then the real climbing begins, a steep 1,500-foot hoof up

to the mountain, where you can see remnants of the lookout cabin. As with all trails affected by the fire, it's a good idea to check with the Forest Service for current conditions.

User groups: Hikers, dogs, and horses. No mountain bikes are allowed. No wheelchair access.

Permits: A federal Northwest Forest pass is required to park here. The cost is $5 for a day pass or $30 for an annual pass. You can buy a day pass at ranger stations, from private vendors, or through Nature of the Northwest Information Center.

Maps: For a map of the Siskiyou National Forest, contact the Nature of the Northwest Information Center. For a topographic map, ask the USGS for Collier Butte.

Directions: From Brookings, drive east on County Road 784 (marked as Constitution Avenue) for 16 miles (it becomes Forest Service Road 1376 at the forest boundary). Turn left at the T-junction to continue on gravel Road 1376 for 14.5 miles. The trailhead and parking are on the left side of the road.

Contact: Siskiyou National Forest, Chetco Ranger District, P.O. Box 4580, 539 Chetco Avenue, Brookings, OR 97415, 541/412-6000.

31 MISLATNAH TRAIL
6.6 mi/3.5 hrs

northeast of Brookings in the Kalmiopsis Wilderness of Siskiyou National Forest

Map 1.6, page 25

Mislatnah Trail, sharing Tincup Trail for more than a mile, starts off as a gentle descent to Mislatnah Creek. Then it says "later" to Tincup (take the left junction) to climb to 3,124-foot Mislatnah Peak, where great views from the former lookout site await and the trail ends. Look out over the deep canyons of the Big Craggies Botanical Area, the only view of the area that is accessible by trail. You'll have to ford the creek, and, as water levels can get high in the winter and early spring, it's best to tackle this one in the late spring or summer. As this trail is within the 2002 Biscuit Fire region, it's a good idea to check current conditions before you head out.

User groups: Hikers, dogs, and horses. No mountain bikes are allowed. No wheelchair access.

Permits: A federal Northwest Forest pass is required to park here. The cost is $5 for a day pass or $30 for an annual pass. You can buy a day pass at the trailhead, at ranger stations, from private vendors, or through Nature of the Northwest Information Center.

Maps: For a map of the Siskiyou National Forest, contact the Nature of the Northwest Information Center. For a topographic map, ask the USGS for Big Craggies.

Directions: From Brookings, drive 25.3 miles on County Road 784 (marked as Constitution Avenue in town), which becomes Forest Service Road 1376 at the forest boundary to the junction with Forest Service Road 360. Turn right on 360 and drive 1.5 miles to Forest Service Road 365. Turn right and drive .8 mile to the end of the road and the trailhead.

Contact: Siskiyou National Forest, Chetco Ranger District, P.O. Box 4580, 539 Chetco Avenue, Brookings, OR 97415, 541/412-6000.

32 TINCUP TRAIL
19.4 mi/1.0–2.0 days
northeast of Brookings in the Kalmiopsis Wilderness of Siskiyou National Forest

Map 1.6, page 25

Don't you hate it when you've hiked for miles and finally feel like you're in the middle of nowhere, only to come across a Boy Scout troop who just hiked in one mile from a road nearby? Well, that won't happen when you do Tincup Trail, because it leads into the edge of the Kalmiopsis Wilderness, where no other trails connect to it. It's best to try this in the late spring and summer, because you have to ford Mislatnah Creek, a tributary of the Chetco River, and the water level can't be safely crossed during the winter and early spring. The trail starts off above the water and dips down to a ford of the creek, then follows the Wild and Scenic portions of the Chetco River. Since this

trail is in the 2002 Biscuit Fire region, it's a good idea to check conditions beforehand.

User groups: Hikers, dogs, and horses. No mountain bikes are allowed. No wheelchair access.

Permits: A federal Northwest Forest pass is required to park here. The cost is $5 for a day pass or $30 for an annual pass. You can buy a day pass at the trailhead, at ranger stations, from private vendors, or through Nature of the Northwest Information Center.

Maps: For a map of the Siskiyou National Forest, contact the Nature of the Northwest Information Center. For a topographic map, ask the USGS for Big Craggies.

Directions: From Brookings, drive 25.3 miles on County Road 784 (marked as Constitution Avenue in town), which becomes Forest Service Road 1376 at the forest boundary to the junction with Forest Service Road 360. Turn right on 360 and drive 1.5 miles to Forest Service Road 365. Turn right and drive .8 mile to the end of the road and the trailhead.

Contact: Siskiyou National Forest, Chetco Ranger District, P.O. Box 4580, 539 Chetco Avenue, Brookings, OR 97415, 541/412-6000.

33 JOHNSON BUTTE
12.6 mi/6.5 hrs
northeast of Brookings in the Kalmiopsis Wilderness of Siskiyou National Forest

Map 1.6, page 25

May and June are the best months to hike this scenic ridgeline trail, when the pink, saucer-shaped Kalmiopsis (pronounced kal-mee-OP-sis) plant is in bloom, the namesake of this wilderness area. The trail starts on an abandoned road for the first two miles, then passes two small lakes—Salamander and Valen Lakes—before ending at the junction with the Chetco trail system. This trail was affected by the 2002 Biscuit Fire, so you may have to cross some downed tree trunks. As with all trails affected by the fire, it's a good idea to check with the Forest Service beforehand for up-to-date conditions.

User groups: Hikers, dogs, and horses. No

mountain bikes are allowed. No wheelchair access.

Permits: A federal Northwest Forest pass is required to park here. The cost is $5 for a day pass or $30 for an annual pass. You can buy a day pass at ranger stations, from private vendors, or through Nature of the Northwest Information Center.

Maps: For a map of the Siskiyou National Forest, contact the Nature of the Northwest Information Center. For a topographic map, ask the USGS for Chetco Peak and Tincup Peak.

Directions: From Brookings, drive east on County Road 784 (marked as Constitution Avenue) for 16 miles (it becomes Forest Service Road 1376 at the forest boundary). Turn right onto Forest Service Road 1909 and drive 13.4 miles, then turn left, continuing on Forest Service Road 1909 for 1.7 bumpy miles to the end of the road and the trailhead.

Contact: Siskiyou National Forest, Chetco Ranger District, P.O. Box 4580, 539 Chetco Avenue, Brookings, OR 97415, 541/412-6000.

34 VULCAN PEAK
2.2 mi/1.5 hrs

northeast of Brookings in the Kalmiopsis Wilderness of Siskiyou National Forest

Map 1.6, page 25

It's only 1.1 miles to the top of this 4,655-foot peak, but it's a steep and rocky climb that will leave you breathless at the top. Starting on an abandoned road, you'll soon fork left to hit the top. Stick around for a while, because the views are worth it (and you're likely to have them all to yourself). It's fitting that this is an old fire lookout: It's a perfect perch from which to view the pattern of the Biscuit Fire, which whipped through this area in 2002. Rest here before returning on the rocky descent back to your car.

User groups: Hikers, dogs, and horses. No mountain bikes are allowed. No wheelchair facilities.

Permits: A federal Northwest Forest pass is required to park here. The cost is $5 for a day pass or $30 for an annual pass. You can buy

a day pass at ranger stations, from private vendors, or through Nature of the Northwest Information Center.

Maps: For a map of the Siskiyou National Forest, contact the Nature of the Northwest Information Center. For a topographic map, ask the USGS for Chetco Peak.

Directions: From Brookings, drive east on County Road 784 (marked as Constitution Avenue) for 16 miles (it becomes Forest Service Road 1376 at the forest boundary). Turn right onto Forest Service Road 1909 and drive 13.4 miles, then turn right for less than .1 mile to the end of the road and the trailhead.

Contact: Siskiyou National Forest, Chetco Ranger District, P.O. Box 4580, 539 Chetco Avenue, Brookings, OR 97415, 541/412-6000.

35 VULCAN LAKE
2.8 mi/2.0 hrs

northeast of Brookings in the Kalmiopsis Wilderness of Siskiyou National Forest

Map 1.6, page 25

Desperately seeking solitude? Your search is over. The long, bumpy drive in practically guarantees that you will be on your own, or among only a brave few. The 2002 Biscuit Fire swept through this area, producing an interesting mix of burnt limbs and trunks coexisting peacefully with new and undamaged trees. The trail starts at an elevation of 3,750 feet, which means you'll have views galore as you hike. The path starts on a windswept hill, where you can glimpse the Siskiyou mountain range to the north, and then switchbacks up a hot and dusty trail to a fantastic lookout, where you can view the ocean to the west in the distance. Make sure to watch your step as you take in the view: You'll most likely be hopping over a burnt trunk or three, and the path also has some rocky portions. Keep on truckin', the best is yet to come. Rounding a bend, you'll have yet another view, this time of Little Vulcan Lake and Vulcan Lake, glistening in the sun. The trail descends from here to Vulcan Lake. Stick around to enjoy the solitude before you retrace your steps.

User groups: Hikers and dogs. No mountain bikes or horses are allowed. No wheelchair access.

Permits: A federal Northwest Forest pass is required to park here. The cost is $5 for a day pass or $30 for an annual pass. You can buy a day pass at the trailhead, at ranger stations, from private vendors, or through Nature of the Northwest Information Center.

Maps: For a map of the Siskiyou National Forest, contact the Nature of the Northwest Information Center. For a topographic map, ask the USGS for Chetco Peak.

Directions: From Brookings, drive east on County Road 784 (marked as Constitution Avenue) for 16 miles (it becomes Forest Service Road 1376 at the forest boundary). Turn right onto Forest Service Road 1909 and drive 13.4 miles, then turn left, continuing on Forest Service Road 1909 for 1.7 bumpy miles to the end of the road and the trailhead.

Contact: Siskiyou National Forest, Chetco Ranger District, P.O. Box 4580, 539 Chetco Avenue, Brookings, OR 97415, 541/412-6000.

36 REDWOOD NATURE LOOP
1.2 mi/0.5 hr

northeast of Brookings in Siskiyou National Forest

Map 1.6, page 25

You don't need to head south to Oregon's neighboring state to see these famous trees—we've got a few of our own to show off. This flat, well-marked loop is lined with interpretive signs (pick up a brochure at the trailhead) so you'll know what you're looking at. Old-growth redwoods up to 250 feet tall and 10 feet in diameter join forces with Oregon staples such as Douglas fir, bigleaf maple, Oregon myrtle, and red alder to make you feel like you're walking through a tree museum. This is a great one for kids, or for those who have always wondered how to tell the difference between a fir and a pine.

User groups: Hikers and dogs. No mountain bikes or horses are allowed. No wheelchair access.

Permits: A federal Northwest Forest pass is required to park here. The cost is $5 for a day pass or $30 for an annual pass. You can buy a day pass at the trailhead, at ranger stations, from private vendors, or through Nature of the Northwest Information Center.

Maps: For a map of the Siskiyou National Forest, contact the Nature of the Northwest Information Center. For a topographic map, ask the USGS for Mount Emily.

Directions: From Brookings, drive east on County Road 784 (marked as Constitution Avenue). Continue 8.1 miles; parking and the trailhead are on the left (north) side of the road.

Contact: Siskiyou National Forest, Chetco Ranger District, P.O. Box 4580, 539 Chetco Avenue, Brookings, OR 97415, 541/412-6000.

37 OREGON REDWOODS TRAIL
1.6 mi/1.0 hr

southeast of Brookings in Siskiyou National Forest

Map 1.6, page 25

Hey, who says California has all the big guys? Redwoods are alive and well in southern Oregon, too, but there are only a couple places to view them (see also the Redwood Nature Loop listing in this chapter). In fact, the Siskiyou National Forest has a monopoly on these giants, hosting the only redwoods in the Pacific Northwest. This trail starts out flat and easy, complete with a .8-mile wheelchair-accessible loop. The trail is 1.2 miles one-way, but for an interesting return journey, try the barrier-free route on the return trip for a 1.6-mile loop. Bring your camera; you'll want to get a pic of your hiking partner in the hollowed-out redwoods on this gentle route.

User groups: Hikers and dogs. No mountain bikes or horses are allowed. This trail includes a wheelchair-accessible loop.

Permits: A federal Northwest Forest pass is required to park here. The cost is $5 for a day pass or $30 for an annual pass. You can buy a day pass at the trailhead, at ranger stations, from private vendors, or through Nature of the Northwest Information Center.

Maps: For a map of the Siskiyou National Forest, contact the Nature of the Northwest Information Center. For a topographic map, ask the USGS for Mount Emily.

Directions: From Brookings, drive five miles south on U.S. 101 and turn left on Winchuck Road. Drive 1.5 miles, then turn right on Peavine Ridge Road and drive 4.1 miles to the end of the road and the trailhead.

Contact: Siskiyou National Forest, Chetco Ranger District, P.O. Box 4580, 539 Chetco Avenue, Brookings, OR 97415, 541/412-6000.

38 ELK CREEK FALLS AND BIG TREE
2.6 mi/1.5 hrs

northeast of Gold Beach in Siskiyou National Forest

Map 1.7, page 26

Two short and aptly named trails lead from this trailhead, Elk Creek Falls and Big Tree. For a short and sweet hike to a scenic falls, hit the left trail first for the .2-mile round-trip. Back at the trailhead, take the right trail for a pleasant climb through a lush fern forest as you seek out the largest Port Orford cedar in the world. The trail will seem longer than its 1.2 miles, and at every turn the trees get bigger and bigger. But those are only the bridesmaids—the bride stands tall at 219 feet, measuring in at over 12 feet in diameter. Our favorite part is a viewing platform, made solely so you can behold the Big Tree.

User groups: Hikers and dogs. No mountain bikes or horses allowed. No wheelchair access.

Permits: Permits are not required. Parking and access are free.

Maps: For a map of the Siskiyou National Forest, contact the Nature of the Northwest Information Center. For a topographic map, ask the USGS for China Flat.

Directions: From Powers, drive south for six miles on Powers South Road/Highway 90 (which turns into Highway 33); the trailhead is 1.7 miles after entering Highway 33. The trailhead

and parking area are on the left (east) side of the highway.

Contact: Siskiyou National Forest, Powers Ranger District, Powers, OR 97466, 541/439-3011.

39 PANTHER RIDGE/ HANGING ROCK
14.4 mi/8.0 hrs

northeast of Gold Beach in Siskiyou National Forest

Map 1.7, page 26

Solitude-seekers will enjoy this trail, as it's a long and winding—though thankfully paved—drive up to the ridge. Although the trail is 7.2 miles one-way, one of the highlights is majestic Hanging Rock, roughly two miles in. The rest of the trail is not nearly so scenic, so you may want to call it a day after hitting this giant boulder situated on top of a sheer cliff. Height-lovers who dare take a peek below will be rewarded with a superb view of Eden Valley and the distant Rogue River Canyon. This is definitely one of those "I was here!" moments that cameras are made for.

User groups: Hikers and dogs. No mountain bikes or horses are allowed. No wheelchair access.

Permits: Permits are not required. Parking and access are free.

Maps: For a map of the Siskiyou National Forest, contact the Nature of the Northwest Information Center. For a topographic map, ask the USGS for Eden Valley, Illahe, and Marial.

Directions: From Powers, drive south on Forest Service Road 33 for 12.2 miles to paved Forest Service Road 3348, then turn left. Drive nine miles to Forest Service Road 5520 (ignore the first sign for 5520), turn right and continue 1.1 miles, then turn left onto Spur Road 230 and go .5 mile to the end of the road and the trailhead.

Contact: Siskiyou National Forest, Powers Ranger District, Powers, OR 97466, 541/439-3011.

40 MOUNT BOLIVAR
2.8 mi/2.0 hrs

south of Powers in Siskiyou National Forest

Map 1.7, page 26

If you're the type who likes to see where you're going, you'll appreciate Mount Bolivar. From the trailhead, you can glimpse your destination, so you can use it as a beacon as you start your ascent. As with many of this area's hikes, you'll feel as if you're getting away from it all as you trudge through the old-growth timber and scrub oak trail—mostly because the drive there is never-ending (although thankfully paved). Since you'll be likely to have the 4,319-foot summit to yourself, sit and enjoy the stellar view of Rogue River Valley and Eden Valley below. Also, take in a bit of history while you're there: At the top, a plaque gives a well-deserved nod to Simón Bolívar, who wrested Venezuela away from those pesky Spaniards.

User groups: Hikers and dogs. No mountain bikes or horses are allowed. No wheelchair facilities.

Permits: Permits are not required. Parking and access are free.

Maps: For a map of the Siskiyou National Forest, contact the Nature of the Northwest Information Center. For a topographic map, ask the USGS for Mount Bolivar.

Directions: From Powers, drive south on Forest Service Road 33 for 12.2 miles, and turn left on paved Forest Service Road 3348. Continue almost 20 miles to the parking area and trailhead, on the right side of the road.

Contact: Siskiyou National Forest, Powers Ranger District, Powers, OR 97466, 541/439-3011.

41 BIG PINE INTERPRETIVE LOOP TRAIL
1.1 mi/0.5 hr

west of Grants Pass in Siskiyou National Forest

Map 1.7, page 26

Four teeny loops make up this homage to the

wide world of pines: Creek Loop is .2 mile, Challenge Loop is .75 mile, Sunshine Loop is .5 mile, and, last but not least, Big Pine Loop measures in at a cute .3 mile. The big guy himself stands over 250 feet tall, a height he can lord over all the other ponderosa pines in the world. With benches on which to sit and soak up the essence of all things pine, and eight interpretive signs, this easy and flat stroll through old-growth forest just screams "family outing". It's located conveniently in the Big Pine Campground, so if you're camping, you can make this a short morning walk before hitting other trails nearby.

User groups: Hikers and dogs. No horses or mountain bikes are allowed. The path is wheelchair accessible.

Permits: A federal Northwest Forest pass is required to park here. The cost is $5 for a day pass or $30 for an annual pass. You can buy a day pass at the trailhead, at ranger stations, from private vendors, or through Nature of the Northwest Information Center.

Maps: For a map of the Siskiyou National Forest, contact the Nature of the Northwest Information Center. For a topographic map, ask the USGS for Chrome Ridge.

Directions: From Grants Pass, drive five miles north on I-5 to the Merlin Exit 61. Drive 12.2 miles on Merlin-Galice Road and turn left on Briggs Creek Road/Forest Service Road 25 (a one-lane paved road). Drive 12.4 miles and turn right into Big Pine Campground. The trailhead is straight ahead as you're driving in.

Contact: Siskiyou National Forest, Galice Ranger District, 200 Northeast Greenfield Road, P.O. Box 440, Grants Pass, OR 97526, 541/471-6500.

42 BRIGGS CREEK
19.0 mi/2.0 days

west of Grants Pass in Siskiyou National Forest

Map 1.7, page 26

If you like to get your feet wet or want to take a mid-hike dip, try this creekside trail. You'll have to ford the creek a few times, so the summer and early fall are the best bets for this history-rich area. The Briggs Creek area used to be mining country, and some mining operations are still running today. Four miles in, you'll find the Courier Mine Historic Cabin, a handy destination for the day, or you can continue along the 9.5-mile (one-way) trail and camp along the way (there's a campsite five miles in). It's a relatively view-free hike, but if you want some solo adventuring along the creek, with a little history thrown in for good measure, check this one out.

User groups: Hikers, dogs, mountain bikes, and horses. No wheelchair access.

Permits: Permits are not required. Parking and access are free.

Maps: For a map of the Siskiyou National Forest, contact the Nature of the Northwest Information Center. For a topographic map, ask the USGS for Chrome Ridge and York Butte areas.

Directions: From Grants Pass, drive five miles north on I-5 to the Merlin Exit 61. Drive 12.2 miles on Merlin-Galice Road and turn left on Briggs Creek Road/Forest Service Road 25 (a one-lane paved road). Turn left and drive 13.1 miles to Forest Service Road 2512. Turn right and drive .5 mile, then turn left into Sam Brown Campground. Turn right before the day-use sign and drive to the parking area and trailhead.

Contact: Siskiyou National Forest, Galice Ranger District, 200 Northeast Greenfield Road, P.O. Box 440, Grants Pass, OR 97526, 541/471-6500.

43 BABYFOOT LAKE
2.0 mi/1.0 hr

west of Cave Junction in Kalmiopsis Wilderness of Siskiyou National Forest

Map 1.7, page 26

While many surrounding trails were destroyed in the 2002 Biscuit Fire, Babyfoot Lake Trail is still ticking, and new signs have been erected to show you the way. It's an interesting walk through the remnants of bare tree trunks still singed black, and you can see signs of life slowly returning to the trail as stubborn plants poke their way out of the soil. Despite this, or actually because of it, this burned trail makes for a peaceful walk. When you come to a junction .25 mile in with Babyfoot Lake Rim Trail, turn right to head to the clear green lake, which is an oasis in this wasteland of dead trees. It's one mile total to the lake itself, worth a visit if you're interested in solitude and a bit of natural history along the way.

User groups: Hikers and dogs. No horses or mountain bikes are allowed. No wheelchair facilities.

Permits: Permits are not required. Parking and access are free.

Maps: For a map of the Siskiyou National Forest, contact the Nature of the Northwest Information Center. For a topographic map, ask the USGS for Josephine Mountain.

Directions: From Cave Junction, drive 4.5 miles north on U.S. 199 and turn left onto Eight Dollar Road, which becomes Forest Service Road 4201. Drive 11 miles to Forest Service Road 141, then turn left. Continue for 14.6 miles (3 miles of which is paved) to Forest Service Road 140, then turn left and drive .6 mile to the trailhead and parking area, on the right.

Contact: Siskiyou National Forest, Illinois Valley Ranger District, 26568 Redwood Highway, Cave Junction, OR 97523, 541/592-2166.

Chapter 2

Portland and the Willamette Valley

Chapter 2—Portland and the Willamette Valley

In most cities, you have to plan a three-day weekend to get to trails. Not so with Portland (or PDX for short, a nickname it snagged from the airport). A two-hour cruise to the west takes you to the coast, and most of the trails within the Columbia River Gorge and on Mount Hood are within an easy hour's drive. But there's also plenty in the heart of Portland itself and the Willamette Valley (the pronunciation stumps many a visitor: It's will-AM-et).

First, let's clear up a little something about the rain. Although Portland gets a bad rap for its wet stuff, consider this: The City of Roses gets less annual rainfall than Atlanta, Houston, Indianapolis, or Seattle. How so? Precipitation in Portland tends to be a light daily mist during the October-through-May rainy season, rather than all-out downpours. Consider it a small price to pay for the area's lush green scenery.

Portland is proud of Forest Park, and why not? The biggest city park in the United States within city limits, 5,000-acre Forest Park is an urban trail runner's dream. (Portland also boasts the nation's smallest park, Mills End Park on Front Street along the Willamette River, but its two-foot length would make for a mighty short hike.) When you enter the wilder, northern areas of 30.2-mile Wildwood Trail, you would never know that coffeehouses and brewpubs are just a stone's throw away on ever-trendy Northwest 23rd Avenue. Tryon Creek, Oregon's only state park that is located in a major metropolitan area, is the second-largest hiking area, with eight miles of trails popular with runners and hikers. You can easily never leave the city and still have more trails at your disposal than you'll know what to do with.

Traveling south down the I-5 corridor beyond Portland, there are two state parks that offer some interesting history to ponder as you hike. Willamette Mission Park is the site of the first mission for Native Americans, as well as the landing for the first ferry to carry a covered wagon across the Willamette River; the Champoeg (pronounced sham-POO-ey) State Heritage Area marks the spot where the West Coast's first provisional government was formed, in 1843. Both parks are perfect for families, with easy strolls lined with historical plaques. Farther south is Silver Falls State Park, the largest park in the Oregon state parks system; popular Trail of Ten Falls is just one of its many attractions.

Moseying on down through the state capital of Salem and the Willamette Valley, which is unofficially edging out Napa Valley as a prime winery hot spot, you'll arrive at Eugene and the University of Oregon, famous for being the Running Capital of the World. Legendary U. of O. track star Steve Prefontaine returned from track meets with visions of bark chip–lined trails, and Pre's Trail was born (sadly, he died before he ever saw his dream come true, but the trail lives on in his honor). On the outskirts of Eugene, there are several worthy hikes at Mount Pisgah, Falls Creek, and Elijah Bristow State Park.

This area is more urban than those covered in the other chapters, but don't let that term fool you. Oregon is renowned for liveable big cities that are clean and outdoors-oriented, and most cities have strict urban-growth boundaries—which means you get to enjoy the wilds surrounding the cities for years to come.

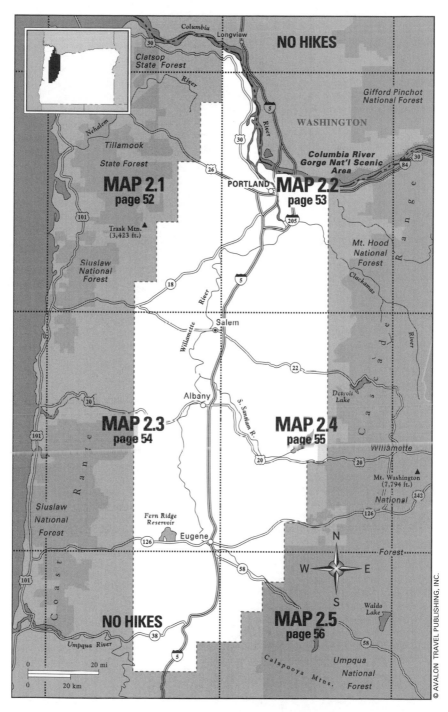

Map 2.1

Hike 1
Page 57

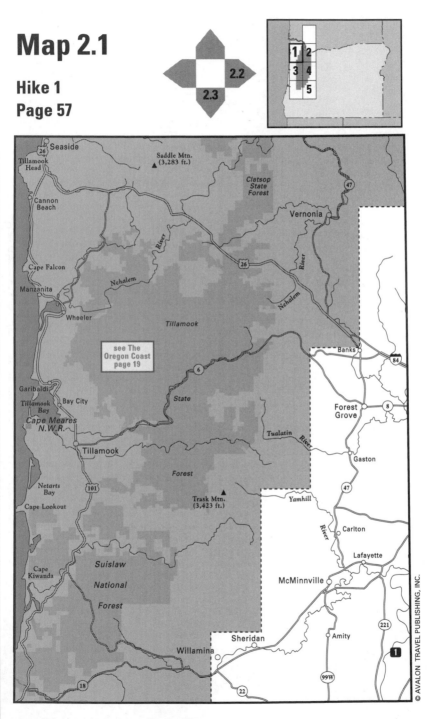

2.2

2.3

1 2
3 4
5

Seaside
Tillamook Head
Saddle Mtn.
(3,283 ft.)
Clatsop State Forest
Cannon Beach
Vernonia
Cape Falcon
Nehalem
River
Manzanita
Nehalem
Wheeler
Tillamook
see The Oregon Coast page 19
Banks
Garibaldi
Bay City
State
Forest Grove
Tillamook Bay
Cape Meares N.W.R.
Tualatin River
Gaston
Tillamook
Forest
Netarts Bay
Trask Mtn.
(3,423 ft.)
Yamhill
Cape Lookout
Carlton
Lafayette
Cape Kiwanda
Suislaw
National
Forest
McMinnville
Sheridan
Amity
Willamina

© AVALON TRAVEL PUBLISHING, INC.

Map 2.2

Hikes 2–5
Pages 57–59

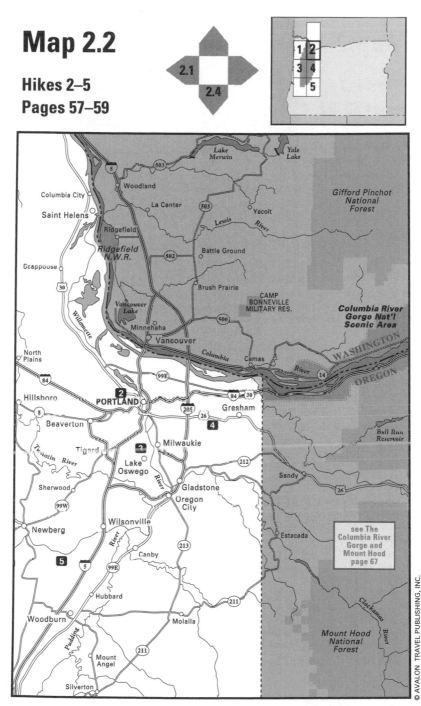

Map 2.3

Hikes 6–7
Pages 59–60

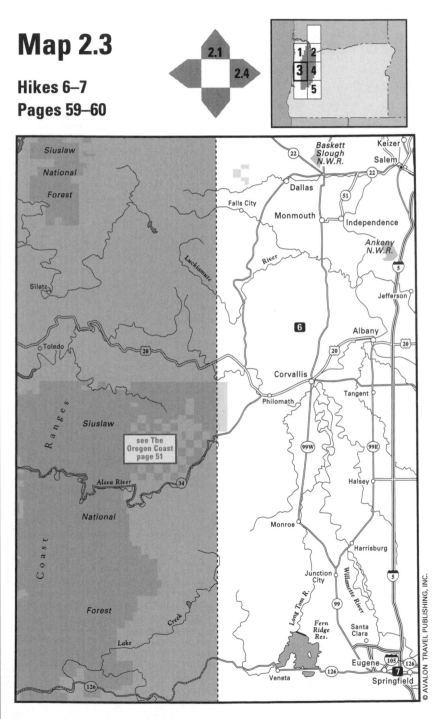

Map 2.4

Hike 8
Page 60

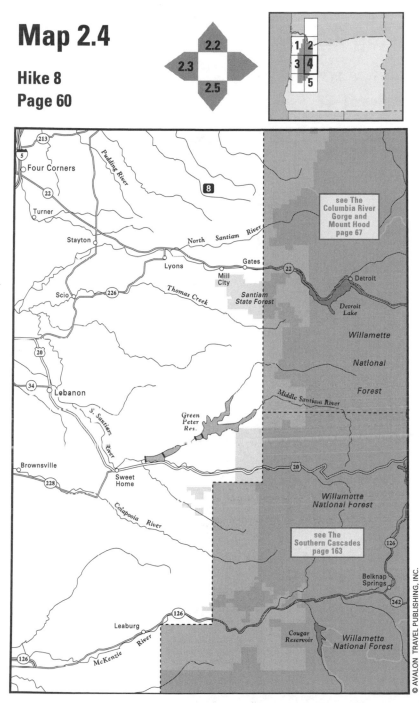

Map 2.5

Hikes 9–11
Pages 61–62

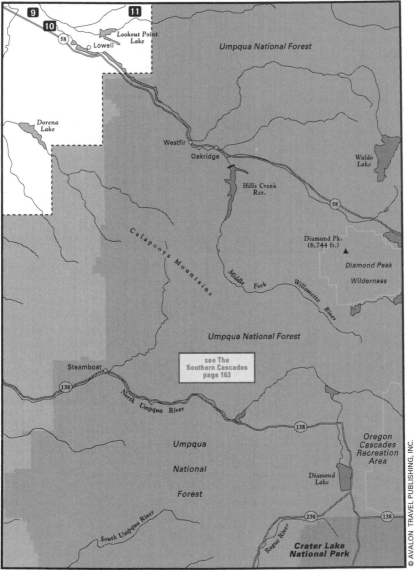

❶ WILLAMETTE MISSION STATE PARK
2.7 mi/1.5 hrs

north of Salem on the Willamette River

Map 2.1, page 52

Ever wonder where the largest black cottonwood rests its roots? Wonder no more: Willamette Mission State Park is the proud soil provider for this thick trunk, measuring in at 26 feet, three inches in circumference. Throw in a free ferry ride, prime picnic spots, and a few history tidbits, and this state park can keep you occupied all day. The loop starts at the Filbert Grove day-use area. It then travels on a biking trail along the Willamette River straight up to the Wheatland ferry landing, which hauled the first covered wagon across the Willamette River in 1844. After your thrill ride, backtrack about a half mile, and hang a left on the hiking trail to hug the side of Mission Lake, passing the Jason Lee Mission monument, a nod to the reverend who in 1834 founded the first mission for Native Americans. The trail ends at the mighty cottonwood itself. Stand and admire its sturdy trunk before continuing straight on the paved road back to your car.

User groups: Hikers, dogs, mountain bikes, and horses. Paved portions are wheelchair accessible.

Permits: Permits are not required. A $3 day-use fee is collected at the park entrance, or you can get an annual Oregon Parks and Recreation pass for $25; contact Oregon Parks and Recreation, 800/551-5949.

Maps: For a free park brochure, contact Oregon Parks and Recreation, 800/551-6949, www.oregonstateparks.org. For a topographic map, ask the USGS for Mission Bottom.

Directions: From Portland, drive on I-5 South for 35 miles to Exit 263, toward Brooks/Gervais. Turn right onto Brooklake Road Northeast and drive 1.7 miles, then turn right onto Wheatland Road North for 2.4 miles to the park entrance. Drive to the Filbert Grove day-use area; the trailhead starts from there.

Contact: Oregon Parks and Recreation Department, 1115 Commercial Street Northeast, Salem, OR 97301, 800/551-6949, www.oregonstateparks.org.

❷ WILDWOOD NATIONAL RECREATION TRAIL
30.2 mi/.5 hr–1.0 day

in Portland's Washington and Forest Parks

Map 2.2, page 53

This is without a doubt the best urban hike you'll find in the entire state, if not the country. Starting in Washington Park and zigzagging through 5,000-acre Forest Park—the largest city park in the United States—Wildwood Trail is a great escape from the city. Sure, you'll hear highway traffic now and then, and you'll see plenty of other hikers and runners, but scenery-wise it's like you just stepped into a national forest. The 30.2-mile trail starts in Washington Park at the Veterans Memorial at the zoo, then travels through Hoyt Arboretum, past the Japanese gardens (check out the Rose Garden while you're here), and then continues north, crossing busy Burnside Street to enter Forest Park. A steep two-mile climb leads you to Pittock Mansion, where you can take a well-deserved break and view the city below. In the northern sections, the trail parallels the Leif Erickson fire road, popular with bikers and runners. Plenty of well-marked side trails branch out from Wildwood, so you can choose loops or just do an out-and-back. The possibilities are endless in this park that just refuses to act like it's in city limits.

User groups: Hikers and dogs. No mountain bikes or horses.

Permits: Permits are not required. Parking and access are free.

Maps: For a free trail map, contact Portland Parks and Recreation, 503/823-PLAY (503/823-7529). For a topographic map, ask the USGS for Portland and Linnton.

Directions: There are many points of access

to Wildwood Trail. To get to the southern trailhead from downtown Portland, drive west on U.S. 26 to Exit 72/Canyon Road. Turn right to enter the Oregon Zoo entrance and the large parking lot. The trail starts to the right of the Vietnam Veterans Memorial. To reach the northern trailhead, drive on U.S. 30 or Skyline Boulevard to Germantown Road and the parking area, on the right.

Contact: Portland Parks and Recreation, 1120 Southwest 5th Avenue, Suite 1302, Portland, OR 97204, 503/823-PLAY (503/823-7529).

3 TRYON CREEK
2.0–8.0 mi/1.0–4.0 hrs

in southwest Portland's Tryon Creek State Park

Map 2.2, page 53

Yet another example of a park-within-the-city that feels worlds away, Tryon Creek offers a perfect escape from the city when you don't feel like driving hours to get there. The 645-acre state park is popular with runners and has eight miles of trails to explore through old-growth forest of red alder, Douglas fir, bigleaf maple, and western red cedar. Before you set out, pick up a trail brochure at the nature center, or check out the handy trail map on the wall nearby. It's pretty tough to get lost here, even if you are directionally challenged, but there are many short, interconnecting trails, all with different names, so you'll want to come up with a game plan before you start your trek. The 1.25-mile Upper Loop connects to many other trails that can extend your trip.

User groups: Hikers and dogs. Mountain bikes and horses are allowed only on certain trails. The .35-mile Trillium Trail is paved and wheelchair accessible.

Permits: Permits are not required. Parking and access are free.

Maps: For a free map, contact Oregon Parks and Recreation, 800/551-6949, www.oregonstateparks.org. For a topographic map, ask the USGS for Lake Oswego.

Directions: From Portland, drive south on I-5

to Exit 297/Terwilliger Boulevard. Keep right at the fork in the ramp, and turn right onto Southwest Barbur Boulevard, then take a slight right onto Southwest Terwilliger Boulevard. Drive 2.3 miles to the park entrance and the large parking area.

Contact: Tryon Creek State Natural Area, 11321 Southwest Terwilliger Boulevard, Portland, OR 97219, 503/636-9886.

4 POWELL BUTTE
3.0 mi/1.5 hrs

between Portland and Gresham south of U.S. 26

Map 2.2, page 53

It may not win the prize for biggest park in Portland (but it is runner-up to the overall winner, Forest Park), but Powell Butte has its own claim to fame: It's an extinct volcano, and just steps from your car you can stand on its top to witness commanding views of five mountains on a clear day. The park contains nine miles of trails, but keep in mind that many are open to horses and it's a popular mountain-biking spot, so watch the signs. For a quick three-mile loop, start on the appropriately named Mountain View Trail, where a plaque points out the various peaks to spot. Then keep straight onto Mount Hood Trail, which heads into the woods (with the steep descent, you can see why it's popular with mountain bikers). Hang a right when you reach the T intersection to return on Cedar Grove Trail, and then turn left onto Meadowland Trail. Don't worry, it's not as confusing as it sounds. Besides, it's pretty difficult to get lost in a city park.

User groups: Hikers, dogs, horses, and mountain bikes. Part of Mountain View Trail is paved and wheelchair accessible.

Permits: Permits are not required. Parking and access are free.

Maps: For a free brochure and map, contact the Portland Parks and Recreation Department, 503/823-PLAY (503/823-7529). For a topographic map, ask the USGS for Gladstone.

Directions: From Portland, drive on I-205 south

to Exit 19. Follow Southeast Powell Boulevard three miles south and turn right onto Southeast 162nd Avenue to the park entrance and the parking area. The trail starts on the west side of the parking area.

Contact: Portland Parks and Recreation, 1120 Southwest 5th Avenue, Suite 1302, Portland, OR 97204, 503/823-PLAY (503/823-7529).

5 CHAMPOEG STATE PARK LOOP
3.0 mi/1.5 hrs

east of Newberg on the south banks of the Willamette River

Map 2.2, page 53

Hikers who like a little history thrown in with their hiking will appreciate this state park. Pronounced sham-POO-ey, the park is the old stomping grounds of Native Americans who found the Willamette River ideal for hunting and fishing. The first provisional government on the West Coast was established on this site in 1843, and in Champoeg's heyday it was a popular stop for stagecoaches and steamboats. Alas, the riverfront location that contributed to its popularity was also its downfall: In 1861, the largest flood ever recorded on the Willamette River submerged the busy town in 23 feet of water, which put a damper on business, to say the least. Although the town was partly rebuilt, it never stood a chance, as floods returned in 1890. Hikers can check out the whole story at the visitors center and at two museums on the state park property. Although the park's scenery isn't exactly mind-blowing, it's the idea that you never know what's around the bend that makes this area a must-visit. The trail passes historical monuments, the Pioneer Mother's cabin museum, and Robert Newell House; strolls down the riverfront (check out the waterfront homes across the river); and winds around a Frisbee Golf course, so your eyes and mind are constantly engaged. A .25-mile nature trail starts from the campground (where you can rent a yurt or cabin), and a paved bike trail extends to the town of Butteville. Pick up a park brochure before you set out to make sure you don't miss any sights.

User groups: Hikers and dogs. Mountain bikes are allowed only on the biking trails. No horses are allowed. Paved portions of the park are wheelchair accessible.

Permits: Permits are not required. A $3 day-use fee is collected at the park entrance, or you can get an annual Oregon Parks and Recreation pass for $25; contact Oregon Parks and Recreation, 800/551-5949.

Maps: For a free park brochure, contact Oregon Parks and Recreation, 800/551-6949, www.oregonstateparks.org. For a topographic map, ask the USGS for Newberg.

Directions: From Portland, drive south on I-5 for 20 miles to Exit 278 for Donald/Aurora. Turn right (west) and drive about six miles to the park entrance. Park in the Riverside Day-Use Area.

Contact: Oregon Parks and Recreation Department, 1115 Commercial Street Northeast, Salem, OR 97301, 800/551-6949, www.oregonstate parks.org.

6 MCDONALD RESEARCH FOREST LOOP
3.5 mi/2.0 hrs

north of Corvallis off Highway 99W

Map 2.3, page 54

This is a college hangout, minus the frat parties. Instead, a different type of celebration is going on here—a festival of forestry. It's a research forest for nearby Oregon State University, with over 60 projects going on at once in this eclectic ecosystem, where even-age, uneven-age, and new-growth stand side by side. Don't know what that means? Don't worry, it makes for an interesting hike anyway. Along the way, you can look out for flags marking various projects (it's like walking through a petri dish). The trails, popular with mountain bikers, also host the locally famous McDonald 50K run every April. You don't need to be in marathon shape or a forestry buff to take advantage of the scenery, though: Within these 11,000 acres, there are several short nature trails, including 1.4-mile

Forest Discovery Trail, a loop that features a tree once used to cure malaria, and trees used to build temples in China. A popular loop is the Section 36/Powder House loop, which offers a good gaze at Soap Creek Valley and a meander near Cronemiller Lake. Pick up a brochure at the Forestry Club Cabin, or check out the detailed map at the trailhead. Not that you good citizens would ever need a reminder, of course, but remember to stick to the trail so as not to disturb the research projects.

User groups: Hikers, dogs, mountain bikes, and horses. (The Section 36/Power House loop is for hikers only, but other trails in the forest allow bikes and horses.) No wheelchair access.

Permits: Permits are not required. Parking and access are free.

Maps: A trail map is available at local outdoor vendors like the Oregon State University bookstore in Corvallis. A brochure is available at the Peavy Arboretum offices in the forest, or online at www.cof.orst.edu. For a topographic map, ask the USGS for Airlie South.

Directions: From Corvallis, drive north on Highway 99W for five miles, and turn left (west) onto Arboretum Road to the park entrance. Park at the day-use parking area.

Contact: Oregon State University, College of Forestry, 8692 Peavy Auditorium Road, Corvallis, OR 97330, www.cof.orts.edu.

7 PRE'S TRAIL
3.8 mi/1.5 hrs

in Eugene's Alton Baker Park

Map 2.3, page 54

Okay, okay, this isn't exactly in the wilderness, but any trail book just isn't complete without a nod to Eugene's famous Pre's Trail. Here's the story: Legendary University of Oregon track star Steve Prefontaine, while traveling in Europe to attend meets, developed a soft spot for European tracks made of bark chip. He dreamed of making a similar surface on his training ground, Alton Baker Park (named after the publisher of Lane County's daily newspaper, the *Register-Guard*). Sadly, Prefontaine died before he got to see his dream realized, but a day after his untimely death in May 1975, the park gave his idea the green light. One trail just doesn't do justice to a guy like Pre, so they decided to give him three short loops in this system, with a total of 3.8 miles. Arrive extra early on a weekend morning to watch locals venturing out of their cars in the still-dark hours, ready to run on the flat, popular trails that meander near the McKenzie River. The trails offer a good way to see some of the campus, too, but avoid game days, when the mighty Ducks take over the park.

User groups: Hikers, dogs, and mountain bikes. No horses allowed. Paved portions of the park are wheelchair accessible.

Permits: Permits are not required. Parking and access are free.

Maps: For a free map online, go to www.oregontrackclub.org. For a topographic map, ask the USGS for Eugene East.

Directions: From downtown Eugene, drive north across the Ferry Street Bridge and turn right onto Centennial Boulevard. Turn right again at the first light and drive a short distance to the Alton Baker Park entrance and the large parking lot.

Contact: City of Eugene Parks and Open Space, Recreation Services Division, 99 West 10th Avenue, Suite 340, Eugene, OR 97401, 541/682-5333.

8 TRAIL OF TEN FALLS/ CANYON TRAIL
7.0 mi/3.5 hrs

east of Salem in Silver Falls State Park

Map 2.4, page 55

Not only is this the Trail of Ten Falls, but it's the Trail of Two Names. Apparently, the namegivers couldn't choose between the glorious falls and the Silver Creek Canyon as the trail's main feature (perhaps an arm-wrestling match ensued, with no clear winner? Just a guess . . .). Like its name suggests, this trail takes you past not one, not two, but—all together now—ten waterfalls before it calls it a loop and heads back to your car. Ranging in height from cute 27-footers to awesome 178-footers you can walk underneath, all the falls come proudly equipped with a handy plaque. Benches along the way invite you to sit and soak (no pun intended) up the scenery of this state park, Oregon's largest. Besides this trail, Silver Falls State Park features camping, cabins, horse trails (and horse rentals), and paved biking trails. Another tidbit of interest: This park was the location of the outdoor scenes in the film *The Hunted,* starring Tommy Lee Jones, where Benicio del Toro played a trained killer gone haywire, killing hunters to save the animals. (Don't worry, hunting isn't allowed here in real life.) Although the scenery is astounding, you're not far from civilization, so those who like post-hike lattes will enjoy the gift shop and café, conveniently located next to the parking lot.

User groups: Hikers only. No dogs, mountain bikes, or horses allowed. The trail is not wheelchair accessible, although there are paved parts of the park that are wheelchair friendly.

Permits: Permits are not required. A $3 day-use fee is collected at the park entrance, or you can get an annual Oregon Parks and Recreation pass for $25; contact Oregon Parks and Recreation, 800/551-5949.

Maps: For a free trail and park brochure, contact Oregon Parks and Recreation, 800/551-6949, www.oregonstateparks.org. For a topographic map, ask the USGS for Drake Crossing.

Directions: From Salem, drive on U.S. 22 five miles to Highway 224. Turn left and drive 15 miles to the park entrance and the large parking lot. The trail starts from behind the lodge.

Contact: Oregon Parks and Recreation Department, 1115 Commercial Street Northeast, Salem, OR 97301, 800/551-6949, www.oregonstateparks.org.

⑨ MOUNT PISGAH SUMMIT
3.0 mi/1.5 hrs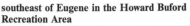

southeast of Eugene in the Howard Buford Recreation Area

Map 2.5, page 56

If you live in or are visiting Eugene and you want a quick getaway, Mount Pisgah is the place to do it. Local legend has it that the earliest Lane County settlers saw the view and named it after the Biblical summit from which Moses himself viewed the Promised Land. In any case, Pisgah is certainly divine. It's a short and sweet climb, gaining 1,000 feet in elevation, and you'll be rewarded with a 360-degree view of the rolling Willamette Valley below, and even the Cascade peaks if you catch it on a clear day. You'll also glimpse plenty of fellow urban-escapers out for a quick jaunt before brunch or football games at nearby University of Oregon. There are many offshoot trails that will take hikers up a more meandering route, but stick to the main summit trail for a well-marked route, which even gives you progress reports on your climb. You won't exactly feel like you're getting away from it all—what with the power lines and fellow hikers—but for a speedy, sweat-inducing jaunt with a view at the top, it's a great pick if you're already in the area.

User groups: Hikers and dogs. No mountain bikes or horses are allowed.

Permits: Permits are not required. From May through August, a $2 parking fee is collected at the park entrance.

Maps: For a free map, contact the Lane County Parks Division, Armitage Park, 90064 Coburg Road, Eugene, OR 97408, 541/682-2000. For a topographic map, ask the USGS for Springfield.

Directions: From the south end of Eugene, take I-5 to the 30th Avenue exit. At the second light, turn left to travel over I-5, and at the stop sign turn left, then turn right onto Franklin Road. In less than .25 mile, turn left onto Seavey Loop Road. Drive 1.5 miles and turn right to the park entrance. Parking is at the end of the road, at the arboretum entrance.

Contact: Lane County Parks Division, Armitage Park, 90064 Coburg Road, Eugene, OR 97408, 541/682-2000.

10 ELIJAH BRISTOW STATE PARK
2.0 mi/1.0 hr   1️⃣ 🥾6

southeast of Eugene on the Middle Fork Willamette River

Map 2.5, page 56

If you're in the mood for a simple Sunday stroll or a picnic with the whole family, Elijah Bristow State Park is a perfect place to spend an afternoon. The riverside park is named after one Elijah Bristow, a pioneer from Virginia who apparently went first to California, which didn't suit this mountain man, and then came north to Lane County, where he raised his hat and exclaimed, "This is my claim! Here I will live, and when I die, here I shall be buried!" (You gotta love the guy's enthusiasm for this great state, no?) Well, at least he got a park out of the deal, with plenty of hiking loops to choose from. A big map will greet you with your choices as you enter the park, so you can take your pick. One option is taking the two-mile Lost Creek Trail, where the easy-to-follow signposts will lead you on your way up Lost Creek and turning right at the junction to reach the Willamette River. (Or, to add a third mile to your hike, continue straight at the intersection to reach the river). The 847-acre park consists of meadows, woodlands, and wetlands, and do we ever mean wet: This is definitely a summer picnicking spot, as the rainy season turns everything into a massive sogfest (let's just say we learned this the hard way, shall we?). Home to several threatened animal species such as the Western pond turtle and the Oregon chub, tree-lovers will be in leafy heaven among the cottonwood, bigleaf maple, western red cedar, Douglas fir, western hemlock, Oregon ash, and white oak. It won't necessarily satisfy the hardy-hiker crowd, and the picnic areas scream "family reunion," but if you are looking for some interesting scenery for your next gathering, Bristow won't disappoint.

User groups: Hikers, dogs, horses, and mountain bikes. No wheelchair facilities.

Permits: Permits are not required. Parking and access are free.

Maps: For a free park brochure, contact the Oregon Parks and Recreation Department, 800/551-6949, www.oregonstateparks.org. For a topographic map, ask the USGS for Lowell.

Directions: From Eugene, drive seven miles on Willamette Highway/Highway 58 and turn left into the park entrance. The trailhead is to the left past the first parking lot, just past the small bridge.

Contact: Oregon Parks and Recreation Department, 1115 Commercial Street Northeast, Salem, OR 97301, 800/551-6949, www.oregonstateparks.org.

11 FALL CREEK NATIONAL
RECREATION TRAIL
13.7 mi one-way/6.0 hrs   2️⃣ 🥾7

southeast of Eugene near the Middle Fork Willamette River

Map 2.5, page 56

You may feel like you've just entered a Dr. Suess book with all the dripping, mossy tentacles of the Douglas fir and maple trees along this scenic route. The undulating trail—mostly flat, except for a healthy climb near the Bedrock campground—is easy to follow. You'll have plenty of company along the way: This is a popular stomping ground on sunny weekends, especially because it crosses Forest Service Road 18 several times, providing several access points. Trails lead down to the clear, green Fall Creek for fishing, swimming, and picnic spots. Seasonal camping is provided nearby, so you can take full advantage of this scenic spot.

User groups: Hikers and dogs. No horses or mountain bikes are allowed. No wheelchair facilities.

Permits: A federal Northwest Forest pass is required to park here. The cost is $5 for a day pass or $30 for an annual pass. You can buy a day pass at ranger stations, from private vendors, or through Nature of the Northwest Information Center.

Maps: For a map of the Willamette National Forest, contact the Nature of the Northwest Information Center. For a topographic map, ask the USGS for Fall Creek Lake, Saddleback Mountain, and Sinker Mountain.

Directions: From Eugene, drive 15 miles east on Willamette Highway/Highway 58, and turn left on Lowell-Jasper Road (you'll cross the Dexter Reservoir on the bridge towards Lowell). Drive two miles through the town of Lowell and turn right on Fall Creek Road/Forest Service Road 18. Continue 11 miles to the trailhead on the right, just before Dolly Varden campground. If you want to arrange a car shuttle, continue on Forest Service Road 18 for 12 miles to the junction with Forest Service Road 1833. Turn right and cross the bridge over Fall Creek to the trailhead and parking area, on the left.

Contact: Willamette National Forest, Middle Fork Ranger District, Lowell Office, 60 South Pioneer Street, Lowell, OR 97452, 541/937-2129.

 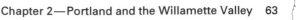

© MEGAN McMORRIS

The Columbia River
Gorge and Mount Hood

Chapter 3—The Columbia River Gorge and Mount Hood

L ooming large as a constant presence for Portlanders (and, on clear days, for those living to the south as well), 11,239-foot Mount Hood is the tallest peak in Oregon and is the second-most climbed mountain in the world (after Mount Fuji in Japan). Although scaling its heights requires mountaineering skills and equipment, you can easily access its slopes and foothills for seemingly endless miles. Mount Hood's Timberline Ski Resort offers the only year-round ski season in North America, and many elite skiers and snowboarders use Mount Hood's slopes for training. Mount Hood has an unbelievable number of trails within its boundaries, most of which are right off Highways 26 and 35. Timberline Trail is the mightiest of them all, a strenuous 40.7-mile loop circling Mount Hood. And though many of the higher-elevation trails remain snow-covered until July, there are plenty of lower trails you can explore year-round.

Just north of Mount Hood is the Columbia River Gorge National Scenic Area, which slices the border between Oregon and Washington. The Gorge, as the locals call it, is lined with trails right off I-84. (Drive down the highway on a summer weekend and you'll see cars with license plates from all over the country packed into parking areas.) The Pacific Crest Trail makes its Oregon debut in the Gorge, extending from the Bridge of the Gods in Cascade Locks to Timberline Lodge in Mount Hood. Popular for its easy access to trails and cliffside scenery, the area is known for its waterfalls and tough peak climbs, with 4,960-foot Mount Defiance being the toughest of the bunch. But by far, the hot tamale of the Gorge is Multnomah Falls, the fourth-largest waterfall in the country. The area is also known for stiff breezes: The wind rushing through the Gorge has turned the area into "the windsurfing capital of the world." On a summer day, you'll see sail- and kiteboarders zipping through the water.

The Columbia Gorge Scenic Area extends 70 miles from Corbett to Cascade Locks to The Dalles, with outdoors hub Hood River being the unofficial capital of it all. Bed-and-breakfasts, historic hotels, upscale restaurants, and downscale brewpubs offer great stopping points after a long day of hiking. (Treat yourself to a swirl cone at the East Wind Drive-In, in Cascade Locks—just look for the ever-present line snaking in front of the walk-up window.)

Water is also a big selling point of this area, from the white-water Clackamas River west of Mount Hood—popular with rafters and kayakers—to the Columbia River itself, to plenty of waterfalls, mountain lakes, and smaller creeks. Speaking of water, the rainy season tends to be October through May, so come prepared if you want to head out on the trails during the wet months.

Extending to the south, this chapter also includes the northern sections of Willamette National Forest and the Mount Jefferson Wilderness Area. At 10,497 feet, Mount Jefferson is the second-highest peak in Oregon, adding wildflower meadows and backcountry wilderness to this fine mix, while nearby Detroit Reservoir is a campground mecca for day hikers.

Overall, the hikes in this chapter range from many short waterfall and riverfront strolls right off the highway to tough day hikes up a cliff, to backpacking adventures in the backcountry. There are so many loops and interconnecting trails, the hiking possibilities truly seem endless. All this within an easy drive of Portland and surrounding cities! Seem too good to be true? It isn't.

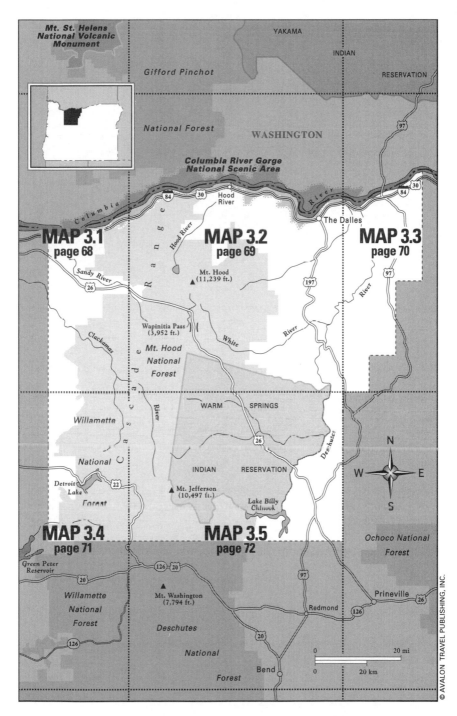

MAP 3.1
page 68

MAP 3.2
page 69

MAP 3.3
page 70

MAP 3.4
page 71

MAP 3.5
page 72

Mt. St. Helens
National Volcanic
Monument

Gifford Pinchot

National Forest

WASHINGTON

YAKAMA

INDIAN

RESERVATION

Columbia River Gorge
National Scenic Area

Hood
River

The Dalles

Columbia

Hood River

River

Mt. Hood
(11,239 ft.)

Sandy River

Wapinitia Pass
(3,952 ft.)

White

River

Mt. Hood
National
Forest

Clackamas

River

Cascade

Range

WARM   SPRINGS

Willamette

National

INDIAN   RESERVATION

Detroit
Lake

Mt. Jefferson
(10,497 ft.)

Lake Billy
Chinook

Deschutes

Forest

N
W   E
S

Green Peter
Reservoir

Willamette

National

Forest

Mt. Washington
(7,794 ft.)

Ochoco National
Forest

Prineville

Redmond

Deschutes

National

Forest

Bend

0   20 mi

0   20 km

© AVALON TRAVEL PUBLISHING, INC.

Map 3.1

Hikes 1–11
Pages 73–78

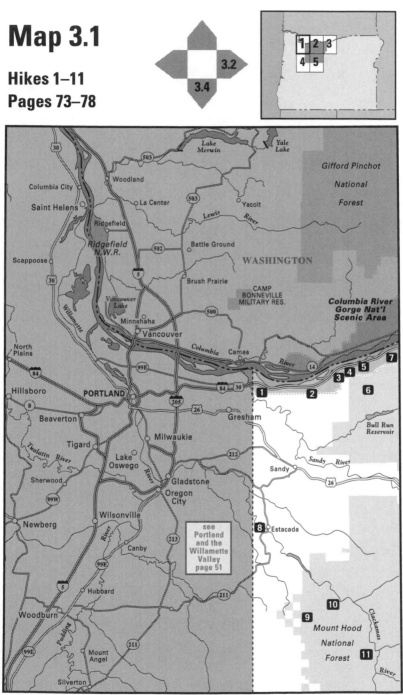

© AVALON TRAVEL PUBLISHING, INC.

Map 3.2

Hikes 12–48
Pages 78–100

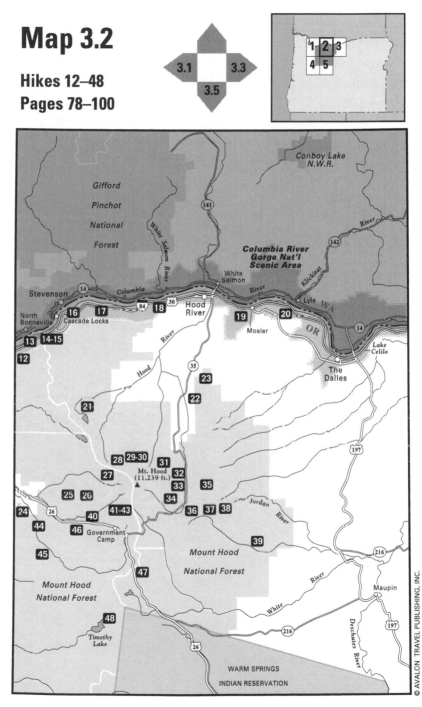

3.1 3.3
3.5

© AVALON TRAVEL PUBLISHING, INC.

Map 3.3

Hike 49
Page 100

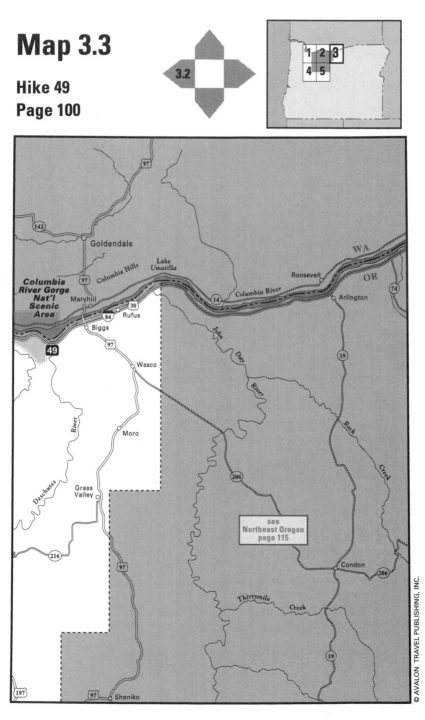

Map 3.4

Hikes 50–59
Pages 101–106

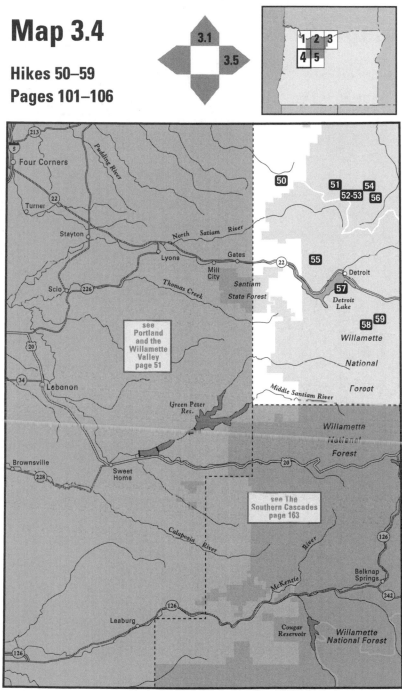

Map 3.5

Hikes 60–67
Pages 107–110

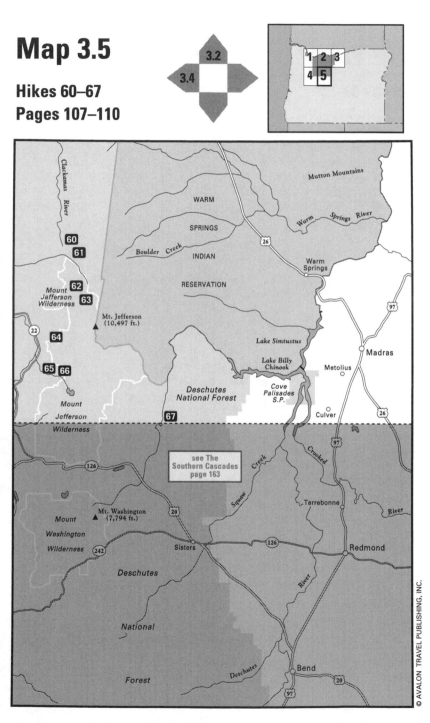

◼1 LEWIS AND CLARK NATURE TRAIL
4.0 mi/2.0 hrs

in Lewis & Clark State Park on the west side of the Columbia River Gorge

Map 3.1, page 68

In an area that's filled with references to intrepid explorers Lewis and Clark, this is the ultimate trail, where they ended their journey. Clark reportedly attempted to wade across the Sandy River here but found the bottom was quicksand, so they named it Quicksand River. (Thankfully, that name has changed!) This two-mile nature trail is lined with interpretive signs, courtesy of a local Girl Scout troop. Botanical highlights of the trail include Oregon grape (the state flower), wild ginger, Oregon white oak, bigleaf maple, and Oregon crabapple. Detect a theme? Oregonians are notorious for their pride in native status, and local plants are included in the glory. After a flat nature exhibit, the trail heads into the forest before flattening out again. Another short but rocky trail in this state park leads up to Broughton's Bluff, a popular climbing spot. The trail is short but requires some scrambling on the rocks, so skip it on a wet day. Although this is probably the least scenic trail in the Gorge, it's a good leg-stretcher if you're already in the area, are bringing the kids along, or want to work off that potato salad after a picnic.

User groups: Hikers and dogs. No mountain bikes or horses are allowed. No wheelchair access.

Permits: Permits are not required. Parking and access are free.

Maps: For a map of the Columbia River Gorge, contact Nature of the Northwest Information Center. For a topographic map, ask the USGS for Washougal.

Directions: From Portland, drive east on I-84 for 20 miles to Exit 18 and follow signs less than .1 mile to Lewis & Clark State Park and the parking lot. The trail starts on the southwest side of the parking lot.

Contact: Oregon Parks and Recreation Department, 1115 Commercial Street Northeast, Salem, OR 97301, 800/551-6949, www.oregonstateparks.org.

◼2 LATOURELL FALLS
2.1 mi/1.0 hr

east of Crown Point in the Columbia River Gorge

Map 3.1, page 68

Latourell Falls is so easygoing: It doesn't make you drive far (it's the closest of the Gorge falls to Portland) or walk far (it's an easy two-mile loop). So do it a favor and pay it a visit. Starting from the parking lot, you'll climb up a short paved trail for about .5 mile to a lookout over the falls, then the pavement ends and a path continues to Upper Latourell Falls, where a footbridge spans Latourell Creek right in front of the falls, a perfect place to snap some shots. Great viewpoints line this short and sweet trip. Add in the nearby Bridal Veil (a popular one-mile round-trip) waterfall for another short and scenic hike. Be warned, though: Because they are so convenient to the highway and close to Portland, these easy trails can get packed with families and tourists on summer weekends.

User groups: Hikers and dogs. No mountain bikes or horses are allowed. No wheelchair access.

Permits: Permits are not required. Parking and access are free.

Maps: For a map of the Columbia River Gorge, contact Nature of the Northwest Information Center. For a topographic map, contact Green Trails, Inc. (ask for Bridal Veil, map number 428), 206/546-MAPS (206/546-6277), www.greentrails.com; or ask the USGS for Bridal Veil.

Directions: From Portland, drive about 25 miles east on I-84 to Bridal Veil Falls/Exit 28. Continue down the historic Columbia River Scenic Highway for 2.5 miles to the trailhead and parking area on the right.

Contact: Columbia River Gorge National Scenic Area, 902 Wasco Avenue, Suite 200, Hood River, OR 97031, 541/386-2333.

3 ANGEL'S REST
4.5 mi/2.5 hrs

on the Columbia River Scenic Highway in the Columbia River Gorge

Map 3.1, page 68

This would rate a higher score scenery-wise if it weren't for the fact that it's such a popular spot. You'll also hear highway traffic pretty much the whole way, so it's not exactly back-country solitude. Still, if you have visitors—or are a visitor yourself—you should definitely check this one out. It offers great views of the Gorge, a waterfall, friendly Oregonians (you'll encounter a lot), and offshoot lookout trails. About a half mile in, you'll come across 150-foot Coopey Falls, and then the true switch-backing continues up to the 1,600-foot viewpoint. When you reach a rock field at the top, don't stop: Continue straight across the rock field and climb on. At the top, pick your pleasure of rock formations for a picnic spot and a rest before heading back down the way you came. This trail also continues for 1.8 miles to Wahkeena Falls (see listing in this chapter) and another 1.6 miles to Devil's Rest Viewpoint so you can keep on pushing if you want to make a day of it.

User groups: Hikers and dogs. No mountain bikes or horses are allowed. No wheelchair access.

Permits: Permits are not required. Parking and access are free.

Maps: For a map of the Columbia River Gorge, contact Nature of the Northwest Information Center. For a topographic map, contact Green Trails, Inc. (ask for Bridal Veil, map number 428), 206/546-MAPS (206/546-6277), www.green trails.com; or ask the USGS for Bridal Veil.

Directions: From Portland, drive about 25 miles east on I-84 to Exit 28/Bridal Veil. Drive off the exit to the junction with Columbia River Scenic Highway. The trailhead starts on the south side of the junction.

Contact: Columbia River Gorge National Scenic Area, 902 Wasco Avenue, Suite 200, Hood River, OR 97031, 541/386-2333.

4 WAHKEENA FALLS LOOP
4.7 mi/2.5 hrs

west of Multnomah Falls in the Columbia River Gorge

Map 3.1, page 68

Most people just saunter up to the falls and then return to their cars, but they're missing out on the good stuff. For a true waterfall fiesta, you can hit several falls on this loop hike and escape the crowds, to boot. Start on the short .5-mile trip up to pleasant Wahkeena Falls, and then continue up the trail another mile to Wahkeena Springs. Take a left (east) when you hit the springs for .5 mile on Wahkeena Trail. If you have enough juice, try the switchbacks up to the viewpoint at 2,400 feet by turning right at the junction at this point. Or continue straight for another 1.2 miles, then turn left for the return trip home on Larch Mountain Trail (see listing in this chapter), which descends past upper Multnomah Falls areas, like Ecola Falls and Weisendanger Falls, before reaching the dizzying Multnomah Falls overlook on a short side trail. Continue back to the Multnomah Falls lodge and return along the highway to find the .6-mile return trail back to the parking area.

User groups: Hikers and dogs. No mountain bikes or horses are allowed.

Permits: Permits are not required. Parking and access are free.

Maps: For a map of the Columbia River Gorge, contact Nature of the Northwest Information Center. For a topographic map, contact Green Trails, Inc. (ask for Bridal Veil, map number 428), 206/546-MAPS (206/546-6277), www.green trails.com; or ask the USGS for Bridal Veil and Multnomah Falls.

Directions: From Portland, drive about 25 miles east on I-84 to Bridal Veil Falls/Exit 28. Turn left on the historic Columbia River Scenic Highway for 2.5 miles to the parking area on the left; the trailhead is across the highway on the right.

Contact: Columbia River Gorge National Scenic Area, 902 Wasco Avenue, Suite 200, Hood River, OR 97031, 541/386-2333.

5 MULTNOMAH FALLS
2.4 mi/1.5 hrs

on the Columbia River Scenic Highway in the Columbia River Gorge

Map 3.1, page 68

If you were the second-highest year-round waterfall in the country, wouldn't you want a nice shiny plaque proudly proclaiming the fact? I guess they figure the 620-foot falls speak for themselves, but still. Multnomah does receive plenty of attention, though, so here's a word to the wise: Don't even think about visiting Multnomah Falls on a sunny weekend. It's the number-one tourist attraction in the state, and the parking lot fills quickly. Better to hit some of the lesser-known falls in this chapter, and save the Big One for a weekday if you can swing it. (I know, the job does tend to get in the way of such outings, but it's worth it.) The paved trail leads up to a viewpoint at Benson Bridge, just .5 mile up, to behold the falls (those prone to dizziness should skip this). You can also continue to the top of the trail for an overlook above the falls, for a 2.4-mile round-trip hike. The trail also continues another five miles up to Larch Mountain and connects with Wahkeena Falls Trail for a five-mile loop (see listings in this chapter).

User groups: Hikers and dogs. No mountain bikes or horses are allowed.

Permits: Permits are not required. Parking and access are free.

Maps: For a map of the Columbia River Gorge, contact Nature of the Northwest Information Center. For a topographic map, contact Green Trails, Inc. (ask for Bridal Veil, map number 428), 206/546-MAPS (206/546-6277), www.green trails.com; or ask the USGS for Multnomah Falls.

Directions: From Portland, drive about 30 miles east on I-84 to Multnomah Falls/Exit 31. Park in the large parking lot and go under a short tunnel to the falls and the well-marked trailhead.

Contact: Columbia River Gorge National Scenic Area, 902 Wasco Avenue, Suite 200, Hood River, OR 97031, 541/386-2333.

6 LARCH MOUNTAIN LOOP
5.4 mi/3.0 hrs

above Multnomah Falls in the Columbia River Gorge

Map 3.1, page 68

You can walk 6.8 miles one-way up to Larch Mountain from Multnomah Falls, but there's a better way to get there: Start from the top of the mountain itself for great Gorge views right off the bat (check out the .25-mile trail to scenic Sherrard's Point from the parking lot first), then descend into the Gorge for 1.5 miles. Head east (right) at a junction onto Multnomah Creek Way to cross the creek, and then head north (right) to let the climbing begin, for 2.5 miles. Take another right on Oneonta Trail to complete the loop. Alternatively, keep going straight when you come upon the junction to reach Multnomah Falls, and make it a shuttle hike.

User groups: Hikers, dogs, and mountain bikes. No horses are allowed. No wheelchair access.

Permits: A federal Northwest Forest pass is required to park here. The cost is $5 for a day pass or $30 for an annual pass. You can buy a day pass at ranger stations, from private vendors, or through Nature of the Northwest Information Center.

Maps: For a map of Mount Hood National Forest, contact Nature of the Northwest Information Center. For a topographic map, contact Green Trails, Inc. (ask for Bridal Veil, number 428), 206/546-MAPS (206/546-6277), www.greentrails.com; or ask the USGS for Multnomah Falls.

Directions: From Portland, drive east for about 20 miles on I-84 to Exit 22/Corbett. Drive up the Corbett hill for one mile, then turn left on the historic Columbia River Highway for two miles, and turn right on Larch Mountain Road for 12 miles to the end of the road and the parking area and well-marked trailhead.

Contact: Columbia River Gorge National Scenic Area, 902 Wasco Avenue, Suite 200, Hood River, OR 97031, 541/386-2333.

7 ONEONTA/HORSETAIL FALLS LOOP
2.7 mi/1.5 hrs

east of Multnomah Falls in the Columbia River Gorge

Map 3.1, page 68

Dare I say there are cooler falls than Mult-nomah? I dare. Although they may not be as large as their flashier sister next door, these falls are more scenic simply because the crowds are busy ooh-ing and ah-ing at the Big M. This trail hits three lesser-known falls (add 2.4 miles to your hike to throw in an extra one for good measure). Start off beside Horsetail Falls and then take a right (west) after .2 mile onto Horse-tail Falls Trail to arrive at Bachelor Number Two: Upper Horsetail Falls, a.k.a. Ponytail Falls. Here you can actually walk behind the falls in a cavern before continuing on for more than a mile to Oneonta Trail, which heads into the Oneonta Gorge and spits you out at Oneon-ta Falls. If you want to reach Triple Falls (which sounds like the name suggests and is worth the trip), 1.2 miles down, take a left at Oneonta Falls. Otherwise, turn right here to complete the loop back to the highway and a .5-mile walk back to your car.

User groups: Hikers and dogs. No mountain bikes or horses are allowed. No wheelchair access.

Permits: Permits are not required. Parking and access are free.

Maps: For a map of the Columbia River Gorge, contact Nature of the Northwest Information Center. For a topographic map, contact Green Trails, Inc. (ask for Bridal Veil, map number 428), 206/546-MAPS (206/546-6277), www.green trails.com, or ask the USGS for Multnomah Falls.

Directions: From Portland, drive about 35 miles east on I-84 to Ainsworth State Park/Exit 35. Drive 1.5 miles west on the historic Columbia River Scenic Highway to the large parking area on the north side of the highway. The trail starts across the road.

Contact: Columbia River Gorge National Scenic Area, 902 Wasco Avenue, Suite 200, Hood River, OR 97031, 541/386-2333.

8 MILO McIVER STATE PARK
4.5 mi/2.0 hrs

northwest of Estacada off Highway 211

Map 3.1, page 68

A remote wilderness excursion this is not. Between the Frisbee golf, fish hatchery, horse-back riding, fishing, massive campground, and even a model-airplane field, this is a mecca for the whole family. The "main drag" is a 4.5-mile loop, but the trail markings aren't exact-ly bountiful, if even present. Still, even if you're not quite the wizard with directions, you'll be hard-pressed to stray far, as all the paths con-nect. A scenic riverside stroll along the Clacka-mas River and a one-mile nature trail round out the trails in the park, where you'll spot tril-lium and purple foxglove, and maybe even a curious deer wondering what all the ruckus is about. Pick up a map at the park entrance to plan your route. A word to the wise: Make advance camping reservations because the campground fills up fast.

User groups: Hikers, dogs, and horses. Moun-tain bikes are not allowed. Wheelchair access is on paved portions of the trail.

Permits: A $3 day-use fee is collected at the park entrance, or you can get an annual Ore-gon Parks and Recreation pass for $25; con-tact Oregon Parks and Recreation, 800/551-6949, www.oregonstateparks.org.

Maps: Free brochures are available at the park entrance and through Oregon Parks and Recre-ation Department, 800/551-6949, www.ore-gonstateparks.org. For a topographic map, ask the USGS for Estacada.

Directions: From Portland, drive 25 miles east on U.S. 26 to Highway 211 (two miles past Estacada). Turn right (south) on Highway 211 to Hayden Road. After one mile, turn right on Spring Water Road and continue 1.2 miles to the well-marked park entrance. The loop starts in the southern day-use area; the nature and riverside trails start in the northern day-use area.

Contact: Oregon Parks and Recreation Department, 1115 Commercial Street Northeast, Salem, OR 97301, 800/551-6949, www.oregonstate parks.org.

9 MEMALOOSE LAKE
2.6 mi/1.5 hrs

southeast of Estacada in the Clackamas River area of Mount Hood National Forest

Map 3.1, page 68

This easy stroll follows Memaloose Creek to a pretty lake at 4,100 feet (elevation gain is 500 feet). You'll walk through beautiful old-growth forest on your way to the lake, and you'll feel like you're miles from anywhere (even though you're only about an hour's drive from Portland). Keep in mind that the trail can be snowy through the end of June, so it's best to try this trail later in the season if you don't want to drive—or walk—through the white stuff.

User groups: Hikers, dogs, mountain bikes, and horses. No wheelchair access.

Permits: Permits are not required. Parking and access are free.

Maps: For a map of Mount Hood National Forest, contact Nature of the Northwest Information Center. For a topographic map, contact Green Trails, Inc. (ask for Fish Creek Mountain, map number 492), 206/546-MAPS (206/546-6277), www.greentrails.com; or ask the USGS for Wanderers Peak.

Directions: From Estacada, drive southeast on Highway 224 for nine miles to Memaloose Road/Forest Service Road 45. Turn right and drive 11.2 miles until the pavement ends, then keep right to drive on a gravel road for another .9 mile to a small parking pullout and the trailhead on the left.

Contact: Mount Hood National Forest, Clackamas River Ranger District, Estacada Ranger Station, 595 Northwest Industrial Way, Estacada, OR 97023, 503/630-6861.

10 CLACKAMAS RIVER
7.8 mi one-way/3.5 hrs

on the Clackamas River between Fish Creek and Indian Henry Campgrounds in Mount Hood National Forest

Map 3.1, page 68

This trail winds along the scenic Clackamas River, which makes for a great and simple getaway from Portland. The river is popular with white-water kayakers and rafters, so you may glimpse a few along the way. Extending from Fish Creek campground to Indian Henry campground, the trail travels through old-growth forest and passes by beaches and waterfalls. You can do this hike as a shuttle, or for a seven-mile round-trip, hike from the lower trailhead (from Fish Creek Campground) to Pup Creek Falls, a 100-foot waterfall with a half-cave you can hike through. Plenty of fishing and picnic spots line the way, for a perfect year-round weekend escape.

User groups: Hikers and dogs. No mountain bikes or horses are allowed. No wheelchair access.

Permits: A federal Northwest Forest pass is required to park here. The cost is $5 for a day pass or $30 for an annual pass. You can buy a day pass at ranger stations, from private vendors, or through Nature of the Northwest Information Center.

Maps: For a map of Mount Hood National Forest, contact Nature of the Northwest Information Center. For a topographic map, contact Green Trails, Inc. (ask for Fish Creek Mountain, map number 492), 206/546-MAPS (206/546-6277), www.greentrails.com; or ask the USGS for Beford Point, Three Lynx, and Fish Creek Mountain.

Directions: From Estacada, drive 15 miles southeast on Highway 224 to Fish Creek Road/Forest Service Road 54. Turn right and drive .2 mile to the parking lot on the right. The trail starts from the far end of the parking lot and crosses the road to the actual trailhead.

Contact: Mount Hood National Forest, Clackamas River Ranger District, Estacada Ranger

Station, 595 Northwest Industrial Way, Estacada, OR 97023, 503/630-6861.

11 RIVERSIDE NATIONAL RECREATION TRAIL
4.0 mi one-way/2.0 hours

on the Clackamas River between Rainbow and Riverside Campgrounds in Mount Hood National Forest

Map 3.1, page 68

No fancy monikers here: Riverside Trail's name is plain Jane and it likes it that way, thanks very much. If you want an easy stroll but don't feel like dealing with other pleasure-seekers, paved paths, or super-short hikes, this riverside amble along the mighty shores of the Clackamas River aims to please. The river provides white noise, and the cool forest air and river breeze refreshes on a scorching day. Mossy trees and ferns line the route, and it's a shade of green you can't get in a box of crayons. You can access the river at several spots, so bring along lunch—you probably won't have to share your spot with others, since it's not nearly as crowded as other area trails. A relatively flat trail extending from Rainbow camp to Riverside camp, it's a good way to put in some mileage without having to climb too much. You can do this as a four-mile one-way hike, an eight-mile round-trip, or anything in between.

User groups: Hikers, dogs, mountain bikes, and horses. No wheelchair access.

Permits: A federal Northwest Forest pass is required to park here. The cost is $5 for a day pass or $30 for an annual pass. You can buy a day pass at the trailhead, at ranger stations, from private vendors, or through Nature of the Northwest Information Center.

Maps: For a map of Mount Hood National Forest, contact Nature of the Northwest Information Center. For a topographic map, contact Green Trails, Inc. (ask for Fish Creek Mountain, map number 492), 206/546-MAPS (206/546-6277), www.greentrails.com; or ask the USGS for Fish Creek Mountain.

Directions: From Estacada, drive southeast on Highway 224 for 25.5 miles to Rainbow Camp on the right, at the junction with Forest Service Road 46. Drive in the campground entrance and park to the left of site 14 in the small parking area. The trailhead isn't noticeable as you're driving in, so park here and walk a short distance to the sign straight ahead. To reach the trailhead from Riverside Campground, continue on Forest Service Road for four miles; the campground and trailhead are on the right side of the road.

Contact: Mount Hood National Forest, Clackamas River Ranger District, Estacada Ranger Station, 595 Northwest Industrial Way, Estacada, OR 97023, 503/630-6861.

12 NESMITH POINT
9.2 mi/6.5 hrs

between Multnomah Falls and Bonneville in the Columbia River Gorge

Map 3.2, page 69

Feel like climbing a few feet? How about 3,800? Then check out Nesmith Point, the highest point along the Gorge cliffs (it doesn't snag the Gorge's ultimate highest title, though—Mount Defiance has that glory). It's a great escape from crowds, as it's a tough one and not as well known as other trails in the Gorge. The switchbacks through this box canyon are steep, but most of the climbing is in the first three miles, then you'll reach the top of the canyon and gradually ascend the ridgeline to the former lookout site. Keep right at the intersection with an abandoned road to reach the lookout. Once on top, give a friendly wave to Oregon's next-door neighbor, Washington, and its Beacon Rock and Mount Adams. This trail also connects to Horsetail Falls and Oneonta Trails (see listing in this chapter) by turning left (west) .3 mile before the summit when you reach the abandoned road.

User groups: Hikers and dogs. No mountain bikes or horses are allowed. No wheelchair access.

Permits: Permits are not required. Parking and access are free.

Maps: For a map of the Columbia River Gorge, contact Nature of the Northwest Information Center. For a topographic map, contact Green Trails, Inc. (ask for Bridal Veil, map number 428), 206/546-MAPS (206/546-6277), www.green trails.com; or ask the USGS for Bridal Veil.

Directions: From Portland, drive east on I-84 for 35 miles to Exit 35/Ainsworth State Park. Turn left toward Dodson for a short distance, then turn right onto Frontage Road and drive two miles to Yeon Park trailhead and the parking area.

Contact: Columbia River Gorge National Scenic Area, 902 Wasco Avenue, Suite 200, Hood River, OR 97031, 541/386-2333.

13 WAHCLELLA FALLS
1.8 mi/1.0 hr

near Bonneville Dam in the Columbia River Gorge

Map 3.2, page 69

The trail may not get off to a great start—it begins on an old gated road—but it makes up for it later on. You'll pass by a small dam for the Bonneville Fish Hatchery before entering a canyon to arrive at this spectacular two-tiered, 350-foot waterfall, which shows off for you and thanks you for visiting it by splashing dramatically into a pool below. After .7 mile, the trail forks—it's a loop, so take your pick. Once you arrive at the falls, you'll cross a bridge at Tanner Creek with a good view of the water display before returning to complete the loop.

User groups: Hikers and dogs. No mountain bikes or horses are allowed. No wheelchair access.

Permits: A federal Northwest Forest pass is required to park here. The cost is $5 for a day pass or $30 for an annual pass. You can buy a day pass at ranger stations, from private vendors, or through Nature of the Northwest Information Center.

Maps: For a map of the Columbia River Gorge, contact Nature of the Northwest Information Center. For a topographic map, contact Green Trails, Inc. (ask for Bonneville Dam, map num-

ber 429), 206/546-MAPS (206/546-6277), www.greentrails.com; or ask the USGS for Tanner Butte.

Directions: From Portland, drive about 40 miles east on I-84 to Bonneville Dam/Exit 40 and drive south (away from the dam) a short distance to the parking area and trailhead.

Contact: Columbia River Gorge National Scenic Area, 902 Wasco Avenue, Suite 200, Hood River, OR 97031, 541/386-2333.

14 WAUNA VIEWPOINT
3.6 mi/2.0 hrs

near Bonneville Dam in the Columbia River Gorge

Map 3.2, page 69

It's a short climb up 950 feet to the Wauna Viewpoint, where you can gaze down at the Bonneville Dam and the Gorge in all its glory. You'll cross a 200-foot suspension bridge at the start of the trail before switchbacking through Douglas fir forest to the bluff, where you can pretend the power lines don't exist. A mile down, the trail reaches a junction with Gorge Trail, where you should fork left for the last push uphill. Once on top, enjoy the scenery and check out the wildflowers (in spring and summer), such as red paintbrush and orange tiger lily.

User groups: Hikers and dogs. No mountain bikes or horses are allowed. No wheelchair access.

Permits: A federal Northwest Forest pass is required to park here. The cost is $5 for a day pass or $30 for an annual pass. You can buy a day pass at ranger stations, from private vendors, or through Nature of the Northwest Information Center.

Maps: For a map of the Columbia River Gorge, contact Nature of the Northwest Information Center. For a topographic map, contact Green Trails, Inc. (ask for Bonneville Dam, map number 429), 206/546-MAPS (206/546-6277), www.greentrails.com; or ask the USGS for Bonneville Dam and Tanner Butte.

Directions: From Portland, drive about 40

miles east on I-84 to Eagle Creek/Exit 41. Turn right (south) and drive past the Bonneville Fish Hatchery, parking on the left by the picnic area.

Contact: Columbia River Gorge National Scenic Area, 902 Wasco Avenue, Suite 200, Hood River, OR 97031, 541/386-2333.

15 EAGLE CREEK TO TUNNEL FALLS

12.0 mi/7.0 hrs

east of Bonneville Dam in the Columbia River Gorge

Map 3.2, page 69

Eagle Creek is a popular out-and-back trail for runners, backpackers, and those who are just out for a short stroll. Like the name suggests, it travels along Eagle Creek for 13.2 miles to Wahtum Lake, where there are campsites if you want to make this a two-day trip. For day hikers, there is plenty to see along the way. First on the itinerary is Punchbowl Falls, a 25-foot fall plunging into a blue-green pool. That's the turn-around point for many people, for a 4.2-mile round-trip. Three words if you're thinking about doing the same: Don't do it! Hike another mile and you'll cross High Bridge, a suspension bridge 150 feet over the Gorge. The scenery gets better the more you hike in, and at times you'll be tempted to hold on to the wall because it's a long drop below (at precarious points, there are handrails to grasp onto). The coolest part on the trail is the amazing Tunnel Falls, named for the tunnel you walk through underneath the falls. Even if you're cool as a cucumber with heights, you may find yourself holding on a little too tightly to the handrails once you get to the falls, and it's an exhilarating experience. The total elevation gain is about 1,000 feet, parceled out gently on the six-mile stretch.

User groups: Hikers and dogs. No mountain bikes or horses are allowed. No wheelchair access.

Permits: A federal Northwest Forest pass is required to park here. The cost is $5 for a day pass or $30 for an annual pass. You can buy a day pass at ranger stations, from private vendors, or through Nature of the Northwest Information Center.

Maps: For a map of the Columbia River Gorge, contact Nature of the Northwest Information Center. For a topographic map, contact Green Trails, Inc. (ask for Bonneville Dam, map number 429), 206/546-MAPS (206/546-6277), www.greentrails.com; or ask the USGS for Wahtum Lake.

Directions: From Portland, drive about 40 miles east on I-84 to Eagle Creek/Exit 41 and turn right to drive a mile to the large parking area and the well-marked trailhead.

Contact: Columbia River Gorge National Scenic Area, 902 Wasco Avenue, Suite 200, Hood River, OR 97031, 541/386-2333.

16 HERMAN CREEK/NICK EATON RIDGE LOOP

8.0 mi/5.0 hrs

between Cascade Locks and Wyeth in the Columbia River Gorge

Map 3.2, page 69

The Herman Creek area has tons of intersecting trails and options, and unlike some of the Gorge trails to the west, the area typically isn't as crowded. For both of these reasons, it can be helpful to bring along a map to check your progress if you don't like to spend your time scratching your head and wondering if you're on the right trail. In any case, here's one option for a tough climb up to Indian Point: At the first junction, at .7 mile, keep to the left, climbing up an old road for another mile to Herman Camp and a clearing. Stay to the left to pick up Gorton Creek Trail (Herman Creek Trail, to the right, heads eight miles to Wahtum Lake for an overnight option). Gorton Creek Trail climbs for another three miles up some tough switchbacks; elevation gain on the entire trail is about 2,700 feet. Enjoy the scenery of the Douglas fir forest, but keep your head up, because the Ridge Cut-Off Trail junction can be hard to miss. You'll turn right about

3.5 miles after the last junction to climb about 100 feet, then you'll descend two miles back to the Herman Camp clearing, where you first took Gorton Creek Trail, and return from there the way you came. It's a tough climb with great views, and you're likely to encounter few people on the way.

User groups: Hikers, dogs, and horses. No mountain bikes are allowed. No wheelchair access.

Permits: A federal Northwest Forest pass is required to park here. The cost is $5 for a day pass or $30 for an annual pass. You can buy a day pass at ranger stations, from private vendors, or through Nature of the Northwest Information Center.

Maps: For a map of the Columbia River Gorge, contact Nature of the Northwest Information Center. For a topographic map, contact Green Trails, Inc. (ask for Bonneville Dam, map number 429), 206/546-MAPS (206/546-6277), www.greentrails.com; or ask the USGS for Carson and Wahtum Lake.

Directions: From Portland, drive about 45 miles east on I-84 to Cascade Locks/Exit 44. Drive under the highway and through Cascade Locks for 1.8 miles to the eastbound entrance ramp. At the stop sign, cross the road and drive 1.6 miles toward Oxbow Fish Hatchery, and turn right into the Herman Creek Campground. Drive through the campground to the parking area and the trailhead a short distance down at the end of the road.

Contact: Columbia River Gorge National Scenic Area, 902 Wasco Avenue, Suite 200, Hood River, OR 97031, 541/386-2333.

◼17 MOUNT DEFIANCE/
STARVATION RIDGE
11.4 mi/1.0 day
at Starvation Creek rest area east of Wyeth in the Columbia River Gorge

Map 3.2, page 69

Even its name is bold: Mount Defiance is the tallest peak in the Gorge, standing proud over all the little people. This renowned sweat bonan-

za requires climbing almost 5,000 feet in five miles (no, that's not a typo). Be prepared for a heart-pounding trip—the view up top is worth the aching in your quads (just pretend those TV antennas don't exist). If the climb doesn't get to you, the poison oak that grows along the trail might, so be careful.

Right after leaving your car, you'll pass by Cabin Creek Falls, just 200 feet from the trailhead. Stop here to enjoy the scenery before tackling the climb ahead. If the falls look familiar, it's because they are—they're the image on the cover of this book.

There are two ways to reach the top: the rockier, steeper Starvation Ridge and the well-maintained but still steep Mount Defiance Trail. (There's no way to get around that elevation gain, unless you drive directly to the top, which is possible, by the way.) It's a good idea to climb up the Starvation Ridge route, because all the loose rock makes for a nasty descent. If you value the cartilage in the ol' knees, try it this way: After reaching the summit, and stopping to catch your breath, of course, head east past Warren Lake to reach Mount Defiance Trail, turning right for the 5.5-mile return trip to your car. There are several good camping spots at Warren Lake if you want to make it an overnight trip, although one could think of easier things to do than hauling a heavy pack up this ridge.

User groups: Hikers and dogs. No mountain bikes or horses are allowed. No wheelchair access.

Permits: Permits are not required. Parking and access are free.

Maps: For a map of the Columbia River Gorge, contact Nature of the Northwest Information Center. For a topographic map, contact Green Trails, Inc. (ask for Hood River, map number 430), 206/546-MAPS (206/546-6277), www.greentrails.com; or ask the USGS for Mount Defiance.

Directions: From Portland, drive about 50 miles to Starvation Creek State Park exit, just after Wyeth Exit 51. Turn into the rest area;

the trailheads are on the right (west) side of the parking lot.

Contact: Columbia River Gorge National Scenic Area, 902 Wasco Avenue, Suite 200, Hood River, OR 97031, 541/386-2333.

18 WYGANT POINT
8.0 mi/5.5 hrs

between Viento State Park and Hood River in the Columbia River Gorge

Map 3.2, page 69

Wygant Point is the often-overlooked middle child of the Columbia River Gorge—not as mighty as its neighbor Mount Defiance, not as flashy as Multnomah Falls. But Wygant Point is proud of its understated, strong and silent status. You'll huff and puff up this switchback-happy trail to the 2,200-foot summit. Just when you feel like you're getting the hang of this switchback thing, the trail flattens for a bit before the real climbing begins. Outstanding viewpoints of the Gorge await you along the way, and you'll discover see why the area is sometimes called "the windsurfing capital of the world." (Hold on to anything that isn't attached to your body or it will be gone with the wind.) You've probably been wringing your hands in anticipation of the grand finale of views at the point, but it's kind of a buzz-kill when you finally reach it. A bunch of rocks marks the spot (I'd prefer a plaque myself, but that's just me). You can return the way you came or on Chetwoot Trail, which goes through the Perham Creek area (and lacks the great viewpoints).

User groups: Hikers and dogs. No mountain bikes or horses are allowed. No wheelchair access.

Permits: Permits are not required. Parking and access are free.

Maps: For a map of the Columbia River Gorge, contact Nature of the Northwest Information Center. For a topographic map, contact Green Trails, Inc. (ask for Hood River, map number 430), 206/546-MAPS (206/546-6277), www.greentrails.com; or ask the USGS for Hood River and Mount Defiance.

Directions: From Portland, drive east on I-84 for about 55 miles to Exit 58/Mitchell Point Overlook. Park in the large parking area at the well-marked trailhead. Note: This exit is accessible only to eastbound traffic. If you're coming from Hood River, travel 5.5 miles to Exit 56/Viento State Park and re-exit the highway going east.

Contact: Oregon Parks and Recreation Department, 1115 Commercial Street Northeast, Salem, OR 97301, 800/551-6949, www.oregonstateparks.org.

19 MOSIER TWIN TUNNELS
4.5 mi one-way/2.0 hrs

between Mosier and Hood River

Map 3.2, page 69

Traveling along historic Old Columbia River Highway, the first complete road built though the Columbia Gorge, this bike and hike path has a lot of history behind it, although the restoration of the trail itself didn't start until 1995. The trail extends from Mosier to Hood River for 4.5 miles, but the best part is the Mosier Twin Tunnels, just .9 mile from the trailhead in Mosier. They're called twins, though they really are one long tunnel with a short roadway between the two. Construction of the tunnels began in 1921 and took—appropriately enough—two long years to complete. The whole trail is paved and wide, making it a hit with bikers. It's a great way to take in spectacular views without having to exert a lot (or really any) effort to reach the vantage point, since you start high above the river. Stop and watch for sail- and kiteboarders slicing across the river—this area is "the windsurfing capital of the world." You'll find out why it's such a popular water-sports place when you reach the blustery tunnels (bring warm clothes, even on a hot day).

User groups: Hikers, dogs, and mountain bikes. No horses are allowed. The entire trail is wheelchair accessible, and there is a separate parking area for wheelchair users.

Permits: Permits are not required. A $3 day-use fee is collected at the park entrance, or you can get an annual Oregon Parks and Recreation pass for $25; contact Oregon Parks and Recreation, 800/551-6949.

Maps: For a map of the Historic Columbia River Highway State Trail, contact Oregon Parks and Recreation Department, 800/551-6949, www.oregonstateparks.org. For a topographic map, ask the USGS for White Salmon and Hood River.

Directions: From Hood River, travel five miles east on I-84 to Exit 69. Before you hit the town of Mosier, turn left onto Rock Creek Road and drive one mile to the Mark O. Hatfield parking entrance, on the left. Follow the well-marked trail along the paved Rock Creek Road, and then cross the street to the wheelchair parking area, where the trail officially begins.

Contact: Oregon Parks and Recreation Department, 1115 Commercial Street Northeast, Salem, OR 97301, 800/551-6949, www.oregonstateparks.org.

20 TOM MCCALL PRESERVE
5.0 mi/3.0 hrs

east of Hood River at the Rowena Crest Viewpoint in the Columbia River Gorge

Map 3.2, page 69

Named after a former Oregon governor, Tom McCall Preserve offers something different than other Gorge trails. Two trails leave from Rowena Crest: One is an easy one-mile stroll out past two lakes before ending at a cliffside viewpoint; the other leads up to McCall Point (open May through November), gaining 1,000 feet in elevation to a view of the Gorge and the wildflowers that cover the area in the spring and summer. More than 300 plant species live here, and you can't blame them for setting up camp at this scenic spot. Although this is a good place to bring the kids, you should leave your furry friends at home.

User groups: Hikers only. No dogs, mountain bikes, or horses are allowed. No wheelchair access.

Permits: Permits are not required. Parking and access are free.

Maps: Brochures are available (when supplies last) at the trailhead. For a topographic map, ask the USGS for White Salmon.

Directions: From Portland, drive 65 miles east on I-84 to Mosier/Exit 69 and follow signs for 6.5 miles to Rowena Crest Viewpoint. Park at the Rowena Viewpoint parking area, where both trails start.

Contact: The Nature Conservancy of Oregon, 821 Southeast 14th Avenue, Portland, OR 97214, 503/230-1221.

21 LOST LAKE LOOP
3.2 mi/1.5 hrs

southwest of Hood River in Mount Hood National Forest

Map 3.2, page 69

Lost Lake doesn't seem to mind that it's lost, sitting in such a beautiful area. With Mount Hood as the backdrop, this trail follows the lakeshore for an easy loop that everyone can—and will want to—do. The lake is a happenin' place, with a store, a huge campground, canoe rental, and, of course, hiking. Pick up a self-guided nature tour brochure at the store before you head out. If you want to put a little more legwork and add some even cooler scenery into the whole affair, you can add four miles to the trip by heading to 4,468-foot Lost Lake Butte (the trailhead starts from the northeast corner of the lake). Since the lake's elevation is 3,100 feet, it's best to hit this area from June through September, as it can be snowbound the rest of the year.

User groups: Hikers and dogs. Mountain bikes are not allowed. Horses are not allowed.

Permits: Permits are not required. Parking and access are free.

Maps: For a map of Mount Hood National Forest, contact Nature of the Northwest Information Center. For a topographic map, contact Green Trails, Inc. (ask for Government Camp, map number 461), 206/546-MAPS (206/546-6277), www.greentrails.com; or ask the USGS for Bull Run Lake.

Directions: From Portland, drive about 40 miles east on Highway 26 to Zigzag, and turn left onto East Lolo Pass Road/Forest Service Road 18. After 10.5 miles, turn right onto McGee Creek Road/Forest Service Road 1810 for 7.5 miles until it rejoins Forest Service Road 18. Continue another seven miles and turn left onto Forest Service Road 13 to the Lost Lake entrance. The trailhead starts at the picnic area near the parking lot.

Contact: Mount Hood National Forest, Hood River Ranger District, 6780 Highway 35, Mount Hood-Parkdale, OR 97041, 541/352-6002.

22 OAK RIDGE TO BALD BUTTE/RIMROCK
8.2–9.2 mi/5.0–6.0 hrs
east of Highway 35 in Mount Hood National Forest

Map 3.2, page 69

Robert Frost knew a thing or two when he wrote "The Road Not Taken." He took the lesser-known path when encountering two roads diverging in the woods, and look what happened to him—he's famous! You'll have a chance to solve the same dilemma when you encounter two paths here, each to a viewpoint. There are no guarantees that either path will necessarily be less traveled, as they hit the popular Surveyor's Ridge (see listing in this chapter). Starting at an open grassy area, the trail soon enters the oak and fir forest, and then you start to climb up switchbacks. At 2.3 miles, Oak Ridge Trail officially ends, but your trip has only begun: Turn right for another 2.3 miles south to hit 4,300-foot Rimrock, or head left to reach the 3,779-foot Bald Butte, to the north. Take your pick, or do them both if one viewpoint just isn't enough for you. Clear views of Mount Hood, Mount Adams, Mount St. Helens, Mount Rainier, and the Hood River Valley are your reward for the tough climb up.

User groups: Hikers, dogs, mountain bikes, and horses. No wheelchair access.

Permits: Permits are not required. Parking and access are free.

Maps: For a map of Mount Hood National Forest, contact Nature of the Northwest Information Center. For a topographic map, contact Green Trails, Inc. (ask for Hood River, map number 430), 206/546-MAPS (206/546-6277), www.greentrails.com; or ask the USGS for Parkdale.

Directions: From Hood River, drive 15 miles south on Highway 35 and turn left on Smullin Road. Drive .2 mile to an unmarked gravel road, turn left, and drive less than .1 mile to the small parking area and well-marked trailhead, on the right.

Contact: Mount Hood National Forest, Hood River Ranger District, 6780 Highway 35, Mount Hood-Parkdale, OR 97041, 541/352-6002.

23 SURVEYOR'S RIDGE
13.0 mi one-way/ 1.0–2.0 days
east of Highway 35 in Mount Hood National Forest

Map 3.2, page 69

The name says it all: This is a ridgeline trail from which to survey the land below. And what a land it is. From this popular trail, you can spy on Mount Hood, Mount St. Helens, Mount Rainier, Mount Adams, and the upper Hood River Valley. This trail has an interesting weather pattern, as it's the dividing line between the wet weather of the Columbia River Gorge and Hood River Valley to the west and the dry climate of the desert to the east. Surveyor's Ridge is well known in the area, especially to mountain bikers, so expect some company along the way. The path also hits Gibson Prairie Horse Camp five miles down the way, so you may also see some four-legged friends. There are several access points and campsites along the way, so you can do this as a shuttle or an out-and-back overnight trip. The trail also hits Bald Butte and intersects Oak Ridge Trail (see listing in this chapter).

User groups: Hikers, dogs, horses, and mountain bikes. No wheelchair access.

Permits: A federal Northwest Forest pass is

required to park here. The cost is $5 for a day pass or $30 for an annual pass. You can buy a day pass at ranger stations, from private vendors, or through Nature of the Northwest Information Center.

Maps: For a map of Mount Hood National Forest, contact Nature of the Northwest Information Center. For a topographic map, contact Green Trails, Inc. (ask for Hood River and Mount Hood, map numbers 430 and 462), 206/546-MAPS (206/546-6277), www.greentrails.com; or ask the USGS for Parkdale and Dog River.

Directions: From Hood River, drive south on Highway 35 for 15 miles to Pinemont Drive/Forest Service Road 17. Turn left and drive six miles to Spur Road 630. Turn right and drive four miles to the parking area on the left, a short distance past the fork in the road; take the right fork. (Before the road forks, you'll pass another small parking area; keep going until you come to the small parking area on the left, under the power lines.) To reach the south trailhead, drive south on Highway 35 from Hood River for 25 miles. Between mileposts 70 and 71, turn left onto paved Forest Service Road 44. Drive for 3.5 miles to the junction with Road 620. Park on the side of the road; the trailhead is on the left.

Contact: Mount Hood National Forest, Hood River Ranger District, 6780 Highway 35, Mount Hood-Parkdale, OR 97041, 541/352-6002.

24 HUCKLEBERRY MOUNTAIN
10.5 mi/6.0 hrs

south of Highway 26 in the Salmon Huckleberry Wilderness of Mount Hood National Forest

Map 3.2, page 69

A popular stomping ground for Portlanders, Huckleberry Mountain offers choices on how to visit it. Most people access the 4,000-foot summit from Wildwood Recreation Area, which means that it can get crowded—but not too crowded, as the trail is a hefty hike. Starting from Boulder Ridge Trail, the path switchbacks

up through Douglas fir forest, where views get better with each step (remember to look behind you once in a while to glimpse Mount Hood). At the 4.2-mile mark, turn right onto Plaza Trail for another mile to reach the summit. Return the same way, or continue along the mountain's ridge to turn right at Bonanza Mine Trail for five miles to the eastern trailhead (arrange a pick-up if you take this route, as parking can be tough at the trailhead).

User groups: Hikers, dogs, and horses. No mountain bikes are allowed. No wheelchair access.

Permits: A federal Northwest Forest pass is required to park here. The cost is $5 for a day pass or $30 for an annual pass. You can buy a day pass at ranger stations, from private vendors, or through Nature of the Northwest Information Center.

Maps: For a map of Mount Hood National Forest and Salmon Huckleberry Wilderness, contact Nature of the Northwest Information Center. For a topographic map, contact Green Trails, Inc. (ask for Cherryville and Government Camp, map numbers 460 and 461), 206/546-MAPS (206/546-6277), www.greentrails.com; or ask the USGS for Wildcat Mountain and Rhododendron.

Directions: From Portland, drive about 40 miles east on U.S. 26 to Zigzag. Just past the town, turn right (south) on Salmon River Road and drive 6.7 miles (paved for the first 5.1 miles) to the small parking area on the left. The trailhead starts across the street on an unmarked spur road.

Contact: Mount Hood National Forest, Zigzag Ranger District, 70220 East Highway 26, Zigzag, OR 97049, 503/622-3191.

25 ZIGZAG MOUNTAIN LOOP
11.0 mi/8.0 hrs

west of Mount Hood in the Mount Hood Wilderness

Map 3.2, page 69

One peak not enough for you? Double your pleasure (and pain) with this challenging mountain loop that hits both East and West Zigzag summits. Starting from Burnt Lake Trail (from the other direction than the one in this chapter's listing), the trail starts off on an abandoned road up through Devil's Meadow, filled with wildflowers in the summer. For a shorter loop that shaves 2.5 miles from your trip, you can take the first junction you come across, the Devil's Tie Trail, but then you'd be missing out on the East Zigzag peak. Instead continue straight for another 1.3 miles, turning left to head up the ridge to the peak (4,980 feet) for a peek down into Burnt Lake and, of course, across to Mount Hood. Continue downhill and consider how you're feeling: If you want to take your time, you can add another mile round-trip by heading to Cast Lake for a rest stop. Otherwise, continue just past the lake junction and turn right (west) on Zigzag Mountain Trail another 3.8 miles to the West Zigzag Mountain lookout, passing Horseshoe Ridge Trail to your second lookout. The beauty of this trail is that you're not locked into your distance—if you've had enough, you can always continue straight to return three miles back to your car at this point, turning right at Burnt Lake Trail for an eight-mile loop. If you want to say you bagged two peaks in one day, though, and you're up for a challenge, the entire loop is worth the trip. After reaching the summit of West Zigzag (passing the return trail to your left about .1 mile from the summit), backtrack to West Zigzag Trail for a 2.3-mile descent.

User groups: Hikers, dogs, and horses. No mountain bikes are allowed. No wheelchair access.

Permits: A federal Northwest Forest pass is required to park here. The cost is $5 for a day pass or $30 for an annual pass. You can buy a day pass at ranger stations, from private vendors, or through Nature of the Northwest Information Center.

Maps: For a map of Mount Hood Wilderness and Mount Hood National Forest, contact Nature of the Northwest Information Center. For a topographic map, contact Green Trails, Inc. (ask for Government Camp, map number 461), 206/546-MAPS (206/546-6277), www.greentrails.com; or ask the USGS for Government Camp.

Directions: From Portland, drive east on U.S. 26 for about 45 miles, passing through the town of Rhododendron. Turn left on Forest Service Road 27, and drive .5 mile to Forest Service Road 207. Turn left and drive 4.5 rough miles to the trailhead and the parking area at the end of the road.

Contact: Mount Hood National Forest, Zigzag Ranger District, 70220 East Highway 26, Zigzag, OR 97049, 503/622-3191.

26 BURNT LAKE
6.0 mi/3.0 hrs

west of Mount Hood in Mount Hood National Forest

Map 3.2, page 69

Burnt Lake sure got the short end of the stick when it came to naming. But there's a good reason for the unfortunate moniker: an old fire that left an interesting display of burned tree trunks you can step inside. A couple miles in, look for a short side trail to the left to find Lost Creek Falls before continuing the climb. You'll get a good workout on the way up, as the trail ascends about 1,500 feet through a mixture of old- and new-growth forest to the lake with a great view of Mount Hood. This trail also continues past the lake less than a mile to Zigzag Mountain Trail (see listing in this chapter).

User groups: Hikers and dogs. No horses or mountain bikes are allowed. No wheelchair access.

Permits: A federal Northwest Forest pass is required to park here. The cost is $5 for a day pass or $30 for an annual pass. You can buy a day pass at ranger stations, from private vendors, or through Nature of the Northwest Information Center.

Maps: For a map of Mount Hood National Forest, contact Nature of the Northwest Information Center. For a topographic map, contact Green Trails, Inc. (ask for Government

Camp, map number 461), 206/546-MAPS (206/546-6277), www.greentrails.com; or ask the USGS for Government Camp.

Directions: From Portland, drive east on Highway 26 for about 40 miles to the town of Zigzag. Turn left onto East Lolo Pass Road/Forest Service Road 18 and drive 4.2 miles to a fork in the road. Stay to the right, turning onto Forest Service Road 1825. Drive 2.5 miles, and just past the Lost Creek Campground entrance, turn left onto a gravel road for 1.3 miles to the small parking area and well-marked trailhead at the end of the road.

Contact: Mount Hood National Forest, Zigzag Ranger District, 70220 East Highway 26, Zigzag, OR 97049, 503/622-3191.

27 RAMONA FALLS
7.1 mi/3.0 hrs

south of Bald Mountain in Mount Hood National Forest

Map 3.2, page 69

For a well-marked loop to remarkable falls, this is a pleasant day trip. It can get a smidge crowded, though, as the falls are a popular destination. Rhododendron blooms here in the summer, keeping you company as you stroll down this relatively easy path to the falls. Travel one mile to a bridge (which is removed every fall to prevent damage from the high water levels, then reinstalled in the spring), and you'll come to a fork. The right fork is slightly shorter and easier, reaching Ramona in two miles, but it's a sandy trail popular with horses. The left fork wants to be fashionably late, arriving at the falls in 2.3 miles. When you get there, you can see why it's such a popular place. Unlike other waterfalls, which show off with one giant explosion of water, Ramona takes a more dainty approach: Trickling cascades of water rush down the entire rock wall. It's a sight worth seeing, despite the crowds. Complete the loop to travel back to the trailhead. You can lengthen the hike by adding a six-mile loop to Bald Mountain: When you reach the falls, turn north onto Pacific Crest Trail for

4.8 miles, then keep left at the junction to return back to Ramona Falls Trail. You'll have to cross Muddy Fork River, which is lower earlier in the day, so keep that in mind when you arrange your trip.

User groups: Hikers and horses. No mountain bikes are allowed. No wheelchair access.

Permits: A federal Northwest Forest pass is required to park here. The cost is $5 for a day pass or $30 for an annual pass. You can buy a day pass at ranger stations, from private vendors, or through Nature of the Northwest Information Center.

Maps: For a map of Mount Hood National Forest, contact Nature of the Northwest Information Center. For a topographic map, contact Green Trails, Inc. (ask for Government Camp, map number 461), 206/546-MAPS (206/546-6277), www.greentrails.com; or ask the USGS for Government Camp.

Directions: From Portland, drive east on Highway 26 for about 40 miles to the town of Zigzag. Turn left onto East Lolo Pass Road/Forest Service Road 18 and drive 4.2 miles to a fork in the road. Stay to the right, turning onto Forest Service Road 1825. Continue another 2.4 miles, turning left at the sign for Ramona Falls, and drive .4 mile to the large parking area and the well-marked trailhead.

Contact: Mount Hood National Forest, Zigzag Ranger District, 70220 East Highway 26, Zigzag, OR 97049, 503/622-3191.

28 VISTA RIDGE TO EDEN PARK, CAIRN, AND WY'EAST BASINS
8.0 mi/5.0 hrs

on the northwest slope of Mount Hood

Map 3.2, page 69

The scenic ridgeline (yep, the trail is aptly named) is an easy way to access Timberline Trail to three wildflower meadows: Eden Park, Cairn, and Wy'east Basins. It starts on an old road for a few hundred feet before heading into the hemlock forest, with views of Mount Hood peeking out here and there when you least expect it. It climbs to 5,700 feet (total elevation gain is 900 feet) for 2.5 miles and then comes to the Timberline Trail junction. From here, you can do a three-mile loop to access the attractions. First, head right (west) to Eden Park and Cairn Basin, turning left at both junctions as you head back to Wy'east Basin, and turn left again to complete the loop (remember, when in doubt after that first right, take a left). These meadows afford stellar views of mighty Mount Hood and are worth the trip in. The trail also connects to Elk Cove, two miles to the east (to the left when you first hit Timberline Trail; see listing in this chapter), so you can add another four miles to your trip if you're a fool for alpine beauty.

User groups: Hikers and dogs. No mountain bikes or horses are allowed.

Permits: A federal Northwest Forest pass is required to park here. The cost is $5 for a day pass or $30 for an annual pass. You can buy a day pass at ranger stations, from private vendors, or through Nature of the Northwest Information Center.

Maps: For a map of Mount Hood National Forest, contact Nature of the Northwest Information Center. For a topographic map, contact Green Trails, Inc. (ask for Mount Hood, map number 462), 206/546-MAPS (206/546-6277), www.greentrails.com; or ask the USGS for Mount Hood North.

Directions: From Portland, drive about 40 miles east on U.S. 26 to East Lolo Pass Road/Forest Service Road 18 and drive 10.5 miles to McGee Creek Road/Forest Service Road 1810. Turn right and drive until the road rejoins Forest Service Road 18, 7.5 miles down, and continue another 3.5 miles and turn right on Forest Service Road 16. Drive 5.5 miles and turn left onto Forest Service Road 1650, following signs another four miles to the end of the rough road and the trailhead.

Contact: Mount Hood National Forest, Hood River Ranger District, 6780 Highway 35, Mount Hood-Parkdale, OR 97041, 541/352-6002.

29 TIMBERLINE TRAIL TO ELK COVE
9.8 mi/6.0 hrs

on the north slope of Mount Hood

Map 3.2, page 69

Ready for a close-up of Mount Hood? Try this 4.9-mile stretch of Timberline Trail to Elk Cove, a meadowed basin of "Da Hood" itself. Along the challenging and exhilarating hike, you'll cross several streams then descend before the steep, rocky climb to the cove. You'll know you've arrived when you hit the remains of a stone shelter. Wildflowers complete the photo op–filled hike in July and August (it can be snowbound through July, so it's best to hit this one later in the season).

User groups: Hikers and dogs. No mountain bikes or horses are allowed.

Permits: A federal Northwest Forest pass is required to park here. The cost is $5 for a day pass or $30 for an annual pass. You can buy a day pass at ranger stations, from private vendors, or through Nature of the Northwest Information Center.

Maps: For a map of Mount Hood National Forest, contact Nature of the Northwest Information Center. For a topographic map, contact Green Trails, Inc. (ask for Mount Hood, map number 462), 206/546-MAPS (206/546-6277), www.greentrails.com; or ask the USGS for Mount Hood North.

Directions: From Hood River, drive 23 miles south on Highway 35. At the sign for Cooper Spur Ski Area, turn right onto Cooper Spur Road. Drive 2.3 miles and turn left at the sign for Cloud Cap, onto Forest Service Road 3512. Drive 10.2 miles up the narrow, winding road (paved road turns into gravel after 1.4 miles) to the end of the road and the large parking pullout by the restroom. The trailhead is on the right as you're driving in. Look for the sign to Timberline Trail, and take the right fork heading west.

Contact: Mount Hood National Forest, Hood River Ranger District, 6780 Highway 35, Mount Hood-Parkdale, OR 97041, 541/352-6002.

30 COOPER SPUR
6.8 mi/4.0 hrs

on the north slope of Mount Hood

Map 3.2, page 69

One of the highest trails on Mount Hood, Cooper Spur Trail climbs to 8,514 feet, gaining almost 2,000 feet in elevation. Remember to pack along warm clothes, since it can get a bit nippy at that altitude. You'll walk on Timberline Trail (ignore the right fork heading to Eliot Glacier) for more than a mile before reaching a rock shelter and the junction with Cooper Spur Trail, and then the true climbing begins. Continue until you've reached Tie-In Rock, your beacon in this lonely and beautiful alpine wilderness. The trail is usually snowed in through late July, so it's best to tackle the grueling route later in the season (which will give you all summer to get in shape for it).

User groups: Hikers and dogs. No mountain bikes or horses are allowed. No wheelchair access.

Permits: A federal Northwest Forest pass is required to park here. The cost is $5 for a day pass or $30 for an annual pass. You can buy a day pass at ranger stations, from private vendors, or through Nature of the Northwest Information Center.

Maps: For a map of Mount Hood National Forest, contact Nature of the Northwest Information Center. For a topographic map, contact Green Trails, Inc. (ask for Mount Hood, map number 462), 206/546-MAPS (206/546-6277), www.greentrails.com; or ask the USGS for Mount Hood North.

Directions: From Hood River, drive 23 miles south on Highway 35. At the sign for Cooper Spur Ski Area, turn right onto Cooper Spur Road. Drive 2.3 miles and turn left at the sign for Cloud Cap, onto Forest Service Road 3512. Drive 10.2 miles up the narrow, winding road (paved road turns into gravel after 1.4 miles) to the end of the road and the large parking pullout by the restroom. The trailhead is on the right as you're driving in.

Contact: Mount Hood National Forest, Hood River Ranger District, 6780 Highway 35, Mount Hood-Parkdale, OR 97041, 541/352-6002.

31 TILLY JANE SKI TRAIL/ POLALLIE RIDGE TO CLOUD CAP
6.0 mi/3.5 hrs

between Cooper Spur Ski Area and Cloud Cap on the northeastern slope of Mount Hood

Map 3.2, page 69

Want to say you've climbed up to the country's oldest alpine ski cabin? (You can also say you drove to it, but that doesn't have quite the same ring to it.) Cloud Cap cabin was built in 1889, and a large section of this area has been listed on the National Registry of Historic Places since 1981. Tilly Jane Ski Trail was nominated in August 2003 for a place of her own on the list. The historic ski trail extends 2.5 miles up to the Tilly Jane shelter and old amphitheater, which was first used in 1920, and then continues for another .5 mile to Cloud Cap. Tilly Jane Ski Trail is one of those continuous, sneaky ascents where, if it weren't for your racing heart, you might not realize you're going uphill. The trail is popular in the winter—all the more reason to hike it in the summer, when you may have it all to yourself. Close to the top, you'll come to a clearing with wildflowers where you can view the valley spread out before you. After exploring Cloud Cap, return to the Tilly Jane shelter and follow the sign marked "Tilly Jane Trail #600A," taking that trail back to Polallie Ridge Trail for the return loop back.

User groups: Hikers, dogs, mountain bikes, and horses. No wheelchair access.

Permits: A federal Northwest Forest pass is required to park here. The cost is $5 for a day pass or $30 for an annual pass. You can buy a day pass at ranger stations, from private vendors, or through Nature of the Northwest Information Center.

Maps: For a map of Mount Hood National Forest, contact Nature of the Northwest Information Center. For a topographic map, contact Green Trails, Inc. (ask for Mount Hood, map number 462), 206/546-MAPS (206/546-6277), www.greentrails.com; or ask the USGS for Mount Hood North.

Directions: From Hood River, drive 23 miles south on Highway 35. At the sign for Cooper Spur Ski Area, turn right onto Cooper Spur Road. Drive 2.3 miles to Cloud Cap Road, following signs to the Cooper Spur Ski Area for 1.4 miles. Park in the small parking area on the right; the trailhead is across the road on the left.

Contact: Mount Hood National Forest, Hood River Ranger District, 6780 Highway 35, Mount Hood-Parkdale, OR 97041, 541/352-6002.

32 TAMANAWAS FALLS
4.0 mi/2.0 hrs

off Highway 35 north of Sherwood campground in Mount Hood National Forest

Map 3.2, page 69

You'll get tongue-tied pronouncing the name (ta-MA-na-was, a Native American word meaning "spiritual guardian"), but you'll be speechless when you reach the 100-foot falls. Starting from the East Fork trailhead, the trail starts by crossing a log bridge over East Fork Hood River and then following the creek to the falls (total elevation gain: about 450 feet). A canopy of Douglas fir cools your route, and the flowing creek drowns out all other sounds. You'll be tempted to stop for a picnic and soak up the scenery, but hold your hunger: The best is yet to come. When you finally round a bend and see the falls (two miles in), remember not to gape and walk at the same time—you'll need to watch where you're going. It's a sketchy final climb through boulder fields to the falls, but it's worth the effort: Standing under the cave as water pours down in front of you is like having a slice of your own private Oregon. Well, kind of, as the trail can get crowded. After lingering in the cool mist, return on the same route. Feeling extra energetic? Add 1.5 miles for a loop off the beaten path: Turn left after the second boulder field on your return trip,

which takes you up to Polallie Overlook, where you can view the 1980 flood's path of destruction. Return along East Fork Trail, following the signs back to Tamanawas Trail.

User groups: Hikers and dogs. No horses or mountain bikes are allowed. No wheelchair access.

Permits: A federal Northwest Forest pass is required to park here. The cost is $5 for a day pass or $30 for an annual pass. You can buy a day pass at ranger stations, from private vendors, or through Nature of the Northwest Information Center.

Maps: For a map of Mount Hood National Forest, contact Nature of the Northwest Information Center. For a topographic map, contact Green Trails, Inc. (ask for Mount Hood, map number 462), 206/546-MAPS (206/546-6277), www.greentrails.com; or ask the USGS for Dog River.

Directions: From Hood River, drive 25 miles south on Highway 35 to the trailhead on the right side of the highway, just before Sherwood Campground.

Contact: Mount Hood National Forest, Hood River Ranger District, 6780 Highway 35, Mount Hood-Parkdale, OR 97041, 541/352-6002.

33 EAST FORK TRAIL
6.0 mi one-way/3.0 hrs

west of Highway 35 along the East Fork Hood River

Map 3.2, page 69

Traveling along the East Fork Hood River, this trail is a popular one with mountain bikers for the rolling hills and great single-track trail. Although the entire length is six miles, the trail gets extremely sandy from a washout leading up to Robinhood Campground (the southern trailhead), so unless you feel like a sandy stroll, you should turn around at this point. Still, most of the trail is a scenic walk along the rushing waters of Hood River, and there are plenty of top-notch campsites across the river. The beauty of this camping spot is that it's convenient, right by the highway, but the water drowns out the highway traffic, so you feel as if you're in the middle of the wilderness. Also, it's not nearly as crowded as nearby Tamanawas Falls, where the northern trailhead is located, making it a good choice after hitting the falls to see more of this beautiful area.

User groups: Hikers, dogs, and mountain bikes. Horses are not allowed. No wheelchair access.

Permits: A federal Northwest Forest pass is required to park here. The cost is $5 for a day pass or $30 for an annual pass. You can buy a day pass at ranger stations, from private vendors, or through Nature of the Northwest Information Center.

Maps: For a map of Mount Hood National Forest and Salmon Huckleberry Wilderness, contact Nature of the Northwest Information Center. For a topographic map, contact Green Trails, Inc. (ask for Mount Hood, map number 462), 206/546-MAPS (206/546-6277), www.greentrails.com; or ask the USGS for Dog River and Badger Lake.

Directions: From Hood River, drive 25 miles south on Highway 35 to the trailhead on the right side of the highway, just before Sherwood Campground.

Contact: Mount Hood National Forest, Hood River Ranger District, 6780 Highway 35, Mount Hood-Parkdale, OR 97041, 541/352-6002.

34 ELK MEADOWS LOOP
7.8 mi/4.0 hrs

on the southeast side of Mount Hood

Map 3.2, page 69

Leading up to a wildflower meadow, this trail is popular with not only other hikers but also with other trails, as many other routes connect to it. The route starts in Clark Creek Sno-Park, leading into a fir forest. At the one-mile point, hikers reach a junction with Newton Creek Trail. Keep going straight, crossing the creek over logs and rocks (it's best to hit this early in the day, when water levels are lower). Then the switchbacks begin, gaining 1,500 feet in elevation en route to the 5,900-foot meadows.

Once at the top, you'll arrive at a four-way junction, where you have plenty of options. You can either do a loop around the meadows by heading straight, or turn left (west) to tackle Gnarl Ridge and a tough climb up to 6,500-foot Lamberson Butte. This option will pile five more miles on to your trip. Otherwise, circle the meadows and return the way you came for a long and exhilarating downhill hike.

User groups: Hikers, dogs, and horses. No mountain bikes are allowed. No wheelchair access.

Permits: A federal Northwest Forest pass is required to park here. The cost is $5 for a day pass or $30 for an annual pass. You can buy a day pass at ranger stations, from private vendors, or through Nature of the Northwest Information Center.

Maps: For a map of Mount Hood National Forest, contact Nature of the Northwest Information Center. For a topographic map, contact Green Trails, Inc. (ask for Mount Hood, map number 462), 206/546-MAPS (206/546-6277), www.greentrails.com; or ask the USGS for Mount Hood South and Badger Lake.

Directions: From Hood River, drive 35 miles on Highway 35 to Clark Creek Sno-Park, on the right. (Note: You can also start from Hood River Meadows, which is another mile down Highway 35 on the right.)

Contact: Mount Hood National Forest, Hood River Ranger District, 6780 Highway 35, Mount Hood-Parkdale, OR 97041, 541/352-6002.

35 HIGH PRAIRIE TRAIL TO LOOKOUT MOUNTAIN
2.4 mi/2.0 hrs

east of Mount Hood in Mount Hood National Forest

Map 3.2, page 69

So many trailheads lead to Lookout Mountain that it would almost take a book to cover all of them. One longer route starts from Highway 35 and ascends steeply up 2.4 long miles to Gumjuwac Saddle, then another 2.2 miles on Divide Trail up to Lookout Mountain. Another route starts from Fifteenmile Campground and treks for 2.1 miles before hitting Divide Trail for another 1.5 miles. But why mess around with switchbacks? To cut to the chase, take High Prairie Trail for a gentle 600-climb to the top, after which you can check out the surrounding areas. The trail starts on the not-so-scenic old summit road, which can be snow-covered through July, so it's best to leave this one until later in the season. After 1.2 miles you'll reach a junction with Divide Trail; turn left for the summit, just 200 yards away. The views extend as far as Mount Rainier and the Three Sisters. Stick around once you've reached the ridge to explore other attractions, like Oval Lake (about 1.5 miles past the summit, off a short side trail to the left), Palisade Point (another great viewpoint, just past Oval Lake), and Flag Point (about two more miles from Palisade Point). You can just line up your attractions in a row and decide how many you have the energy to hit in one day.

User groups: Hikers, dogs, and horses. No mountain bikes are allowed. No wheelchair access.

Permits: A federal Northwest Forest pass is required to park here. The cost is $5 for a day pass or $30 for an annual pass. You can buy a day pass at ranger stations, from private vendors, or through Nature of the Northwest Information Center.

Maps: For a map of Mount Hood National Forest, contact Nature of the Northwest Information Center. For a topographic map, contact Green Trails, Inc. (ask for Mount Hood, map number 462), 206/546-MAPS (206/546-6277), www.greentrails.com; or ask the USGS for Badger Lake.

Directions: From Hood River, drive south on Highway 35 for about 30 miles to paved Dufur Mill Road/Forest Service Road 44, between mileposts 70 and 71. Turn left (east) and drive 3.8 miles to High Prairie Road/Forest Service Road 4410. Turn right and go 4.7 miles to a T-junction. Turn left and continue .1 mile to the small parking area on the left. The trailhead is across the road from the parking area.

Contact: Mount Hood National Forest, Hood River Ranger District, 6780 Highway 35, Mount Hood-Parkdale, OR 97041, 541/352-6002.

36 GUMJUWAC SADDLE/ GUNSIGHT BUTTE/DIVIDE TO BADGER LAKE
5.4–9.2 mi/3.0–5.0 hrs   4 8

east of Highway 35 in the Badger Creek Wilderness of Mount Hood National Forest

Map 3.2, page 69

There are approximately 9,845 routes to Badger Lake (give or take). Okay, there are really only four, if you count the bumpy and often snowy road that leads directly to the lake, but once you're up there it seems like the possibilities are endless. Here are your options: Divide Trail, the easiest path and gentlest on your knees, leads 2.7 miles and 600 feet directly down to the lake. In the middle-of-the-road category with a view to kill, there's Gunsight Trail, which follows the ridgeline for 3.3 miles to Gunsight Butte, which then connects with Badger Creek Trail for 1.3 miles to the lake (elevation loss is also 600 feet but it's a longer route). For the final option, tougher Gumjuwac Saddle Trail offers a challenge, shooting down 1,300 feet in 2.2 miles, then connecting with Badger Creek Trail for two miles to the lake. If you want to get to the lake directly and get a workout hiking back up, try Divide Trail down to the lake and return on Gumjuwac Saddle Trail via Badger Creek Trail for a 6.9-mile loop. (Don't try the loop around the lake itself, though, as it's not maintained.) You can make this an overnight trip by camping at the lake, where there are developed campsites. It's a good idea to get a map of this area before you start off; although the trails are usually marked, it can get confusing at times with all the options. Also, be warned that the road to this trail is rough and often snowed in through July, so check ahead of time to make sure it's clear.

User groups: Hikers, dogs, and horses. Mountain bikes are allowed only on Gunsight Trail. No wheelchair access.

Permits: Permits are not required. Parking and access are free.

Maps: For a map of Mount Hood National Forest and Badger Creek Wilderness, contact Nature of the Northwest Information Center. For a topographic map, contact Green Trails, Inc. (ask for Mount Hood, map number 462), 206/546-MAPS (206/546-6277), www.green-trails.com; or ask the USGS for Badger Lake.

Directions: From Hood River, drive about 30 miles south on Highway 35 to Dufur Mill Road/Forest Service Road 44, between mileposts 70 and 71. Turn left (east) and drive 3.8 miles to High Prairie Road/Forest Service Road 4410. Turn right and drive 4.5 miles and then turn right on the rough, dirt Bennett Pass Road/Forest Service Road 3350 for 3.5 miles to the trailheads. Gunsight Trail starts on the right side of the road, while Gumjuwac Saddle and Divide Trails start from the left side of the road.

Contact: Mount Hood National Forest, Barlow Ranger District, Dufur Ranger Station, 780 Northeast Court Street, Dufur, OR 97021, 541/467-2291.

③⑦ FLAG POINT/GORDON BUTTE
7.0 mi/3.5 hrs

east of Highway 35 in the Badger Creek Wilderness of Mount Hood National Forest

Map 3.2, page 69

Your car does most of the work on the bumpy ride in to this 5,651-foot lookout tower, but it's worth the effort: You can climb up stairs to the top of Flag Point Lookout (which is available for rental), where northern views extend to Mount Rainier and Mount Adams in Washington. For a sweeping southern view, head to the south of the A-frame building to pick up the .5-mile round-trip West Point Trail, where the ranger on duty takes a daily pilgrimage to check out how the south side is faring. Once you've seen both sides of the picture, return to the lookout and pick up Douglas Cabin Trail. It leads 3.5 miles down 800 feet to 4,820-foot Gordon Butte for more southern exposure (there may be some logs on the route; check to see if

it's clear if you don't want to hop the obstacles). Be warned: The road leading to this trail is often snowed in through July, so unless you enjoy plowing through snow on a bumpy road with a cliff on one side—which, I found out while driving through this area, some people actually do enjoy—you'd be wise to steer (no pun intended) clear until it's snow-free. Check conditions with the Forest Service before heading out.

User groups: Hikers, dogs, and horses. No mountain bikes are allowed. No wheelchair access.

Permits: Permits are not required. Parking and access are free.

Maps: For a map of Mount Hood National Forest and Badger Creek Wilderness, contact Nature of the Northwest Information Center. For a topographic map, contact Green Trails, Inc. (ask for Flag Point, map number 463), 206/546-MAPS (206/546-6277), www.green-trails.com; or ask the USGS for Flag Point.

Directions: From Hood River, drive 30 miles south on U.S. 35. Turn left (east) on Forest Service Road 44/Dufur Mill Road, between mileposts 70 and 71. Drive 8.5 miles to Forest Service Road 4420. Turn right and continue two miles to a fork, turning left onto Forest Service Road 2730, which turns into a narrow, one-lane paved road. Drive 3.4 miles to Forest Service Road 200 and turn right. Continue 3.1 miles to the Flag Point trailhead at the end of the road. (Note: Road 200 is bumpy and often snowed in through July.)

Contact: Mount Hood National Forest, Barlow Ranger District, Dufur Ranger Station, 780 Northeast Court Street, Dufur, OR 97021, 541/467-2291.

③⑧ SCHOOL CANYON/BALL POINT
6.5 mi/3.5 hrs

east of Highway 35 in the Badger Creek Wilderness of Mount Hood National Forest

Map 3.2, page 69

Walking up the dusty old road that starts off School Canyon Trail, you get a sneaking suspicion that you've just stepped out of the Mount

Hood area. You have, kind of. The Badger Creek Wilderness area is typically drier than its brethren to the west, and you'll notice a change in the scenery, with scrub alpine hinting at the desert landscape just east. You'll know you're still in the Mount Hood area, though, because of the views. They begin almost as soon as you leave your car, extending to Mount Jefferson to the south. Leading up a mile just before 3,959-feet Ball Point summit, the trail goes on another three miles to amazing views on a cliff just past the junction with Little Badger Creek Trail. Turn around here, or return on Little Badger Creek Trail for a shuttle hike just three miles down from where you started.

User groups: Hikers, dogs, and horses. No mountain bikes are allowed. No wheelchair access.

Permits: A federal Northwest Forest pass is required to park here. The cost is $5 for a day pass or $30 for an annual pass. You can buy a day pass at ranger stations, from private vendors, or through Nature of the Northwest Information Center.

Maps: For a map of Mount Hood National Forest and Badger Creek Wilderness, contact Nature of the Northwest Information Center. For a topographic map, contact Green Trails, Inc. (ask for Flag Point, map number 463), 206/546-MAPS (206/546-6277), www.green trails.com; or ask the USGS for Flag Point and Friend.

Directions: From the intersection of U.S. 26 and U.S. 35 (about three miles east of Government Camp), drive 3.5 miles north on U.S. 35 toward Hood River. Turn right on Forest Service Road 48 at the sign for Rock Creek Reservoir. Drive 24.5 miles on paved Forest Service Road 48 and turn left on Forest Service Road 4810 at the sign for Bonney Creek Crossing (keeping to the right when the road veers left); drive two miles to Forest Service Road 4811. Continue 1.2 miles to Forest Service Road 2710 and turn right, continuing 5.7 miles to a junction. Turn right and stay on the gravel road for three miles to Forest Service Road 27. Turn left and drive two miles to the trailhead and parking pullout on the left.

Contact: Mount Hood National Forest, Barlow Ranger District, Dufur Ranger Station, 780 Northeast Court Street, Dufur, OR 97021, 541/467-2291.

39 BADGER CREEK TRAIL
12.2 mi one-way/2.0 days   3   8

between Badger Lake and Bonney Crossing Campground in the Badger Creek Wilderness of Mount Hood National Forest

Map 3.2, page 69

This is the longest and probably the most popular trail in the Badger Creek Wilderness, connecting with plenty of other trails, so you can choose to shorten the route or make it an overnight trip; there are prime creekside camping spots along the way. The east side of Mount Hood can get hot and dry in the summer (look out for rattlesnakes), so the creekside access is refreshing on a scorching day. This is also a longer and, for the most part, gentler access route to Badger Lake (although there are some steep climbs along the way on the upper part of the route). Badger Lake is about 11 miles down the trail.

User groups: Hikers, dogs, and horses. No mountain bikes are allowed. No wheelchair access.

Permits: A federal Northwest Forest pass is required to park here. The cost is $5 for a day pass or $30 for an annual pass. You can buy a day pass at ranger stations, from private vendors, or through Nature of the Northwest Information Center.

Maps: For a map of Mount Hood National Forest and Badger Creek Wilderness, contact Nature of the Northwest Information Center. For a topographic map, contact Green Trails, Inc. (ask for Mount Hood and Flag Point, map numbers 462 and 463), 206/546-MAPS (206/546-6277), www.greentrails.com; or ask the USGS for Flag Point and Badger Lake.

Directions: From the U.S. 26/Highway 35 intersection (about three miles east of Government Camp), drive 3.5 miles north on U.S. 35 toward Hood River. Turn right on paved Forest Service Road 48 at the sign for Rock Creek Reservoir. Drive 24.5 miles and turn left on Forest Service Road 4810 at the sign for Bonney Creek Crossing, staying to the right when the road forks. Drive two miles to Forest Service Road 4811 and turn right. Continue 1.2 miles to gravel Forest Service Road 2710. Turn right and drive 1.8 miles to the trailhead at Bonney Crossing campground. The small parking lot and trailhead begin just after you drive across the bridge on the left side of the road.

Contact: Mount Hood National Forest, Barlow Ranger District, Dufur Ranger Station, 780 Northeast Court Street, Dufur, OR 97021, 541/467-2291.

40 HIDDEN LAKE
4.0 mi/2.5 hrs
north of Government Camp in the Mount Hood Wilderness of Mount Hood National Forest

Map 3.2, page 69

It's hidden all right, and views are hidden from it. It's not the most scenic lake you'll ever come across, but the pink rhododendrons lining the trail in June make up for it. You also won't be hidden from the sound of highway traffic, which accompanies you for about half of the hike. It's a gentle switchbacking trail that will give you some exercise without leaving you a sweating mess. Once you reach the lake, you can take a rest and turn around from here, or you can continue on for a super-challenging 13-mile loop: Continue past the lake for three miles, then turn left when you reach Pacific Crest Trail. Wind through Zigzag Canyon for 2.5 miles until you reach Paradise Park Trail, then return the five miles back to the road and the trailhead, which ends on Kiwanis Camp Road, about a mile from the trailhead you started from.

User groups: Hikers, dogs, and horses. No mountain bikes are allowed. No wheelchair access.

Permits: A federal Northwest Forest pass is required to park here. The cost is $5 for a day pass or $30 for an annual pass. You can buy a day pass at ranger stations, from private vendors, or through Nature of the Northwest Information Center.

Maps: For a map of Mount Hood National Forest, contact Nature of the Northwest Information Center. For a topographic map, contact Green Trails, Inc. (ask for Mount Hood and Government Camp, map numbers 461 and 462), 206/546-MAPS (206/546-6277), www.green trails.com; or ask the USGS for Mount Hood South and Government Camp.

Directions: From Portland, drive about 50 miles east on Highway 26 to about two miles past Rhododendron. Turn left onto Kiwanis Camp Road/Forest Service Road 2639 and drive two miles to the large parking area and trailhead on the left.

Contact: Mount Hood National Forest, Zigzag Ranger District, 70220 East Highway 26, Zigzag, OR 97049, 503/622-3191.

41 TIMBERLINE LODGE TO ZIGZAG CANYON/PARADISE PARK
4.4–12.3 mi/2.5–8.0 hrs
west of Mount Hood's Timberline Lodge in Mount Hood National Forest

Map 3.2, page 69

Simply put, this section of Pacific Crest Trail is a beaut, but don't let her looks fool you: She's also out to kill (or maybe just maim a little). It's a tough climb through Zigzag Canyon and up through Paradise Park, but it's well worth the grunts and curses. The views of Mount Hood can't be beat, and you'll feel like you're walking through a vast expanse all to yourself. You may encounter a few other people along the way, but overall it's surprisingly uncrowded. If you just want a taste of the scenery without too much effort, you can turn around when you hit the Zigzag Canyon viewpoint, 2.2 miles down the trail (you'll know it when you see it; the zigging and zagging is impossible to miss). If you want to keep on going, you'll have to descend into the canyon and climb up the other side, which is no easy feat. When you reach Paradise Park Trail, about 3.5 miles in, turn right to continue the scenic tour of alpine wildflower meadows. The trail starts and ends at the massive yet cozy Timberline Lodge, where you can end your day with a meal. Locals know it as the place where exterior shots in *The Shining* were filmed (the interior and other exterior shots were filmed in Colorado and England), but the lodge itself doesn't broadcast this information. Maybe they think it would spook overnight guests? Anyway, the lodge is a great destination in and of itself, so if camping isn't your thing, treat yourself to a night of luxury.

User groups: Hikers, dogs, and horses. No mountain bikes are allowed. No wheelchair access.

Permits: Permits are not required. Parking and access are free.

Maps: For a map of Mount Hood National Forest, contact Nature of the Northwest Information Center. For a topographic map, contact Green Trails, Inc. (ask for Mount Hood, map number 462), 206/546-MAPS (206/546-6277), www.greentrails.com; or ask the USGS for Mount Hood South.

Directions: From Portland, drive about 55 miles east on Highway 26 to Government Camp. Following signs to Timberline Lodge, turn left onto Timberline Road, and drive six miles to the road's end and the large parking lot. The trail starts from behind the lodge; look for signs for Timberline Trail, and head west (left) as it travels under a chairlift to start the trail.

Contact: Mount Hood National Forest, Zigzag Ranger District, 70220 East Highway 26, Zigzag, OR 97049, 503/622-3191.

42 MOUNTAINEER TRAIL TO SILCOX HUT

2.0 mi/1.5 hrs

from Timberline Lodge to Silcox Hut on the south slope of Mount Hood

Map 3.2, page 69

Built in 1939, Silcox Hut was named after Ferdinand Silcox, who reigned supreme as chief of the National Forest Service in the 1930s. In its infancy, it was used as a warming hut for the ski area's original Magic Mile chairlift, the second chairlift in the country. It was brushed aside for a fancier, shinier Magic Mile chairlift and a new warming hut, but it wasn't entirely left out in the cold: The 13-room hut with sleeping bunks is now available for rent, with your own chef and bartender for group parties. The trail heads straight up for 1,000 feet (you may wonder why you're breathless so quickly; remember, you're *starting* at 6,000 feet). The mile-long trail is mostly on a Snowcat road, but the trail is not the main attraction here. It's worth the trip just to be hiking alongside skiers and snowboarders in the middle of the summer (Mount Hood is renowned for offering year-round snow, and the national teams often flock here because of that). Once you reach the hut, park yourself on the picnic bench and enjoy the ridiculously cool views of the Mount Hood area. You really have to see it to believe it, and all that for chump change, as far as mileage goes! Return the way you came, or continue west just past the hut to return on a Snowcat road back down to the lodge. It's hard to get lost on this one. Use the hut as your beacon to the top and the lodge as your beacon to the bottom. Pack warm clothes—it can get gusty at the top.

User groups: Hikers and dogs. No mountain bikes or horses are allowed. No wheelchair access.

Permits: Permits are not required. Parking and access are free.

Maps: For a map of Mount Hood National Forest, contact Nature of the Northwest Information Center. For a topographic map, contact Green Trails, Inc. (ask for Mount Hood, map number 462), 206/546-MAPS (206/546-6277), www.greentrails.com; or ask the USGS for Mount Hood South.

Directions: From Portland, drive about 55 miles east on Highway 26 to Government Camp. Following signs to Timberline Lodge, turn left onto Timberline Road and drive six miles to the road's end and the large parking lot. The trail starts from the east (right) side of the lodge. Look for signs to Mountaineer Trail. **Contact:** Mount Hood National Forest, Zigzag Ranger District, 70220 East Highway 26, Zigzag, OR 97049, 503/622-3191.

43 TIMBERLINE TRAIL
40.7 mi/4.0–5.0 days

around the rim of Mount Hood

Map 3.2, page 69

Mighty Timberline Trail is a famous notch in any backpacker's belt. Circling Mount Hood, the path travels partly on Pacific Crest Trail. If you're looking for the Ultimate Experience, you should try this trail. Keep several things in mind, though: It's not for the novice, the faint of heart, the faint of lungs, or the directionally challenged. Absolutely bring along a map and compass (and know how to use them), and realize that conditions change quickly on the mountain. Come prepared with plenty of warm clothes and emergency survival equipment. It can still be snowy through July, so plan accordingly. If you're tough enough, you'll be rewarded with amazing views the whole way, not to mention bragging rights. The average elevation on the trail is 5,000 feet, with ranges from 3,000 to 7,000 feet, so you'll be doing a lot of climbing and descending along the way—and that's why you get to brag about it when all is said and done.

User groups: Hikers and dogs. No mountain bikes. Horses are allowed only on Pacific Crest Trail portions of the trail. No wheelchair access.

Permits: No permits are required at Timberline Lodge. At other trailheads, a federal Northwest Forest pass is required to park there; the cost is $5 for a day pass or $30 for an annual pass. You can buy a day pass at ranger stations, from private vendors, or through Nature of the Northwest Information Center.

Maps: For a map of Mount Hood National Forest, contact Nature of the Northwest Information Center. For a topographic map, con-

tact Green Trails, Inc. (ask for Government Camp and Mount Hood, map numbers 461 and 462), 206/546-MAPS (206/546-6277), www.greentrails.com; or ask the USGS for Mount Hood North, Mount Hood South, and Bull Run Lake.

Directions: There are several access points. The most popular starting point from the south is Timberline Lodge: From Portland, drive about 55 miles east on Highway 26 to Government Camp. Following signs to Timberline Lodge, turn left onto Timberline Road, and drive six miles to the road's end and the large parking lot. The trail starts behind the lodge and is marked as the Pacific Crest Trail. The most popular starting point from the north is Cloud Cap (see listing in this chapter for directions).

Contact: Mount Hood National Forest Information Center, 65000 East Highway 26, Welches, OR 97067, 503/622-7674.

44 OLD SALMON RIVER/ DEVIL'S PEAK
16.0 mi one-way/ 1.0–2.0 days

south of Highway 26 in the Salmon Huckleberry Wilderness of Mount Hood National Forest

Map 3.2, page 69

Plenty of spots access the scenic shores of the Old Salmon River, and plenty of people do just that. Traveling the river for almost its entirety, minus a slight climb in the northern region to cliffside views, the riverside trail is a good one for the whole family. Be warned: Because it's so easy to get to, it can get crowded on sunny weekends. The trail follows the road for almost three miles, then leaves civilization behind to pass by waterfalls and deep canyons, with plenty of camping sites along the way. You can also get some climbing in on this trail, if the flat route just isn't putting enough strain on your hamstrings. About 10 miles from the original trailhead, the trail forks to the left to climb 3.5 miles to 5,045-foot Devil's Peak Lookout, where there are views of the Cascade peaks and the Salmon River Valley. One option is to start from the Upper Salmon River trailhead (see directions, below) and hike in about five miles to one of the many riverside camp spots, then tackle Devil's Peak on the next day. (Or do it all in one day if you have to be like that.) Unlike many of the trails in the Mount Hood area, this one is quite simple to follow: Keep the river at your side and you can't go wrong. If you want a simple yet scenic stroll, Old Salmon has got your back.

User groups: Hikers and dogs. Mountain bikes are allowed on the lower portion of the trail. No horses are allowed. No wheelchair access.

Permits: A federal Northwest Forest pass is required to park here. The cost is $5 for a day pass or $30 for an annual pass. You can buy a day pass at ranger stations, from private vendors, or through Nature of the Northwest Information Center.

Maps: For a map of Mount Hood National Forest and Salmon Huckleberry Wilderness, contact Nature of the Northwest Information Center. For a topographic map, contact Green Trails, Inc. (ask for Government Camp and High Rock, map numbers 461 and 493), 206/546-MAPS (206/546-6277), www.green-trails.com; or ask the USGS for Rhododendron, High Rock, and Wolf Peak.

Directions: From Portland, drive about 40 miles east on U.S. 26 to Zigzag. Just past the town, turn right (south) on Salmon River Road. The first trailhead and parking area is 2.7 miles down the road on the right. Other access points are farther down the road and tend to be less crowded: Continue another two miles down Salmon River Road to the Upper Salmon River Bridge, where parking and the trail are on the left.

Contact: Mount Hood National Forest, Zigzag Ranger District, 70220 East Highway 26, Zigzag, OR 97049, 503/622-3191.

45 SALMON BUTTE
8.4 mi/5.0 hrs

south of Highway 26 in the Salmon Huckleberry Wilderness of Mount Hood National Forest

Map 3.2, page 69

When the snow is away, the flowers will play: In June, when the snow typically melts from the area, the rhododendrons are in bloom as you hike up to the former lookout site. At about four miles, the trail connects to an old road that leads you to the 4,877-foot summit for views of Mount Hood, Mount Jefferson, Mount St. Helens, and the Salmon River Valley below. The trailhead can be a little confusing: You first walk on an old road for .25 mile, and when you come to a clearing, the trailhead is on the left. It's typically not as crowded as other trails in the area, so you may have a view for one (or two, if you bring a friend to share the glory with).

User groups: Hikers, dogs, and horses. No mountain bikes are allowed. No wheelchair access.

Permits: A federal Northwest Forest pass is required to park here. The cost is $5 for a day pass or $30 for an annual pass. You can buy a day pass at ranger stations, from private vendors, or through Nature of the Northwest Information Center.

Maps: For a map of Mount Hood National Forest and Salmon Huckleberry Wilderness, contact Nature of the Northwest Information Center. For a topographic map, contact Green Trails, Inc. (ask for Government Camp and High Rock, map numbers 461 and 493), 206/546-MAPS (206/546-6277), www.green-trails.com; or ask the USGS for Rhododendron and High Rock.

Directions: From Portland, drive about 40 miles east on U.S. 26 to Zigzag. Just past the town, turn right (south) on Salmon River Road and drive 6.7 miles (paved for the first 5.1 miles) to the small parking area on the left. The trailhead starts across the street on an unmarked spur road.

Contact: Mount Hood National Forest, Zigzag Ranger District, 70220 East Highway 26, Zigzag, OR 97049, 503/622-3191.

46 MIRROR LAKE
3.2 mi/2.0 hrs

west of Government Camp off U.S. 26 in Mount Hood National Forest

Map 3.2, page 69

Convenience is the spice of life (or something like that), and this trail is made for those who want to get in and out quickly. Starting right off the highway on a narrow footbridge, the wide and well-maintained trail switchbacks gently for 1.4 miles, just enough to make you feel like you're getting a workout. There are campsites along the picturesque lakeshore, and plenty of picnic stops and access points. Although it's just a stone's throw from the highway, you may as well have hiked in 10 miles, because it seems so remote. The only clue that it's a short hike is the number of other people who are also attracted to this hot spot. Take a .4-mile loop around the lake and head back the way you came for a quick and easy hike to a grand locale. If that wasn't enough, you can also visit your three buds Tom, Dick, and Harry: As you start to circle the lake, take a right onto Wind Creek Trail when the trail forks, continuing 1.8 miles up to a viewpoint on Tom, Dick, and Harry Mountain (which has to win the "weirdest mountain name" contest) and views of Mount Hood. Return the way you came, continue circling the lake, and head back to the trailhead.

User groups: Hikers and dogs. No mountain bikes or horses are allowed. No wheelchair access.

Permits: A federal Northwest Forest pass is required to park here. The cost is $5 for a day pass or $30 for an annual pass. You can buy a day pass at ranger stations, from private vendors, or through Nature of the Northwest Information Center.

Maps: For a map of Mount Hood National Forest, contact Nature of the Northwest Information Center. For a topographic map, con-

tact Green Trails, Inc. (ask for Government Camp, map number 461), 206/546-MAPS (206/546-6277), www.greentrails.com; or ask the USGS for Government Camp.

Directions: From Portland, drive about 50 miles east on Highway 26, between mileposts 51 and 52, about two miles west of Government Camp. The small parking area and the well-marked trailhead are on the right side of the highway.

Contact: Mount Hood National Forest, Zigzag Ranger District, 70220 East Highway 26, Zigzag, OR 97049, 503/622-3191.

47 TWIN LAKES
5.0 mi/2.5 hrs

south of Mount Hood in Mount Hood National Forest

Map 3.2, page 69

As with many trails that lead directly from the highway, this trail tends to be busy, especially to the lower lake. It's an easy hike to two clear, pristine lakes, and you can also include Palmateer Point to add four more miles to your trip. From the trailhead, start off on Pacific Crest Trail for the first 1.5 miles, turning right at the junction to the lower lake. Circle the one mile perimeter, and if you want to escape the crowds, continue around the lake to turn right and hit the upper lake after another .5 mile. If you're looking for a good swimming spot, this is the place to stop for a while. After you've had your fill, continue on the trail you started from, turning left and hiking .5 mile to the junction with Pacific Crest Trail; then turn left again to complete the loop. If you want to add some views of Mount Hood and some muscle power to your trip, continue on past the upper lake for a steep, rocky climb on Palmateer Trail another mile to the crest, then return the way you came, or continue past the point for a mile to the Pacific Crest Trail junction, turning left to complete the loop.

User groups: Hikers, dogs, and horses. No mountain bikes are allowed. No wheelchair access.

Permits: A federal Northwest Forest pass is

required to park here. The cost is $5 for a day pass or $30 for an annual pass. You can buy a day pass at ranger stations, from private vendors, or through Nature of the Northwest Information Center.

Maps: For a map of Mount Hood National Forest, contact Nature of the Northwest Information Center. For a topographic map, contact Green Trails, Inc. (ask for Mount Hood and Mount Wilson, map numbers 462 and 494), 206/546-MAPS (206/546-6277), www.greentrails.com; or ask the USGS for Mount Hood South.

Directions: From Portland, drive about 60 miles east on U.S. 26, about eight miles past Government Camp, and turn into the Frog Lake Sno-Park parking area on the right. The trailhead, marked as the Pacific Crest Trail, is on the left side of the parking lot.

Contact: Mount Hood National Forest, Hood River Ranger District, 6780 Highway 35, Mount Hood-Parkdale, OR 97041, 541/352-6002.

48 TIMOTHY LAKE LOOP
12.0 mi/6.5 hrs

around Timothy Lake south of Mount Hood in Mount Hood National Forest

Map 3.2, page 69

Tired of sweet little two-mile saunters around cute little lakes? Timothy is your man! As far as lakes go in the Mount Hood area, this is the Master of the Loops, the Big Loopola, the Loop to End Them All. This 12-mile flat loop circles this scenic lake with Mount Hood as a backdrop. You'll travel on Timothy Lake Trail and catch the Pacific Crest Trail; it's all straightforward, no navigation required. The lake is popular for camping and fishing, with several campgrounds on the shores. Hiking the well-maintained trail, you can actually feel like you've gotten some exercise for the day (and have earned that cold beverage at your campsite). What else do you need? Well, maybe to have it to yourself, but 'dems the breaks.

User groups: Hikers, dogs, mountain bikes, and horses. There is wheelchair access at several points.

Permits: A federal Northwest Forest pass is required to park here. The cost is $5 for a day pass or $30 for an annual pass. You can buy a day pass at ranger stations, from private vendors, or through Nature of the Northwest Information Center.

Maps: For a map of Mount Hood National Forest, contact Nature of the Northwest Information Center. For a topographic map, contact Green Trails, Inc. (ask for High Rock and Mount Wilson, numbers 493 and 494), 206/546-MAPS (206/546-6277), www.greentrails.com; or ask the USGS for Wolf Peak and Timothy Lake.

Directions: From Portland, drive east on U.S. 26 past Mount Hood, between mileposts 65 and 66. Turn right at the sign for Timothy Lake onto Skyline Road, and continue for four miles. Turn right onto Abbott Road/Forest Service Road 58, and drive 1.5 miles to the trailhead at the eastern end of the campground loop at Little Crater Campground.

Contact: Mount Hood National Forest, Zigzag Ranger Station, 70220 East Highway 26, Zigzag, OR 97049, 503/622-3191.

49 LOWER DESCHUTES RIVER
4.0 mi/2.0 hrs

at the confluence of the Columbia and Deschutes Rivers in the eastern Columbia River Gorge

Map 3.3, page 70

Commonly known as the Gateway to the Desert (okay, I actually just made that up—but I did see a tumbleweed as I drove in), this area is where the Deschutes meets the Columbia River. (Deschutes, meet Columbia. Columbia, meet Deschutes.) It's also the beginning of the desert environment, a stark contrast to the lush forest areas of the western Gorge trails. Between the campground and fishing spots and horseback riding, there's a lot going on in Deschutes State Park, where the trail is located, but keep your focus to find the easy-to-miss trailhead. The first part of the trail is just a faint path through the grass directly in front of the second day-use parking area (on the south end of the campground). Just trod on through to spot the trail sign, visible across the meadow. There are two trails that connect for a four-mile loop. Start on the lower trail along the Deschutes River for a pleasant riverside saunter, then head back on the easy-to-find middle trail for a two-mile trek back through the desert shrubs and a view of the bald peaks on the Washington side of the Gorge. Hikers can also share the 16 miles of biking trails here.

User groups: Hikers and dogs. Horses and mountain bikes are allowed on separate trails in the park. No wheelchair access.

Permits: Permits are not required. Parking and access are free.

Maps: For a free brochure, contact Oregon Parks and Recreation Department, 800/551-6949, www.oregonstateparks.org. For a topographic map, ask the USGS for Emerson.

Directions: From The Dalles (85 miles east of Portland), drive east on I-84 for 12 miles to Exit 97/Deschutes Park, following signs for three miles to the park entrance. Drive past the campground (you'll pass one day-use parking area on your right), and park in the southern end of the campground in the day-use parking area, to the left of the tent camping spot. The trailhead is straight ahead, across the meadow.

Contact: Oregon Parks and Recreation Department, 1115 Commercial Street Northeast, Salem, OR 97301, 800/551-6949, www.oregonstateparks.org.

50 TABLE ROCK
7.6 mi/3.5 hrs

east of Salem off Highway 22 in the Table Rock Wilderness

Map 3.4, page 71

Since it's the highest point in the Table Rock Wilderness, the 4,881-foot sheer granite wall gets a wilderness named after it. As well it should. The sweeping view from the top peeks into California and Washington, and surveys the Cascade range. The trail starts off gently on a gravel road, with buttercups, Indian paintbrush, and rhododendrons lining the way. It climbs steeper in the last .5 mile, when you turn left to switchback and scramble up a rocky scree slope to reach the summit (the overall elevation gain along the trail is 1,200 feet). A landslide now covers part of the road, but determined hikers have beaten a path through the forest; take that trail, to the right, hike around the slide, and continue up the main road again before reaching the trail to the right again after a mile. Because the route can be confusing at times, get a trail map before you set out. Once you reach the summit, backtrack to the main trail again, and head over to Table Rock's runner-up in the tallest-peak division: Rooster Rock, standing proud at 4,663 feet. Return to the saddle junction and continue straight across the saddle to add three miles to your trip.

User groups: Hikers, dogs, and horses. No mountain bikes are allowed. No wheelchair access.

Permits: Permits are not required. Parking and access are free.

Maps: For a map of the Table Rock Wilderness, contact Nature of the Northwest Information Center. For a topographic map, ask the USGS for Rooster Rock.

Directions: From Molalla, drive .5 mile east on Highway 211 to South Mathias Road. Turn right and drive .2 mile to South Feyrer Park Road, taking a slight left. Drive 1.6 miles to South Dickie Prairie Road, and then turn right. Continue 5.3 miles and turn right to cross a bridge over the Molalla River. Drive 12.8 miles to a fork and veer left onto gravel Middle Fork Road. Go another 2.6 miles and turn right on Table Rock Road. The road dead-ends at a landslide at 4.3 miles. Park on the side of the road and hike up the road.

Contact: Bureau of Land Management, Salem District, 1717 Fabry Road Northeast, Salem, OR 97306, 503/375-5646.

51 BAGBY HOT SPRINGS
3.0 mi/1.5 hrs

on the Hot Springs Fork of the Collawash River in the Bull of the Woods Wilderness in Mount Hood National Forest

Map 3.4, page 71

As the Monty Python saying goes, "And now for something completely different." This is definitely a different type of hike than any others, which you'll notice as soon as you reach the trailhead. That's because the main gig here isn't the hike itself, but the Bagby Hot Springs. Soooo, let's just say you'll encounter all types on this gentle hike: couples, groups of teenagers, and folks who look like they are quite comfy on the back of a Harley. Here, backpacks are swapped for towels and loungewear—or no wear at all. Check your modesty at the trailhead: These are hot springs, after all, and people don't necessarily wear clothing when bathing in them. The path is amazingly well maintained, with logs on either side of the mostly gravel path and mini-bridges spanning each and every steam, lest your dainty feet get soaked. Kinda defeats the purpose, seeing as you're about to dip into the springs, but what the heck. You'll cross a bridge over a little waterfall when you're almost there, and you can see the clear, green water, a glimpse of things to come. If you're interested in taking a dip in the springs, which are all enclosed in little cabins, you may have to wait in line on a weekend, because it can get packed. The trail also leads six miles to Silver King Mountain, connecting to the Whetstone Mountain trail system for endless loop and backpacking options if you want to use the hot springs as a setting-off point further into the Bull of the Woods Wilderness.

User groups: Hikers and dogs. Mountain bikes and horses are not allowed. No wheelchair access.

Permits: A federal Northwest Forest pass is required to park here. The cost is $5 for a day pass or $30 for an annual pass. You can buy a day pass at ranger stations, from private vendors, or through Nature of the Northwest Information Center.

Maps: For a map of the Bull of the Woods Wilderness, contact Nature of the Northwest Information Center. For a topographic map, contact Green Trails, Inc. (ask for Battle Ax, map number 524), 206/546-MAPS (206/546-6277), www.greentrails.com; or ask the USGS for Bagby Hot Springs.

Directions: From Estacada, drive 25.5 miles southeast on Highway 224 to the junction with Forest Service Road 46 (Highway 224 ends here). Turn right (south) and drive 3.5 miles, then turn right on Forest Service Road 63. Go 3.5 miles, then turn right on Forest Service Road 70. Continue for six miles to the trailhead and large parking area, to the left.

Contact: Mount Hood National Forest, Clackamas River Ranger District, Estacada Ranger Station, 595 Northwest Industrial Way, Estacada, OR 97023, 503/630-6861.

52 PANSY LAKE
4.0 mi/2.0 hrs

in the Bull of the Woods Wilderness in Mount Hood National Forest

Map 3.4, page 71

An easy lake stroll means it's popular on a sunny weekend, but don't rule it out: It's worth a trip, and you can turn this into a challenging loop up to Bull of the Woods Lookout if you want to escape the crowds. Start with a 500-foot elevation climb up to the lake, ignoring a junction to the right, which leads down an abandoned trail. Continue to the lake, which will be on your right, and stop here to decide your attack plan. If the lake is your thing, stick around and then return the way you came. If you want more, continue 1.3 miles to the junction with Mother Lode Trail, then turn left and climb about 1.3 miles to reach the Bull of the Woods Lookout for views of Mount Hood, Mount Jefferson, Three Sisters, and Three Fingered Jack from the 5,523-foot summit. Total elevation gain for this loop is about 2,000 feet. After enjoying the view from the top, continue down Bull of the Woods Trail to reach a junction with the return route; turn left here to return to the trailhead.

User groups: Hikers, dogs, and horses. No mountain bikes are allowed. No wheelchair access.

Permits: A free wilderness permit is required to hike here, available shortly after entering the trailhead. In addition, a federal Northwest Forest pass is required to park here. The cost is $5 for a day pass or $30 for an annual pass. You can buy a day pass at ranger stations, from private vendors, or through Nature of the Northwest Information Center.

Maps: For a map of the Bull of the Woods Wilderness, contact Nature of the Northwest Information Center. For a topographic map, contact Green Trails, Inc. (ask for Battle Ax, map number 524), 206/546-MAPS (206/546-6277), www.greentrails.com; or ask the USGS for Bull of the Woods.

Directions: From Estacada, drive 27 miles southeast on Highway 224, which becomes Forest Service Road 46. Continue on Forest Service Road 46 for three miles to paved Forest Service Road 63. Turn right and drive six miles, then turn right on gravel Forest Service Road 6340. Drive 9.5 miles to the trailhead and the parking pullout, on the right side of the road.

Contact: Mount Hood National Forest, Clackamas River Ranger District, Estacada Ranger Station, 595 Northwest Industrial Way, Estacada, OR 97023, 503/630-6861.

53 BULL OF THE WOODS LOOKOUT
6.4 mi/3.5 hrs

in the Bull of the Woods Wilderness in Mount Hood National Forest

Map 3.4, page 71

This relatively easy hike gains just 900 feet in elevation to the Bull of the Woods Lookout, where you can mosey on up to spend some quality time with the Indian paintbrush and rhododendrons, along with views of Mount Hood, Mount Jefferson, Three Sisters, and

Three Fingered Jack along the trail and at the 5,523-foot summit. This trail can also be combined with Pansy Lake for a loop (see listing in this chapter), starting at the Pansy Lake trailhead. If you see hikers traveling up from that more strenuous side, try not to be too smug about your easier route.

User groups: Hikers, dogs, and horses. No mountain bikes are allowed. No wheelchair access.

Permits: A federal Northwest Forest pass is required to park here. The cost is $5 for a day pass or $30 for an annual pass. You can buy a day pass at ranger stations, from private vendors, or through Nature of the Northwest Information Center.

Maps: For a map of the Bull of the Woods Wilderness, contact Nature of the Northwest Information Center. For a topographic map, contact Green Trails, Inc. (ask for Battle Ax, map number 524), 206/546-MAPS (206/546-6277), www.greentrails.com; or ask the USGS for Bull of the Woods.

Directions: From Estacada, drive 27 miles southeast on Highway 224, which becomes Forest Service Road 46. Continue on Forest Service Road 46 for three miles to paved Forest Service Road 63. Turn right and drive six miles, then turn right on gravel Forest Service Road 6340. Drive 9.5 miles to the trailhead and parking pullout on the right side of the road.

Contact: Mount Hood National Forest, Clackamas River Ranger District, Estacada Ranger Station, 595 Northwest Industrial Way, Estacada, OR 97023, 503/630-6861.

54 DICKEY CREEK TO BIG SLIDE LAKE
11.0 mi/5.5 hrs

north of Bull of the Woods Wilderness in Mount Hood National Forest

Map 3.4, page 71

This trail has it all: a forested valley, sweeping valley views, and a lake. Oh, yeah, and switchbacks. After an initial descent, the trail levels out and then the climbing begins, topping out at Big Slide Lake (total elevation gain is 2,200 feet). You can also access the Bull of the Woods Lookout or Big Slide Mountain by taking Schreiner Peak Trail about four miles round-trip for each option (as if 11 miles weren't enough): For the mountain, turn left onto Schreiner Peak Trail, and for the lookout, keep right at all junctions. Keep in mind that Schreiner Peak may not be maintained, so you should check before you go if you want to try the longer route. It's not as crowded as other nearby trails, so if you want some solitude, this is a good choice.

User groups: Hikers, dogs, and horses. No mountain bikes are allowed. No wheelchair access.

Permits: Permits are not required. Parking and access are free.

Maps: For a map of Mount Hood National Forest and Bull of the Woods Wilderness, contact Nature of the Northwest Information Center. For a topographic map, contact Green Trails, Inc. (ask for Battle Ax, map number 524), 206/546-MAPS (206/546-6277), www.greentrails.com; or ask the USGS for Bull of the Woods.

Directions: From Estacada, drive southeast on Highway 224 for 27 miles. When it turns into Forest Service Road 46, continue three more miles to paved Forest Service Road 63. Turn right and drive six miles to gravel Forest Service Road 6340. Turn right and drive three miles to dirt Spur Road 140. Turn left and drive 1.5 miles to the trailhead and the road's end.

Contact: Mount Hood National Forest, Clackamas River Ranger District, Estacada Ranger Station, 595 Northwest Industrial Way, Estacada, OR 97023, 503/630-6861.

55 PHANTOM BRIDGE
5.2 mi/2.5 hrs

north of Detroit in Willamette National Forest

Map 3.4, page 71

Ready for your close-up? Then bring your camera (and a friend) and head to this natural arch-

way that you can peek through. Traveling along French Creek Ridge Trail, you'll pass by Dog Tooth Rock one mile up on your left, squeeze past tiny Cedar Lake, and then climb for another mile to a natural bridge you just have to see to believe. The beauty of it all? Unlike many other attractions in the state, it's not right off the highway, and there's no tram or paved walkway leading to a platform. Translation: You may just have the scenery all to yourself. The total elevation gain is about 400 feet.

User groups: Hikers, dogs, horses, and mountain bikes. No wheelchair access.

Permits: Permits are not required. Parking and access are free.

Maps: For a map of Willamette National Forest, contact Nature of the Northwest Information Center. For a topographic map, contact Green Trails, Inc. (ask for Battle Ax, map number 524), 206/546-MAPS (206/546-6277), www.greentrails.com; or ask the USGS for Battle Ax.

Directions: From the west end of Detroit on Highway 22, turn north onto French Creek Road. Drive 4.1 miles to Forest Service Road 2207, and turn right. Continue 3.6 miles to the parking area on the right. The trail is confusing here, because the French Creek Ridge passes through here. Don't take the trail leading from the parking lot. Instead, cross the road from the parking lot to the other French Creek Ridge trail marker.

Contact: Willamette National Forest, Detroit Ranger District, HC 73, Mill City, OR 97360, 503/854-3366.

56 RHODODENDRON RIDGE TO HAWK MOUNTAIN
10.0 mi/5.0 hrs

on Rhododendron Ridge in the southern portion of Mount Hood National Forest

Map 3.4, page 71

For a little something different, try the more remote Hawk Mountain, where an old fire lookout cabin commands views of Mount Jefferson and Mount Washington. But you don't need to walk far in order to capture some scenery, thanks to the new-growth pine trees: Their little heads just aren't tall enough to obstruct your view of Mount Hood or of the rhododendrons lining the way. Lest you think this is a walk in the park, take note: It's strongly encouraged that you get a map of the area before setting out, because the trail stops at an abandoned road after about a mile, and you have to walk for roughly a mile before continuing through the trail. After five miles total, veer left at an unmarked trail to climb up about .5 mile to Hawk Mountain. It's worth the trip to see the cabin and its scenic neighborhood, and you're likely to have it all to yourself, but take a map along to guide your way.

User groups: Hikers, dogs, mountain bikes, and horses. No wheelchair access.

Permits: Permits are not required. Parking and access are free.

Maps: For a map of Mount Hood National Forest, contact Nature of the Northwest Information Center. For a topographic map, contact Green Trails, Inc. (ask for Breitenbush, map number 525), 206/546-MAPS (206/546-6277), www.greentrails.com; or ask the USGS for Mount Lowe and Breitenbush Hot Springs.

Directions: From Estacada, drive southeast on Highway 224 for 27 miles. When it turns into Forest Service Road 46, continue another 3.5 miles to Forest Service Road 63. Turn right and drive 8.9 miles to Forest Service Road 6350. Turn left and drive 1.2 miles to a fork, veering right at the fork and continuing another 4.5 miles on the gravel road. Turn left at the fork and drive one mile to the trailhead and small parking area on the right.

Contact: Mount Hood National Forest, Clackamas River Ranger District, Estacada Ranger Station, 595 Northwest Industrial Way, Estacada, OR 97023, 503/630-6861.

57 STAHLMAN POINT
5.0 mi/2.5 hrs

on the south side of Detroit Reservoir in Willamette National Forest

Map 3.4, page 71

For a convenient hike near the Detroit Reservoir camping areas, try this climb through younger Douglas fir forest to a former lookout site. It gains 1,300 feet in 2.5 miles, the last 200 of which are rocky, so watch your step. From the top you can look 3,000 feet over the towns of Detroit and Idanha, Detroit Lake, and Mount Jefferson (hey, it wouldn't be a former lookout site if it didn't have any views, after all). The lake, actually a man-made reservoir created in 1955, has been a popular fishing, boating, and camping spot ever since. After gazing out and pondering how different Detroit, Oregon is from Detroit, Michigan, start your descent to enjoy all the area has to offer.

User groups: Hikers and dogs. No mountain bikes or horses are allowed. No wheelchair access.

Permits: Permits are not required. Parking and access are free.

Maps: For a map of the Willamette National Forest, contact Nature of the Northwest Information Center. For a topographic map, contact Green Trails, Inc. (ask for Detroit, map number 556), 206/546-MAPS (206/546-6277), www.greentrails.com; or ask the USGS for Detroit.

Directions: From the east end of Detroit (50 miles east of Salem on Highway 22), turn right on Blowout Road and drive 3.5 miles. The well-marked trailhead and large parking area are on the left side of the road.

Contact: Willamette National Forest, Detroit Ranger District, HC 73, P.O. Box 320, Mill City, OR 97360, 503/854-3366.

58 COFFIN MOUNTAIN
3.0 mi/2.0 hrs

south of Highway 22 in Willamette
National Forest

Map 3.4, page 71

It's an unfortunate but strangely fitting name, as you sometimes feel like you're on a death march on this hot, exposed trail. There's a reason for that: You're starting at 4,800 feet elevation and climbing 1,000 feet, so pack plenty o' H$_2$0 for this. Gorgeous views on both sides will serve to distract you—Mount Jefferson and Three Fingered Jack to the north and the southern Cascade range to the south. As you creep up the unrelenting switchbacks along the exposed and wildflower-filled mountain, a rocky overhang makes you think it's your destination, which is the ultimate psych-out; you can't see Coffin Mountain until you round the final bend and see the lookout tower. A viewing platform awaits you on the top of the 5,771-foot peak, and here, Mount Hood joins the view gang. Head back the way you came for the return trip.

User groups: Hikers, dogs, mountain bikes, and horses. No wheelchair access.

Permits: Permits are not required. Parking and access are free.

Maps: For a map of the Willamette National Forest, contact Nature of the Northwest Information Center. For a topographic map, contact Green Trails, Inc. (ask for Detroit, map number 556), 206/546-MAPS (206/546-6277), www.greentrails.com; or ask the USGS for Coffin Mountain.

Directions: From Salem, drive 50 miles east on Highway 22 to Detroit and continue another 18.9 miles to Straight Creek Road/Forest Service Road 11. Turn right and drive 4.2 miles to Forest Service Road 1168 (don't turn at the first 1168 sign). Turn right and drive 3.8 miles to Forest Service Road 450. Turn left and drive less than .1 mile to the parking area and the trailhead on your right.

Contact: Willamette National Forest, Detroit Ranger District, HC 73, P.O. Box 320, Mill City, OR 97360, 503/854-3366.

59 BACHELOR MOUNTAIN
3.8 mi/2.5 hrs

south of Highway 22 in Willamette
National Forest

Map 3.4, page 71

Interesting name choices—Bachelor and neighboring Coffin Mountain. Both definitely convey the sense of aloneness you'll get when you hike these trails. Bachelor is not a long trail, but since you start at 4,800 feet you may get a sudden case of the "are we there yet" (funny how altitude is the great equalizer, no?). The Douglas fir forest trail gains 900 feet in elevation, and the last .5 mile is a steep and rocky climb. You'll come to a junction with Bruno Meadows Trail at the 1.5 mile mark, but just keep on trucking straight to the top. When you reach the former lookout site, you can take a gander at the panoramic view, or snap a shot of it if you have one of them thar newfangled cameras that offer that feature. Once you've impressed your friends with your zoom lens and put away all your equipment, head back down the way you came.

User groups: Hikers, dogs, horses, and mountain bikes. No wheelchair access.

Permits: A federal Northwest Forest pass is required to park here. The cost is $5 for a day pass or $30 for an annual pass. You can buy a day pass at ranger stations, from private vendors, or through Nature of the Northwest Information Center.

Maps: For a map of the Willamette National Forest, contact Nature of the Northwest Information Center. For a topographic map, contact Green Trails, Inc. (ask for Detroit, map number 556), 206/546-MAPS (206/546-6277), www.greentrails.com; or ask the USGS for Coffin Mountain.

Directions: From Salem, drive 50 miles east on Highway 22 to Detroit and continue another 18.9 miles to Straight Creek Road/Forest Service Road 11. Turn right and drive 4.2 miles to Forest Service Road 1168 (don't turn at the first 1168 sign). Turn right and drive 4.4 miles to Forest Service Road 430. Turn left and continue .5 mile to the end of the road and the parking area and trailhead.

Contact: Willamette National Forest, Detroit Ranger District, HC 73, P.O. Box 320, Mill City, OR 97360, 503/854-3366.

60 RED LAKE TRAIL TO POTATO BUTTE
7.2 mi/3.5 hrs

north of Mount Jefferson in the Olallie Lake Scenic Area

Map 3.5, page 72

There are actually many lakes along this trail, but Red Lake gets top billing because it's the first you pass. There are hundreds of lakes in the Olallie Lake Scenic Area, and here is a great way to get a sample platter of them (pass the salt). At 1.5 miles, you'll pass Red Lake herself, and then all lined up in a nice orderly fashion for you are Averill, Wall, and Sheep Lakes within one more mile. At Sheep Lake, turn left to head up to 5,310-foot Potato Butte for scenic views of Mount Hood all the way up the steep climb. Turn back the way you came, turning right at Sheep Lake and return the way you came. Red Lake Trail also extends to the Olallie Lake area.

User groups: Hikers, dogs, mountain bikes, and horses. No wheelchair access.

Permits: Permits are not required. Parking and access are free.

Maps: For a map of Mount Hood National Forest and the Olallie Lake Scenic Area, contact Nature of the Northwest Information Center. For a topographic map, contact Green Trails, Inc. (ask for Breitenbush, map number 525), 206/546-MAPS (206/546-6277), www.green trails.com; or ask the USGS for Olallie Butte.

Directions: From Estacada, drive 27 miles southeast on Highway 224 to Forest Service Road 46. Continue straight on Forest Service Road 46, and drive 26.5 miles to the sign for Red Lake Trail (gravel Forest Service Road 380, which is unmarked). Park in a small pull-out on the side of the road .9 mile up; the trailhead is on the left.

Contact: Mount Hood National Forest, Clacka-

mas River Ranger District, Estacada Ranger Station, 595 Northwest Industrial Way, Estacada, OR 97023, 503/630-6861.

61 SOUTH BREITENBUSH GORGE
4.9 mi one-way/2.5 hrs

on the northwest side of Mount Jefferson in Willamette National Forest

Map 3.5, page 72

There are several things to enjoy along this easy riverside trail. For starters, there's the gorge, where the river passes through a 300-foot basalt narrow (a short, marked side trail leads down to the view). Then there's the soothing sound of the river itself, rushing along as a backdrop through this dense Douglas fir and western hemlock forest. There are a few spots to access this trail as a shuttle hike, but it's short and flat enough to do the whole shebang if you have the urge. Don't miss the log footbridge over Roaring Creek for a good photo-snapping spot.

User groups: Hikers and dogs. No horses or mountain bikes are allowed. No wheelchair access.

Permits: A federal Northwest Forest pass is required to park here. The cost is $5 for a day pass or $30 for an annual pass. You can buy a day pass at ranger stations, from private vendors, or through Nature of the Northwest Information Center.

Maps: For a map of Willamette National Forest, contact Nature of the Northwest Information Center. For a topographic map, ask the USGS for Breitenbush Hot Springs.

Directions: From Salem, drive 50 miles east on Highway 22 to Detroit, and turn left (north) onto paved Forest Service Road 46. Drive 11 miles and turn right onto gravel Forest Service Road 4685. To reach the main trailhead, ignore the first two signs (at .5 mile and 1.5 miles) and drive 2.2 miles to the pullout and trailhead on the right.

Contact: Willamette National Forest, Detroit Ranger District, HC 73, P.O. Box 320, Mill City, OR 97360, 503/854-3366.

62 TRIANGULATION PEAK
4.2 mi/2.5 hrs

northwest of Mount Jefferson in the Mount Jefferson Wilderness of Willamette National Forest

Map 3.5, page 72

If you're the type who likes a nice warm-up before hitting the heavy-duty climbing, this hike is for you. The first 1.5 miles are easy hiking through Douglas fir and western hemlock, with wildflowers and plenty of views through clearings of Mount Hood to the north. You'll see a rocky protrusion jutting up in the distance, a false alarm that's not your destination: Instead, it's Spire Rock, and you'll come face to face with it after 1.5 miles. Warmed up yet? Good, but you'll need some reserves in your tank to climb the switchbacks up to the 5,400-foot peak, where great views of the Mount Jefferson Wilderness are yours for the taking. Keep in mind that since you're starting at well over 4,000 feet of elevation, this trail can still be snowy through July, so save it for later in the season.

User groups: Hikers, dogs, and horses. No mountain bikes are allowed. No wheelchair access.

Permits: A free wilderness permit is required to hike here and is available at the trailhead. No Northwest Forest pass is required.

Maps: For a map of the Mount Jefferson Wilderness, contact Nature of the Northwest Information Center. For a topographic map, contact Green Trails, Inc. (ask for Mount Jefferson, map number 557), 206/546-MAPS (206/546-6277), www.greentrails.com; or ask the USGS for Mount Bruno and Mount Jefferson.

Directions: From Salem, drive 50 miles east on Highway 22 to Detroit, and continue another 6 miles to McCoy Road/Forest Service Road 2233. Turn left and drive eight miles to a junction, and turn right to continue for another 1.2 miles. Turn right onto Forest Service Road 635; the trailhead and small parking area are on the right side of the road, just past the junction.

Contact: Willamette National Forest, Detroit Ranger District, HC 73, P.O. Box 320, Mill City, OR 97360, 503/854-3366.

63 WHITEWATER TO JEFFERSON PARK
10.2 mi/6.0 hrs

on the north side of Mount Jefferson in the Mount Jefferson Wilderness in Willamette National Forest

Map 3.5, page 72

You don't have to walk far to get good views of Mount Jefferson—thar she blows as soon as you step on the trail. This is the easiest route to the popular Mount Jefferson Wilderness, and the area is already showing signs of overuse. Mount Jefferson came in a close second in the competition for tallest mountain in the state, edged out by 742 feet by Mount Hood. You start off by entering the cool old-growth Douglas fir forest for 1.5 miles before you reach a trail junction. Turn right to climb the ridgeline for another mile before leveling out. Continue a few more miles, and turn left at the junction with Pacific Crest Trail to come upon the alpine lakes and open wildflower-filled meadows of Jefferson Park. Everyone seems to know about this trail, so it's guaranteed to be filled to the max on sunny weekends. The trail can be snow-covered through July, so either come early in the season if you don't mind some snow (and missing out on the wildflowers) or wait until fall to have a little elbow room.

User groups: Hikers, dogs, and horses. No mountain bikes are allowed. No wheelchair access.

Permits: Free wilderness permits are required, available at the trailhead. In addition, a federal Northwest Forest pass is required to park here. The cost is $5 for a day pass or $30 for an annual pass. You can buy a day pass at ranger stations, from private vendors, or through Nature of the Northwest Information Center.

Maps: For a map of the Mount Jefferson Wilderness, contact Nature of the Northwest Information Center. For a topographic map, contact

Green Trails, Inc. (ask for Mount Jefferson, map number 557), 206/546-MAPS (206/546-6277), www.greentrails.com; or ask the USGS for Mount Bruno and Mount Jefferson.

Directions: From Salem, drive 50 miles east on Highway 22 to Detroit, and continue another 10.3 miles to Whitewater Road/Forest Service Road 2243. Turn left and drive 7.5 miles to the parking area at the end of the road and the well-marked trailhead.

Contact: Willamette National Forest, Detroit Ranger District, HC 73, P.O. Box 320, Mill City, OR 97360, 503/854-3366.

64 PAMELIA LAKE/GRIZZLY PEAK
10.2 mi/6.5 hrs

on the southwest side of Mount Jefferson in the Mount Jefferson Wilderness of Willamette National Forest

Map 3.5, page 72

This is a prime overnight spot, but as there are few campsites in the lake area, other people have the same idea, so you probably won't be solo-ing it. Whether you choose to do this as a day hike or a two-day trek, two things are guaranteed: You're in for a killer workout and some knockout views of Mount Jefferson. Start off through the cool, refreshing old-growth Douglas fir, hemlock, and western red cedar forest along rushing Pamelia Creek, a pretty and peaceful 2.3-mile stroll that gains 800 feet in elevation. That was just a warm-up: Once you hit the lake, take a right to the junction with 2.8-mile Grizzly Peak Trail for a nearly 2,000-foot climb to the 5,800-foot summit. Turn around here and camp near Pamelia Lake, or return the way you came if you prefer to call it a day.

User groups: Hikers, dogs, and horses. No mountain bikes are allowed. No wheelchair access.

Permits: An free overnight wilderness permit is required to camp here. Contact the Detroit Ranger District, HC 73, P.O. Box 320, Mill City, OR 97360, 503/854-3366. In addition, a federal Northwest Forest pass is required to park here. The cost is $5 for a day pass or $30

for an annual pass. You can buy a day pass at ranger stations, from private vendors, or through Nature of the Northwest Information Center.

Maps: For a map of the Mount Jefferson Wilderness, contact Nature of the Northwest Information Center. For a topographic map, contact Green Trails, Inc. (ask for Mount Jefferson, map number 557), 206/546-MAPS (206/546-6277), www.greentrails.com; or ask the USGS for Mount Jefferson.

Directions: From Salem, drive 50 miles east on Highway 22 to Detroit and continue another 11.9 miles to Forest Service Road 2246. Turn left and drive 3.7 miles to the parking area at the end of the road and the well-marked trailhead.

Contact: Willamette National Forest, Detroit Ranger District, HC 73, P.O. Box 320, Mill City, OR 97360, 503/854-3366.

65 INDEPENDENCE ROCK LOOP
1.7 mi/1.5 hrs

east of Marion Forks off Highway 22 in Willamette National Forest

Map 3.5, page 72

Unlike neighboring Marion Lake, this trail doesn't attract hordes of people, which means it's overgrown in parts, but the overgrown ground plants make a nice contrast to the tall old-growth trunks. The sweet smell of gorgeous pink rhododendrons also contrasts well to the pine scent, making this easy trail a feast for the senses. A small side trail leads up to Independence Rock itself in all its glory (those scared of heights may not share the love, because footing can be a little sketchy). Turn back the way you came, or continue on the trail for a 1.7-mile loop. If you choose the loop, you'll have to walk more than .5 mile on the road back to your car.

User groups: Hikers, dogs, mountain bikes, and horses. No wheelchair access.

Permits: Permits are not required. Parking and access are free.

Maps: For a map of Willamette National Forest, contact Nature of the Northwest Information Center. For a topographic map, contact

Green Trails, Inc. (ask for Mount Jefferson, map number 557), 206/546-MAPS (206/546-6277), www.greentrails.com; or ask the USGS for Marion Forks.

Directions: From Salem, drive 50 miles east on Highway 22 to Detroit, and continue another 16.8 miles to Forest Service Road 2255 (at Marion Forks). Turn left and drive .1 mile to a small turnout on the side of the road to the right. The trailhead is across the road, on the left side as you're driving in.

Contact: Willamette National Forest, Detroit Ranger District, HC 73, P.O. Box 320, Mill City, OR 97360, 503/854-3366.

66 MARION LAKE LOOP
5.4 mi/2.5 hrs

on the southwest side of Mount Jefferson in the Mount Jefferson Wilderness of Willamette National Forest

Map 3.5, page 72

You need only to pull up to the parking lot to get a sense that this is a popular trail. Families flock to this lake because it's an easy two miles in to its shores. The well-maintained, wooded trail doesn't actually circle the lake itself, but you can make a little loop of your own by going right at the junction about .5 mile after passing by Lake Ann, and making another right to view Marion Falls. Return to the trail, then keep left at the junction to travel past the northwest lakeshore, then turn left again to head back the way you came. If you want more solitude and views of Mount Jefferson, head up to Marion Mountain: Instead of turning left to reach the lakeshore, turn right onto Blue Ridge Trail for 1.8 miles, then turn left at Pine Ridge Trail for one mile, turning left again to climb .8 mile to the 5,400-foot peak of Marion Mountain. The trail also connects to the Eight Lakes Basin trail system for an eight-mile loop. As with many of this area's trails, there are endless possibilities if you want to backpack.

User groups: Hikers, dogs, and horses. Mountain bikes are not allowed. No wheelchair access.

Permits: A free wilderness permit is required to hike here and is available at the trailhead. In addition, a federal Northwest Forest pass is required to park here. The cost is $5 for a day pass or $30 for an annual pass. You can buy a day pass at ranger stations, from private vendors, or through Nature of the Northwest Information Center.

Maps: For a map of the Mount Jefferson Wilderness and Willamette National Forest, contact Nature of the Northwest Information Center. For a topographic map, contact Green Trails, Inc. (ask for Mount Jefferson, map number 557), 206/546-MAPS (206/546-6277), www.greentrails.com; or ask the USGS for Marion Forks and Marion Lake.

Directions: From Salem, drive 50 miles east on Highway 22 to Detroit and continue another 16.8 miles to Forest Service 2255 (at Marion Forks). Turn left and drive 4.5 miles to the end of the road and the trailhead.

Contact: Willamette National Forest, Detroit Ranger District, HC 73, P.O. Box 320, Mill City, OR 97360, 503/854-3366.

67 METOLIUS RIVER TRAIL
5.0–11.5 mi/–5.5 hrs

northwest of Sisters in Deschutes National Forest

Map 3.5, page 72

One of the largest spring-fed rivers in the country, the Metolius is a popular camping area. In such a hot and dry area, it's also refreshing—if you're camping nearby, enjoy a soak in the river. The dusty and flat path is good for both running and meandering. From the trailhead at Canyon Creek campground, hike 2.5 miles to the Wizard Falls Hatchery, where you can take a self-guided tour and see why this is a hot spot for fly-fishing: rainbow, brook, brown and trophy trout, as well as kokanee and Atlantic salmon, mingle with the three million other fish here. (Kids Day is the second Saturday of June, so plan accordingly.) You can either turn back here or continue past the hatchery for three more miles to the Lower Bridge Campground, where you can cross the bridge and continue on the other side (crossing again when you hit the hatchery) for an additional 6.5-mile loop.

User groups: Hikers and dogs. No mountain bikes or horses are allowed. No wheelchair access.

Permits: Permits are not required. Parking and access are free.

Maps: For a map of the Deschutes National Forest, contact Nature of the Northwest Information Center. For a topographic map, contact Green Trails, Inc. (ask for Whitewater River, map number 558), 206/546-MAPS (206/546-6277), www.greentrails.com; or ask the USGS for Black Butte, Candle Creek, and Prairie Farm Spring.

Directions: From Sisters, drive nine miles west on Highway 20 to paved Forest Service Road 14. Turn right and drive 2.6 miles to a right fork. Keep going straight at this point, continuing on Forest Service Road 1419 for 2.2 miles, and keep going straight as it changes to paved Forest Service Road 1420. Drive 3.3 miles, and turn right on Forest Service Road 400. Drive .8 mile to the Canyon Creek Campground. The parking area and trailhead are on the far side of the campground.

Contact: Deschutes National Forest, Sisters Ranger District, Highway 20/Pine Street, P.O. Box 249, Sisters, OR 97759, 541/549-7700.

© MEGAN McMORRIS

Chapter 4

Northeast Oregon

Chapter 4—Northeast Oregon

op quiz: What's the deepest canyon in North America? Wrong. It's actually Hells Canyon, which plummets 7,900 feet between Seven Devil's Mountain in western Idaho and Wallowa Mountain in northeastern Oregon. (Your likely first guess, the Grand Canyon, is actually 2,600 feet shy of this.) Snaking through it all is, well, the Snake River (popular with white-water rafters), which you can walk along on several of this chapter's shorter hikes or arrange a longer backpacking trip along its shores. One of the short hikes in Hells Canyon, Stud Creek, is only accessible from the Idaho border, and getting there is one of the most scenic drives in this book.

Probably the best hiking in the region is in the Wallowa-Whitman National Forest and Eagle Cap Wilderness, just west of the Idaho/Oregon border. The Wallowas (as the locals call it) are known as the Alps of Oregon, with nearly 20 peaks that stand over 8,000 feet. The area is famous for its Lakes Basin Loop, high-alpine lakes surrounded by wildflower meadows, as well as for many other backpacking trips. Keep your head up here, because black bears, elk, and deer proliferate in these parts. (The cute town of Joseph, nearby, is home to the World's Best Ice Cream, at Joe's Place, on the main drag, but you won't find that in any reference book except this one.) Scenic Wallowa Lake, from where Lakes Basin Trail and other high-alpine lake trailheads start, is a popular destination, with camping, cabins, boating, horseback riding, restaurants, and even a wedding chapel. The entire Wallowa-Whitman forest offers plenty of other high-alpine lake trailheads, too, if you prefer to avoid the circuslike (but cool) atmosphere at Wallowa Lake.

Its neighbor to the northwest is the remote Umatilla National Forest (pronounced YOU-ma-TILL-a) and North Fork John Day Wilderness, known for wildlife like deer and Rocky Mountain elk, as well as for the popular and scenic South Fork Walla Walla Trail. If solitude is your goal, you're likely to find it in this forest.

Umatilla National Forest also extends south, cutting across the Blue mountain range. Lining the Blue Mountain Scenic Byway are trails galore right off the highway and surrounding the Anthony Lakes Ski Area, from long easy strolls along North Fork John Day River to intense climbs leading to high alpine lakes and mountain meadows.

Farther south, we come to the drier, dustier Strawberry Mountain Wilderness, in Malheur National Forest, which is packed with miles of trails both remote and not-so-remote, and even a climb up to the summit of 9,039-foot Strawberry Mountain. The Strawberry Lakes Basin is an especially big hit among the crowds, who come here for short loops around the lake with a backdrop of Strawberry Mountain looking over the proceedings.

Finally, for some short and sweet trips, you need to take in the scene that is the John Day Painted Desert Area, and the Fossil Monument Areas, where you can see colorful layers of volcanic ash and preserved fossils on a trip that will take you back in time (well before your time, that is). To the west is Ochoco National Forest, where you can get up-close and personal with red rock Twin Pillars and Stein's Pillar, jutting up 200 feet in the air.

So, to recap: In this chapter you'll find the Alps of Oregon, the deepest gorge in North America, short history-filled strolls through volcanic ash formations, scenic white-water river hikes, and a couple of red-rock pillars thrown in for good measure. From remote excursions to filled-to-the-gill hot spots, you'll find everything you ever wanted in this diverse part of the state. And more.

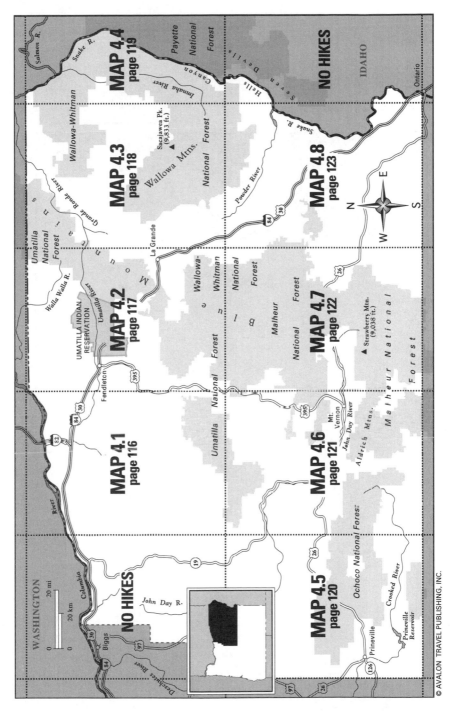

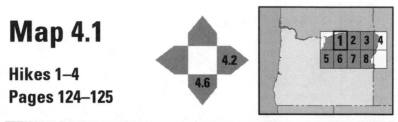

Map 4.1

Hikes 1–4
Pages 124–125

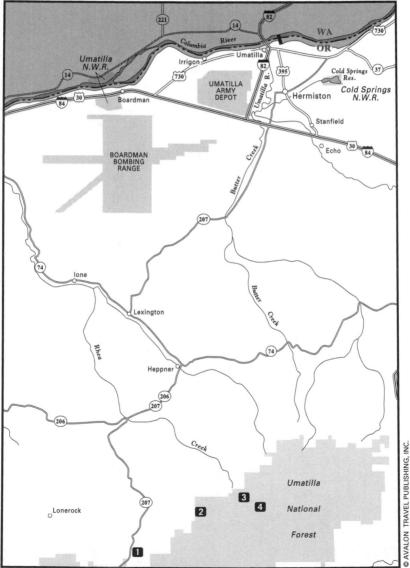

© AVALON TRAVEL PUBLISHING, INC.

Map 4.2

Hikes 5–14
Pages 125–131

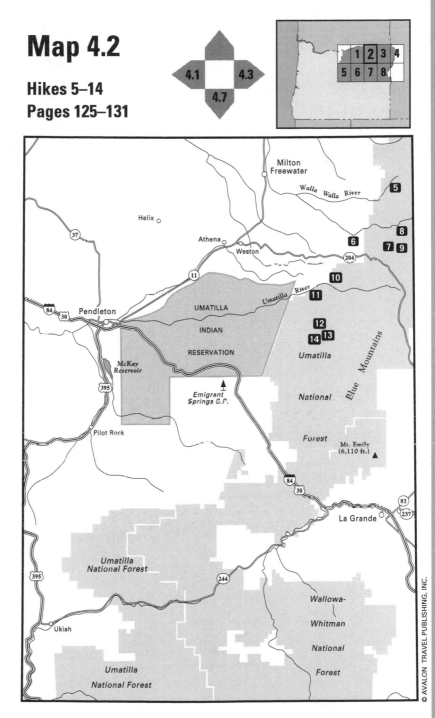

Map 4.3

Hikes 15–30
Pages 131–140

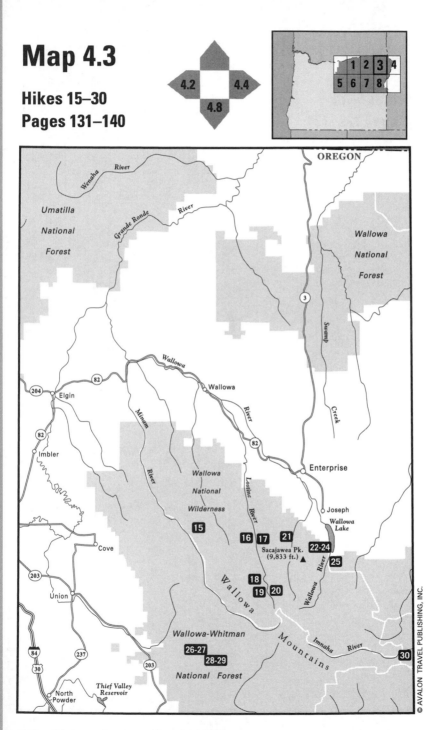

Map 4.4

Hikes 31–33
Pages 140–142

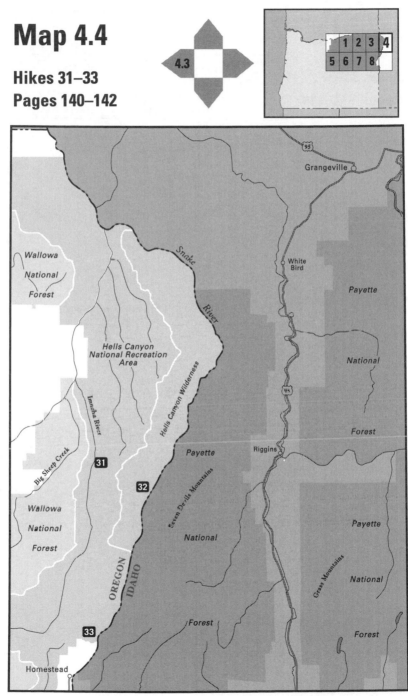

Map 4.5

Hikes 34–37
Pages 142–144

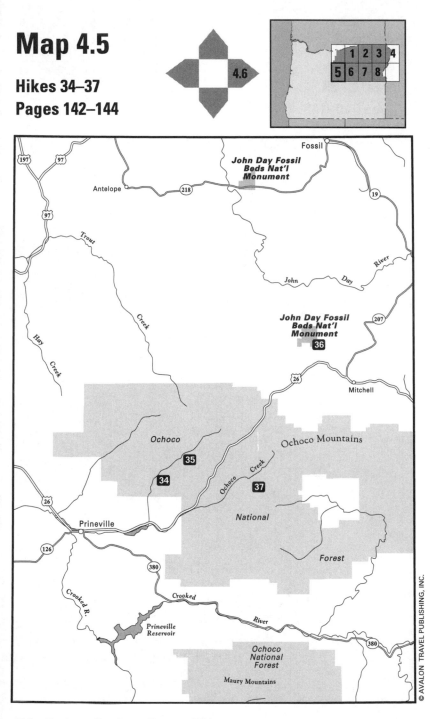

© AVALON TRAVEL PUBLISHING, INC.

Map 4.6

Hikes 38–41
Pages 144–146

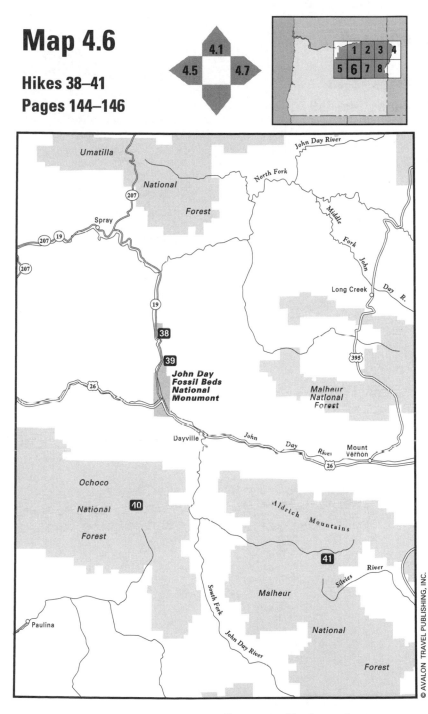

© AVALON TRAVEL PUBLISHING, INC.

Map 4.7

Hikes 42–68
Pages 146–159

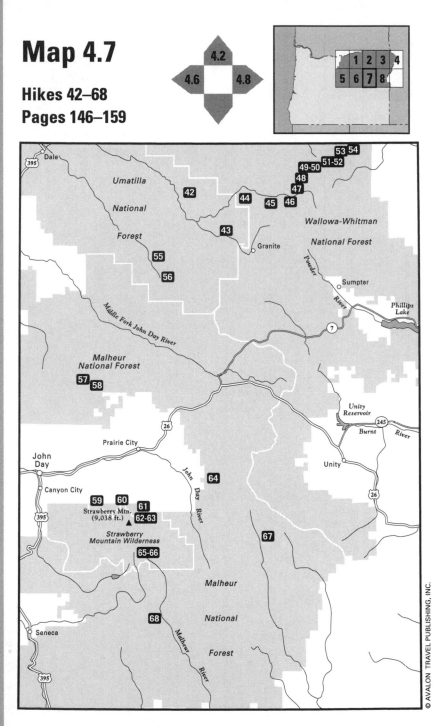

Map 4.8

Hike 69
Page 159

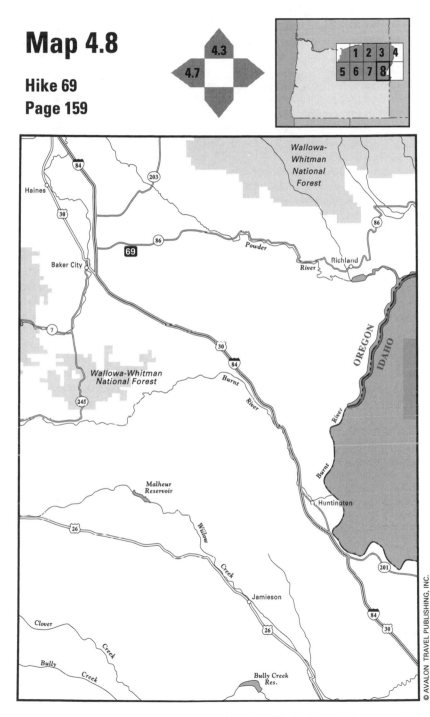

◼1 BULL PRAIRIE LAKE
0.5 mi/0.5 hr

**south of Heppner off Highway 207 in
Umatilla National Forest**

Map 4.1, page 116

In the remote and wild Umatilla Forest, you sometimes may wonder where everyone is. Well, wonder no more: They're all packed into this pretty and popular lake. (Okay, not everyone, but still.) Surrounded by willows and wildflowers, Bull Prairie Lake is all the rage as a prime trout fishing spot, complete with floating piers. The flat .5-mile gravel path is fine for families who want to add in a leg-stretcher while camping nearby or fishing at the lake.

User groups: Hikers and dogs. No mountain bikes or horses are allowed. No wheelchair access.

Permits: Permits are not required. Parking and access are free.

Maps: For a map of Umatilla National Forest, contact Nature of the Northwest Information Center. For a topographic map, ask the USGS for Whitetail Butte.

Directions: From Heppner, drive 40 miles south on Highway 207. At the sign for Bull Prairie Recreation Area, turn left (east) onto Forest Service Road 2039. Drive one mile to the recreation area on the right. There is no official trailhead, but there are many access points around the lake.

Contact: Umatilla National Forest, Heppner Ranger District, P.O. Box 7, Heppner, OR 97836, 541/676-9187.

◼2 MADISON BUTTE LOOKOUT
TRAIL TO TUPPER BUTTE
2.0 mi/1.0 hr

**south of Heppner in Umatilla
National Forest**

Map 4.1, page 116

For a one-mile jaunt to a knockout view all to yourself, head up to Tupper Butte. And we're talking up: The trail can't be bothered with gentle switchbacks; instead, it climbs straight up an old jeep trail 1,800 feet to the 5,184-foot summit of Tupper Butte. Near the top, the trail forks; take the left fork to reach a meadow packed with flowers such as daisies and Indian paintbrush, to mention just a few. (The path straight ahead to Madison Butte is not passable at this writing.) Stick around and check out the view of Umatilla National Forest, as well as a healthy chunk of northeastern Oregon.

User groups: Hikers, dogs, and horses. No mountain bikes are allowed. No wheelchair access.

Permits: Permits are not required. Parking and access are free.

Maps: For a map of Umatilla National Forest, contact Nature of the Northwest Information Center. For a topographic map, ask the USGS for Madison Butte.

Directions: From Heppner, drive 26 miles south on Highway 207, .25 mile past Anson Wright Park, and turn left (east) onto Sunflower Flat Road/Forest Service Road 22. Drive four miles and turn left onto Forest Service Road 2119. Continue 3.5 miles and turn left onto Forest Service Road 21. Drive .7 mile to the trailhead on the left (park at the side of the road), starting from the locked gate on the abandoned road.

Contact: Umatilla National Forest, Heppner Ranger District, P.O. Box 7, Heppner, OR 97836, 541/676-9187.

◼3 SKOOKUM TRAIL
5.0 mi/2.5 hrs

south of Heppner in Umatilla National Forest

Map 4.1, page 116

Following an old jeep road at the beginning, Skookum Trail climbs steeply up to Madison Butte, gaining a cool 1,000 feet in elevation in just one mile. Up for it? Well, that's not all . . . This trail is not currently maintained, which is good news for solitude-seekers and not-so-good news for those who like a well-marked trail with a plaque thrown in every once in a while. It's best to pick up a map if you want to check out this area, because there are a few junctions that begin to look the same after awhile, and they tend to be unmarked. Here's a quick peek at the trail: After climbing, you'll head left (west) at Copple Butte Trail to Madison Butte for great views of the valley below. After enjoying the vista laid out before you, retrace your steps. You can combine this trail with Alder Creek for a 5.5-mile loop (and a gentler descent your knees will thank you for).

User groups: Hikers, dogs, and horses. No mountain bikes are allowed. No wheelchair access.

Permits: Permits are not required. Parking and access are free.

Maps: For a map of Umatilla National Forest, contact Nature of the Northwest Information Center. For a topographic map, ask the USGS for Madison Butte.

Directions: From Heppner, drive 26 miles south on Highway 207, .25 mile past Anson Wright Park, and turn left (east) onto Sunflower Flat Road/Forest Service Road 22. Drive four miles and turn left onto Forest Service Road 2119. Continue 3.5 miles and turn left onto Forest Service Road 21, continuing for 5.8 miles to Forest Service Road 140. Turn left and drive for .5 mile to the road's end and the trailhead.

Contact: Umatilla National Forest, Heppner Ranger District, P.O. Box 7, Heppner, OR 97836, 541/676-9187.

◢ ALDER CREEK
6.0 mi/3.0 hrs

south of Heppner in Umatilla National Forest

Map 4.1, page 116

If you love to whip out a map to blaze your own trail, try this guy. When last visited, it was in need of some sprucing up and trimming around the edges. The good news, oh, map lover, is that you are roughly 99.7 percent guaranteed not to run into another soul out here. The trail starts out as a cool and shaded path along its namesake, Alder Creek, crossing over the creek twice before heading up for a long but relatively gentle climb, gaining 800 feet in the final two miles. Although there are steep

sections, the challenge on this trail is due more to the obstacles along the way, as there are a few logs and branches to hop over, around, and sometimes even scoot under. The trail is also overgrown in parts, but luckily (or unluckily, depending on your take) a barbed wire fence runs along the right side of the trail for the entire time, which comes in handy, although barbed wire does tend to detract from the scenery a smidge. Once at the top, enjoy the view of the valleys below before returning the way you came, or bushwhack and scramble to the top of Madison Butte for a better glimpse. The trail also connects with Skookum Trail (see listing in this chapter for that loop option), but it's easier to navigate from the other direction, as there are no signs and it's easy to get disoriented in this remote area.

User groups: Hikers, dogs, and horses. No mountain bikes are allowed. No wheelchair access.

Permits: Permits are not required. Parking and access are free.

Maps: For a map of Umatilla National Forest, contact Nature of the Northwest Information Center. For a topographic map, ask the USGS for Madison Butte.

Directions: From Heppner, drive 26 miles south on Highway 207, .25 mile past Anson Wright Park, and turn left (east) onto Sunflower Flat Road/Forest Service Road 22. Drive four miles and turn left onto Forest Service Road 2119. Continue 3.5 miles and turn left onto Forest Service Road 21, continuing for 5.8 miles to Forest Service Road 140. Turn left and drive for .5 mile to the road's end and the trailhead.

Contact: Umatilla National Forest, Heppner Ranger District, P.O. Box 7, Heppner, OR 97836, 541/676-9187.

◪ NORTH FORK WALLA WALLA
11.0 mi one-way/1.0 day

southeast of Walla Walla, Washington, in Umatilla National Forest

Map 4.2, page 117

This is the more remote side to the Walla

Walla River, mainly because of the hard-to-find trailhead and the long, dramatic (one might even say death-defying) drive on the twisty, dusty road in. You'll feel like you've arrived at a true adventure before you've even left your car, so if that's your bag, dive on in, because the Walla Walla awaits (how can you resist repeating that name? It means "place of many waters," in case you were wondering). Once you've arrived, the trail doesn't even make it easy for you, dropping quickly through thick forest to a small stream crossing and then an open meadow (when you reach a junction with an old jeep road, keep going straight). You won't likely encounter many hikers, but it is a popular mountain and dirt-biking area. It's probably best to get a map of the area before you venture out, not only for the drive in but for the hike itself, as it comes to junctions with roads at times, and it's not the most well-marked trail in the area. Still, there are places to fish and camp along the way, so if you want to take a walk on the wilder side of the Walla Walla (there it is again!), you might just find what you're looking for here.

User groups: Hikers, dogs, horses, and mountain bikes. No wheelchair access.

Permits: Permits are not required. Parking and access are free.

Maps: For a map of Umatilla National Forest, contact Nature of the Northwest Information Center. For a topographic map, ask the USGS for Big Meadows.

Directions: From Walla Walla, Washington, drive 14 miles east on Mill Creek Road to the junction with Forest Service Road 65. Turn right and drive 9.2 miles to the junction with unmarked Forest Service Road 65-040. The trailhead is on the right, about 50 yards from the junction.

Contact: Umatilla National Forest, Walla Walla Ranger District, 1415 West Rose Street, Walla Walla, WA 99362, 509/522-6290.

6 SOUTH FORK WALLA WALLA
19.0 mi one-way/
1.0–2.0 days

southeast of Milton-Freewater in Umatilla National Forest

Map 4.2, page 117

The Walla Walla is not only fun to say, but fun to hike. And bike. And camp. And fish. And even motorbike. Yep, it gets a mite crowded in these parts on a sunny day, and it's not hard to see why it wins the popularity contest. The trail hugs the riverbank for several miles and climbs up the valley walls occasionally to give you a glimpse of the river and valley below before dropping back to the shaded riverside. There are plenty of prime camping and fishing spots along the way, so you can explore the trail at your leisure. (Unfortunately, along with the easy access to this hot spot is the bane of every outdoor-lover's existence: litter!) About 1.5 miles in, look for the old foundation and chimney of Demaris Cabin, and continue on, exploring the volcanic cliffs forming the canyon walls. Keep your ears open for rattling and buzzing, as the trail is also popular with rattlesnakes and yellowjackets. Shuttle hikers can access the trail from the upper trailhead for a 19-mile hike one-way.

User groups: Hikers, dogs, mountain bikes, and horses. No wheelchair access.

Permits: Permits are not required. Parking and access are free.

Maps: For a map of Umatilla National Forest, contact Nature of the Northwest Information Center. For a topographic map, ask the USGS for Bone Springs, Tollgate, and Jubilee Lake.

Directions: From the south end of Milton-Freewater, turn east onto 14th Street (which quickly runs into 15th Street) and follow signs to Harris County Park. Drive for 13 miles (the road turns into Walla Walla River Road). Just past Harris County Park, you'll arrive at the parking lot and the trailhead at the road's end. To reach the upper trailhead, follow directions to the North Fork Walla Walla, turning left to continue on Forest Service Road 65 at the road junction and North Fork trailhead. Continue another three miles to Deduct Pond and the trailhead, on the right side of the road.

Contact: Umatilla National Forest, Walla Walla Ranger District, 1415 West Rose Street, Walla Walla, WA 99362, 509/522-6290.

7 BURNT CABIN
8.0 mi/4.0 hrs

north of Tollgate in Umatilla National Forest

Map 4.2, page 117

Sometimes it's the simple rules of life that are so easy to forget when you're caught up in an outdoors adventure, so this bears repeating: What goes up must come down. Simple, yes, but you'll want to keep this in mind when you descend the four steep switchbacking miles down (2,300 feet, to be exact), because you'll need to conserve your energy for the hike back up. Just enjoy the scenery while you still have the strength for it—the views of the steep brown cliffs of the valley make it worth your while. Be on the lookout for rattlesnakes in this area, and bring plenty of water, as it can get scorching here. The narrow and often rocky trail finally lets up near the end of the trail and spits you out at the South Fork Walla Walla River (see listing in this chapter); you can explore the river before you start your climb up. Once you're back at the trailhead, stick around for a history lesson: The trail starts near the Target Meadow Campground, which was used as a camp and target range for soldiers from Old Fort Walla Walla from the late 1800s to 1906. You can still see damage to the trees, and the target mound itself.

User groups: Hikers, dogs, mountain bikes, and horses. No wheelchair access.

Permits: A federal Northwest Forest pass is required to park here. The cost is $5 for a day pass or $30 for an annual pass. You can buy a day pass at the trailhead, at ranger stations, from private vendors, or through Nature of the Northwest Information Center.

Maps: For a map of Umatilla National Forest, contact Nature of the Northwest Information Center. For a topographic map, ask the USGS for Tollgate.

Directions: From Tollgate, turn left (north) onto Forest Service Road 64. Drive .2 mile to a junction with the Target Meadow Camp Road/Forest Service Road 6401. Turn left at the junction and drive 1.5 miles to Forest Service Road 6401-050. Turn right and continue one mile to the Target Meadow campground. At the campground, the road forks—stay to the left and drive another .5 mile until the road's end, the parking area, and the trailhead. The trail starts about 50 yards from the trail marker (it can be hard to find). Note: The road can be closed through mid-June due to snow, so check ahead before you venture out.

Contact: Umatilla National Forest, Walla Walla Ranger District, 1415 West Rose Street, Walla Walla, WA 99362, 509/522-6290.

8 ROUGH FORK
6.4 mi/3.5 hrs

northeast of Tollgate in Umatilla National Forest

Map 4.2, page 117

If you want to dip straight down into the South Fork Walla Walla River and ditch the crowds near the river trailhead, try this steep descent. You'll plunk down about 13 miles from the lower river trailhead and about 6 miles from the upper trailhead, so chances are you'll be on your own—except for the deer and rattlesnakes, that is (keep your eye out for the latter). Also, remember to bring water with you, because it's a hot and dusty trail. Oh yeah, and don't forget about the 1,780-foot climb back to your car after you reach the river. It's a speedy descent to the river, with views of the brown and green valley walls, and the rushing river itself. The Mottet Campground is a cute and remote site, so stick around if you want to make a weekend out of the trip (or if you need to rest after the steep climb up).

User groups: Hikers, dogs, mountain bikes, and horses. No wheelchair access.

Permits: A federal Northwest Forest pass is required to park here. The cost is $5 for a day pass or $30 for an annual pass. You can buy a day pass at the trailhead, at ranger stations, from private vendors, or through Nature of the Northwest Information Center.

Maps: For a map of Umatilla National Forest, contact Nature of the Northwest Information Center. For a topographic map, ask the USGS for Tollgate.

Directions: From Tollgate, drive 12 miles north on dirt Forest Road 64 to the junction with Jubilee Lake. After the lake junction, drive another 3.5 miles to a sign for Rough Fork. Turn left onto Forest Service Road 6411 (which is a rough road) and drive 1.3 miles to an unmarked fork just before Mottet Campground. Turn right onto unmarked Forest Service Road 6403 and drive less than .1 mile (keeping to the left at another unmarked fork) to the trailhead. Note: The road in is often closed to snow through mid-June, so call ahead to make sure it's open before heading out.

Contact: Umatilla National Forest, Walla Walla Ranger District, 1415 West Rose Street, Walla Walla, WA 99362, 509/522-6290.

9 JUBILEE LAKE NATIONAL RECREATION TRAIL
2.6 mi/1.5 hrs

northeast of Tollgate in Umatilla National Forest

Map 4.2, page 117

For a relatively flat lake loop, you can't go wrong with Jubilee Lake (you also can't go wrong with the name, which is all about fun). Although it can be a popular lake, with a large campground, it's surprisingly solitary, since most people prefer to hit the great fishing spots rather than take a stroll. Well, they're missing out. It's a trail for taking it easy and enjoying the scenery without putting in too much effort, and plenty of benches line the route so you can do just that. On the north shore, there are

private nooks for casting in the stocked lake. Note to spring trail-seekers: Jubilee Lake is closed through June due to snow, so call ahead before you arrive.

User groups: Hikers and dogs. No mountain bikes or horses are allowed. The south shore of the lake is paved and wheelchair accessible.

Permits: A $3 day-use fee is collected at the entrance.

Maps: For a map of Umatilla National Forest, contact Nature of the Northwest Information Center. For a topographic map, ask the USGS for Jubilee Lake.

Directions: From Tollgate, drive 12 miles north on dirt Forest Road 64 to the Jubilee Lake Campground. The trailhead leaves from the boat ramp.

Contact: Umatilla National Forest, Walla Walla Ranger District, 1415 West Rose Street, Walla Walla, WA 99362, 509/522-6290.

10 LICK CREEK/ GROUSE MOUNTAIN
7.0 mi/3.5 hrs

southeast of Tollgate in the North Fork Umatilla Wilderness of Umatilla National Forest

Map 4.2, page 117

Starting at 4,050 feet in elevation, the upper trailhead offers unobstructed insta-views of the North Fork Umatilla Valley and sprawling grassy wildflower meadows and hills. It can be hot, dry, and exposed at first, so remember to bring water and sunscreen. After about a mile, you'll start to descend through forest, where it gets cooler and shadier with each step, as the trail leads down to the North Fork Umatilla River. It's a remote trail, and the only people you're likely to encounter are morel mushroom seekers, who flock to the area in the summer. The trail passes through Grouse Mountain saddle, where a faint trail leads up to the peak. If you're interested in this more adventurous feat, pick up a map before you go, because the route is not well marked or maintained. You can also access the trail from the lower trailhead if you'd rather climb to the top.

User groups: Hikers, dogs, and horses. No mountain bikes are allowed. No wheelchair access.

Permits: Permits are not required. Parking and access are free.

Maps: For a map of the North Fork Umatilla Wilderness and Umatilla National Forest, contact Nature of the Northwest Information Center. For a topographic map, ask the USGS for Bingham Springs and Blalock Mountain.

Directions: From Weston, drive 14.8 miles east on Highway 402 and turn right on McDougall Camp Road/Forest Service Road 3715. Drive three miles to the end of the road and the small parking pullout. To reach the lower trailhead, drive seven miles east from Pendleton on I-84 to Exit 216. Turn left (north) toward Walla Walla for 2.1 miles, then turn right on Mission Road. Drive 1.6 miles, then turn left on Cayuse Road for 10.8 miles. Turn right onto Bingham Road (which turns into Forest Service Road 32), and continue for 15.5 miles to the Corporation Guard Station and the parking area, to the left.

Contact: Umatilla National Forest, Walla Walla Ranger District, 1415 West Rose Street, Walla Walla, WA 99362, 509/522-6290.

⑪ NORTH FORK UMATILLA
9.8 mi one-way/
5.0 hrs–2.0 days

east of Pendleton in the North Fork Umatilla Wilderness of Umatilla National Forest

Map 4.2, page 117

As you can see above, it's tricky to gauge just how long it will take the average hiker to explore this area, because that's up to you. For a peaceful stroll along the river, check out the first four miles of this trail. This section gains just 450 feet in elevation and saunters along the rushing water on a narrow dirt path filled with flitting butterflies and the sounds of chirping birds. The trail leaves the river to climb Coyote Ridge for the last five miles, gaining 2,000

feet in elevation to views of the river below and the Umatilla wilderness area. So take your pick: You can either turn around before the climb for a pleasant eight-mile round-trip, or continue on for the steep trip up the ridge for a shuttle hike to the upper trailhead, or do it as an out-and-back backpacking trip.

User groups: Hikers, dogs, and horses. No mountain bikes are allowed. No wheelchair access.

Permits: A federal Northwest Forest pass is required to park here. The cost is $5 for a day pass or $30 for an annual pass. You can buy a day pass at ranger stations, from private vendors, or through Nature of the Northwest Information Center.

Maps: For a map of the North Fork Umatilla Wilderness and Umatilla National Forest, contact Nature of the Northwest Information Center. For a topographic map, ask the USGS for Bingham Springs and Andies Prairie.

Directions: From Pendleton, drive seven miles east to Exit 216. Turn left (north) toward Walla Walla for 2.1 miles, then turn right on Mission Road. Drive 1.6 miles, then turn left on Cayuse Road for 10.8 miles. Turn right onto Bingham Road (which turns into Forest Service Road 32), and continue for 15.6 miles, turning left into the Umatilla Forks day-use pullout and parking area. The trailhead is to the left of the sign. To reach the upper trailhead from Tollgate, drive one mile east on Highway 204 and turn south onto Forest Service Road 3719. Drive two miles and turn right onto Forest Service Road 041, continuing another two miles to the end of the road and the trailhead at Coyote Ridge.

Contact: Umatilla National Forest, Walla Walla Ranger District, 1415 West Rose Street, Walla Walla, WA 99362, 509/522-6290.

⑫ NINE MILE RIDGE
13.6 mi/7.0 hrs

east of Pendleton in the North Fork Umatilla Wilderness of Umatilla National Forest

Map 4.2, page 117

Okay, so it's called the Nine Mile Ridge, and

the length is actually 6.8 miles one-way, but who's to quibble? Climbing up this first section will make it seem like it's nine miles anyway, as it gains 1,800 feet in the first two miles. The trail is overgrown in parts, so true adventurers will love it (while those who prefer a well-maintained trail may not be sharing the joy). After the first two strenuous miles, the trail levels off to the ridgecrest, where you can enjoy views of the Umatilla wilderness valley below, and maybe some local wildlife like elk, deer, black bears, and cougars. It's best to bring along a detailed map for this one, because sometimes trail signs are missing in this area.

User groups: Hikers, dogs, and horses. No mountain bikes are allowed. No wheelchair access.

Permits: Permits are not required. Parking and access are free.

Maps: For a map of the North Fork Umatilla Wilderness and Umatilla National Forest, contact Nature of the Northwest Information Center. For a topographic map, ask the USGS for Bingham Springs and Andies Prairie.

Directions: From Pendleton, drive seven miles east to Exit 216. Turn left (north) toward Walla Walla for 2.1 miles, then turn right on Mission Road. Drive 1.6 miles, then turn left on Cayuse Road for 10.8 miles. Turn right onto Bingham Road (which turns into Forest Service Road 32), and continue for 16.1 miles. Turn left at the junction, .25 mile past the Umatilla Forks Campground, before the South Fork Umatilla bridge, and drive .1 mile up a rough side road to a small parking area on the left. (To the right is a short access road to the Kiwanis clubhouse; the gate is sometimes locked.) The trail begins to the left as you're driving in (in front of the parking turnout). When you come to a trail junction shortly after entering, take the left junction (the sign may be missing).

Contact: Umatilla National Forest, Walla Walla Ranger District, 1415 West Rose Street, Walla Walla, WA 99362, 509/522-6290.

13 BUCK CREEK
7.0 mi/3.5 hrs

east of Pendleton in the North Fork Umatilla Wilderness of Umatilla National Forest

Map 4.2, page 117

This lightly used trail meanders down Buck Creek for 3.5 miles, crossing it several times. Since it gains only 800 feet in elevation, it's a good choice for those who want to explore the wilderness without having to hoof it up nearby Buck Mountain (see listing in this chapter). It can be overgrown in parts, but it's a simple trail to follow. If you like to feel as if you're in the middle of the deep wilds, this is worth checking out. Locals in this part of the Umatilla Forest include coyotes, elk, black bears, and deer, so you may have a chance to see a few natives while you explore.

User groups: Hikers, dogs, and horses. No mountain bikes are allowed. No wheelchair access.

Permits: Permits are not required. Parking and access are free.

Maps: For a map of the North Fork Umatilla Wilderness and Umatilla National Forest, contact Nature of the Northwest Information Center. For a topographic map, ask the USGS for Bingham Springs.

Directions: From Pendleton, drive seven miles east to Exit 216. Turn left (north) toward Walla Walla for 2.1 miles, then turn right on Mission Road. Drive 1.6 miles, then turn left on Cayuse Road for 10.8 miles. Turn right onto Bingham Road (which turns into Forest Service Road 32), and continue for 16.1 miles. Turn left at the junction, .25 mile past the Umatilla Forks Campground, before the South Fork Umatilla bridge, and drive .1 mile up a rough side road to a small parking area, on the left. (To the right is a short access road to the Kiwanis clubhouse; the gate is sometimes locked.) The trail begins to the left as you're driving in (in front of the parking turnout). When you come to a trail junction shortly after entering, stay on the trail straight ahead that travels along the creek.

Contact: Umatilla National Forest, Walla Walla

Ranger District, 1415 West Rose Street, Walla Walla, WA 99362, 509/522-6290.

14 BUCK MOUNTAIN
7.0 mi/3.5 hrs

east of Pendleton in the North Fork Umatilla Wilderness of Umatilla National Forest

Map 4.2, page 117

This lightly used trail doesn't give you time to warm up. Instead, it shoots straight uphill for almost 2,000 feet for the first 1.5 miles. Then you catch a break, gaining only 300 feet in elevation to reach the summit, surrounded by meadows. The trail continues for a total of 7.5 miles, ending at a junction with Lake Creek Trail, where you can do a 12-mile loop to Buck Creek to return to the trailhead. Otherwise, if the view is your goal, head back when you reach the summit about 3.5 miles down the trail. Word of warning before you set out: You'll be lucky if the signs are still in place, as some of them look like they've been used as target practice or are missing altogether. Also, the trail can be overgrown and faint in parts, so you'd be smart to get a map before you set out. Even the trailhead is tricky to find. But if you like the challenge of route-finding and setting off into parts unknown to many, this may be your ticket.

User groups: Hikers, dogs, and horses. No mountain bikes are allowed. No wheelchair access.

Permits: Permits are not required. Parking and access are free.

Maps: For a map of the North Fork Umatilla Wilderness and Umatilla National Forest, contact Nature of the Northwest Information Center. For a topographic map, ask the USGS for Bingham Springs.

Directions: From Pendleton, drive seven miles east to Exit 216. Turn left (north) toward Walla Walla for 2.1 miles, then turn right on Mission Road. Drive 1.6 miles, then turn left on Cayuse Road for 10.8 miles. Turn right onto Bingham Road (which turns into Forest Service Road 32), and continue for 16.1 miles.

Turn left at the junction, .25 mile past the Umatilla Forks Campground, before the South Fork Umatilla bridge, and drive .1 mile up a rough side road to a small parking area on the left. (To the right is a short access road to the Kiwanis clubhouse; the gate is sometimes locked.) The trail begins to the left as you're driving in (in front of the parking turnout). Take the right fork of the trail to Buck Mountain (the sign may be missing).

Contact: Umatilla National Forest, Walla Walla Ranger District, 1415 West Rose Street, Walla Walla, WA 99362, 509/522-6290.

15 BEARWALLOW TO
STANDLEY CABIN
9.6 mi/5.0 hrs

south of Minam in Eagle Cap Wilderness of Wallowa-Whitman National Forest

Map 4.3, page 118

Starting at over 6,000 feet in elevation sure has its advantages: You get great views right off the bat of the Wallowa mountain range and the valley below with little exertion on your part. Since you're so far off the beaten path, this is prime time for wildlife viewing—give my regards to my bear friend there, and tell him next time I'm in the area, we'll do berries. Bears are quite common in the Wallowa Mountains, as are deer, elk, cougars, and woodpeckers. The trail starts along a forested ridgeline as you travel nearly 1,000 feet up to the 7,200-foot Standley Cabin, an old cabin from the early 1900s. You probably won't see anyone else while you're here, since the road in is long and rough. For this reason, it can be handy to bring a friend along to hop out and remove any obstacles in the road, and to unclench your fingers from the steering wheel after you've arrived at the trailhead. The road tends to be blocked through June due to snow, so make sure all is clear before you head out.

User groups: Hikers, dogs, and horses. Mountain bikes are not allowed. No wheelchair access.

Permits: A free wilderness permit is required to hike here and is available at the trailhead. A federal Northwest Forest pass is also required to park here. The cost is $5 for a day pass or $30 for an annual pass. You can buy a day pass at the trailhead, at ranger stations, from private vendors, or through Nature of the Northwest Information Center.

Maps: For a map of Eagle Cap Wilderness and Wallowa-Whitman National Forest, contact Nature of the Northwest Information Center. For a topographic map, ask the USGS for Mount Moriah.

Directions: From Wallowa, drive about 17 miles west on Highway 82 to mile marker 35. Turn left (south) onto Big Canyon Road and drive 10 miles. Turn left and drive another six miles on Forest Service Road 050 to the end of the road and the trailhead.

Contact: Wallowa-Whitman National Forest, Wallowa Valley Ranger District, 88401 Highway 82, Enterprise, Oregon 97828, 541/426-4978.

16 BOWMAN TRAIL TO CHIMNEY/WOOD LAKES
14.8 mi/1.0–2.0 days

south of Wallowa in Eagle Cap Wilderness of Wallowa-Whitman National Forest

Map 4.3, page 118

This trail is a feast for the senses: For the ears, you have the Lostine River white-water rapids. For the eyes, you have the snowcapped Wallowa Mountains behind you as you hike, which you will want to rest and take a look at here and there on the steep climb. And for the nose, a pine scent fills the air. It's hard to talk about this neck of the woods without lapsing into superlatives. The trailhead starts at 5,200 feet, so take it easy as you start the ascent, which starts gradually but quickly becomes steeper as you climb 2,000 feet in 3.5 miles, when you'll come upon a junction. Turn right for another 1.5 miles, passing Laverty Lakes (or stopping there if you like) to Chimney Lake, a perfect place to stop and rest, with the Wallowa Mountains as the backdrop. It's just a taste of the mountain lakes, though, because in another .5 mile is Hobo Lake, followed by Wood Lake another two miles down.

The total mileage from the trailhead to Wood Lake is 7.4 miles. Return the way you came after drinking in the view, or camp here for the night. The trail also continues past the junction with Chimney Lake to cross alpine meadows to the North Minam River (total trip is 20 miles round-trip). Whichever route you take, you should bring a map and water along for this area, as the many intersecting trails can be confusing (although they tend to be well marked).

User groups: Hikers, dogs, and horses. No mountain bikes are allowed. No wheelchair access.

Permits: A free wilderness permit is required to hike here and is available at the trailhead. A federal Northwest Forest pass is also required to park here. The cost is $5 for a day pass or $30 for an annual pass. You can buy a day pass at the trailhead, at ranger stations, from private vendors, or through Nature of the Northwest Information Center.

Maps: For a map of the Eagle Cap Wilderness and Wallowa-Whitman National Forest, contact Nature of the Northwest Information Center. For a topographic map, ask the USGS for North Minam Meadows.

Directions: From Wallowa, drive 7.6 miles south on Highway 82 to Lostine, and turn right on Lostine River Road (a paved two-lane road). Drive for 14.7 miles (after seven miles it turns into good gravel and dirt road), and park in the well-marked Bowman trailhead parking area to the left. The well-marked trailhead is to your right as you're walking from the parking lot back to the road.

Contact: Wallowa Mountains Visitor Center, Eagle Cap Ranger District, 88401 Highway 82, Enterprise, OR 97828, 541/426-5546.

17 FRANCES LAKE
18.2 mi/1.0–2.0 days

south of Wallowa in Eagle Cap Wilderness of Wallowa-Whitman National Forest

Map 4.3, page 118

If you plan to head to Frances Lake, be warned right off the bat: It's long. It's uphill. It gains

3,300 feet in elevation. And considering you're already starting from 5,200 feet, you will definitely be feeling the altitude (unless you've climbed Everest recently, in which case this will be a breeze). But it's also worth it, with views of the Eagle Cap peaks and Chimney Lake (see listing in this chapter) across the Lostine River canyon, brook trout fishing, and camping spots around the lake. Along the way, look out for deer, elk, black bears, and mountain goats. Although it's do-able in one day, it's a good trail for an overnight backpacking trip, because it would be a long haul back to your car in one day. At the very least, start off first thing in the morning, if you're not planning to camp, to give yourself plenty of time. This trail is maintained, but heavy storms sometimes make it hard to pass by the many felled trees (more so than on other trails). Make sure you check beforehand that all is well before you head out.

User groups: Hikers, dogs, and horses. No mountain bikes are allowed. No wheelchair access.

Permits: A free wilderness permit is required to hike here and is available at the trailhead. A federal Northwest Forest pass is also required to park here. The cost is $5 for a day pass or $30 for an annual pass. You can buy a day pass at the trailhead, at ranger stations, from private vendors, or through Nature of the Northwest Information Center.

Maps: For a map of the Eagle Cap Wilderness and Wallowa-Whitman National Forest, contact Nature of the Northwest Information Center. For a topographic map, ask the USGS for North Minam Meadows and Chief Joseph Mountain.

Directions: From Wallowa, drive 7.6 miles south on Highway 82 to Lostine, and turn right on Lostine River Road (a paved two-lane road). Drive for 14.7 miles (after seven miles it turns into good gravel and dirt road), and park in the well-marked Bowman trailhead parking area to the left. The trail starts to the left as you're walking back from the parking area to the road, crossing a meadow before it hits the true trailhead.

Contact: Wallowa Mountains Visitor Center, Eagle Cap Ranger District, 88401 Highway 82, Enterprise, OR 97828, 541/426-5546.

18 MAXWELL LAKE
8.0 mi/4.5 hrs

south of Wallowa in Eagle Cap Wilderness of Wallowa-Whitman National Forest

Map 4.3, page 118

If you want to check out one of the many Wallowa mountain lakes but don't feel like hauling up a 10-mile trail to get there, you'll like Maxwell Lake. The trail starts out on a gentle switchbacking, but the climb steepens later on (total elevation gain: 2,300 feet). You'll want to keep your head up, because sometimes the trail can be hard to follow after a bad storm before it's been maintained. But you'll want to keep your head up anyway, to let the views sink in. Before you turn on the first switchback, turn around to view the snowcapped Wallowa peaks behind you for the first good photo op. Save some camera film, though, there's more to come. The small lake sits at 7,729 feet, which means more views ahead—and all that for a four-mile price of admission.

User groups: Hikers, dogs, and horses. No mountain bikes are allowed. No wheelchair access.

Permits: A free wilderness permit is required to hike here and is available at the trailhead. A federal Northwest Forest pass is also required to park here. The cost is $5 for a day pass or $30 for an annual pass. You can buy a day pass at the trailhead, at ranger stations, from private vendors, or through Nature of the Northwest Information Center.

Maps: For a map of the Eagle Cap Wilderness and Wallowa-Whitman National Forest, contact Nature of the Northwest Information Center. For a topographic map, ask the USGS for North Minam Meadows.

Directions: From Wallowa, drive 7.6 miles south on Highway 82 to Lostine, and turn right on

Lostine River Road (a paved two-lane road). Drive for 17.4 miles (after seven miles it turns into good gravel and dirt road) to the parking area on the left. The trail starts across the road in Shady Campground.

Contact: Wallowa Mountains Visitor Center, Eagle Cap Ranger District, 88401 Highway 82, Enterprise, OR 97828, 541/426-5546.

19 WEST FORK LOSTINE TO MINAM/BLUE LAKES
14.2 mi/7.5 hrs

south of Wallowa in Eagle Cap Wilderness of Wallowa-Whitman National Forest

Map 4.3, page 118

Blue Lake sits apart from the other Lakes Basin trails, so it doesn't always get the attention it deserves—which is a good thing for hikers craving solitude. Shortly after the trailhead, the trail comes to a well-marked junction. Take the right fork to travel along and over the West Fork Lostine River, heading through the Douglas fir forest for a gentle ascent (total elevation gain is 2,200 feet for the entire 7.1-mile trip). Views of 9,595-foot Eagle Cap and the Lostine Valley get better with every step, and you'll arrive at Minam Lake at 6.1 miles. You can stay here or travel another one mile to Blue Lake, which is the smaller and more remote of the two sister lakes. Camping spots are limited at Blue Lake but more numerous at Minam Lake (and at the trailhead) if you want to stay overnight. As with all the trails in the Lakes Basin area, although the trails tend to be well marked, there are a lot of options for longer loops, so get a map before you set out.

User groups: Hikers, dogs, and horses. No mountain bikes are allowed. No wheelchair access.

Permits: A free wilderness permit is required to hike here and is available at the trailhead. A federal Northwest Forest pass is also required to park here. The cost is $5 for a day pass or $30 for an annual pass. You can buy a day pass at the trailhead, at ranger stations, from private vendors, or through Nature of the Northwest Information Center.

Maps: For a map of the Eagle Cap Wilderness and Wallowa-Whitman National Forest, contact Nature of the Northwest Information Center. For a topographic map, ask the USGS for Steamboat Lake and Eagle Cap.

Directions: From Wallowa, drive 7.6 miles south on Highway 82 to Lostine, and turn right on Lostine River Road (a paved two-lane road). Drive for 18.1 miles (after seven miles it turns into good gravel and dirt road) to the end of the road and the large parking area at Two Pan trailhead. The trail starts at the end of the parking area, to the left of the Two Pan trailhead sign.

Contact: Wallowa Mountains Visitor Center, Eagle Cap Ranger District, 88401 Highway 82, Enterprise, OR 97828, 541/426-5546.

20 EAST LOSTINE RIVER TO MIRROR LAKE
14.6 mi/7.5 hrs

south of Wallowa in Eagle Cap Wilderness of Wallowa-Whitman National Forest

Map 4.3, page 118

One of many access routes to the Lakes Basin area, this one isn't as populated as other trailheads. It does tend to be snowed in later than its surrounding cousins, though, so check to make sure the white stuff is out of there before deciding on this route. The river sounds like a highway, but the only traffic jams here are of the elk, deer, and bears that populate the area. At the marked junction shortly after the trailhead, take the left fork to lead up to short switchbacks through the forest before entering a lush meadow filled with wildflowers and a sneak peek at Eagle Cap itself, standing at a majestic 9,595 feet. There are places to camp at Mirror Lake, along the way, and at the trailhead if you want to stick around (which you will). Pick up a map before you go, because although the trails tend to be well marked in this area, there are plenty of intersecting trails and longer loop possibilities.

User groups: Hikers, dogs, and horses. No mountain bikes are allowed. No wheelchair access.

Permits: A free wilderness permit is required to hike here and is available at the trailhead. A federal Northwest Forest pass is also required to park here. The cost is $5 for a day pass or $30 for an annual pass. You can buy a day pass at the trailhead, at ranger stations, from private vendors, or through Nature of the Northwest Information Center.

Maps: For a map of the Eagle Cap Wilderness and Wallowa-Whitman National Forest, contact Nature of the Northwest Information Center. For a topographic map, ask the USGS for Steamboat Lake and Eagle Cap.

Directions: From Wallowa, drive 7.6 miles south on Highway 82 to Lostine, and turn right on Lostine River Road (a paved two-lane road). Drive for 18.1 miles (after seven miles it turns into good gravel and dirt road) to the end of the road and the large parking area at Two Pan trailhead. The trail starts at the end of the parking area, to the left of the Two Pan trailhead sign.

Contact: Wallowa Mountains Visitor Center, Eagle Cap Ranger District, 88401 Highway 82, Enterprise, OR 97828, 541/426-5546.

21 HURRICANE CREEK TO ECHO LAKE
16.0 mi/2.0 days

south of Enterprise in Eagle Cap Wilderness of Wallowa-Whitman National Forest

Map 4.3, page 118

A popular access trail to the Lakes Basin area, the crowds thin out as you head up to Echo Lake, and there's a reason for that: It's a steep, rocky, and sometimes unmaintained climb up to the lake. Start off early if you plan to make this a day hike; if you want to stay overnight, there are plenty of places to camp along the trail and at the lake. After five miles, you come to the junction with Echo Lake Trail and then climb another 2,400 feet in three miles. While you're walking along the creek, you'll have

views of the two highest peaks in the Eagle Cap Wilderness to your left across the valley: 9,839-foot Sacajawea and 9,832-foot Matterhorn peaks, followed by the 9,595-foot Eagle Cap. Although the trail tends to be free of snow earlier than others in the area, it's a flash flood area, and mountain runoff makes some creeks uncrossable, so it's best to hit this later in the season or at least check ahead before you head out.

User groups: Hikers, dogs, and horses. No mountain bikes are allowed. No wheelchair access.

Permits: A free wilderness permit is required to hike here and is available at the trailhead. A federal Northwest Forest pass is also required to park here. The cost is $5 for a day pass or $30 for an annual pass. You can buy a day pass at the trailhead, at ranger stations, from private vendors, or through Nature of the Northwest Information Center.

Maps: For a map of the Eagle Cap Wilderness and Wallowa-Whitman National Forest, contact Nature of the Northwest Information Center. For a topographic map, ask the USGS for Chief Joseph Mountain and Eagle Cap.

Directions: From Enterprise, drive south on Hurricane Creek Road for 8.8 miles (it's a paved two-lane road for the first five miles, then turns into a gravel road for 1.5 miles, then a one-lane paved road). Park at the entrance to Hurricane Creek trailhead and the parking area. The well-marked trail is to the left of the parking lot as you're driving in from the road.

Contact: Wallowa Mountains Visitor Center, Eagle Cap Ranger District, 88401 Highway 82, Enterprise, OR 97828, 541/426-5546.

22 ICE LAKE
15.8 mi/9.0 hrs

south of Joseph in Eagle Cap Wilderness of Wallowa-Whitman National Forest

Map 4.3, page 118

Starting from the popular West Fork Wallowa trailhead to the high alpine lake, the trail is a long but beautiful climb up. After 2.8 miles, the trail forks to the left to start Ice Lake Trail. It's another 5.1 miles up to Ice Lake, with views of the Matterhorn and surrounding 9,000-foot Wallowa peaks, plus the wildflower meadows and of course Ice Lake itself, sitting pretty at a cool 7,920 feet. You can also hit the Matterhorn summit from here if you're really aching for adventure (but get a detailed map before you go, because it's not as heavily used as the lower trails). Before you get all hot and bothered around the collar and decide to jump in, remember two things: As with all trails in this scenic area, the area can be crowded, especially on holiday weekends. It's also at high altitude, so you should expect snow at least through June (check ahead to make sure trails are clear). For both of those reasons, shoot for later in the season, preferably midweek (yeah, yeah, the job gets in the way, I know).

User groups: Hikers, dogs, and horses. No mountain bikes are allowed. No wheelchair access.

Permits: A free wilderness permit is required to hike here, available at the trailhead. Parking and access are free.

Maps: For a map of the Eagle Cap Wilderness and Wallowa-Whitman National Forest, contact Nature of the Northwest Information Center. For a topographic map, ask the USGS for Joseph, Aneroid Lake, and Eagle Cap.

Directions: From Enterprise, drive 12.4 miles south on Highway 82 to Wallowa Lake State Park. Continue past Wallowa Lake and head straight (passing the campground entrance sign to the right) to the end of the road. Park at the parking area on the right side of the road, and walk across the street to the trailhead, forking to the right after the trailhead sign.

Contact: Wallowa Mountains Visitor Center, Eagle Cap Ranger District, 88401 Highway 82, Enterprise, OR 97828, 541/426-5546.

23 LAKES BASIN LOOP
22.7 mi/2.0 days

south of Joseph in Eagle Cap Wilderness of Wallowa-Whitman National Forest

Map 4.3, page 118

Welcome to the ultimate experience. The Lakes Basin is one of the most popular destinations in the state, where people flock to hit the high alpine lakes surrounded by snowcapped peaks, where you can see why the Wallowa Mountains are often referred to as the Alps of Oregon. The trail can be packed at the start, where horseback riders and hikers from the nearby campground hit the trailhead for shorter hikes. Only the true adventure-seekers make it to the top, though (and a surprising amount actually do just that). The trail starts out along the West Fork Wallowa River, up through the valley meadows, climbing almost 4,000 feet, where an 11-mile loop starts around the alpine lakes with backdrops of 9,000-plus-foot Eagle Cap, Sentinel Peak, East Peak (and the list goes on), and plenty of camping spots along the way. Keeping in mind that this area is often snowed in through June, so check ahead to make sure the trails are snow-free. The Lakes Basin is also accessible from Hurricane Creek and the East Fork Lostine River (see listings in this chapter), and shorter loop possibilities are endless. Or at least they seem that way.

User groups: Hikers, dogs, and horses. No mountain bikes are allowed. No wheelchair access.

Permits: A free wilderness permit is required to hike here and is available at the trailhead. Parking and access are free.

Maps: For a map of the Eagle Cap Wilderness and Wallowa-Whitman National Forest, contact Nature of the Northwest Information Center. For a topographic map, ask the USGS for Joseph, Aneroid Lake, and Eagle Cap.

Directions: From Enterprise, drive 12.4 miles south on Highway 82 to Wallowa Lake State Park. Continue past Wallowa Lake and head straight (passing the campground entrance sign to the right) to the end of the road. Park at the parking area on the right side of the road, and walk across the street to the trailhead, forking to the right after the trailhead sign.

Contact: Wallowa Mountains Visitor Center, Eagle Cap Ranger District, 88401 Highway 82, Enterprise, OR 97828, 541/426-5546.

24 HAWKINS PASS
24.0 mi/2.0 days

south of Joseph in Eagle Cap Wilderness of Wallowa-Whitman National Forest

Map 4.3, page 118

The Lakes Basin is a popular area, and one way to go right through it without passing Go is to follow the West Fork Wallowa River right to its end, 8,330-foot Hawkins Pass. Of course, in order to get there you need to invest a healthy climb of 4,685 feet. But no need to do it all in one swoop—you have a good 12 miles to get there. Climbing up the West Fork Wallowa River, you'll pass the Lakes Basin in all its wildflower-meadow and alpine-lake glory; continue straight when the loop forks to the right, passing scenic Frazier Lake before climbing straight up to Hawkins Pass. Camping spots abound in this area, but realize that it can get a smidge crowded, especially on a holiday weekend. Also, you should always check ahead to make sure these high-altitude trails are snow-free, as they can be blocked through June.

User groups: Hikers, dogs, and horses. No mountain bikes are allowed. No wheelchair access.

Permits: A free wilderness permit is required to hike here and is available at the trailhead. Parking and access are free.

Maps: For a map of the Eagle Cap Wilderness and Wallowa-Whitman National Forest, contact Nature of the Northwest Information Center. For a topographic map, ask the USGS for Joseph, Aneroid Lake, and Eagle Cap.

Directions: From Enterprise, drive 12.4 miles south on Highway 82 to Wallowa Lake State Park. Continue past Wallowa Lake and head straight (passing the campground entrance sign to the right) to the end of the road. Park at

the parking area on the right side of the road, and walk across the street to the trailhead, forking to the right after the trailhead sign.

Contact: Wallowa Mountains Visitor Center, Eagle Cap Ranger District, 88401 Highway 82, Enterprise, OR 97828, 541/426-5546.

25 EAST FORK WALLOWA
14.0 mi/8.0 hrs

south of Joseph in Eagle Cap Wilderness of Wallowa-Whitman National Forest

Map 4.3, page 118

Popular and right off Wallowa Lake, this trail is shared by hikers and horses at the start (watch your step), not to mention the buzzing of a hydroelectric plant. Be patient, because soon you'll leave the ruckus behind and start your ascent. After the trailhead sign, fork left to head up the East Fork Wallowa, which flows along the entire route. You'll pass through wildflower meadows with views of the 9,000-plus-foot Wallowa peaks as you climb up the nearly 4,000 feet to Tenderfoot Pass, where the trail ends. Aneroid Lake, sitting in the basin surrounded by the high alpine peaks, is six miles from the trailhead, where you can camp for the night if you want to make it an overnight trip. But first, continue past the lakes to 8,500-foot Tenderfoot Pass and the trail's end for even better views from above. Like many of this area's trails, there are plenty of loop options here, and the trails tend to be well marked; get a map to explore your options in this cool area. Also, the trails can be snowbound through June, so check ahead to make sure the paths are snow-free.

User groups: Hikers, dogs, and horses. No mountain bikes are allowed. No wheelchair access.

Permits: A free wilderness permit is required to hike here, available at the trailhead. Parking and access are free.

Maps: For a map of the Eagle Cap Wilderness and Wallowa-Whitman National Forest, contact Nature of the Northwest Information Center. For a topographic map, ask the USGS for Joseph and Aneroid Mountain.

Directions: From Enterprise, drive 12.4 miles south on Highway 82 to Wallowa Lake State Park. Continue past Wallowa Lake and head straight (passing the campground entrance sign to the right) to the end of the road. Park at the parking area on the right side of the road, and walk across the street to the trailhead, forking to the left after the trailhead sign.

Contact: Wallowa Mountains Visitor Center, Eagle Cap Ranger District, 88401 Highway 82, Enterprise, OR 97828, 541/426-5546.

26 EAGLE CREEK TO DIAMOND LAKE
18.0 mi/2.0 days

northeast of Baker City in Eagle Cap Wilderness of Wallowa-Whitman National Forest

Map 4.3, page 118

Following West Fork Eagle Creek for the first couple of miles, the trail gets off to a slow start and holds no hint of the good things to come. Horses share the trail for the first portion, so it can be dusty and muddy in parts as you pass by an open meadow. Creek crossings can be difficult when the runoff is high, so you should probably plan to hit this one later in the season. Just when you started to get the hang of things, the trail changes gears on you, climbing up switchbacks almost 2,000 feet. The trail forks to the left before hitting Echo Lake (see following listing), when you'll turn left and head straight up to higher ground, climbing about 3,000 feet in elevation when all is said and done. You'll probably have the alpine lake all to yourself, as most people visiting the area head to the Lakes Basin area.

User groups: Hikers, dogs, and horses. No mountain bikes are allowed. No wheelchair access.

Permits: A federal Northwest Forest pass is required to park here. The cost is $5 for a day pass or $30 for an annual pass. You can buy a day pass at the trailhead, at ranger stations, from private vendors, or through Nature of the Northwest Information Center.

Maps: For a map of the Eagle Cap Wilderness and Wallowa-Whitman National Forest, contact Nature of the Northwest Information Center. For a topographic map, ask the USGS for Steamboat Lake and Bennet Peak.

Directions: From Medical Springs, drive 1.6 miles south on Forest Service Road 70. Turn left onto Forest Service Road 67 and drive 13.9 miles to Forest Service Road 77. Turn left and continue 5.1 miles to Forest Service Road 77-500. Turn right, and the trailhead and parking area are on the left. Note: The last few miles of this are rough but passable road.

Contact: Wallowa Mountains Visitor Center, Eagle Cap Ranger District, 88401 Highway 82, Enterprise, OR 97828, 541/426-5546.

27 EAGLE CREEK TO ECHO/TRAVERSE LAKE
13.0 mi/7.0 hrs

northeast of Baker City in Eagle Cap Wilderness of Wallowa-Whitman National Forest

Map 4.3, page 118

Traveling along West Fork Eagle Creek, this trail starts off with several stream crossings that can be tricky in the early summer, so it's best to visit when the runoff has calmed down. The trail starts off on a dusty and often muddy path (you can thank the horses for that) crossing through an open meadow—watch for deer, at least when the horses aren't around—before starting the switchback routine. It's five uphill miles to Echo Lake, which sits at 7,220 feet, where you can camp for the night or continue another 1.5 miles to Traverse Lake. Either way, you'll be likely to have the digs to yourself, as the crowds tend to descend upon the nearby Lakes Basin area. This trail also accesses Diamond Lake (see Eagle Creek to Diamond Lake listing in this chapter) at a junction before you reach Echo Lake. Total elevation gain is about 3,000 feet, and the fact that the trailhead already starts at 5,451 feet means you'll be feeling every step of the way.

User groups: Hikers, dogs, and horses. No

mountain bikes are allowed. No wheelchair access.

Permits: A federal Northwest Forest pass is required to park here. The cost is $5 for a day pass or $30 for an annual pass. You can buy a day pass at the trailhead, at ranger stations, from private vendors, or through Nature of the Northwest Information Center.

Maps: For a map of the Eagle Cap Wilderness and Wallowa-Whitman National Forest, contact Nature of the Northwest Information Center. For a topographic map, ask the USGS for Bennet Peak.

Directions: From Medical Springs, drive 1.6 miles south on Forest Service Road 70. Turn left onto Forest Service Road 67 and drive 13.9 miles to Forest Service Road 77. Turn left and continue 5.1 miles to Forest Service Road 77–500. Turn right, and the trailhead and parking area are on the left. Note: The last few miles of this are rough but passable.

Contact: Wallowa Mountains Visitor Center, Eagle Cap Ranger District, 88401 Highway 82, Enterprise, OR 97828, 541/426-5546.

28 EAGLE LAKE
14.0 mi/7.0 hrs

northeast of Baker City in Eagle Cap Wilderness of Wallowa-Whitman National Forest

Map 4.3, page 118

Starting on a sandy trail shared by horses, Main Eagle Trail eases you into things by starting out flat so you can warm up before climbing almost 2,500 feet to Eagle Lake. It travels along Eagle Creek for its entire length, through meadows and across footbridges, to reach a trail junction at 5.8 miles. Turn right to continue just over a mile to the lake. Trail junctions tend to be well marked in this area, but as there are so many intersecting trails (such as Lookingglass Lake Trail, covered in this chapter, which shares the first four miles with Eagle Lake), it's a good idea to bring along a map. While you're at it, bring along your camera, because the 9,000-plus-foot tall Wallowas reign supreme

in this area, always mugging for the camera. You can camp along the trail and at the lake if you want to make this an overnight stop.

User groups: Hikers, dogs, and horses. No mountain bikes are allowed. No wheelchair access.

Permits: A federal Northwest Forest pass is required to park here. The cost is $5 for a day pass or $30 for an annual pass. You can buy a day pass at the trailhead, at ranger stations, from private vendors, or through Nature of the Northwest Information Center.

Maps: For a map of the Eagle Cap Wilderness and Wallowa-Whitman National Forest, contact Nature of the Northwest Information Center. For a topographic map, ask the USGS for Bennet Peak and Krag Peak.

Directions: From Medical Springs, drive 1.6 miles south on Forest Service Road 70. Turn left onto Forest Service Road 67 and drive 13.9 miles to Forest Service Road 77. Turn left, continue .7 miles, and keep straight to continue onto Forest Service Road 7755. Drive 3.6 miles to the road's end and the trailhead.

Contact: Wallowa Mountains Visitor Center, Eagle Cap Ranger District, 88401 Highway 82, Enterprise, OR 97828, 541/426-5546.

29 LOOKINGGLASS LAKE
14.0 mi/7.0 hrs

northeast of Baker City in Eagle Cap Wilderness of Wallowa-Whitman National Forest

Map 4.3, page 118

Starting off as a hot, sandy path, the trail soon heads into the cool confines of Eagle Creek. It's a gentle path that will give you energy to enjoy the scenery of waterfalls and meadows before the real climbing begins. At 4.1 miles, you'll reach a junction with Lookingglass Lake Trail. Take a right here to travel almost three miles to the lake, where you'll see that it's called Lookingglass because of the constant view it enjoys (okay, I just made that up, but still). This area is crawling with hot campsites, so you can make it an overnight trip if you want, and you'll probably have it all to yourself because it's not as highly traveled as other parts of this scenic area. This trail shares the first four miles with Eagle Lake Trail (see listing in this chapter).

User groups: Hikers, dogs, and horses. No mountain bikes are allowed. No wheelchair access.

Permits: A federal Northwest Forest pass is required to park here. The cost is $5 for a day pass or $30 for an annual pass. You can buy a day pass at the trailhead, at ranger stations, from private vendors, or through Nature of the Northwest Information Center.

Maps: For a map of the Eagle Cap Wilderness and Wallowa-Whitman National Forest, contact Nature of the Northwest Information Center. For a topographic map, ask the USGS for Bennet Peak and Krag Peak.

Directions: From Medical Springs, drive 1.6 miles south on Forest Service Road 70. Turn left onto Forest Service Road 67, and drive 13.9 miles to Forest Service Road 77. Turn left, continue .7 mile, and keep straight to continue onto Forest Service Road 7755. Drive 3.6 miles to the road's end and the trailhead.

Contact: Wallowa Mountains Visitor Center, Eagle Cap Ranger District, 88401 Highway 82, Enterprise, OR 97828, 541/426-5546.

30 SOUTH FORK IMNAHA
34.6 mi/3.0 days

north of Richland in Eagle Cap Wilderness of Wallowa-Whitman National Forest

Map 4.3, page 118

The mileage may look daunting at first glance, but you don't need to travel far to reach great views, and then you can turn around where you started. Following the South Fork Imnaha River, the easy path starts off as a wide, dusty, flat trail. If a scenic and flat trip is what you're after, you can head just two miles in to Blue Hole, where the river shoots through the rocky gorge. If a strenuous backpacking trip is what you're after, keep on going, because the trail gets steeper at the end, gaining 4,000 feet in elevation up to 8,330-foot Hawkins Pass,

in the Lakes Basin. Camp here for views of the 9,000-plus-foot Wallowa peaks.

User groups: Hikers, dogs, and horses. No mountain bikes are allowed. No wheelchair access.

Permits: A federal Northwest Forest pass is required to park here. The cost is $5 for a day pass or $30 for an annual pass. You can buy a day pass at ranger stations, from private vendors, or through Nature of the Northwest Information Center.

Maps: For a map of the Eagle Cap Wilderness and Wallowa-Whitman National Forest, contact Nature of the Northwest Information Center. For a topographic map, ask the USGS for Deadman Point, Cornucopia, Krag Peak, Eagle Cap, and Aneroid Mountain.

Directions: From Richland, drive east on Highway 86 to the junction with Wallowa Mountain Loop Road/Forest Service Road 39. Turn left and drive 23.1 miles, then turn left on Imnaha River Road/Forest Service Road 3960. Drive 8.6 miles to the road's end and the trailhead (the road turns to gravel for last .2 mile, but otherwise, the whole route is paved).

Contact: Wallowa Mountains Visitor Center, Eagle Cap Ranger District, 88401 Highway 82, Enterprise, OR 97828, 541/426-5546.

31 SADDLE CREEK TO FREEZEOUT SADDLE/SNAKE RIVER
4.0–22.0 mi/ 2.5 hrs–2.0 days

east of Joseph in Hells Canyon National Recreation Area of Wallowa-Whitman National Forest

Map 4.4, page 119

This is the trail of many names and many routes. Saddle Creek Trail leads two miles up to Freezeout Saddle via a grassy mountain, where you can see the switchbacks ahead and behind you (remember to keep looking behind you for the views down, because you quickly gain 3,000 feet in elevation). Reaching a rock cairn marking the saddle, the trail then continues another nine miles to Snake River. If you're turning back here, cross the summit ridge (turning right) for some even better views of the Hells Canyon gorges and Wallowa peaks. No offense to trees, but there's something to be said for crisscrossing up a treeless domain, because, well, there's nothing to get in the way of the glorious views. From the saddle, the trail also continues straight for nine miles, plunging a healthy 5,000 feet to Snake River, so you can also extend this trip into a two-day affair and camp at the river. And then we come to option number three, taking the high road (or trail as the case may be): Continuing on Saddle Creek Trail after reaching the summit, you'll come across the High Trail junction after another two miles, which is a daunting 36.6 miles one-way, with views of the spectacular canyon and Seven Devil's peaks across the border in Idaho. The fourth and final option is to continue across the ridgeline to do a loop back to the right fork at the trailhead, but it's not recommended, because the trail can be sparse at times; if you choose this route, you should have your bearings. Whatever route you take will be lined with views the entire time in this sparse area, so you can't go wrong.

User groups: Hikers, dogs, and horses. No mountain bikes are allowed. No wheelchair access.

Permits: A federal Northwest Forest pass is required to park here. The cost is $5 for a day pass or $30 for an annual pass. You can buy a day pass at ranger stations, from private vendors, or through Nature of the Northwest Information Center.

Maps: For a map of the Hells Canyon National Recreation Area and Wallowa-Whitman National Forest, contact Nature of the Northwest Information Center. For a topographic map, ask the USGS for Sheep Creek Divide, Hat Point, and Old Timer Mountain.

Directions: From Joseph, drive 40 miles east on Highway 350 to Imnaha. Turn south on Imnaha River Road/County Road 727 and drive 12.5 miles to Forest Service Road 4230.

Turn left and drive 2.7 miles to the end of the road and the trailhead.

Contact: Wallowa Mountains Visitor Center, Hells Canyon National Recreation Center, 88401 Highway 82, Enterprise, OR 97828, 541/426-5546.

32 STUD CREEK
2.0 mi/1.5 hrs

along the Snake River in Hells Canyon National Recreation Area in Wallowa-Whitman National Forest

Map 4.4, page 119

Many trails in the Hells Canyon area seem to go on forever, but you don't need to spend an entire day to explore America's deepest canyon: This trail is short and sweet (although rather rocky), traveling along the Snake River for two miles to a pebble beach. It starts near the Hells Canyon Visitors Center and the dam itself, which offers guided tours and is a popular launching point for white-water rafting trips. (One cool thing about the dam is you can only reach it via the Idaho side, so you get to slip into another state for a beautiful drive in.) Though the area is hot, you should absolutely, positively wear long pants, because if the desert brush doesn't kill you, the poison oak that cloaks the area sure will. The trail travels along a rocky cliff for views that will make you want to throw yourself over said cliff if you didn't bring along a camera. Once you've hit the rocky beach, turn back the way you came and spend some time at the visitors center, getting to know your canyon. Hey, you just trekked through its lovely territory, you owe it a favor.

User groups: Hikers, dogs, and horses. No mountain bikes are allowed. No wheelchair access.

Permits: Permits are not required. Parking and access are free.

Maps: For a map of the Hells Canyon National Recreation Center and Wallowa-Whitman National Forest, contact Nature of the Northwest Information Center. For a topographic map, ask the USGS for Squirrel Prairie.

Directions: From Richland, drive 30 miles east on Highway 86 to Copperfield. Drive across the Snake River Bridge to Idaho and turn left (north) onto Forest Service Road 454. Drive 21.9 miles to Hells Canyon Dam. Turn left and cross the dam into Oregon, and turn right (north). Drive .9 mile to the visitors center parking. The trailhead starts just west of the boat ramp.

Contact: Wallowa Mountains Visitor Center, Hells Canyon National Recreation Center, 88401 Highway 82, Enterprise, OR 97828, 541/426-5546.

33 HELLS CANYON RESERVOIR
9.6 mi/9.5 hrs

north of Copperfield in Hells Canyon National Recreation Area of Wallowa-Whitman National Forest

Map 4.4, page 119

Scooting along the Snake River (which, incidentally, is aptly named—look out for rattlers), this trail is a walk on the wild side. First off the bat, you need to find the trail, which is across a small rock field at the parking lot. Then you need to skirt some nasty poison oak that thrives here, so bring long pants. Finally, you have to do all of that and soak in the scenery of the purple-hued rocks and wild sunflowers and the deep gorge, viewing Idaho's fine contribution to Hells Canyon across the white-water river. Although trails tend to be well marked in this area, and the trail is rather straightforward (along the river, followed by along the river), the path is overgrown toward the end and may be a little faint because it's lightly used, so turn back when the trail ends.

User groups: Hikers, dogs, and horses. No mountain bikes are allowed. No wheelchair access.

Permits: Permits are not required. Parking and access are free.

Maps: For a map of the Hells Canyon National Recreation Area and Wallowa-Whitman National Forest, contact Nature of the North-

west Information Center. For a topographic map, ask the USGS for Homestead.

Directions: From Richland, drive 30 miles east on Highway 86 to Copperfield. Turn left (north) on Homestead Road and drive 9.1 miles to the road's end and the parking area. Note: The trailhead is tricky to find. It starts to the north of the road's end, across a small rock field.

Contact: Wallowa Mountains Visitor Center, Hells Canyon National Recreation Center, 88401 Highway 82, Enterprise, OR 97828, 541/426-5546.

34 STEIN'S PILLAR
4.0 mi/2.0 hrs

northeast of Prineville in Mill Creek Wilderness of Ochoco National Forest

Map 4.5, page 120

Poor Stein's doesn't have a twin pillar to keep it company, unlike its neighbor Twin Pillars, but then again, it doesn't have to share all the attention, which it basks in quite a bit, as it's a popular destination. The trail starts off as a hot and dusty route, with the smell of juniper to keep you company, and slips in and out of desert terrain and cool forest for a change of pace at almost every step. A viewpoint of the spindly and rather slender pillar arrives shortly before the end of the trail, where you can stop here or continue on for a rocky scramble to bring you face to face with the 200-foot red rock pillar. It's just one of many attractions in the unique and rugged Ochoco Mountains and is worth the quick trip in to see it.

User groups: Hikers, dogs, and horses. No mountain bikes are allowed. No wheelchair access.

Permits: Permits are not required. Parking and access are free.

Maps: For a map of Ochoco National Forest, contact Nature of the Northwest Information Center. For a topographic map, ask the USGS for Stein's Pillar.

Directions: From Prineville, drive nine miles east on U.S. 26 to Mill Creek Road/Forest Service Road 33 and turn left (north). Drive

6.7 miles and turn right over a bridge to Forest Service Road 3300-500. Drive two miles (exactly, check your odometer) to the unmarked gravel parking circle, on the left. It can be tricky to find—if you miss it, you'll soon come to the end of the road. The trailhead is on far end (east side) of the pullout.

Contact: Ochoco National Forest, P.O. Box 490, Prineville, OR 97754, 541/416-6500.

35 TWIN PILLARS
11.0 mi/6.0 hrs

northeast of Prineville in Mill Creek Wilderness of Ochoco National Forest

Map 4.5, page 120

Jutting 200 sheer cliff feet in the air, the Twin Pillars are a sight to see, and it's even better when you can hike to visit them, so you can enjoy the view as you rest from the nearly 2,000-foot climb. The trail starts off relatively easy for the first mile but then shifts into high gear as you climb to views of the Mill Creek Valley. Several stream crossings may be dicey in the spring, so check ahead to make sure all is well in the area before setting off.

User groups: Hikers, dogs, and horses. No mountain bikes are allowed. No wheelchair access.

Permits: Permits are not required. Parking and access are free.

Maps: For a map of Ochoco National Forest, contact Nature of the Northwest Information Center. For a topographic map, ask the USGS for Stein's Pillar.

Directions: From Prineville, drive nine miles east on U.S. 26 to Mill Creek Road/Forest Service Road 33. Turn left (north) and drive 10.7 miles to the Wildcat Campground parking area on the right. The trail begins on the north side of the parking area, just to the left of the trailhead sign.

Contact: Ochoco National Forest, P.O. Box 490, Prineville, OR 97754, 541/416-6500.

36 JOHN DAY PAINTED HILLS
2.5 mi/1.5 hrs

in John Day Fossil Beds National Monument west of Mitchell off Highway 26

Map 4.5, page 120

If you really want to feel like a spring chicken, take a stroll through the Painted Hills trails, which have you beat by a good 39 million years (give or take). Four mini-trails lead through this area. Even if you snored through geology class, you can't help but be fascinated by the colorful hills, whose hues constantly change depending on the time of day and weather. Plants steer clear of the hills because of their poor nutrient makeup, which leaves the hills bald and beautiful, perfect for your viewing pleasure. The first trail is 1.5-mile Carroll Rim Trail, a gentle climb to a viewing bench. Next up is Painted Hills Overlook Trail, lined with benches and another vantage point of the colorful hills. The highlight of the trip is coming up, the .25-mile loop through Painted Cove, where you can actually walk on a footbridge right through the red hill, lined with interpretive signs to fill your head with all the geology facts to dazzle your friends with over dinner. The last stop is the .25-mile Leaf Fossil Loop, which may not be visually interesting upon first glance until you notice the fossils on display at the trailhead and the fossils littering the hill (respect the fossils—they are your elders, remember—and don't pick one up). So, let's recap: Climb to two viewpoints to get a feel for the situation, loop around and through a brilliant rust-colored hill, and then take a peek at some fossil collections. You won't exactly get a workout on these hikes, but it's a perfect place to bring kids if they're starting to yawn through their science classes. This place can be packed with families from all over on a sunny day.

User groups: Hikers and dogs (remember to keep them leashed). No mountain bikes or horses are allowed. No wheelchair access.

Permits: Permits are not required. Parking and access are free.

Maps: A free trail brochure is available at the Painted Hills Overlook trailhead. For a topographic map, ask the USGS for Painted Hills.
Directions: From Mitchell, drive three miles west on U.S. 26 (about 50 miles east of Prineville) and turn north on Burnt Ranch Road. Drive 5.6 miles, then turn left on Bear Creek Road and drive 1.1 miles. To reach Painted Hills Overlook Trail, turn left to the large parking lot and well-marked trailhead on the west side of the lot. Carroll Rim Trail starts across the street from the parking lot. To reach Painted Cove Trail, continue down Bear Creek Road for another .6 mile, turn right at the fork, and drive .4 mile to the well-marked trailhead and parking area to the left. To reach Leaf Hill Fossil Loop, backtrack to Bear Creek Road, and turn right at the fork for one mile. The well-marked trailhead and parking area are on the right.
Contact: John Day Fossil Beds National Monument, 32651 Highway 19, Kimberly, OR 97848, 541/987-2333.

37 LOOKOUT MOUNTAIN
16.0 mi/8.0 hrs

east of Prineville in Ochoco National Forest

Map 4.5, page 120

With a name like Lookout, it better be good, right? Well, it is, in more than one way. First, it's a good sweat-inducing climb of nearly 3,000 feet before reaching the 6,900-foot summit, where you'll encounter the second good thing: the view of the Cascade Range. Along the way, don't get so bogged down with the climb that you miss out on the wildflower meadows and the four-footed locals, like deer and elk. Remember to bring water and sunscreen, as it can get scorching in this area.
User groups: Hikers, dogs, mountain bikes, and horses. No wheelchair access.
Permits: Permits are not required. Parking and access are free.
Maps: For a map of Ochoco National Forest, contact Nature of the Northwest Information

Center. For a topographic map, ask the USGS for Ochoco Butte and Lookout Mountain.
Directions: From Prineville, drive east on U.S. 26 for 16 miles, and fork right onto Forest Service Road 22. Drive eight miles, and park in the small pullout to the right (just past the Ochoco ranger station, on your left).
Contact: Ochoco National Forest, P.O. Box 490, Prineville, OR 97754, 541/416-6500.

38 FLOOD OF FIRE/ STORY IN STONE
1.0 mi/0.5 hr

northwest of Dayville in the John Day Fossil Beds National Monument

Map 4.6, page 121

Talk about your identity crisis: The John Day Valley has seen it all in its years, playing host to a subtropical forest, massive lava flows, and hardwood forests—not to mention the locals (including rhinos, camel, and early elephants) trampling through its delicate earth. After all that prehistoric rolling with the punches, it's come out on the flip side to reveal dramatic red and white cliffs against gray valley walls, and you can walk right through them (just don't trample the earth like those inconsiderate rhinos used to). The .25-mile Flood of Fire Trail extends to cliffside views of the John Day River, while the Story in Stone Trail's .25 mile offers up a touch exhibit with replica fossils. Though the area is a magnet for tourists, who flock from all over to visit, even native Oregonians—or those who never thought they would get excited about a couple of fossils—will be gawking at this sight (just don't embarrass yourself; keep your mouth firmly shut at all times). Blue Basin and Island of Time Trails (see listings in this chapter) are nearby, so you can stick around for the day to get the full picture—and more pictures.
User groups: Hikers and dogs (remember to keep them leashed). No mountain bikes or horses are allowed. No wheelchair access.
Permits: Permits are not required. Parking and access are free.

Maps: Trail brochures are available at the trailhead. For a topographic map, ask the USGS for Mount Misery.

Directions: From Dayville, drive five miles west on U.S. 26 to Highway 19. Turn right (north) and drive 12.5 miles to the "John Day Fossil Beds National Monument" sign (passing the first sign). Turn right and drive a short distance to the parking area and both trailheads.

Contact: John Day Fossil Beds National Monument, 32651 Highway 19, Kimberly, OR 97848, 541/987-2333.

39 BLUE BASIN OVERLOOK/ ISLAND OF TIME
4.0 mi/2.0 hrs

northwest of Dayville in the John Day Fossil Beds National Monument

Map 4.6, page 121

Who needs South Dakota when we have the Badlands of Oregon right in our backyard? Colorful cliffs of blue, green, red, and white line this dramatic valley, and you can see it all on these relatively short trails. Get ready for an information overload, because everything you ever wanted to know about the area is available at the trail signs. A somewhat steep climb starts off the three-mile Blue Basin Overlook loop, where you can check out the multilayered cliffs and examine the fossil beds (just remember to keep your grubby paws off of them). After you've looped back, climb up the .5-mile Island of Time, which jets out to beat Overlook Trail at its game, peering over the middle of the trail. The John Day Fossil Beds area is a plethora of geology lessons, and even the most jaded will find themselves in awe. Bring a camera, because even if you've never felt compelled to snap a shot, you will here. Also bring water, because the area is hot and dry. These trails are near Flood of Fire and Story in Stone Trails (see listings in this chapter); don't go away until you've tried them all, because you'll want as many different perspectives on this unique area as possible.

User groups: Hikers and dogs (remember to keep them leashed). No mountain bikes or horses are allowed. No wheelchair access.

Permits: Permits are not required. Parking and access are free.

Maps: Trail brochures are available at the trailhead. For a topographic map, ask the USGS for Picture Gorge West.

Directions: From Dayville, drive five miles west on U.S. 26 to Highway 19. Turn right (north) and drive six miles to the "John Day Fossil Beds National Monument" sign. Turn right and drive a short distance to the parking area and both trailheads.

Contact: John Day Fossil Beds National Monument, 32651 Highway 19, Kimberly, OR 97848, 541/987-2333.

40 BLACK CANYON
25.0 mi/2.0 days

south of Highway 26 in the Black Canyon Wilderness of Ochoco National Forest

Map 4.6, page 121

Snaking for 14.5 miles through the Black Canyon Wilderness, Black Canyon Trail is wilderness at its best—which often means dealing with the elements. In this case, the elements include a grand total of 12 creek crossings, so come prepared. Just getting into the wilderness can be tricky: You'll need to cross the John Day River to start on the trail, and you may find other area trails are not well marked or maintained, or the road in is rough. Here's the best access route: Start from Boeing Field Trail, which plops you .5 mile into the canyon roughly two miles from the trailhead and lets you explore the 6,000-foot canyon cliffs and the wildlife of this remote area, including elk, black bears, cougars, and deer. Watch out for rattlesnakes. If you're not up for the full length of the trail, or if the creek crossings are getting to you, there are plenty of spots to camp for the night, or you can turn around and make it as long or as short of a hike as you want. A bonus about the tricky entrances is that you're bound to have it all to yourself, so you may want to plan for an overnight trip while you're there.

User groups: Hikers, dogs, and horses. No mountain bikes are allowed. No wheelchair access.

Permits: Permits are not required. Parking and access are free.

Maps: For a map of Ochoco National Forest, contact Nature of the Northwest Information Center. For a topographic map, ask the USGS for Wolf Mountain and Aldrich Gulch.

Directions: From John Day, drive about 40 miles west on U.S. 26 to Forest Service Road 12. Turn left and drive 19 miles (the first 6.9 are paved) and turn left on Forest Service Road 38. After 8.3 miles, turn right onto Forest Service Road 5810. The Boeing Field trailhead is one mile down on the left side, starting in a meadow. Park at the side of the road.

Contact: Ochoco National Forest, Paulina Ranger District, 7803 Beaver Creek Road, Paulina, OR 97751, 541/477-6900.

41 MYRTLE CREEK
15.8 mi/8.0 hrs

north of Burns in Malheur National Forest

Map 4.6, page 121

Following its namesake, this 7.9-mile trail through ponderosa pine forest is relatively gentle, climbing less than 1,000 feet along its course. Why the higher rating for difficulty, you ask? Because it's not exactly a snap to find, and light use in the area makes for light trails in spots. If you do venture out, make sure to bring along a map of the area, because side trails do take off from here, and the markings aren't always in place. Even the Forest Service signs are sometimes missing. But you're guaranteed some peace and quiet, and if you want an adventure, Myrtle is your ticket.

User groups: Hikers, dogs, mountain bikes, and horses. No wheelchair access.

Permits: Permits are not required. Parking and access are free.

Maps: For a map of Malheur National Forest, contact Nature of the Northwest Infor-

mation Center. For a topographic map, ask the USGS for Myrtle Park Meadows.

Directions: From Burns, drive 17.9 miles north on U.S. 395 to the unmarked junction with Forest Service Road 31 (just north of Devine Summit). Turn left (west) and drive 13.1 miles to Forest Service Road 3100-226. Turn left and drive to the road's end and the trailhead.

Contact: Malheur National Forest, Emigrant Creek Ranger District, 265 Highway 20 South, Hines, OR 97738, 541/573-4300.

42 SOUTH WINOM TRAIL
8.0 mi/4.0 hrs

southeast of Ukiah in the North Fork John Day Wilderness of Umatilla National Forest

Map 4.7, page 122

This trail sits front and center of the OHV trail system, but they're not allowed on this trail, so you can have it all to yourself. And you probably will: It travels through a burned area from the '90s, with the bare, slender tree trunks giving you a clear view of the Winom Creek Valley you're hiking through. It's a pleasant and gentle walk along South Winom Creek and a chance to view the burned sections up close. The trail is better maintained than some of its neighbors that didn't fare so well in the fire, and it's a pretty straightforward route, but be aware that it may be faint in parts. Keep your eyes peeled for the locals who wander through the John Day wilderness area, like mule deer and Rocky Mountain elk.

User groups: Hikers, dogs, and horses. No mountain bikes are allowed. No wheelchair access.

Permits: Permits are not required. Parking and access are free.

Maps: For a map of North Fork John Day Wilderness and Umatilla National Forest, contact Nature of the Northwest Information Center. For a topographic map, ask the USGS for Pearson Ridge and Kelsay Butte.

Directions: From Ukiah, drive 22.6 miles southeast on the Blue Mountain Scenic Byway/Forest Service Road 52 to the junction with Forest

Service Road 440. Turn right and drive .7 mile. At the fork leading to the South Winom Campground, turn left and continue .2 mile to the parking pullout on the right. The trailhead is across the road on the left.

Contact: Umatilla National Forest, North Fork John Day Ranger District, P.O. Box 158, Ukiah, OR 97880, 541/427-3231.

43 GRANITE CREEK
6.8 mi/3.5 hrs

northwest of Granite in the North Fork John Day Wilderness of Umatilla National Forest

Map 4.7, page 122

Descending along Granite Creek to the North Fork John Day River, this relatively gentle trail is a great spot to escape the more popular riverside crowds while still accessing the river itself. The trail loses only 400 feet in its 3.4-mile length, so it's an easy jaunt along a scenic creek before hitting the river. Since you'll reach the river at the trail's halfway point, you're likely to see fewer people than if you started at the North Fork John Day trailhead. When you arrive at the trailhead, there are two forks: The one to the left goes down an old mining road, and you can use this as a return trip for a loop. The decaying mining operations here are evidence of the once-booming gold mines in the area, so if that kind of stuff does it for you, it's worth the trip in—just remember to leave any objects that you see behind.

User groups: Hikers, dogs, and horses. No mountain bikes are allowed. No wheelchair access.

Permits: Permits are not required. Parking and access are free.

Maps: For a map of the North Fork John Day Wilderness and Umatilla National Forest, contact Nature of the Northwest Information Center. For a topographic map, ask the USGS for Desolation Butte.

Directions: From Granite, drive 1.5 miles west on Forest Service Road 10. Turn right onto Granite Creek Road/Forest Service Road 1035.

Drive 4.3 miles, then turn left onto a spur road for .2 mile, to the parking area and trailhead, straight ahead at the road's end. (Start on the trailhead to the right.)

Contact: Umatilla National Forest, North Fork John Day Ranger District, P.O. Box 158, Ukiah, OR 97880, 541/427-3231.

44 NORTH FORK JOHN DAY RIVER
22.9 mi one-way/
2.0 days

at the junction of Highways 52 and 73 in the North Fork John Day Wilderness of Umatilla National Forest

Map 4.7, page 122

There's something to be said for meandering trails along scenic rivers. You don't have to think too much about whether you're on the right trail, you just keep the river at your side and enjoy the scenery. Wildflower meadows start the peaceful walk, and good ol' John Day himself keeps you company along the way. The river's quite the spot for fishing, camping, and picnicking, as well as for natives like elk, deer, black bears, and bald eagles. Evidence of the area's 1860s gold-mining boom pops up along the trail, so keep an eye out (just leave everything you see behind). It's a long haul down the river, but it's worth it. One option is to leave a car at Granite Creek, a closer trailhead than the lower trailhead, which intersects the trail about halfway.

User groups: Hikers, dogs, and horses. No mountain bikes are allowed. No wheelchair access.

Permits: A federal Northwest Forest pass is required to park here. The cost is $5 for a day pass or $30 for an annual pass. You can buy a day pass at ranger stations, from private vendors, or through Nature of the Northwest Information Center.

Maps: For a map of the North Fork John Day Wilderness and Umatilla National Forest, contact Nature of the Northwest Information Center. For a topographic map, ask the USGS for Desolation Butte and Olive Lake.

Directions: From Ukiah, drive about 43 miles southeast on the Blue Mountain Scenic Byway/Forest Service Road 52 to the North Fork John Day campground. Drive .1 mile and park in the trailhead parking area to the right. The well-marked trailhead is to the right as you're driving in.

Contact: Umatilla National Forest, North Fork John Day Ranger District, P.O. Box 158, Ukiah, OR 97880, 541/427-3231.

45 BALDY LAKE
14.0 mi/7.0 hrs

west of Baker City in the North Fork John Day Wilderness of Wallowa-Whitman National Forest

Map 4.7, page 122

Traveling through the Baldy Creek drainage, the seven-mile Baldy Creek Trail climbs almost 2,000 feet through spruce, fir, and pine forest before hitting the lake, which rests in a basin below Mount Ireland. Just before you reach the lake, take a short detour on an abandoned road for a view of the historic Cable Cove mining area and the valley below. Keep in mind that, like many trails in this area, the road in is often closed through July, so hit this one later in the season.

User groups: Hikers, dogs, and horses. No mountain bikes are allowed. No wheelchair access.

Permits: A federal Northwest Forest pass is required to park here. The cost is $5 for a day pass or $30 for an annual pass. You can buy a day pass at ranger stations, from private vendors, or through Nature of the Northwest Information Center.

Maps: For a map of the North Fork John Day Wilderness and Wallowa-Whitman National Forest, contact Nature of the Northwest Information Center. For a topographic map, ask the USGS for Crawfish Lake and Mount Ireland.

Directions: From Baker City, drive north on U.S. 30 about 10 miles to Haines and turn left (west) onto Elkhorn Scenic Highway (which becomes Anthony Lakes Highway after 1.8

miles and Forest Service Road 73 after 14.8 miles). Drive for a total of 35.7 miles to Forest Service Road 395. Turn left and drive .1 mile to the end of the road and the parking area. The trailhead is on the left side of the road as you're driving in.

Contact: Wallowa-Whitman National Forest, Baker City Ranger District, 3165 10th Street, Baker City, OR 97814, 541/523-4476.

46 PEAVY TRAIL
8.0 mi/4.0 hrs

west of Baker City in the North Fork John Day Wilderness of Wallowa-Whitman National Forest

Map 4.7, page 122

Driving in can be a little rough, so you would think you'd have the place all to yourself. Surprisingly, there are a fair number of solitude-seekers camping along the meadows of this remote area. Part of the reason is that nearby Peavy Cabin is available for rent, which you'll pass on the way to the trail. Once you hit the trail, you're likely to have it all to yourself, though. The path travels through a 1996 fire zone, which at times makes the trail a little faint; on the way, you'll pass Cunningham Cove Trail, which at this writing was too faint to follow through the sparse forest. But if you want a little something different—or if you plan to rent the cabin for an overnight stay—try this trail, which follows the North Fork John Day River drainage along an abandoned road. After two miles, the trail climbs about 1,500 feet to a meadow, where you can camp for the night to escape the campers nearby. Keep in mind that the road in is often snowy through July, so check conditions before you head out.

User groups: Hikers, dogs, and horses. No mountain bikes are allowed. No wheelchair access.

Permits: A federal Northwest Forest pass is required to park here. The cost is $5 for a day pass or $30 for an annual pass. You can buy a day pass at ranger stations, from private vendors, or through Nature of the Northwest Information Center.

Maps: For a map of the North Fork John Day Wilderness and Wallowa-Whitman National Forest, contact Nature of the Northwest Information Center. For a topographic map, ask the USGS for Crawfish Lake and Anthony Lakes.

Directions: From Baker City, drive north on U.S. 30 about 10 miles to Haines and turn left (west) onto Elkhorn Scenic Highway (which becomes Anthony Lakes Highway after 1.8 miles and Forest Service Road 73 after 14.8 miles). Drive for a total of 35.4 miles to Forest Service Road 380. Turn left and drive three miles to the road's end and the parking area. (Note: This road is rough, and a sign says it's not recommended for passenger cars. It's passable, but slow-going.) The trail starts directly in front of you as you're driving in.

Contact: Wallowa-Whitman National Forest, Baker City Ranger District, 3165 10th Street, Baker City, Oregon 97814, 541/523-4476.

47 CRAWFISH LAKE
3.0 mi/1.5 hrs

west of Baker City in Wallowa-Whitman National Forest

Map 4.7, page 122

There are actually two ways to get to Crawfish Lake. They're both roughly the same distance, but the lower trailhead is slightly shorter and steeper. Either way, it's a three-mile round-trip trek through fir, spruce, and pine forest, traveling through a burned section from a 1986 fire, where you can still see bare trunks and scorched bark. For the shorter and steeper route, take the lower trailhead, which starts on an old rocky road before the trail narrows and enters the forest. Even though you're gaining only 300 feet in elevation, keep in mind you're starting at 6,800 feet, so don't be surprised (and don't let your ego get bruised) if you break a sweat on the trip up. Finally it levels out near the lake and arrives at a rock field on the left (thankfully, there's no need to pass through

that; the trail is rocky enough as it is). Pack your bug repellent, because mosquitoes thrive in the lake area. This area is often snowed in through July, so it's a good idea to check ahead to see if the roads are clear.

User groups: Hikers, dogs, and horses. No mountain bikes are allowed. No wheelchair access.

Permits: A federal Northwest Forest pass is required to park here. The cost is $5 for a day pass or $30 for an annual pass. You can buy a day pass at ranger stations, from private vendors, or through Nature of the Northwest Information Center.

Maps: For a map of the Wallowa-Whitman National Forest, contact Nature of the Northwest Information Center. For a topographic map, ask the USGS for Crawfish Lake.

Directions: From Baker City, drive north on U.S. 30 about 10 miles to Haines and turn left (west) onto Elkhorn Scenic Highway (which becomes Anthony Lakes Highway after 1.8 miles and Forest Service Road 73 after 14.8 miles). Drive for a total of 33.4 miles, and turn left less than .1 mile to the large parking area. Trailhead is at the end of the parking area, to the right of the sign along an abandoned road.

Contact: Wallowa-Whitman National Forest, Baker City Ranger District, 3165 10th Street, Baker City, OR 97814, 541/523-4476.

48 LAKES LOOKOUT
1.4 mi/1.5 hrs

west of Baker City in Wallowa-Whitman National Forest

Map 4.7, page 122

It may be short, but don't discount this little guy, because he's also tough. It's a quad-killer that leaves you reaching for the oxygen tank, because you begin at no less than 7,800 feet of elevation. The trail starts up an abandoned road then quickly narrows, leveling out so you can catch your breath before the final push to the top (nice of it, don't you think?). You'll have to scramble over boulders at the top of the trail before you reach the summit, where the wall is etched with wilderness graffiti, as people took it upon themselves to stake claim with "I was here" signs and "Betty loves Tommy." Pass that by for the view from the 8,552-foot old fire lookout (used in the early 1900s), where you can see where it got its name. It's an incredible view that seems to stretch forever (okay, maybe just into the neighboring counties), where you can see the many lakes and peaks of the Anthony Lakes area. Like many trails in this area, it's often snowed in through July, so check on road conditions beforehand.

User groups: Hikers, dogs, and horses. No mountain bikes are allowed. No wheelchair access.

Permits: No passes are required. Parking and access are free.

Maps: For a map of the Wallowa-Whitman National Forest, contact Nature of the Northwest Information Center. For a topographic map, ask the USGS for Anthony Lakes.

Directions: From Baker City, drive north on U.S. 30 about 10 miles to Haines and turn left (west) onto Elkhorn Scenic Highway (which becomes Anthony Lakes Highway after 1.8 miles and Forest Service Road 73 after 14.8 miles). Drive for a total of 27.5 miles to Forest Service Road 210. Turn left and drive 1.6 miles, then turn right at the T-junction for .3 mile. Park to the left in a pullout, and the trail starts to the right along an old road. (It can be tricky to find since the trailhead sign is near the parking area. As you're facing the summit, the trail starts to the right—south—of you.) Note: Road 210 is rough along a steep cliff, but passable for passenger cars.

Contact: Wallowa-Whitman National Forest, Baker City Ranger District, 3165 10th Street, Baker City, OR 97814, 541/523-4476.

49 ANTHONY LAKE SHORELINE/ HOFFER LAKES
3.0 mi/1.5 hrs
west of Baker City in Wallowa-Whitman National Forest

Map 4.7, page 122

You can stroll along the gravel path of Antho-ny Lakes with interpretive signs introducing you to locals like Jacob's Ladder and Jeffrey's Shooting Star, but why not hit two lakes for the price of one? Make that three lakes, since Hoffer Lakes is actually now divided into two lakes by a meadow, due to sediment creeping up. Start along the Anthony Lake shoreline, with 8,000-plus-foot Gunsight Butte and Angell Peak as backdrops. Then hit the well-marked Hoffer Lakes Trail on the south shore, taking a right if you're touring the lake counterclockwise to extend your trip another two miles round-trip, heading back after viewing the lakes to continue the lakeshore loop. It's an easy stroll with views, and camping is available at nearby Anthony Lakes Campground. The trail is usually snowed in through July, so unless you want to make this a snowshoe trek, it's best to wait until late in the season.

User groups: Hikers, dogs, and horses. No mountain bikes are allowed. No wheelchair access.

Permits: No passes are required. Parking and access are free.

Maps: For a map of the Wallowa-Whitman National Forest, contact Nature of the Northwest Information Center. For a topographic map, ask the USGS for Anthony Lakes.

Directions: From Baker City, drive north on U.S. 30 about 10 miles to Haines and turn left (west) onto Elkhorn Scenic Highway (which becomes Anthony Lakes Highway after 1.8 miles and Forest Service Road 73 after 14.8 miles). Drive for a total of 23.8 miles to Forest Service Road 170 at the well-marked Anthony Lakes Campground. Before hitting the campground, turn right to the parking area on the left across from the guard station (which is not marked as such; just look for the cabin). There's no official trailhead, but this is a good spot to start your loop, traveling counterclockwise to reach Hoffer Lakes Trail, on the other side of the lake.

Contact: Wallowa-Whitman National Forest, Baker City Ranger District, 3165 10th Street, Baker City, OR 97814, 541/523-4476.

50 BLACK LAKE
2.0 mi/1.0 hr

west of Baker City in Wallowa-Whitman
National Forest

Map 4.7, page 122

You can reach Black Lake via Elkhorn Crest Trail (see listing in this chapter) because the trails intersect halfway up the one-mile gentle ascent, but then you'd be missing out on Lilypad Lake, which is covered in yellow water-lily blossoms all summer. The trail passes Lilypad Lake after only .25 mile and then connects with Elkhorn Crest Trail before veering off to Black Lake, which sits at 7,344 feet. It's a good way to enjoy some of the many lakes in the area without spending all day to get there (but this does mean it could attract more crowds). Hit this hike after June, because the road up to the trail tends to be snowed in before then.

User groups: Hikers, dogs, and horses. No mountain bikes are allowed. No wheelchair access.

Permits: Permits are not required. Parking and access are free.

Maps: For a map of the Wallowa-Whitman National Forest, contact Nature of the Northwest Information Center. For a topographic map, ask the USGS for Anthony Lakes.

Directions: From Baker City, drive north on U.S. 30 about 10 miles to Haines and turn left (west) onto Elkhorn Scenic Highway (which becomes Anthony Lakes Highway after 1.8 miles and Forest Service Road 73 after 14.8 miles). Drive for a total of 23.8 miles to Anthony Lakes Campground. Turn left, and just before you reach the campground, turn left into the parking area and the well-marked trailhead.

Contact: Wallowa-Whitman National Forest, Baker City Ranger District, 3165 10th Street, Baker City, Oregon 97814, 541/523-4476.

51 SUMMIT LAKE
25.0 mi/2.0 days

west of Baker City in Wallowa-Whitman
National Forest

Map 4.7, page 122

Traveling along Elkhorn Crest National Recreation Trail, the path quickly ascends 1,000 feet in the first two miles to reach Elkhorn Ridge and views of the Blue and Wallowa Mountains and the Baker Valley below. The trail itself is 22.6 miles one-way, but one good choice for an overnight stop is Summit Lake, which sits surrounded by sheer cliff walls on three sides. Deer, elk, and mountain goats aren't dummies, either; they know this is a great spot to catch some views, so you may see some along the way. After 5.5 miles, the trail leads to an old road, which you cross to pick up Summit Lake Trail for another 1.5 miles to the lake. Keep in mind that this trail is often blocked by snow through July, so check ahead before you set out.

User groups: Hikers, dogs, and horses. No mountain bikes are allowed. No wheelchair access.

Permits: A federal Northwest Forest pass is required to park here. The cost is $5 for a day pass or $30 for an annual pass. You can buy a day pass at ranger stations, from private vendors, or through Nature of the Northwest Information Center.

Maps: For a map of the Wallowa-Whitman National Forest, contact Nature of the Northwest Information Center. For a topographic map, ask the USGS for Anthony Lakes and Bourne.

Directions: From Baker City, drive north on U.S. 30 about 10 miles to Haines and turn left (west) onto Elkhorn Scenic Highway (which becomes Anthony Lakes Highway after 1.8 miles and Forest Service Road 73 after 14.8 miles). Drive for a total of 23.8 miles to the trailhead just before you reach Anthony Lakes Campground. The large parking area and Elkhorn Crest trailhead are on the left side of the highway.

Contact: Wallowa-Whitman National Forest,

Baker City Ranger District, 3165 10th Street, Baker City, OR 97814, 541/523-4476.

52 ELKHORN CREST NATIONAL RECREATION TRAIL TO LOST LAKE
14.0 mi/7.0 hrs

west of Baker City in Wallowa-Whitman National Forest

Map 4.7, page 122

The highest trail in the Blue Mountains, the 22.6-mile Elkhorn Crest National Recreation Trail climbs 1,000 feet in the first two miles for views of the Wallowa and Blue Mountains and the Baker Valley. But you don't need to walk 43-some-odd miles (unless you feel compelled, in which case there are plenty of campsites along the way). You may have company along the way, as deer, elk, and mountain goats like the views too and often travel through the path. The trail hits six lakes along its course, including a side trail (trails tend to be well marked in this area) to Lost Lake, surrounded by wildflower meadows. This is a good turnaround point for a day hike (for an overnight option on this trail, see the Summit Lake listing in this chapter). Plan this hike for later in the season: Although the road in tends to open earlier than others in the area, the high altitude (up to 8,000 feet on the trail) means it's often snowy through July.

User groups: Hikers, dogs, and horses. No mountain bikes are allowed. No wheelchair access.

Permits: A federal Northwest Forest pass is required to park here. The cost is $5 for a day pass or $30 for an annual pass. You can buy a day pass at ranger stations, from private vendors, or through Nature of the Northwest Information Center.

Maps: For a map of the Wallowa-Whitman National Forest, contact Nature of the Northwest Information Center. For a topographic map, ask the USGS for Anthony Lakes.

Directions: From Baker City, drive north on U.S. 30 about 10 miles to Haines and turn left

(west) onto Elkhorn Scenic Highway (which becomes Anthony Lakes Highway after 1.8 miles and Forest Service Road 73 after 14.8 miles). Drive for a total of 23.8 miles to the trailhead just before you reach Anthony Lakes Campground. The large parking area and trailhead are on the left side of the highway.

Contact: Wallowa-Whitman National Forest, Baker City Ranger District, 3165 10th Street, Baker City, OR 97814, 541/523-4476.

53 VAN PATTEN LAKE
3.0 mi/1.5 hrs

west of Baker City in Wallowa-Whitman National Forest

Map 4.7, page 122

The trail is only .5 mile each way to the lake, so you'd think it would be packed. But then you have to consider the drive in: The mile-long road to the top is so steep, rough, and rutted that unless you have a monster truck, there's no way you'll want to hazard driving it. It's recommended that you start instead one mile down on foot and begin a slow climb up the rough road to the actual trailhead. You'll feel as if you're in the middle of nowhere and think there's no way a trail actually exists, when suddenly there's a sign announcing that you've arrived. The trail itself gains 1,000 feet in elevation in just .5 mile (!), another way that it weeds out the crowds. The panoramic view of the Wallowa Mountains will be yours, all yours. Although the road up to this trail tends to be clear of snow earlier than others in the area, you should check ahead of time before heading out.

User groups: Hikers, dogs, and horses. No mountain bikes are allowed. No wheelchair access.

Permits: Permits are not required. Parking and access are free.

Maps: For a map of the Wallowa-Whitman National Forest, contact Nature of the Northwest Information Center. For a topographic map, ask the USGS for Anthony Lakes.

Directions: From Baker City, drive north on

U.S. 30 about 10 miles to Haines and turn left (west) onto Elkhorn Scenic Highway (which becomes Anthony Lakes Highway after 1.8 miles and Forest Service Road 73 after 14.8 miles). Drive for a total of 20.9 miles and turn left onto Forest Service Road 130. Park at the side of the road (there's plenty of room) and walk up the rough road for one mile to the trailhead; you'll want to take the road that leads up and to the left as you're driving in.

Contact: Wallowa-Whitman National Forest, Baker City Ranger District, 3165 10th Street, Baker City, Oregon 97814, 541/523-4476.

54 DUTCH FLAT
16.8 mi/8.0 hrs

west of Baker City in Wallowa-Whitman National Forest

Map 4.7, page 122

Climbing through a forest of spruce, larch, ponderosa pine, and lodgepole pine, you'll catch glimpses of the meadows right off the bat through clearings. The trail climbs steadily, gaining 3,200 of elevation on its way to Dutch Flat Meadows (a great camping spot if you want to stay overnight) and Dutch Flat Lake before the final steep and rocky push to Dutch Flat Saddle. The beauty of gaining elevation is that the views only get better with every step.

User groups: Hikers, dogs, and horses. No mountain bikes are allowed. No wheelchair access.

Permits: A federal Northwest Forest pass is required to park here. The cost is $5 for a day pass or $30 for an annual pass. You can buy a day pass at ranger stations, from private vendors, or through Nature of the Northwest Information Center.

Maps: For a map of the Wallowa-Whitman National Forest, contact Nature of the Northwest Information Center. For a topographic map, ask the USGS for Anthony Lakes and Rock Creek.

Directions: From Baker City, drive north on U.S. 30 about 10 miles to Haines, and turn left

(west) onto Elkhorn Scenic Highway (which becomes Anthony Lakes Highway after 1.8 miles and Forest Service Road 73 after 14.8 miles). Drive for a total of 17.7 miles and turn left onto Forest Service Road 7307. Drive 1.2 miles to the end of the road and the well-marked trailhead straight ahead, behind the restroom as you're driving in.

Contact: Wallowa-Whitman National Forest, Baker City Ranger District, 3165 10th Street, Baker City, OR 97814, 541/523-4476.

55 SOUTH FORK DESOLATION
16.2 mi/8.0 hrs

southeast of Dale in Umatilla National Forest

Map 4.7, page 122

Starting through a sparse forest, this trail climbs up to 7,400 feet (gaining almost 2,000 feet in elevation) as it follows Desolation Creek. Views of the Umatilla mountain range and valleys await you at the top. Its name may be desolate, which is fitting in some way considering that you're escaping the crowds who flock to nearby Olive Lake, but you won't be missing any company when you have the views to yourself. Like many of this area's trails, the path can be faint at times, so you should definitely bring a map along for this one.

User groups: Hikers, dogs, horses, and mountain bikes. No wheelchair access.

Permits: Permits are not required. Parking and access are free.

Maps: For a map of Umatilla National Forest, contact Nature of the Northwest Information Center. For a topographic map, ask the USGS for Desolation Butte.

Directions: From Dale, drive 21.1 miles east on Forest Service Road 10, and turn right on Forest Service Road 45. Drive one mile and park in the pullout to the right; the trailhead begins to the left.

Contact: Umatilla National Forest, North Fork John Day Ranger District, P.O. Box 158, Ukiah, OR 97880, 541/427-3231.

56 OLIVE LAKE
2.5 mi/1.5 hrs

southeast of Dale in Umatilla National Forest

Map 4.7, page 122

Olive Lake is better known for its campground, but there's also a gentle wooded trail surrounding it that is surprisingly uncrowded (if you don't count the people fishing on the banks here and there). A few gentle hills allow you to gain a better glimpse of the shimmering water below, and you cross a footbridge to head into an overgrown portion of the trail nearly at the end. It's simple to follow, gets you away from the campsite, is easy enough for kids, and offers plenty of spots to plop down and dip your feet in the water. It's not exactly a wilderness excursion, but if you're already camping in the area and want to walk off some of those s'mores, this is a great lakeshore loop.

User groups: Hikers, dogs, mountain bikes, and horses. No wheelchair access.

Permits: Permits are not required. Parking and access are free.

Maps: For a map of Umatilla National Forest, contact Nature of the Northwest Information Center. For a topographic map, ask the USGS for Olive Lake.

Directions: From Dale, drive 26.9 miles east on Forest Service Road 10, then turn right into the Olive Lake Campground onto Forest Service Road 430 for .3 mile. Turn left into the day-use parking area near the lake. The trail starts at the lake (there's no official trailhead).

Contact: Umatilla National Forest, North Fork John Day Ranger District, P.O. Box 158, Ukiah, OR 97880, 541/427-3231.

57 MAGONE SLIDE
1.5 mi/1.0 hr

north of John Day in Malheur National Forest

Map 4.7, page 122

Is it just me, or does the Magone (pronounced ma-GO-nee) Slide sound like a popular dance step? The lake is a popular spot for fishing and picnicking, but to escape the action try this nearby trail. Along the way, you'll walk past ponderosa pines that look like they've been doing a little sliding recently themselves, growing at odd angles and sometimes even just lying in the path (the nerve). Nearby Magone Lake was formed by a landslide in the 1860s, and this is a great spot to check out where it all happened; you can see evidence of the slide where terraces were formed by all that sliding around. Wildflowers line the area, and you'll end up climbing 300 feet to reach two viewpoints along cliffs, where you can see the lake below, the Strawberry Mountains, and the John Day Valley. Feel free to dance at the top.

User groups: Hikers and dogs. No mountain bikes or horses are allowed. No wheelchair access.

Permits: Permits are not required. Parking and access are free.

Maps: For a map of Malheur National Forest, contact Nature of the Northwest Information Center. For a topographic map, ask the USGS for Magone Lake.

Directions: From John Day, drive nine miles east on U.S. 26 and turn left (north) onto County Road 18. Drive 12.4 miles to Forest Service Road 3620, a one-lane paved road, and turn left to drive 1.3 miles to Forest Service Road 3618. Turn right and drive 1.2 miles to a small parking pullout and the trailhead on the right (it can be tricky to find, but there is a sign).

Contact: Malheur National Forest, Blue Mountain Ranger District, 431 Patterson Bridge Road, P.O. Box 909, John Day, OR 97845, 541/575-3000.

58 MAGONE LAKE
1.5 mi/1.0 hr

north of John Day in Malheur National Forest

Map 4.7, page 122

Back in the 1880s, former Civil War officer Major Joseph Magone (pronounced ma-GO-nee, so you don't embarrass yourself) was known for his BYOF (bring your own fish) policy: He'd haul bucketfuls of his own fish and dump 'em in the lake so he could fish in his favorite spot. Today, those fish are long gone, but their descendants remain, and many people take advantage of the bounty of rainbow and brook trout. It's a veritable zoo of creatures, with beavers, mule deer, woodpeckers, chipmunks, and mallards among the locals. The simple, partly paved trail loops the 5,000-foot in elevation lake, and a campground is nearby if you want to spend some time partaking in ol' Magone's favorite pastime.

User groups: Hikers and dogs. No mountain bikes or horses are allowed. Wheelchair accessible.

Permits: Permits are not required. Parking and access are free.

Maps: For a map of Malheur National Forest, contact Nature of the Northwest Information Center. For a topographic map, ask the USGS for Magone Lake.

Directions: From John Day, drive nine miles east on U.S. 26 and turn left (north) onto County Road 18. Drive 12.4 miles to Forest Service Road 3620, a one-lane paved road, and turn left and drive 1.3 miles to Forest Service Road 3618. Turn right and drive one mile to the Magone Lake day-use area, on the left, and the trail (there is no official trailhead).

Contact: Malheur National Forest, Blue Mountain Ranger District, 431 Patterson Bridge Road, P.O. Box 909, John Day, OR 97845, 541/575-3000.

59 PINE CREEK
21.0 mi/1.0–2.0 days

southeast of John Day in the Strawberry Mountain Wilderness of Malheur National Forest

Map 4.7, page 122

Getting into the remote Strawberry Mountains is no easy task. Here's a back-door route: Traversing the spiny backbone of the Strawberry mountain range, this trail switchbacks up to cross over Bald Mountain (total elevation gain is 800 feet) and comes to an end at a three-

way junction with Onion Creek and Buckhorn Meadows Trails (see listings in this chapter); you can camp along the trail if you want to make this a two-day trip. Like many of the Strawberry Mountain Wilderness trails, this one can be hot and dry, so bring plenty of water. Trails are also not always marked in this area, so come prepared with a map.

User groups: Hikers, dogs, and horses. No mountain bikes are allowed. No wheelchair access.

Permits: Permits are not required. Parking and access are free.

Maps: For a map of the Strawberry Mountain Wilderness and Malheur National Forest, contact Nature of the Northwest Information Center. For a topographic map, ask the USGS for Pine Creek Mountain.

Directions: From Prairie City, drive 6.5 miles west on U.S. 26 and turn left (south) onto Pine Creek Road/County Road 54. Follow Pine Creek Road for 8.5 miles to the end of the road and the trailhead (the road may be gated at the trailhead; the trail starts here).

Contact: Malheur National Forest, Blue Mountain Ranger District, 431 Patterson Bridge Road, P.O. Box 909, John Day, OR 97845, 541/575-3000.

60 INDIAN CREEK
12.8 mi/6.5 hrs

south of Prairie City in the Strawberry Mountain Wilderness of Malheur National Forest

Map 4.7, page 122

Want an up-close view of Strawberry Mountain without having to hike all day (or camp overnight)? Try Indian Creek Trail, which climbs through alpine meadows and wild onion fields (gaining 2,600 feet in elevation along the entire trail) to get a closer peak at the namesake of this wilderness area. Turn back whenever you want, because the trail then ends at a junction with Pine Creek (see listing in this chapter), so you can add mileage to the trip if you're not ready to head back into civilization yet. If you do decide to add on to the trip, you should definitely bring a map, because trail signs may be missing in this area (road signs too, for that matter, so add a road atlas to that list).

User groups: Hikers, dogs, and horses. No mountain bikes are allowed. No wheelchair access.

Permits: Permits are not required. Parking and access are free.

Maps: For a map of the Strawberry Mountain Wilderness and Malheur National Forest, contact Nature of the Northwest Information Center. For a topographic map, ask the USGS for Strawberry Mountain.

Directions: From Prairie City, drive 4.5 miles west on U.S. 26 to Indian Creek Road/County Road 55. Turn left (south) and follow Indian Creek Road eight miles to the trailhead on the right. Park at the side of the road.

Contact: Malheur National Forest, Prairie City Ranger District, P.O. Box 337, Prairie City, OR 97869, 541/820-3311.

61 ONION CREEK TO STRAWBERRY MOUNTAIN
9.0 mi/5.5 hrs

south of Prairie City in the Strawberry Mountain Wilderness of Malheur National Forest

Map 4.7, page 122

Most of the crowds descend upon nearby Strawberry Lake area, but not many try the summit of the mountain itself. Following Onion Creek Trail, the path climbs 3,600 feet, with the final push to the summit topping the total off at an even 4,000. As if that's not hard enough, the trail gets a little faint at times once it hits the open alpine meadows, so look for rock cairns along the way. Stand on top of the 9,039-foot peak and take in the views of the Eagle Cap and Elkhorn Mountains. Keep in mind that because of the high elevation, the trail can be snowy through July, so check ahead to make sure it's clear. Onion Creek Trail continues another two miles, passing by Strawberry Basin Trail to end at Pine Creek (see listings in this chapter).

User groups: Hikers, dogs, and horses. No mountain bikes are allowed. No wheelchair access.

Permits: Permits are not required. Parking and access are free.

Maps: For a map of the Strawberry Mountain Wilderness and Malheur National Forest, contact Nature of the Northwest Information Center. For a topographic map, ask the USGS for Strawberry Mountain.

Directions: From Prairie City, drive south on County Road 60 for 12 miles to the trailhead on the right.

Contact: Malheur National Forest, Prairie City Ranger District, P.O. Box 337, Prairie City, OR 97869, 541/820-3311.

62 STRAWBERRY LAKE/ LITTLE STRAWBERRY LAKE
6.4 mi/3.0 hrs

south of Prairie City in the Strawberry Mountain Wilderness of Malheur National Forest

Map 4.7, page 122

Just when you were wondering where all the people are in the remote Strawberry wilderness, you suddenly find out as you enter Strawberry Campground (read: avoid this place on a holiday weekend if you prefer a little elbow room). The trail starts on Strawberry Basin Trail from the campground, leading one mile to a junction with Slide Basin Trail. Keep to the right to pass along the western shore of Strawberry Lake for .8 mile, then continue along another .8 mile to visit Strawberry's little sis, passing by Strawberry Falls on the way before forking to the left for .6-mile Little Strawberry Lake Trail. You can't loop around her (she's too little and dainty), but you can stand and admire the Lake with the Cutest Name on Earth, which is surrounded by meadows and onion fields (what, no strawberry fields?). Retrace your steps, completing the loop of Strawberry Lake by turning right to trace the eastern shore. The total elevation gain is 1,200 feet, with views of Strawberry peak nearby. Strawberry Basin Trail extends three more miles to end at Onion Creek Trail (see listing in this chapter).

User groups: Hikers, dogs, and horses. No mountain bikes are allowed. No wheelchair access.

Permits: Permits are not required. Parking and access are free.

Maps: For a map of the Strawberry Mountain Wilderness and Malheur National Forest, contact Nature of the Northwest Information Center. For a topographic map, ask the USGS for Strawberry Mountain.

Directions: From Prairie City, drive south on County Road 60 for 12 miles to the road's end and Strawberry Campground. Park in the day-use area, where the trail begins.

Contact: Malheur National Forest, Prairie City Ranger District, P.O. Box 337, Prairie City, OR 97869, 541/820-3311.

63 SLIDE LAKE
7.6 mi/4.0 hrs

south of Prairie City in the Strawberry Mountain Wilderness of Malheur National Forest

Map 4.7, page 122

Starting for the first mile on the popular Strawberry Basin Trail, Slide Basin Trail then veers to the left (east), traveling through the forest and climbing up almost 2,000 feet to open views of Strawberry Mountain, Slide Creek Basin, and the John Day Valley. The trail then passes Slide Falls and connects with Skyline Trail and Slide Lake Trail to slide down (sorry, can't resist) to the lake itself. The wildflowers are especially brilliant in mid-July, which is when you should plan a visit, because the trails tend to be snowed in through June.

User groups: Hikers, dogs, and horses. No mountain bikes are allowed. No wheelchair access.

Permits: Permits are not required. Parking and access are free.

Maps: For a map of the Strawberry Mountain Wilderness and Malheur National Forest, con-

tact Nature of the Northwest Information Center. For a topographic map, ask the USGS for Strawberry Mountain.

Directions: From Prairie City, drive south on County Road 60 for 12 miles to Strawberry Campground and park in the day-use area, where Strawberry Basin Trail begins.

Contact: Malheur National Forest, Prairie City Ranger District, P.O. Box 337, Prairie City, OR 97869, 541/820-3311.

64 REYNOLDS CREEK
3.0 mi/1.5 hrs

southeast of Prairie City in the Strawberry Mountain Wilderness of Malheur National Forest

Map 4.7, page 122

While waiting for the other trails in the area to open up already, try some spring training on Reynolds Creek Trail. It starts at 4,300 feet, so it's usually open earlier than its neighbors standing on a higher ground. Plus, it's short and sweet, with a gentle ascent of 600 feet, so you can break yourself into summer shape gently. It travels along Reynolds Creek through the Baldy Mountain area and through old-growth forest, just a taste of what lies ahead when the area's longer trails are snow-free.

User groups: Hikers and dogs. No mountain bikes or horses are allowed. No wheelchair access.

Permits: Permits are not required. Parking and access are free.

Maps: For a map of the Malheur National Forest, contact Nature of the Northwest Information Center. For a topographic map, ask the USGS for Isham Creek and Deardorff Mountain.

Directions: From Prairie City, drive 7.5 miles west on County Road 62/Forest Service Road 14. Turn left onto Forest Service Road 2635 and drive four miles to the trailhead.

Contact: Malheur National Forest, Prairie City Ranger District, P.O. Box 337, Prairie City, OR 97869, 541/820-3311.

65 MUD LAKE
7.0 mi/3.5 hrs

south of Prairie City in the Strawberry
Mountain Wilderness of Malheur
National Forest

Map 4.7, page 122

It's easy to see how this one got its name, as it can get a touch soggy in parts. It's best to hit this one later in the season, when everything has had a chance to dry off. Whenever you go, you're practically guaranteed solitude, because it's a remote area. If you're looking for a relatively short day hike with a little climbing involved (elevation gain is 1,700 feet) and a lakeside view, check this one out. Just be warned: The drive in is rough, which seals the promise of solitude.

User groups: Hikers, dogs, and horses. No mountain bikes are allowed. No wheelchair access.

Permits: Permits are not required. Parking and access are free.

Maps: For a map of the Malheur National Forest, contact Nature of the Northwest Information Center. For a topographic map, ask the USGS for Strawberry Mountain.

Directions: From Prairie City, drive 22 miles south on County Road 62/Forest Service Road 14 to Summit Prairie. Turn right (west) onto Forest Service Road 16 and continue five miles to Forest Service Road 1648. Turn right (north) and drive 2.5 miles to Forest Service Road 924-021. Turn right and drive 1.4 miles, then turn left onto Forest Service Road 039 for .8 mile to the trailhead.

Contact: Malheur National Forest, Prairie City Ranger District, P.O. Box 337, Prairie City, OR 97869, 541/820-3311.

66 MEADOW FORK
9.2 mi/4.5 hrs

south of Prairie City in the Strawberry
Mountain Wilderness of Malheur
National Forest

Map 4.7, page 122

Climbing through old-growth pine and fir forest, you'll get a chance to reflect without hearing other people yammering away, because this is a lightly used trail (and better maintained than its neighbors). You won't have views to distract you from your inner thoughts until the upper part of the trail, when you're tired of your own inner voice anyway and just want to soak in the scenery of the Strawberry mountain range and the valleys below. The trail gains 1,300 feet in elevation, and it's a hot and dry area, so bring some water for the road.

User groups: Hikers, dogs, and horses. No mountain bikes are allowed. No wheelchair access.

Permits: Permits are not required. Parking and access are free.

Maps: For a map of Malheur National Forest, contact Nature of the Northwest Information Center. For a topographic map, ask the USGS for Strawberry Mountain and Logan Valley West.

Directions: From Prairie City, drive 22 miles south on County Road 62/Forest Service Road 14 to Summit Prairie. Turn right (west) onto Forest Service Road 16, and continue five miles to Forest Service Road 1648. Turn right (north) and drive 2.5 miles to Forest Service Road 924-021. Turn right and drive 1.4 miles, then turn left onto Forest Service Road 039 for .8 mile to the trailhead.

Contact: Malheur National Forest, Prairie City Ranger District, P.O. Box 337, Prairie City, OR 97869, 541/820-3311.

67 NORTH FORK MALHEUR
12.4 mi one-way/2.0 days

southeast of Prairie City in the Strawberry
Mountain Wilderness of Malheur
National Forest

Map 4.7, page 122

Crossing a footbridge over the North Fork Malheur River at the trailhead, this ambling riverside stroll is like many of the trails in this area: lightly used. But it's maintained better than many in the area (which have been left out of this book due to fire damage or overgrowth), so you'll have a good shot at seeing no one except for the bighorn sheep, mule deer, and Rocky Mountain elk that roam the region. You may choose to turn back halfway for a day hike, or to camp along the river. There's also a sweet camping spot at North Fork Campground, one mile before the trailhead, off the road.

User groups: Hikers, dogs, horses, and mountain bikes. No wheelchair access.

Permits: Permits are not required. Parking and access are free.

Maps: For a map of Malheur National Forest, contact Nature of the Northwest Information Center. For a topographic map, ask the USGS for Flag Prairie and Buck Trough Spring.

Directions: From Prairie City, drive south on County Road 62/Forest Service Road 14 to Deardorff Creek. Turn left onto Forest Service Road 13 and drive 16.4 miles. Turn right at a T-intersection onto Forest Service Road 16 and drive 2.2 miles, then turn left onto Forest Service Road 1675. Drive 3.5 miles to the trailhead (note: this last road is rough), one mile past North Fork Campground.

Contact: Malheur National Forest, Prairie City Ranger District, P.O. Box 337, Prairie City, OR 97869, 541/820-3311.

68 MALHEUR RIVER NATIONAL RECREATION TRAIL
15.2 mi/7.5 hrs
southeast of Seneca in Malheur National Forest

Map 4.7, page 122

Deer, bighorn sheep, and elk roam this national recreation trail (okay, they don't exactly follow the trail, but they're entitled to take shortcuts), which travels along the scenic Malheur River, with great fishing spots along the banks. Though it attracts a few more visitors than other area trails, you'll still feel far, far away from the "real world" as you travel through the ponderosa pine forest along the riverbank.

User groups: Hikers, dogs, and horses. No mountain bikes are allowed. No wheelchair access.

Permits: Permits are not required. Parking and access are free.

Maps: For a map of Malheur National Forest, contact Nature of the Northwest Information Center. For a topographic map, ask the USGS for Dollar Basin.

Directions: From Seneca, drive 16.5 miles east on Logan Valley Road/Forest Service Road 16 to Forest Service Road 1643. Turn right (south) and continue 10 miles to Dollar Basin. Turn left to continue on Forest Service Road 1643 and drive one mile to the Malheur River and the trailhead.

Contact: Malheur National Forest, Emigrant Creek Ranger District, 265 Highway 20 South, Hines, OR 97738, 541/573-4300.

69 HISTORIC OREGON TRAIL
4.2 mi/2.0 hrs
east of Baker City off Highway 86

Map 4.8, page 123

Back in the 1800s, the Oregon Trail served as a gateway to the west for farmers, missionaries, and people seeking a better life in this fine state. By 1852, so many people had used the corridor that it had turned from a faint path to a real-life wagon road, and an industrious soul by the name of Ezra Meeker sought to place markers along the trail. Way to go, Ezra, because the government saw what he was doing and decided to get in on the action themselves. Poor Ezra was long gone by the time they really got down to business, though, it wasn't until 1978 that the trail was dubbed the Oregon National Historic Trail. While much of the trail has been swallowed by superhighways and maybe a couple of McDonald's, there are still 300 miles of wagon ruts that exist to this day. Check out this interpretive trail for a stroll back in time.

User groups: Hikers and dogs. No horses or mountain bikes are allowed. Wheelchair accessible.

Permits: Permits are not required. A $5 fee is charged at the entrance.

Maps: Free trail maps are available at the entrance and online at www.oregontrail.blm.gov. For a topographic map, ask the USGS for Virtue Flat.

Directions: From Baker City, drive six miles east on Highway 86 to the National Historic Oregon Trails Interpretive Center. The trail begins behind the center.

Contact: National Historic Oregon Trail Interpretive Center, 22267 Oregon Highway 86, P.O. Box 987, Baker City, OR 97814, 541/523-1843.

© KEVIN FOREMAN

Chapter 5

The Southern Cascades

Chapter 5—The Southern Cascades

While Portland has Mount Hood knocking on its door asking for it to come out and play, Bend residents have a similar temptation, times three: The Three Sisters, standing tall at over 10,000 feet, come in just behind Mount Jefferson and Mount Hood in the tallest-peak category, rounding out the top five in the state. They're the centerpiece to the Southern Cascade region and within an easy 20-minute drive of the outdoors mecca and mountain-biking hub Bend. South Sister, standing next to the Mount Bachelor Ski Area, is one of the highest peaks you can climb without any equipment (besides good hiking boots).

But you don't have to tackle a summit to get in a good hike around here. In the surrounding Three Sisters Wilderness of Deschutes National Forest, there are plenty of shorter hikes to viewpoints of the imposing triplets, plus backpacking treks to alpine lakes at their basin.

Crater Lake National Park, in the southern region, is another must-see. The deepest lake in the country, Crater Lake has gotten a clean bill of health as one of the clearest lakes in the world. Go anytime but winter, when the park is closed. The Pacific Crest Trail (PCT) winds through the park, and the most noteworthy PCT hikes are covered in this chapter. From half-mile treks up to viewpoints to backpacking trips into the forest on the PCT, you can do it all in this park, and all within viewing range of the clear, blue lake. The unofficial Most Unusual Hike also exists in this park: You can hike down to the lakeshore, take a boat across to Wizard Island, then hike up to the volcanic peak for a view from inside this massive crater.

Coming in a close second to Crater Lake is Waldo Lake, one of the largest natural bodies of water in the state and the second deepest. Scientists took their clear-lake detection devices down to Waldo Lake in Willamette National Forest and—voilà! It's also one of the clearest lakes in the world. You can do a 22-mile loop around the whole lake if you're looking for a great backpacking adventure.

The northern section covered in this chapter is filled with interesting geological formations, like cinder cone peaks, craters, and rocky cliffs, and peaks that attract climbers from all over. The distinct prominent points of Smith Rock State Park and Three Fingered Jack are omnipresent at viewpoints near and far (that Jack, he tends to hog the attention with his jaunty wave).

Surrounding the west side of Crater Lake is the Rogue River National Forest, where the Rogue River National Recreation Trail extends for a whopping 49 miles down the scenic rushing waters. There are plenty of places to access the river and its surrounding hikes right off Highway 62. The 26.5-mile McKenzie River and 9.1-mile Deschutes River Trails are also popular riverside paths, with many access points along the way. Other water adventures include the second-highest waterfall in Oregon—Salt Creek Falls, in Willamette National Forest—and lake hikes galore, from short trails right off the highway to the more remote Sky Lakes and Mountain Lakes Wilderness Areas of Winema National Forest.

It's hard to pinpoint one cool thing about a region filled with so many adventures, but one noteworthy aspect here is trail accessibility. Unlike other wilderness areas that require a long haul through rough Forest Service roads, most of the hikes in this chapter are just a short drive from the highway, if not right off the highway itself. This only adds to their popularity (read: crowds), but the sights in this interesting area make up for the lack of elbow room.

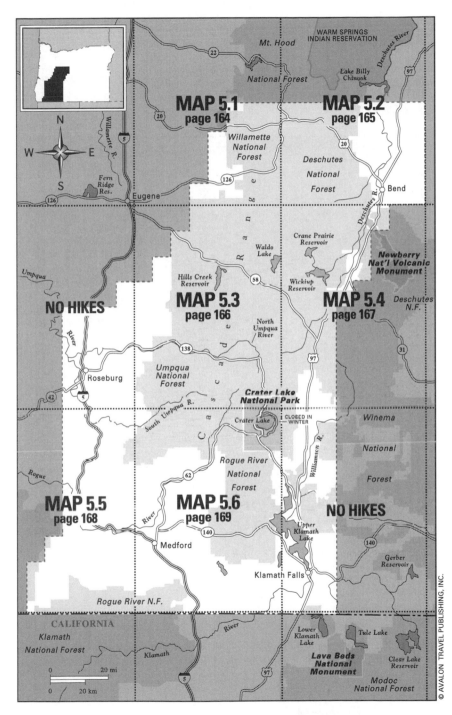

Map 5.1

Hikes 1–8
Pages 170–173

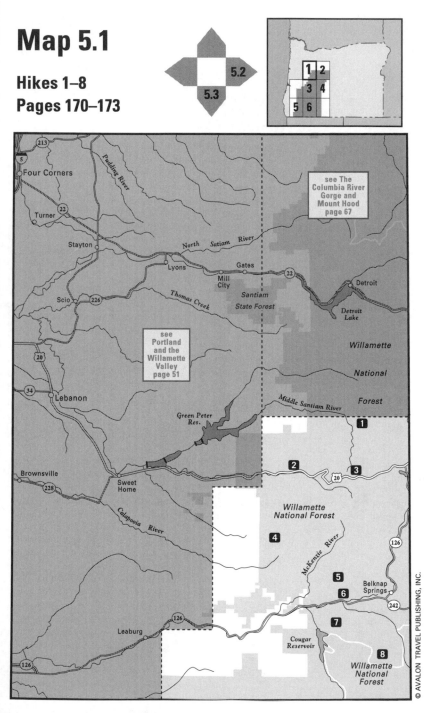

see The
Columbia River
Gorge and
Mount Hood
page 67

see
Portland
and the
Willamette
Valley
page 51

Four Corners

Turner

Stayton

Lyons

Gates

Mill City

Detroit

Detroit Lake

Scio

Thomas Creek

North Santiam River

Santiam State Forest

Willamette

National

Forest

Lebanon

Middle Santiam River

Green Peter Res.

Brownsville

Sweet Home

Calapooia River

Willamette National Forest

McKenzie River

Belknap Springs

Cougar Reservoir

Willamette National Forest

Leaburg

© AVALON TRAVEL PUBLISHING, INC.

Map 5.2

Hikes 9–27
Pages 174–183

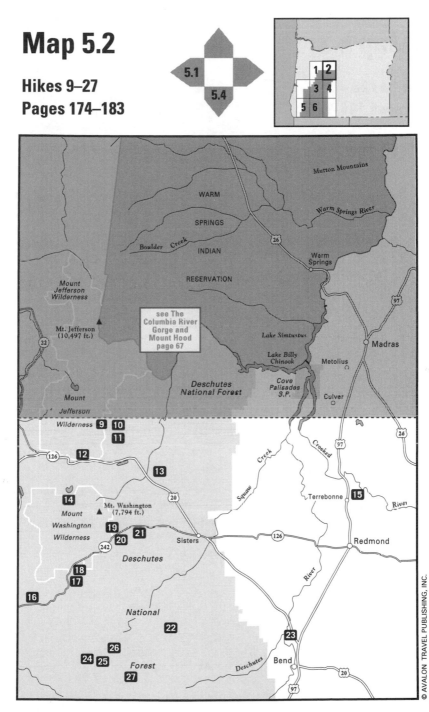

see The Columbia River Gorge and Mount Hood page 67

© AVALON TRAVEL PUBLISHING, INC.

Map 5.3

Hikes 28–45
Pages 184–192

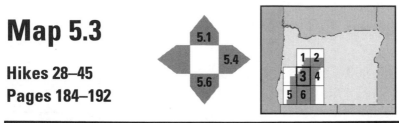

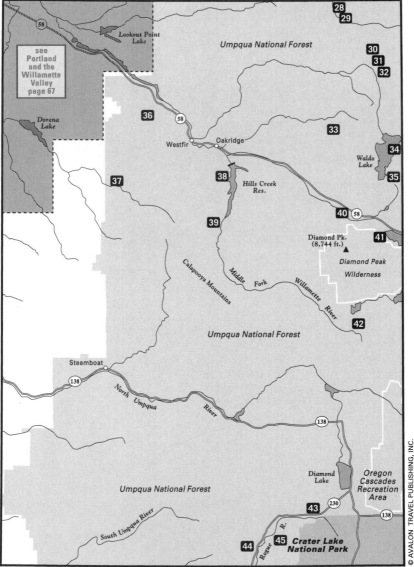

Map 5.4

Hikes 46–52
Pages 193–196

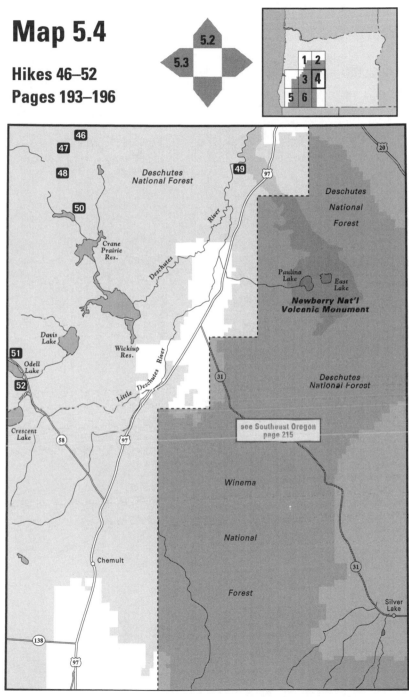

Map 5.5

Hikes 53–60
Pages 196–199

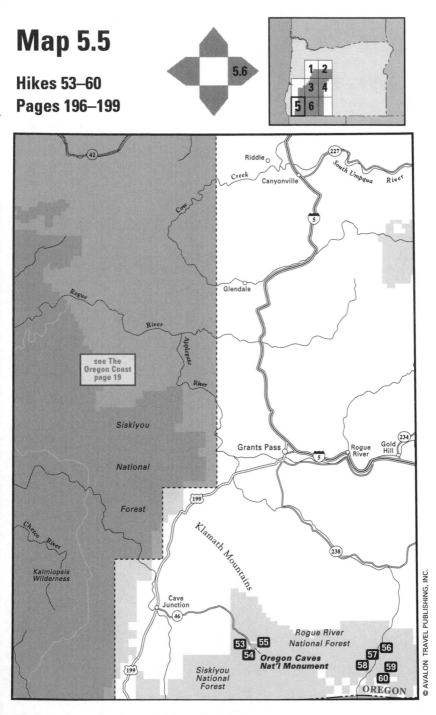

5.6

Map 5.6

Hikes 61–85
Pages 200–211

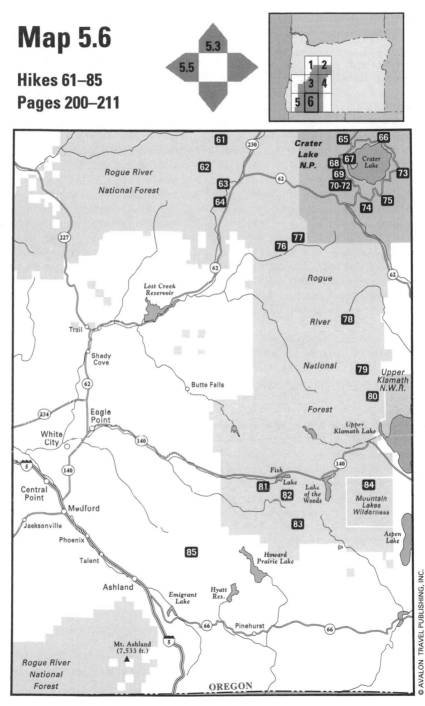

© AVALON TRAVEL PUBLISHING, INC.

1 PYRAMIDS
4.2 mi/2.0 hrs

west of Highway 22 in Willamette
National Forest

Map 5.1, page 164

Sure, the Three Sisters may get most of the fame and fortune, but there is another triple-threat here, with a view that stops traffic. The Three Pyramids stand right in a row, and you can climb up to the remains of their 1934 lookout for panoramic views of the Cascades. The trail gains 1,600 feet in elevation on the climb up to the 5,618-foot lookout. It's a heavily wooded trail that pops out into broad open meadows, adding to your viewing pleasure. South Pyramid Trail also connects to this, but it's not as well maintained as this one, so it's best to stick to the path of least resistance here and head back from the lookout.

User groups: Hikers and dogs. No horses or mountain bikes are allowed. No wheelchair access.

Permits: A federal Northwest Forest pass is required to park here. The cost is $5 for a day pass or $30 for an annual pass. You can buy a day pass at ranger stations, from private vendors, or through Nature of the Northwest Information Center.

Maps: For a map of Willamette National Forest, contact Nature of the Northwest Information Center. For a topographic map, ask the USGS for Coffin Mountain and Echo Mountain.

Directions: From Salem, drive 52 miles east on Highway 22 to Detroit, continuing for another 28 miles. Turn right (south) on Lava Lake Meadow Road, following signs to Old Cascade Crest trails. Continue down the road, turning right at a fork 1.9 miles down. Drive 3.5 miles to the trailhead on the left.

Contact: Willamette National Forest, Sweet Home Ranger District, 3225 Highway 20, Sweet Home, OR 97386, 541/367-5168.

2 ROOSTER ROCK
6.8 mi/4.0 hrs

north of U.S. 20 in the Menagerie
Wilderness of Willamette National Forest

Map 5.1, page 164

The trail up to Rooster Rock walks to the beat of a different drummer. Instead of switchbacking up to a peak, it just keeps going straight. And up. Just when you're getting the hang of the uphill climb, the trail takes it up a notch. It's like an outdoors stair-climber whose ramp level keeps increasing one level at a time. You might also feel like your destination is unknown until you round a bend almost two miles in and you can see the rocky, roosterlike formation through a clearing to the right. The trail is actually called Trout Creek Trail—the actual Rooster Rock Trail starts three miles down the highway, but it gains the same 2,300 feet in just 2.1 miles. Trust one who's been there, you'll want that extra .7 mile to get there, because it's steep enough as it is. You'll hit Rooster Rock Trail .5 mile from the base of the rock, but hold your high-fiving and back-slapping, because the trail must go on. It's just a short (steep) climb to a viewpoint that rocks, so it's worth it. The pillar is also popular with rock climbers, so don't be surprised if you see someone popping their head over the edge from the base itself.

User groups: Hikers and dogs. No mountain bikes or horses are allowed. No wheelchair access.

Permits: A federal Northwest Forest pass is required to park here. The cost is $5 for a day pass or $30 for an annual pass. You can buy a day pass at ranger stations, from private vendors, or through Nature of the Northwest Information Center.

Maps: For a map of Willamette National Forest and the Menagerie Wilderness, contact Nature of the Northwest Information Center. For a topographic map, ask the USGS for Upper Soda.

Directions: From Sweet Home, drive 17.4 miles east on U.S. 20 to the Trout Creek trailhead and the parking area on the left side of the highway.

Contact: Willamette National Forest, Sweet Home Ranger District, 3225 Highway 20, Sweet Home, OR 97386, 541/367-5168.

🔳 IRON MOUNTAIN
3.4 mi/2.0 hrs

north of U.S. 20 in Willamette National Forest

Map 5.1, page 164

The trail up to Iron Mountain starts off gently through wildflower meadows (and all the bugs that go with them). In fact, it starts off so gently you may wonder if you're on the right trail. You are, and you'll start to climb soon enough, so enjoy the stroll while it lasts. After crossing the highway from the short trail leading from the parking lot and entering the meadow, you'll see Iron Mountain to your right, like a castle of rock with proud majestic spires—and even a little white marker on the 5,455 summit. Then leave the meadow behind to dip into the forest for the switchbacks up for views of Mount Jefferson, Three Fingered Jack, and the Three Sisters. A stone bench sits at a viewpoint along the way, so you can rest before the final climb. You'll come to a couple of junctions along this trail, and if you take the 3.5-mile Cone Peak Trail, you'll be in nature heaven as it passes through a nature museum of the 300 species of flowering plants that live on the volcanic slope of Cone Peak. You can also combine the two trails for a 5.5-mile loop—when you return to the Cone Peak trailhead, take Santiam Wagon Trail heading west back to your car. The total elevation gain for both trails is 1,455 feet.

User groups: Hikers and dogs. No mountain bikes or horses are allowed. No wheelchair access.

Permits: A federal Northwest Forest pass is required to park here. The cost is $5 for a day pass or $30 for an annual pass. You can buy a day pass at ranger stations, from private vendors, or through Nature of the Northwest Information Center.

Maps: For a map of the Willamette National Forest, contact Nature of the Northwest Information Center. For a topographic map, ask the USGS for Harter Mountain.

Directions: From Sweet Home, drive 31.8 miles east on U.S. 20 to Forest Service Road 15. Turn right at the Iron Mountain sign, and drive a short distance to the parking area, on the right side of the road. The trail starts on the east side of the parking area.

Contact: Willamette National Forest, Sweet Home Ranger District, 3225 Highway 20, Sweet Home, OR 97386, 541/367-5168.

🔳 TIDBITS MOUNTAIN
3.9 mi/2.0 hrs

north of Blue River Lake in Willamette National Forest

Map 5.1, page 164

Only tidbits remain of Ye Ol' Tidbits Lookout, but the views haven't gone anywhere. A short hike through old-growth forest, with a rocky scramble up to the top, will give you access to a glimpse of the Cascade Range from the 5,185-foot summit (the total elevation gain is 1,200 feet). You'll come to several junctions along the way, so when in doubt, turn left to reach the top (the trails tend to be well marked in this region, but signs can always go AWOL when you least expect it). Retrace your steps, this time turning right at both junctions, to return to your car.

User groups: Hikers, dogs, and mountain bikes. No horses are allowed. No wheelchair access.

Permits: Permits are not required. Parking and access are free.

Maps: For a map of Willamette National Forest, contact Nature of the Northwest Information Center. For a topographic map, ask the USGS for Tidbits Mountain.

Directions: From Eugene, drive 40 miles east on McKenzie Highway/Highway 126 to Blue River. Continue three miles to Forest Service Road 15. Turn left (north) and drive 4.7 miles to Forest Service Road 1509. Drive eight miles to the trailhead parking area on the left. The trail starts a short distance up Spur Road 877.

Contact: Willamette National Forest, McKenzie River Ranger District, 57600 McKenzie Highway, McKenzie Bridge, OR 97413, 541/822-3381.

5 LOOKOUT CREEK OLD-GROWTH TRAIL
7.0 mi/3.5 hrs

north of McKenzie Bridge in H. J. Andrews Experimental Forest of Willamette National Forest

Map 5.1, page 164

If you go ga-ga over old-growth trees, this is your ticket. The 3.5-mile trail gains just 400 feet through, yes, old-growth Douglas fir forest along a scenic wooded trail, with Lookout Creek to keep you company. It's located in the H. J. Andrews Experimental Forest, a living laboratory of ancient forest (don't let the term "laboratory" fool you— no white smocks are required).

User groups: Hikers and dogs. No mountain bikes or horses are allowed. No wheelchair access.

Permits: Permits are not required. Parking and access are free.

Maps: For a free brochure, contact Willamette National Forest, McKenzie River Ranger District, 57600 McKenzie Highway, McKenzie Bridge, OR 97413, 541/822-3381. For a topographic map, ask the USGS for McKenzie Bridge.

Directions: From Eugene, drive 40 miles east on McKenzie Highway/Highway 126 to Blue River. Continue three miles to Forest Service Road 15. Turn left (north) and drive four miles to Forest Service Road 1506. Turn right and drive seven miles to the trailhead and parking area.

Contact: Willamette National Forest, McKenzie River Ranger District, 57600 McKenzie Highway, McKenzie Bridge, OR 97413, 541/822-3381.

6 MCKENZIE RIVER NATIONAL RECREATION TRAIL
26.5 mi one-way/2.0 days

on the McKenzie River between McKenzie Bridge and Clear Lake

Map 5.1, page 164

This is a perfect spring fling to get you ready for all the other trails to shake off their white stuff and open up. The trail follows the white-water McKenzie River the entire length, but hold on to your hat—there's more. Lots more. The trail passes by several waterfalls, reservoirs, lava flows, old-growth forest, and even hot springs—plus plenty of campgrounds along the way, so you can turn the trip into an overnight excursion. There are also a couple of loop options: three-mile Waterfall Loop and five-mile Clear Lake Loop, both of them near the upper trailhead, so you may want to do those for a day hike (although that area tends to be more crowded). Another option is to do the entire length and arrange a car shuttle at the upper trailhead. Unlike some wilderness trails, where you have to drive forever to get from one trail to the other, there are many access points along the route that are right off the highway. The total elevation gain is just 800 feet, just the thing to get your sea (um, river) legs back for hiking again.

User groups: Hikers, dogs, and mountain bikes. No horses are allowed. No wheelchair access.

Permits: Permits are not required. Parking and access are free.

Maps: For a map of Willamette National Forest, contact Nature of the Northwest Information Center. For a topographic map, ask the USGS for McKenzie Bridge, Belknap Springs, Tamolitch Falls, and Clear Lake.

Directions: The trail can be accessed at many places along McKenzie Highway/Highway 126. To reach the lower trailhead from Eugene, drive 50 miles on the McKenzie Highway past the McKenzie Bridge to the trailhead, on the left (north) side of the road, one mile past the McKenzie Bridge Ranger Station. Other marked access points are along the highway.

The upper trailhead is another 25 miles down, at Clear Lake.

Contact: Willamette National Forest, Sweet Home Ranger District, 3225 Highway 20, Sweet Home, OR 97386, 541/367-5168.

7 CASTLE ROCK
2.0 mi/1.0 hrs

south of McKenzie Bridge in Willamette National Forest

Map 5.1, page 164

Lording over the Willamette River Valley, 3,808-foot Castle Rock is easy to get to if you choose the path of least resistance. If you want the red-carpet treatment straight to views of the valley, this trail is perfect for a short leg-stretcher or a warm-up for another hike nearby. Remember not to cackle at those who have chosen the longer path—the locals don't take kindly to that sort of thing. You'll pass the lower trailhead on the route in, which is a 9.2-mile round-trip to the top, so take your pick. The peak is also accessible via the royal King-Castle Trail, which is 15 miles round-trip.

User groups: Hikers, dogs, and mountain bikes. No horses are allowed except on King-Castle Trail. No wheelchair access.

Permits: Permits are not required. Parking and access are free.

Maps: For a map of Willamette National Forest, contact Nature of the Northwest Information Center. For a topographic map, ask the USGS for McKenzie Bridge.

Directions: From Eugene, drive about 42 miles east on McKenzie Highway/Highway 126 to Forest Service Road 19, about five miles west of the McKenzie River Bridge. Turn right (south) and drive one mile, keeping straight to continue on Forest Service Roads 19 and 410 to Forest Service Road 2639. Turn left (east) and drive .5 mile to Forest Service Road 480. Drive six miles to the trailhead at the end of the road. Note: The last miles of this road are rough. To reach the longer lower trailhead, follow the directions above, driving on Forest Service Roads 19 and 410 for two miles, then turn

left onto Forest Service Road 411 and drive 2.7 miles to the parking area on the left side of the road.

Contact: Willamette National Forest, McKenzie River Ranger District, 57600 McKenzie Highway, McKenzie Bridge, OR 97413, 541/822-3381.

8 OLALLIE RIDGE/
OLALLIE MOUNTAIN
9.7 mi one-way/1.0 day

south of McKenzie Bridge on the northern border of the Three Sisters Wilderness in Willamette National Forest

Map 5.1, page 164

So many choices, so little time. It's hard to pick one over another here, so here are all your options. For a shorter trip up to a view, start from the Horsepasture trailhead, and climb 1,400 feet in 1.2 miles up to Horsepasture Mountain for views of the Three Sisters, Mount Washington, Mount Jefferson, Diamond Peak, and Mount Hood. Then return the way you came for a 2.5-mile round-trip. If you're just getting started, continue instead along Olallie Ridge, where wildflowers are at their best in late June. The whole ridgeline is filled with viewpoints, passing Taylor Castle peak in another three miles and continuing to 5,700-foot Olallie Mountain (which is also accessible via another trailhead along the way, which brings you to the mountain in a three-mile round-trip). It's worth it to do the whole ridge, camping overnight along the way, or arrange a shuttle at the Pat Saddle trailhead near Olallie Mountain.

User groups: Hikers, dogs, mountain bikes, and horses. No wheelchair access.

Permits: Permits are not required. Parking and access are free.

Maps: For a map of Willamette National Forest, contact Nature of the Northwest Information Center. For a topographic map, ask the USGS for French Mountain and Chucksney Mountain.

Directions: From Eugene, drive 50 miles east on McKenzie Highway/Highway 126 to Horse

Creek Road/Forest Service Road 2638 at McKenzie Bridge. Turn right (south) and drive two miles to Wapiti Road/Forest Service Road 1993. Turn right and continue 8.5 miles to the Horsepasture Saddle trailhead on the right side of the road. To reach the trailhead near Olallie Mountain: From Eugene, drive 40 miles east on McKenzie Highway/Highway 126 to Blue River. Continue past Blue River, following Cougar Reservoir signs for Forest Service Road 19. Turn right (south) and drive to Cougar Dam. Turn left onto Forest Service Road 1993 across Cougar Dam and continue 15 miles to Pat Saddle Trail on the right side of the road.

Contact: Willamette National Forest, McKenzie River Ranger District, 57600 McKenzie Highway, McKenzie Bridge, OR 97413, 541/822-3381.

9 DUFFY AND MOWICH LAKES
9.0 mi/4.5 hrs

west of Three Fingered Jack in the Mount Jefferson Wilderness

Map 5.2, page 165

Why hit just one lake when you can reach two? You'll pay only two more miles to reach Mowich Lake after Duffy. And it's worth the trip to see both alpine lakes (elevation: 5,000 feet). Since it's a relatively easy jaunt, and since there are so many routes that lead off from here and go deeper into the Jefferson Wilderness, it can be a little crowded at times. But if you want a perfect picnic spot where you can feel like you earned your lunch, this is a good choice. After lunch, you can also add a view to your day by continuing up another 1.5 miles and another 800 feet up to 5,843-foot Red Butte for a view of the Mount Jefferson area and Three Fingered Jack. Note: In August 2003, this area was closed due to the Booth and Bear fires. Check trail conditions before you head out.

User groups: Hikers, dogs, and horses. No mountain bikes are allowed. No wheelchair access.

Permits: A federal Northwest Forest pass is required to park here. The cost is $5 for a day

pass or $30 for an annual pass. You can buy a day pass at ranger stations, from private vendors, or through Nature of the Northwest Information Center.

Maps: For a map of the Mount Jefferson Wilderness and Willamette National Forest, contact Nature of the Northwest Information Center. For a topographic map, ask the USGS for Santiam Junction, Three Fingered Jack, and Marion Lake.

Directions: From Salem, drive 52 miles east on Highway 22 to Detroit, and continue another 27 miles to Big Meadows Road/Forest Service Road 2267. Turn left (east) and drive three miles to the trailhead and parking area at the end of the road.

Contact: Willamette National Forest, Detroit Ranger Station, HC73, P.O. Box 320, Mill City, OR 97360, 503/854-3366.

10 ROCKPILE LAKE
10.0 mi/5.0 hrs

north of Three Fingered Jack in the Mount Jefferson Wilderness

Map 5.2, page 165

Yet another route through the Mount Jefferson Wilderness, this trail accesses the Pacific Crest Trail for countless options (pick up a map of this area before you go; you'll be glad you did). For a day trip to cute Rockpile Lake, nestled at 6,300 feet, try this trail that leads five miles and gains 2,300 feet in elevation to hit the Pacific Crest Trail and the lake itself. From here, you can turn back the way you came or turn left (south) on the PCT to make a loop, keeping left at all junctions and passing by equally tiny Minto Lake to return to the trailhead for a 13.5-mile loop. As with many trails in this area, the choices go on from the trailhead—you can also access the Marion Lake trail system to the west and North Cinder Peaks to the north for backpacking trips. Note: In August 2003, this area was closed and possibly damaged due to the Booth and Bear fires. Check conditions before you head out.

User groups: Hikers, dogs, and horses. No mountain bikes are allowed. No wheelchair access.

Permits: A free wilderness permit is required to hike here and is available at the trailhead. A federal Northwest Forest pass is also required to park here. The cost is $5 for a day pass or $30 for an annual pass. You can buy a day pass at ranger stations, from private vendors, or through Nature of the Northwest Information Center.

Maps: For a map of the Mount Jefferson Wilderness and Deschutes National Forest, contact Nature of the Northwest Information Center. For a topographic map, contact Green Trails, Inc. (ask for Mount Jefferson, map number 557), 206/546-MAPS (206/546-6277), www.greentrails.com, or ask the USGS for Marion Lake.

Directions: From U.S. 20 at Santiam Pass (about 85 miles east of Salem and 22 miles west of Sisters), drive eight miles east to Jack Lake Road/Forest Service Road 12. Turn left (north) and drive four miles to Forest Service Road 1230. Continue straight for 1.7 miles to Forest Service Road 1234, then turn left and drive one mile to Forest Service Road 1235. Turn right and drive four miles to Bear Valley trailhead and the parking area at the end of the road.

Contact: Deschutes National Forest, Sisters Ranger District, Highway 20/Pine Street, P.O. Box 249, Sisters, OR 97759, 541/549-7700.

11 CANYON CREEK MEADOWS LOOP
8.1 mi/4.0 hrs

east of Three Fingered Jack in the Mount Hood Wilderness

Map 5.2, page 165

Traveling through the Canyon Creek Meadows with an up-close view of Three Fingered Jack, this popular loop gives you access to the good stuff without having to hike forever to get there. The well-marked loop is 4.5 miles, unless you want to continue another 1.8 miles (and why not?) straight up the wildflower meadows for the grand finale at the base of 7,841-foot Three Fingered Jack. An extinct volcano with a funny-sounding name and an even fun-

nier look, Three Fingered Jack features three distinct protrusions that are landmarks from viewpoints around the state. Returning back, turn right to complete the loop, keeping left at all junctions to return to the trailhead. Note: In August 2003, this area was closed and possibly damaged due to the Booth and Bear fires. Check conditions before you head out.

User groups: Hikers, dogs, and horses. No mountain bikes are allowed. No wheelchair access.

Permits: A free wilderness permit is required to hike here and is available at the trailhead. A federal Northwest Forest pass is also required to park here. The cost is $5 for a day pass or $30 for an annual pass. You can buy a day pass at ranger stations, from private vendors, or through Nature of the Northwest Information Center.

Maps: For a map of the Mount Jefferson Wilderness and Deschutes National Forest, contact Nature of the Northwest Information Center. For a topographic map, contact Green Trails, Inc. (ask for Whitewater River, map number 558), 206/546-MAPS (206/546-6277), www.greentrails.com, or ask the USGS for Three Fingered Jack.

Directions: From U.S. 20 at Santiam Pass (about 85 miles east of Salem and 22 miles west of Sisters), drive eight miles east to Jack Lake Road/Forest Service Road 12. Turn left (north) and drive four miles to Forest Service Road 1230. Continue straight for 1.7 miles, then turn left onto Forest Service Road 1234 and drive five miles to the trailhead and parking at Jack Lake Campground.

Contact: Deschutes National Forest, Sisters Ranger District, Highway 20/Pine Street, P.O. Box 249, Sisters, OR 97759, 541/549-7700.

12 PACIFIC CREST TRAIL TO THREE FINGERED JACK
10.5 mi/5.5 hrs

on the southern slope of Three Fingered Jack in the Mount Jefferson Wilderness

Map 5.2, page 165

The extinct volcano Three Fingered Jack is

a beacon to climbers, who flock to scale its 7,841-foot height. You can get pretty close to the action on a stellar viewpoint by accessing the Pacific Crest Trail right off the highway. It's a dry, dusty path, so bring water—as well as your camera to snap some shots of this unusual guy. It's a strenuous and sometimes rocky route to a viewpoint right next to Jack himself. You can also do a loop by heading straight to Square Lake, then turning left at all junctions to add another mile to your route. If you're hiking with others who aren't quite as into sweat as you are, they can take an easy stroll to Square and Round Lakes (four miles round-trip) from the same trailhead. Note: In August 2003, this trail was closed and possibly damaged due to the Booth and Bear fires. Check conditions before you try this route.

User groups: Hikers, dogs, and horses. No mountain bikes are allowed. No wheelchair access.

Permits: A federal Northwest Forest pass is required to park here. The cost is $5 for a day pass or $30 for an annual pass. You can buy a day pass at ranger stations, from private vendors, or through Nature of the Northwest Information Center.

Maps: For a map of the Mount Jefferson Wilderness and Deschutes National Forest, contact Nature of the Northwest Information Center. For a topographic map, contact Green Trails, Inc. (ask for Whitewater River, map number 558), 206/546-MAPS (206/546-6277), www.greentrails.com, or ask the USGS for Three Fingered Jack.

Directions: From Salem, drive 52 miles east on Highway 22 to Detroit and continue 36 miles to Santiam Pass (22 miles west of Sisters). Follow signs to the Pacific Crest Trail parking lot on the left (north) side of the road.

Contact: Deschutes National Forest, Sisters Ranger District, Highway 20/Pine Street, P.O. Box 249, Sisters, OR 97759, 541/549-7700.

13 BLACK BUTTE
4.0 mi/2.0 hrs

north of Sisters in Deschutes National Forest

Map 5.2, page 165

The Black Butte volcano has enjoyed quite a bit of attention in the fire lookout station department. Whereas other lookout stations atop fine viewpoints have long since gone by the wayside, 6,436-foot Black Butte has kept Forest Service workers busy for years, making sure she has a nice little lookout on top. In 1910, a platform was built between two trees, where rangers perched to survey the area. The platform endured for 12 years, until a cupola structure was completed in 1922, where it waited to be outdone in 1934 by a bigger, flashier 83-foot lookout tower. The cute cupola got its revenge when the tower collapsed in 2001—but not before an even flashier, shinier tower was built in 1995 and flown in specially to be placed gently on the butte. Got all that? The whole point is, Black Butte is an important lookout site, which means the view can't be beat, from that attention-hogging Three Fingered Jack to the Cascade mountain range. The hike up to the summit gains 1,600 feet in elevation, starting in a ponderosa pine forest and ending up on a hot exposed area.

User groups: Hikers, dogs, and horses. No mountain bikes are allowed. No wheelchair access.

Permits: A federal Northwest Forest pass is also required to park here. The cost is $5 for a day pass or $30 for an annual pass. You can buy a day pass at ranger stations, from private vendors, or through Nature of the Northwest Information Center.

Maps: For a map of Deschutes National Forest, contact Nature of the Northwest Information Center. For a topographic map, ask the USGS for Black Butte.

Directions: From Sisters, drive 6.3 miles northwest on U.S. 20 to Green Ridge Road/Forest Service Road 11. Turn right (north) and continue 3.9 miles to Forest Service Road 1110.

Turn left and drive 5.5 miles to the end of the road and the trailhead.

Contact: Deschutes National Forest, Sisters Ranger District, Highway 20/Pine Street, P.O. Box 249, Sisters, OR 97759, 541/549-7700.

14 PATJENS LAKE LOOP
5.5 mi/2.5 hrs

at Big Lake in the northern Mount Washington Wilderness

Map 5.2, page 165

Accessing three small lakes, the Patjens Lake Loop is a chance to take a dip (literally) in the remote Mount Washington wilderness. Meandering through lodgepole pine, western hemlock, and alpine fir forest, the trail is a relatively easy stroll to these small alpine lakes, which are a perfect setting for a picnic, reflection, or an impromptu dip.

User groups: Hikers, dogs, and horses. No mountain bikes are allowed. No wheelchair access.

Permits: A free wilderness permit is required to hike here and is available at the trailhead.

Maps: For a map of the Mount Washington Wilderness and Willamette National Forest, contact Nature of the Northwest Information Center. For a topographic map, ask the USGS for Clear Lake and Mount Washington.

Directions: From U.S. 20 at Santiam Pass (about 85 miles east of Salem and 22 miles west of Sisters), turn south on Big Lake Road/Forest Service Road 2690 at the sign for Hoodoo Ski Area. Drive one mile past Big Lake Campground to the trailhead on the right side of the road.

Contact: Willamette National Forest, McKenzie River Ranger District, 57600 McKenzie Highway, McKenzie Bridge, OR 97413, 541/822-3381.

15 SMITH ROCK STATE PARK LOOP
4.0 mi/2.0 hrs

northeast of Redmond on the Crooked River off Highway 97

Map 5.2, page 165

How Smith Rock got its name still stymies historians. The optimist side of the camp proclaims that it was named after the pioneer and Oregon legislator John Smith, who discovered the formations in 1867. The pessimist side says it was actually named for a soldier who fell to his death from the highest peak in the 1860s while camping with his company (yikes!). Either way, there were two Smiths involved in some way in the 1860s, so we'll just leave it at that. Two things are clear, though: The park is a sight to behold, and Smith Rock has probably the blandest name in the whole park, what with walls like the Christian Brothers, Morning Glory, Monkey Face, and Misery Ridge (wonder how they got their names?). The park is renowned among climbers, who come from all over to scale the walls. But you don't need to know your way around a carabiner to witness the scene—you can keep both feet firmly planted on the ground and travel along the trail system through the state park. The main drag is a pleasant four-mile loop that brings you up close to the walls and most likely a few climbers.

User groups: Hikers, dogs, horses, and mountain bikes. No wheelchair access.

Permits: A $3 day-use fee is collected at the park entrance, or you can get an annual Oregon Parks and Recreation pass for $25; contact Oregon Parks and Recreation, 800/551-6949.

Maps: For a free park brochure and map, contact Oregon Parks and Recreation Department, 800/551-6949, www.oregonstateparks.org. For a topographic map, ask the USGS for Redmond.

Directions: From Redmond, drive about five miles north on U.S. 97 to Terrebone and turn right (east) on Smith Rock Way, following signs for three miles to the park entrance.

Contact: Oregon Parks and Recreation Department, 1115 Commercial Street Northeast, Salem, OR 97301, 800/551-6949, www.oregonstateparks.org.

16 PROXY FALLS/LINTON LAKE
4.2 mi/2.5 hrs   🥾 ◀8

south of McKenzie Pass Highway in the Three Sisters Wilderness of Willamette National Forest

Map 5.2, page 165

These trails are actually two separate entities altogether, but who's to get technical? They're so close together off Highway 242 that it's simple to do them both. And you'll want to: Start off with a 1.25-mile warm-up to Proxy Falls, where you'll walk through open lava fields and forest on your way to two different falls, each waiting to show off for you. Then head back on the highway to visit Linton Lake in a quick three-mile trip; this is a popular fishing hole for the locals (or for you, if you're into that kind of thing). Two falls, one lake, one lava field, one forest, one small drive, and one picnic later, you can call it a day. Since the trails are right off the highway, they can be a little crowded, but that's the price you pay for convenience. Keep in mind that Highway 242 is often closed until July.

User groups: Hikers and dogs. No horses or mountain bikes are allowed. No wheelchair access.

Permits: A free wilderness permit is required to hike at Linton Lake and is available at the trailhead. A federal Northwest Forest pass is also required to park at both trails. The cost is $5 for a day pass or $30 for an annual pass. You can buy a day pass at ranger stations, from private vendors, or through Nature of the Northwest Information Center.

Maps: For a map of the Three Sisters Wilderness and Willamette National Forest, contact Nature of the Northwest Information Center. For a topographic map, ask the USGS for Linton Lake.

Directions: From Eugene, drive 55 miles east on McKenzie Pass Highway/Highway 126, five miles past the town of McKenzie Bridge, to the junction with Highway 242. Continue east on Highway 242 for nine miles to Proxy Falls Trail on the right (south) side of the road. Lin-

ton Lake Trail is 1.5 miles down the road from Proxy Falls.

Contact: Willamette National Forest, McKenzie River Ranger District, 57600 McKenzie Highway, McKenzie Bridge, OR 97413, 541/822-3381.

17 OBSIDIAN TRAIL LOOP
11.0 mi/4.5 hrs   🥾 ◀8

south of McKenzie Pass Highway in the Three Sisters Wilderness of Willamette National Forest

Map 5.2, page 165

Warning: If you want to hike in this area, you need to get a permit before you enter, because it's now a limited-use area (see information below). Okay, now that we have that out of the way, here's the deal: Gaining 1,200 feet in elevation throughout the hike, you'll pass through a lava field and over the Obsidian Cliffs before hitting a junction with the Pacific Crest Trail. Turn left to pass by the Obsidian Falls, turning left again at the next junction to complete the loop. Remember to bring your camera along; since you were so special to see this cool area, you'll want to show it off to your friends. Keep in mind that Highway 242 is often closed until July, so plan ahead. Restrictions, restrictions.

User groups: Hikers, dogs, and horses. No mountain bikes are allowed. No wheelchair access.

Permits: A free limited-use wilderness permit is required to hike here and is available from Willamette National Forest, McKenzie River Ranger District, 57600 McKenzie Highway, McKenzie Bridge, OR 97413, 541/822-3381. A federal Northwest Forest pass is also required to park here. The cost is $5 for a day pass or $30 for an annual pass. You can buy a day pass at ranger stations, from private vendors, or through Nature of the Northwest Information Center.

Maps: For a map of the Three Sisters Wilderness and Willamette National Forest, contact Nature of the Northwest Information Center.

For a topographic map, ask the USGS for North Sister and Linton Lake.

Directions: From Eugene, drive 55 miles east on McKenzie Pass Highway/Highway 126, five miles past the town of McKenzie Bridge, to the junction with Highway 242. Continue east on Highway 242 for six miles to the Obsidian Trail sign on the right (south) side of the road.

Contact: Willamette National Forest, McKenzie River Ranger District, 57600 McKenzie Highway, McKenzie Bridge, OR 97413, 541/822-3381.

18 SCOTT TRAIL TO FOUR-IN-ONE CONE
10.0 mi/5.0 hrs

west of Sisters in the Three Sisters Wilderness of Willamette National Forest

Map 5.2, page 165

Like Scott Trail's neighbor, Obsidian Trail, this is a fascinating walk through lava flows and alpine meadows. Unlike its neighbor, it doesn't require limited-use permits. Yet. So take a stroll down Scott Trail, named for Felix Scott (hey, at least the trail isn't called Felix), a true trailblazer in his day who led 50 men through the Cascade Mountains in 1862. The trail follows part of his route, and what a route it is—a tough walk through a lava field. No wonder he ended up bagging it to find a new, wagon-friendly course, which became the approximate path of the Willamette Pass Highway. The trail ends at the junction with the Pacific Crest Trail, but remember that to travel south into the Obsidian area, you'll need a permit. Before the end of the trail, though, you'll come across Four-in-One Cone on your right, which you can scramble to the top of for a cool view. Either way, it's best to leave your sandals at home for this one—your ankles will thank you. Keep in mind that Highway 242 is often closed until July.

User groups: Hikers, dogs, and horses. No mountain bikes are allowed. No wheelchair access.

Permits: A free wilderness permit is required to hike here and is available at the trailhead. A federal Northwest Forest pass is also required to park here. The cost is $5 for a day pass or $30 for an annual pass. You can buy a day pass at ranger stations, from private vendors, or through Nature of the Northwest Information Center.

Maps: For a map of the Three Sisters Wilderness and Willamette National Forest, contact Nature of the Northwest Information Center. For a topographic map, ask the USGS for North Sister.

Directions: From Eugene, drive 55 miles east on McKenzie Pass Highway/Highway 126, five miles past the town of McKenzie Bridge, to the junction with Highway 242. Continue east on Highway 242 to the Scott Lake turnoff on the left (north) side of the road. The trail starts across the road.

Contact: Willamette National Forest, McKenzie River Ranger District, 57600 McKenzie Highway, McKenzie Bridge, OR 97413, 541/822-3381.

19 PACIFIC CREST TRAIL TO LITTLE BELKNAP CRATER
4.0 mi/2.0 hrs

west of Sisters in the Mount Washington Wilderness

Map 5.2, page 165

Someday, we'll probably all get a chance to walk on the moon, but why wait another millennium? You'll feel as if you're walking on the moon here when you make your way across the lava field on the Pacific Crest Trail to Little Belknap Crater. The nearby Dee Observatory offers a glimpse through its stone shelter windows of the lava fields and craters in the distance, but they're not so distant that you can't walk to them. It's about two miles to reach the crater summit, and it's unlike any hike around. Thin scraggles of trees struggle to poke up out of the lava surface (you have to admire their determination). The trail is sometimes hard to follow since you're walking right through the lava field, so use the 6,872-foot cinder-and-ash volcanic cone as your beacon, along with its bigger neighbor, the Belknap Crater. From the summit, and actually all throughout the hike, you can see views of the Three Sisters. Just refrain from doing the moonwalk on the crater itself, because it's not the best surface on which to break out the dance moves. If you don't want to risk a twisted ankle on this route, you can also try the paved one-mile Lava River Interpretive Trail, just east of the Dee Observatory.

User groups: Hikers, dogs, and horses. No mountain bikes are allowed. No wheelchair access.

Permits: Permits are not required. Parking and access are free.

Maps: For a map of the Mount Washington Wilderness and Willamette National Forest, contact Nature of the Northwest Information Center. For a topographic map, ask the USGS for Mount Washington.

Directions: From Eugene, drive 50 miles east on McKenzie Highway/Highway 126 to the town of McKenzie Bridge. Continue five miles east to the junction with Highway 242. (From Sisters, drive west about 15 miles on Highway 242.) Continue east on Highway 242 to McKenzie Pass and the Pacific Crest Trail marker on the left (north) side of the road, just before the Dee Wright Observatory. Note: Highway 242 is often closed until July.

Contact: Willamette National Forest, McKenzie River Ranger District, 57600 McKenzie Highway, McKenzie Bridge, OR 97413, 541/822-3381.

20 PACIFIC CREST TRAIL/ MATTHIEU LAKES
6.0 mi/3.0 hrs

west of Sisters in the Three Sisters Wilderness of Deschutes National Forest

Map 5.2, page 165

Traveling along the old Oregon Skyline Trail, which has been replaced by the good ol' PCT, this loop goes to two shimmering lakes with great views of the Sisters peaks, all lined up for your viewing pleasure—although North Sis-

ter is closer, so she kind of hogs the spotlight. You may be sharing the glory with some PCTers and their horses, so just nod and smile and you'll be fine. You'll start from Lava Camp (yes, more lava) and come to a junction with the PCT. Head left to start the loop, keeping straight at the loop junction to continue to North Matthieu Lake, the big bro' of the two lakes. Stick around here to soak in the scenery before continuing the loop to visit the little guy, South Matthieu. Complete the loop by returning to the junction at South Matty, and this time turn right to head back to your car (and some lava walls on the way).

User groups: Hikers, dogs, and horses. No mountain bikes are allowed. No wheelchair access.

Permits: A free wilderness permit is required to hike here and is available at the trailhead. Parking and access are free.

Maps: For a map of the Three Sisters Wilderness and Deschutes National Forest, contact Nature of the Northwest Information Center. For a topographic map, ask the USGS for Mount Washington and North Sister.

Directions: From Eugene, drive 55 miles east on McKenzie Pass Highway/Highway 126, five miles past the town of McKenzie Bridge, to the junction with Highway 242. Continue east for one mile on Highway 242 to Forest Service Road 900 at the sign for Lava Camp Lake. Turn right (south) and drive .3 mile to the Pacific Crest Trail parking area on the right.

Contact: Deschutes National Forest, Sisters Ranger District, Highway 20/Pine Street, P.O. Box 249, Sisters, OR 97759, 541/549-7700.

21 BLACK CRATER
7.6 mi/5.0 hrs

west of Sisters in the Three Sisters Wilderness of Deschutes National Forest

Map 5.2, page 165

Need to break into a hike gently? Then do some jumping jacks at the parking lot, because this trail cuts you no breaks from the get-go. Instead, it just sails on up 2,351 feet (and you'll feel that last foot, too) through thick mountain hemlock forest to reach the 7,251-foot summit, where you can view North Sister, Mount Washington, and a special bird's-eye view of the McKenzie Pass lava flows. In fact, you can even see as far north as Mount Adams on a clear day—just don't pick a day that's scorching, because this area is renowned for hot, dry weather. The only problem is that Highway 242 doesn't tend to open its pearly gates until July 1, so that leaves the hot summer months or the fall. Choose wisely.

User groups: Hikers, dogs, and horses. No mountain bikes are allowed. No wheelchair access.

Permits: A free wilderness permit is required to hike here and is available at the trailhead. A federal Northwest Forest pass is also required to park here. The cost is $5 for a day pass or $30 for an annual pass. You can buy a day pass at ranger stations, from private vendors, or through Nature of the Northwest Information Center.

Maps: For a map of the Three Sisters Wilderness and Deschutes National Forest, contact Nature of the Northwest Information Center. For a topographic map, ask the USGS for Mount Washington and Black Crater.

Directions: From Sisters, drive 11.5 miles west on Highway 242 to the trailhead parking lot on the left (south) side of the road (3.5 miles east of the McKenzie Pass).

Contact: Deschutes National Forest, Sisters Ranger District, Highway 20/Pine Street, P.O. Box 249, Sisters, OR 97759, 541/549-7700.

22 CAMP LAKE/CHAMBERS LAKE BASIN
14.0 mi/7.0 hrs
between the South and Middle Sisters in the Three Sisters Wilderness of Deschutes National Forest

Map 5.2, page 165

Nestled between the South and Middle Sisters (you can still wave at North Sister, but she gets left out of the picture for the most part), the

Chambers Lake Basin is a perfect place to overnight and to wipe the sweat off your brow from a handy water source. Traveling from the Pole Creek trailhead, you'll hike for two miles to catch up to Camp Lake Trail, then turn right to lead five more miles to the lakes. Plan a camping trip here if you can, because unless you actually climb the peaks (more on that later in this chapter), this is the closest you'll come to them. The total elevation gain on the trail is 1,200 feet. Keep in mind Highway 242 is usually closed until July, which makes for a perfect summer getaway.

User groups: Hikers, dogs, and horses. No mountain bikes are allowed. No wheelchair access.

Permits: A free wilderness permit is required to hike here and is available at the trailhead. A federal Northwest Forest pass is also required to park here. The cost is $5 for a day pass or $30 for an annual pass. You can buy a day pass at ranger stations, from private vendors, or through Nature of the Northwest Information Center.

Maps: For a map of the Three Sisters Wilderness and Deschutes National Forest, contact Nature of the Northwest Information Center. For a topographic map, ask the USGS for Trout Creek Butte, Broken Top, and South Sister.

Directions: From Sisters, drive 1.5 miles west on Highway 242 to the junction with Forest Service Road 15. Follow signs to the Pole Creek Trail, 10.5 miles from the junction.

Contact: Deschutes National Forest, Sisters Ranger District, Highway 20/Pine Street, P.O. Box 249, Sisters, OR 97759, 541/549-7700.

23 SHEVLIN PARK LOOP
5.0 mi/2.5 hrs
in Bend's Shevlin Park

Map 5.2, page 165

You're just a javelin's throw away from Bend (well, actually three miles), but you'd never know it. Like many of Oregon's city parks, Shevlin redefines the term "urban" park. If you want to hit some trails and still make it back in time for dinner at the Deschutes Brewery, try the five-mile loop that will take you past and over Tumalo Creek, through Bend's oldest and largest natural park. It's a popular trail with mountain bikers, especially since a paved bike path connects right to the heart of the city.

User groups: Hikers, dogs, and mountain bikes. No wheelchair access.

Permits: Permits are not required. Parking and access are free.

Maps: For a topographic map, ask the USGS for Shevlin Park.

Directions: From downtown Bend, follow Newport Avenue west, which turns into Shevlin Park Road for four miles. Drive across Tumalo Creek to the parking area. Cross the log bridge over Tumalo Creek to start the trail.

Contact: Bend Metro Park and Recreation Department, 200 Northwest Pacific Park Lane, Bend, OR 97701, 541/389-7275.

24 SOUTH SISTER SUMMIT
11.0 mi/1.0 day

the South Sister Summit in Three Sisters Wilderness of Deschutes National Forest

Map 5.2, page 165

Hovering over the little people and its two other sister peaks, 10,538-foot South Sister is the third-tallest peak in the state. It's also The Peak to Climb, because you don't need any shiny equipment to scale her (except some good hiking boots, water, trail treats, and maybe a tune to hum to distract yourself from the brutal climb). Bring warm clothes, because weather conditions can change at any moment. A dormant volcano, South Sister last blew 2,000 years ago, but after the 5.5-mile climb of 4,758 feet, you may feel like you're about to erupt. A gentler option is Moraine Lake Trail (four miles round-trip), which you'll hit before the climbing really gets under way. This is your last chance to back out—or a good option for those saner souls with you who wish to wave at you from the comfort of the trailhead. The trail is usually not clear of snow until July, so

plan accordingly—you'll need the summer to get into shape for it, anyway.

User groups: Hikers and dogs. No mountain bikes or horses are allowed. No wheelchair access.

Permits: A free wilderness permit is required to hike here and is available at the trailhead. A federal Northwest Forest pass is also required to park here. The cost is $5 for a day pass or $30 for an annual pass. You can buy a day pass at ranger stations, from private vendors, or through Nature of the Northwest Information Center.

Maps: For a map of the Three Sisters Wilderness and Deschutes National Forest, contact Nature of the Northwest Information Center. For a topographic map, ask the USGS for South Sister.

Directions: From U.S. 97 in Bend, follow signs for Mount Bachelor Ski Area on Cascade Lakes Highway/Highway 46, driving 33 miles to Devil's Lake Campground, on the left side of the highway, at the sign for Devil's Lake Trail.

Contact: Deschutes National Forest, Bend-Fort Rock Ranger District, 1230 Northeast 3rd Street, Suite A-262, Bend, OR 97701, 541/383-4000.

25 GREEN LAKES LOOP
13.2 mi/7.0 hrs

between Broken Top and South Sister in the Three Sisters Wilderness of Deschutes National Forest

Map 5.2, page 165

You don't need to scale a summit to enjoy the scenery near the Three Sisters. Green Lakes Trail gains only 1,300 feet in elevation (a paltry amount compared to the South Sister haul), yet you get more bang for your buck here: Green Lake, a lava field, and a pass where you can squeeze right in between South Sister and Broken Top and still have energy to spare. Be warned that this trail is heavily used, and you'd be wise to wait until the summer crowds have gone back to their real lives and you can slip out on a September weekday. The loop starts on Fall Creek Trail for six miles to Green Lake, which sits snugly between South Sister and Broken Top. Take a short loop around the lake to get all perspectives of the view before completing the loop by turning left after the lake and keeping to the right at all junctions back to the trailhead. If you want to camp here, keep in mind that camping spots fill up quickly and are restricted to designated campsites only.

User groups: Hikers, dogs, and horses. No mountain bikes are allowed. No wheelchair access.

Permits: A free wilderness permit is required to hike here and is available at the trailhead. A federal Northwest Forest pass is also required to park here. The cost is $5 for a day pass or $30 for an annual pass. You can buy a day pass at ranger stations, from private vendors, or through Nature of the Northwest Information Center.

Maps: For a map of the Three Sisters Wilderness and Deschutes National Forest, contact Nature of the Northwest Information Center. For a topographic map, ask the USGS for Broken Top.

Directions: From U.S. 97 in Bend, follow signs for Mount Bachelor Ski Area on Cascade Lakes Highway/Highway 46, driving 35 miles to the Green Lakes trailhead on the right side of the highway.

Contact: Deschutes National Forest, Bend-Fort Rock Ranger District, 1230 Northeast 3rd Street, Suite A-262, Bend, OR 97701, 541/383-4000.

26 TAM MCARTHUR RIM
5.2 mi/3.0 hrs

west of Bend in the Three Sisters Wilderness in Deschutes National Forest

Map 5.2, page 165

Hey, no need to climb up to a top-notch view here. This trail starts high and stays high, starting at 6,500 feet in elevation and moseying up 1,200 feet along its 2.6-mile length. Don't discount the distance, though, because the altitude can make it feel twice as long, slowing your progress to a crawl. But that just gives you more

time to check out the view: From the rim, you'll peer down at Three Creek Lake and peer over at Broken Top and South Sister, among the countless other sidekicks of the Sisters area. (Yes, that rascal Three Fingered Jack always seems to make it into the equation; give him a wave.) Keep in mind that the trail may be snowy through July, so save this one for later in the season.

User groups: Hikers, dogs, and horses. No mountain bikes are allowed. No wheelchair access.

Permits: A free wilderness permit is required to hike here and is available at the trailhead. A federal Northwest Forest pass is also required to park here. The cost is $5 for a day pass or $30 for an annual pass. You can buy a day pass at ranger stations, from private vendors, or through Nature of the Northwest Information Center.

Maps: For a map of the Three Sisters Wilderness and Deschutes National Forest, contact Nature of the Northwest Information Center. For a topographic map, ask the USGS for Tumalo Falls and Broken Top.

Directions: From downtown Sisters, turn south on Elm Street, following signs for Three Creek Lake. Drive 17 miles on Three Creek Road/Forest Service Road 16. The trailhead parking area is to the right shortly down the entrance road to Driftwood Campground.

Contact: Deschutes National Forest, Sisters Ranger District, Highway 20/Pine Street, P.O. Box 249, Sisters, OR 97759, 541/549-7700.

27 TUMALO MOUNTAIN
3.0 mi/2.0 hrs

north of Mount Bachelor in Deschutes National Forest

Map 5.2, page 165

Climb up to 7,775-foot Tumalo Mountain, and let us count the views: Mount Bachelor, Broken Top, and the Three Sisters. Although the trail is a mere 1.5 miles long, which would be a piece of cake on a flat surface, the trailhead begins at 6,350 feet, so if you're feeling a little loopy as soon as you get out of the car, you'll know why. Add in a 1,200-foot climb, and you have yourself a challenge, unless you happen to be spending your nights in an oxygen-deprivation chamber, in which case this will be breeze. Take it slowly and enjoy the scenery on the way up. Keep in mind that the trail can be snowy through July.

User groups: Hikers and dogs. No mountain bikes or horses are allowed. No wheelchair access.

Permits: A federal Northwest Forest pass is required to park here. The cost is $5 for a day pass or $30 for an annual pass. You can buy a day pass at ranger stations, from private vendors, or through Nature of the Northwest Information Center.

Maps: For a map of Deschutes National Forest, contact Nature of the Northwest Information Center. For a topographic map, ask the USGS for Tumalo Falls and Wanoga Butte.

Directions: From U.S. 97 in Bend, drive on Cascade Lakes Highway/Highway 46 for 27 miles to the Dutchman Sno-Park on the right (north) side of the road.

Contact: Deschutes National Forest, Bend-Fort Rock Ranger District, 1230 Northeast 3rd Street, Suite A-262, Bend, OR 97701, 541/383-4000.

28 FRENCH PETE CREEK
6.0 mi/3.0 hrs

in the South Fork McKenzie River area of Willamette National Forest

Map 5.3, page 166

While the trail actually extends 10 miles one-way, there is a bridgeless creek crossing. Unless you just love to trudge through water, in which case feel free, it's better to turn back at the three-mile mark (you'll know it when you come face-to-face with the river), because the trail isn't maintained after that mark. No worries, though, because you still get to travel through old-growth Douglas fir forest along the rushing French Pete, which makes for a scenic stroll. The total elevation gain is less than 200 feet, so it's just the warm-up you need before hitting other area hikes later in the season. Since

you're at low elevation, this trail tends to open earlier than others in the area, which makes for a perfect antidote to spring fever.

User groups: Hikers and dogs. No mountain bikes or horses are allowed. No wheelchair access.

Permits: A free wilderness permit is required to hike here and is available at the trailhead. A federal Northwest Forest pass is also required to park here. The cost is $5 for a day pass or $30 for an annual pass. You can buy a day pass at ranger stations, from private vendors, or through Nature of the Northwest Information Center.

Maps: For a map of the Three Sisters Wilderness and Willamette National Forest, contact Nature of the Northwest Information Center. For a topographic map, ask the USGS for Cougar Reservoir and French Mountain.

Directions: From Eugene, drive 40 miles on McKenzie Pass Highway/Highway 126 to Blue River. Continue five miles east past Blue River, and turn right (south) onto Forest Service Road 19. Drive 11 miles south to the French Pete Creek trailhead on the left (east) side of the road.

Contact: Willamette National Forest, McKenzie River Ranger District, 57600 McKenzie Highway, McKenzie Bridge, OR 97413, 541/822-3381.

29 REBEL CREEK/ REBEL ROCK LOOP
11.0 mi/6.0 hrs

in the South Fork McKenzie River area of Willamette National Forest

Map 5.3, page 166

Rebel Rock may sound like the new rage in music, but it's also a pleasant jaunt through old-growth forest. But don't set off for a simple creekside stroll just yet: It also gains a smoking 3,000 feet along the way, adding some ridgetop views to the combination platter. Climbing along the forest and out through a meadow, you'll have unobstructed vistas of the Three Sisters and Mount Jefferson. Combine the Rebel Creek and Rebel Rock Trails for an 11-mile loop by following Rebel Rock Trail to its junction with Rebel Creek, then turn left for the return trip along the creek. Simple? Nope. Worth it? Yep.

User groups: Hikers, dogs, and horses. No mountain bikes are allowed. No wheelchair access.

Permits: A free wilderness permit is required to hike here and is available at the trailhead. A federal Northwest Forest pass is also required to park here. The cost is $5 for a day pass or $30 for an annual pass. You can buy a day pass at ranger stations, from private vendors, or through Nature of the Northwest Information Center.

Maps: For a map of Three Sisters Wilderness and Willamette National Forest, contact Nature of the Northwest Information Center. For a topographic map, ask the USGS for Cougar Reservoir, French Mountain, Grasshopper Mountain, and Chucksney Mountain.

Directions: From Eugene, drive 40 miles on McKenzie Pass Highway/Highway 126 to Blue River. Continue five miles east past Blue River, and turn right (south) onto Forest Service Road 19. Drive 14.5 miles to the Rebel Rock trailhead on the left (east) side of the road.

Contact: Willamette National Forest, McKenzie River Ranger District, 57600 McKenzie Highway, McKenzie Bridge, OR 97413, 541/822-3381.

30 CHUCKSNEY MOUNTAIN LOOP
10.5 mi/5.5 hrs

between the Waldo Lake and Three Sisters Wilderness Areas in Willamette National Forest

Map 5.3, page 166

While other, tougher hikes in the area are blanketed in snow, Chucksney Mountain Trail is ready to go. Gaining 2,000 feet in elevation, the trail connects with Grasshopper Trail for a loop that takes you up to 5,760-foot Chucksney Mountain through forests and meadows for views of the Three Sisters and

the South Fork McKenzie River below. Start for .25 mile on Grasshopper Trail, then fork right to start your loop. After descending the mountain, hang a left to meet up with Grasshopper again for a 3.5-mile gentle cooldown back to the trailhead.

User groups: Hikers, dogs, horses, and mountain bikes. No wheelchair access.

Permits: A federal Northwest Forest pass is required to park here. The cost is $5 for a day pass or $30 for an annual pass. You can buy a day pass at ranger stations, from private vendors, or through Nature of the Northwest Information Center.

Maps: For a map of Willamette National Forest, contact Nature of the Northwest Information Center. For a topographic map, ask the USGS for Chucksney Mountain.

Directions: From Eugene, drive 40 miles on McKenzie Pass Highway/Highway 126 to Blue River. Continue five miles east past Blue River, and turn right (south) onto Forest Service Road 19. Drive 26 miles to Box Canyon Horse Camp on the right side of the road.

Contact: Willamette National Forest, McKenzie River Ranger District, 57600 McKenzie Highway, McKenzie Bridge, OR 97413, 541/822-3381.

31 ERMA BELL LAKES
8.5 mi/4.5 hrs

north of Waldo Lake in Willamette National Forest

Map 5.3, page 166

Erma Bell sure is the Belle of the Ball in these parts. Make that Erma Bells, because you'll pass by three lakes on this gentle path through Douglas fir forest. It's a popular haunt due to the easy path and the three lakes to choose from. First up is Lower Erma Lake, just two miles down. Pass her by if you want to hit a more secluded spot, stopping to check out the waterfall first that separates Lower and Middle Erma Lakes. Then continue another 1.5 miles past Upper Erma to a junction with Williams Lake Trail. Turn left here to hit the lake on your right and another easy five miles back to the trailhead, most likely without the crowds on the return trip.

User groups: Hikers, dogs, and horses. No mountain bikes are allowed. The first portion of the trail is wheelchair accessible.

Permits: A free wilderness permit is required to hike here and is available at the trailhead. A federal Northwest Forest pass is also required to park here. The cost is $5 for a day pass or $30 for an annual pass. You can buy a day pass at ranger stations, from private vendors, or through Nature of the Northwest Information Center.

Maps: For a map of Willamette National Forest, contact Nature of the Northwest Information Center. For a topographic map, ask the USGS for Waldo Mountain.

Directions: From Eugene, drive 40 miles on McKenzie Pass Highway/Highway 126 to Blue River. Continue five miles east past Blue River, and turn right (south) onto Forest Service Road 19. Drive 25.5 miles to the junction with Forest Service Road 1957. Turn left and drive 3.5 miles to the trailhead in Skookum Campground.

Contact: Willamette National Forest, Middle Fork Ranger District, 46375 Highway 58, Westfir, OR 97492, 541/782-2283.

32 RIGDON LAKES
8.0 mi/4.0 hrs

north of Waldo Lake in the Waldo Lake Wilderness of Willamette National Forest

Map 5.3, page 166

Waldo Lake may bask in the spotlight with a wilderness to call its own, but there are plenty of smaller lakes worth visiting in the Waldo Lake Wilderness, too. A 1996 fire swept through here, and you can get an up-close view of the blackened trees. This easy loop takes you on a tour of three smaller lakes just a short walk away. Starting along the north shore of Waldo, take a right at the junction with Rigdon Lakes Trail to pass by the Upper and Lower Rigdon and Kiwa Lakes. Keep left at all junctions to complete the simple loop back to your car, and

then stick around to check out Waldo, the second-largest natural lake in Oregon.

User groups: Hikers, dogs, and horses. No mountain bikes are allowed. No wheelchair access.

Permits: A free wilderness permit is required to hike here and is available at the trailhead. A federal Northwest Forest pass is also required to park here. The cost is $5 for a day pass or $30 for an annual pass. You can buy a day pass at ranger stations, from private vendors, or through Nature of the Northwest Information Center.

Maps: For a map of Waldo Lakes Wilderness and Willamette National Forest, contact Nature of the Northwest Information Center. For a topographic map, ask the USGS for Waldo Mountain.

Directions: From Highway 58, three miles west of Willamette Pass, turn north on Waldo Lake Road/Forest Service Road 5897. Drive 12.5 miles, following signs to North Waldo Campground, on Forest Service Roads 5897 and 5898 to the campground. The trail starts near the campground's boat-launch parking area.

Contact: Willamette National Forest, Middle Fork Ranger District, 46375 Highway 58, Westfir, OR 97492, 541/782-2283.

33 WALDO MOUNTAIN
6.0 mi/3.0 hrs

northwest of Waldo Lake in the Waldo Lake Wilderness of Willamette National Forest

Map 5.3, page 166

It's almost a 2,000-foot elevation gain up to 6,357-foot Waldo Mountain Lookout, and it's worth the effort, as you can bear witness to Waldo Lake and its many smaller brothers in the wilderness, as well as its Three Sisters. The trail prefers to save the best for last, so you can concentrate on your climb here, because the views don't start until you get to the top. Retrace your steps here, or if you're feeling particularly energetic, you can add two miles on a loop, taking a right down the east side to hit Waldo Meadows Trail for a return trip.

User groups: Hikers, dogs, and horses. No mountain bikes are allowed. No wheelchair access.

Permits: A free wilderness permit is required to hike here and is available at the trailhead. A federal Northwest Forest pass is also required to park here. The cost is $5 for a day pass or $30 for an annual pass. You can buy a day pass at ranger stations, from private vendors, or through Nature of the Northwest Information Center.

Maps: For a map of the Waldo Lake Wilderness and Willamette National Forest, contact Nature of the Northwest Information Center. For a topographic map, ask the USGS for Blair Lake and Waldo Mountain.

Directions: From Willamette Pass Highway/Highway 58 at Oakridge, turn east on Salmon Creek Road/Forest Service Road 24. Drive 11 miles to a fork in the road, and veer left onto Forest Service Road 2417. Continue six miles to Forest Service Road 2424. Turn right and follow the road four miles to the trailhead on the right side of the road.

Contact: Willamette National Forest, Middle Fork Ranger District, 46375 Highway 58, Westfir, OR 97492, 541/782-2283.

34 WALDO LAKE LOOP
19.6 mi/1.0–2.0 days
around Waldo Lake in Willamette National Forest

The only bummer about this trail is that a large chunk is actually out of view of the lake, and this is a lake you'll want to see. It's the second-deepest natural lake in the state (Crater Lake gets top billing for that prize) and, upon scientific scrutiny, it has been bestowed the honor of being one of the clearest lakes in the world, with water chemistry similar to distilled water's. Cool. But the loop around the lake is still a fabulous one and is quite popular with mountain bikers and runners (many of them training for the Where's Waldo 100K course, which runs in the area, no doubt). It's also relatively gentle, so it's possible as an all-day excursion if you really want

to go for it. Short side trails lead to great views of this pristine water, as well as to views of Mount Bachelor, Broken Top, and the Middle and South Sisters. The trail is part of a large trail system, where you can reach Fuji Mountain, Betty Lake, and others. If you want to break it into a two-day trip, you can camp along the route.

User groups: Hikers, dogs, horses, and mountain bikes. No wheelchair access.

Permits: A federal Northwest Forest pass is required to park here. The cost is $5 for a day pass or $30 for an annual pass. You can buy a day pass at ranger stations, from private vendors, or through Nature of the Northwest Information Center.

Maps: For a map of Willamette National Forest, contact Nature of the Northwest Information Center. For a topographic map, ask the USGS for Waldo Lake.

Directions: From Highway 58, three miles west of Willamette Pass, turn north on Waldo Lake Road/Forest Service Road 5897. Drive 12.5 miles on Forest Service Roads 5897 and 5898, following signs to North Waldo Campground. The trailhead starts from the campground's boat-launch parking area.

Contact: Willamette National Forest, Middle Fork Ranger District, 46375 Highway 58, Westfir, OR 97492, 541/782-2283.

35 THE TWINS
6.6 mi/3.5 hrs
east of Waldo Lake in Willamette National Forest

Map 5.3, page 166

The Twins' cinder cone peaks stand with a view of the Waldo Lake Wilderness, whispering to each other about the local gossip (you know how twins can be), keeping one eye on Waldo and another on the Three Sisters. You can get in on the action yourself by climbing up to the 7,350-foot summit, gaining about 1,500 feet of elevation on the way up this dusty, dry path. From there, you can see their fine view of this interesting wilderness. Take water along, as it can be a hot, dry route.

User groups: Hikers, dogs, and horses. No mountain bikes are allowed. No wheelchair access.

Permits: A free wilderness permit is required to hike here and is available at the trailhead. A federal Northwest Forest pass is also required to park here. The cost is $5 for a day pass or $30 for an annual pass. You can buy a day pass at ranger stations, from private vendors, or through Nature of the Northwest Information Center.

Maps: For a map of Willamette National Forest, contact Nature of the Northwest Information Center. For a topographic map, ask the USGS for Waldo Lake and The Twins.

Directions: From Willamette Pass Highway/Highway 58, three miles west of Willamette Pass, turn north on Waldo Lake Road/Forest Service Road 5897. Drive six miles to the trailhead, on the right side of the road.

Contact: Willamette National Forest, Middle Fork Ranger District, 46375 Highway 58, Westfir, OR 97492, 541/782-2283.

36 MOUNT JUNE/ HARDESTY MOUNTAIN
9.5 mi/5.0 hrs

south of Lookout Point Reservoir in Umpqua National Forest

Map 5.3, page 166

Imagine climbing up almost 4,000 feet to the top of a summit, only to have your view blocked by a bunch of pesky trees. Well, that's kinda what it's like to hike up Hardesty Mountain these days. The better route is a quick, yet sometimes rocky 1.1-mile trip almost 1,000 feet up to its neighbor, Mount June, who welcomes visitors with open arms and open views of the Willamette Valley and Cascade Range. If you want to feel like you've really earned the views, you can continue on Sawtooth Trail on a ridgeline up to Hardesty Mountain just for the workout, if not for the occasional viewpoints along the way. Retrace your steps for a round-trip of 9.5 miles.

User groups: Hikers and dogs. No mountain bikes or horses are allowed. No wheelchair access.

Permits: Permits are not required. Parking and access are free.

Maps: For a map of Umpqua National Forest, contact Nature of the Northwest Information Center. For a topographic map, ask the USGS for Mount June.

Directions: From Cottage Grove Ranger Station, drive 17 miles east on Row River Road/Forest Service Road 2400 to Laying Creek Road/Forest Service Road 17. Turn left and continue five miles to Forest Service Road 1751. Turn left and drive 6.4 miles to Forest Service Road 1721. Turn right and drive two miles to Forest Service Road 941. Turn right, continuing a short distance to the trailhead on the right side of the road.

Contact: Umpqua National Forest, Cottage Grove Ranger District, 78405 Cedar Parks Road, Cottage Grove, OR 97424, 541/942-5591.

37 BRICE CREEK
5.5 mi one-way/3.5 hrs

east of Cottage Grove in Umpqua National Forest

Map 5.3, page 166

Traveling past waterfalls and pools and over footbridges, this easy hike is a great way to spend a summer afternoon. Or spring. Or winter, for that matter, since it's a low-elevation trail that gains only 500 feet along its length. Brice Creek Trail follows in the footsteps of Frank Brice Trail, which accessed the Bohemia Mining District in the early 1900s, way before you were born (unless you're a centenarian). Tunnels and mine shafts still line the trail, but keep those hands to yourself if you please. The last mile follows a ditch. Now, ditches aren't known for their scenic beauty, but this one has an interesting history; it used to carry water to generate electricity for a tram at the mill site. An easy amble, some waterfalls, and some mining history thrown in, and you have reason to stick around.

User groups: Hikers, dogs, mountain bikes, and horses. No wheelchair access.

Permits: Permits are not required. Parking and access are free.

Maps: For a map of Umpqua National Forest, contact Nature of the Northwest Information Center. For a topographic map, ask the USGS for Rose Hill.

Directions: From Cottage Grove Ranger Station, drive 19 miles east on Row River Road/Forest Service Road 2400. Turn right onto Brice Creek Road/Forest Service Road 2470, and drive 3.3 miles to the West trailhead. Other access points along the road include the Cedar Creek Campground, Lund Park trailhead, and Champion Lake trailhead, all within eight miles of the first trailhead parking area.

Contact: Umpqua National Forest, Cottage Grove Ranger District, 78405 Cedar Parks Road, Cottage Grove, OR 97424, 541/942-5591.

38 LARISON CREEK
6.0 mi one-way/3.0 hrs

south of Oakridge in Willamette
National Forest

Map 5.3, page 166

Starting from Larison Cove, the creekside stroll gains only 500 feet in elevation along the way, so it's yet another good trail for all types. Stop halfway in to view a clear pool and prime picnic spot (you have to bushwhack a ways, but it's worth the hassle). The path starts to climb from here, so this is a good stopping point if you want a super-simple hike for a six-mile round-trip. If you're planning to enjoy Larison Cove's water, best to steer clear in August, when many of the lakes in the region are closed to all water use during the height of the blue-green algae blooms. Check on conditions before you set out.

User groups: Hikers, dogs, mountain bikes, and horses. No wheelchair access.

Permits: Permits are not required. Parking and access are free.

Maps: For a map of Willamette National Forest, contact Nature of the Northwest Information Center. For a topographic map, ask the USGS for Oakridge and Holland Point.

Directions: From Oakridge, drive 1.2 miles east

on Willamette Pass Highway/Highway 58 to Kitson Springs Road/Forest Service Road 23 at the sign for Hills Creek Reservoir. Turn right and drive .5 mile, forking right onto Forest Service Road 21. The trailhead is 3.3 miles on the right side of the road, near Larison Cove.

Contact: Willamette National Forest, Middle Fork Ranger District, 46375 Highway 58, Westfir, OR 97492, 541/782-2283.

39 MIDDLE FORK WILLAMETTE RIVER
27.0 mi/1.0 day

south of Oakridge in Willamette
National Forest

Map 5.3, page 166

Extending for 27 miles along the river, a hefty day trip for many (okay, most), this trail can be accessed from many points along the way. You can choose your distance, or choose a slice from the lower trailhead, which tends to open earlier in the year than the snowy-through-June upper stretches. From the lower trailhead, you'll start through a mixed-growth forest of bigleaf maple and cottonwood, traveling along portions of the old Oregon Central Military Wagon Road. Turn back when you've seen what you want to see, and call it a day.

User groups: Hikers, dogs, mountain bikes, and horses. No wheelchair access.

Permits: A federal Northwest Forest pass is required to park here. The cost is $5 for a day pass or $30 for an annual pass. You can buy a day pass at ranger stations, from private vendors, or through Nature of the Northwest Information Center.

Maps: For a map of Willamette National Forest, contact Nature of the Northwest Information Center. For a topographic map, ask the USGS for Warner Mountain, Rigdon Point, Emigrant Butte, and Cowhorn Mountain.

Directions: From Oakridge, drive 1.2 miles east on Willamette Pass Highway/Highway 58 to Kitson Springs Road/Forest Service Road 23 at the sign for Hills Creek Reservoir. Turn right and drive .5 mile, forking right onto Forest

Service Road 21. Drive 10 miles to Sand Prairie Campground and the junction with Forest Service Road 134. Turn right and follow it through the campground to the parking lot at the picnic area near the river. There are several more access points along Forest Service Road 21, and the lower trailhead is located at Indigo Lake Trail (see listing in this chapter).

Contact: Willamette National Forest, Middle Fork Ranger District, 46375 Highway 58, Westfir, OR 97492, 541/782-2283.

40 VIVIAN LAKE/ SALT CREEK FALLS
8.0 mi/4.0 hrs

south of Highway 58 in the Diamond Peak Wilderness of Willamette National Forest

Map 5.3, page 166

Think quick: What's the second-highest waterfall in Oregon? Give up? Roll out the red carpet for 286-foot Salt Creek Falls, which you can see on a short .5-mile trip from the trailhead. It may not be as flashy or get as much attention as certain other falls, but it does get its own observation platform. The most powerful waterfall in Southern Oregon, Salt Creek Falls churns out an average yearly flow of about 50,000 gallons per minute (enough water to supply a town of 180,000 people—take that, Multnomah!). After paying your respects and taking a picture, continue on Diamond Falls Loop, passing Diamond Falls before picking up the junction to Vivian Lake, where you'll pass a series of smaller falls. Got your fill of falls? Then continue to the pretty lake for a prime picnic spot.

User groups: Hikers, dogs, and horses. No mountain bikes are allowed. No wheelchair access.

Permits: A free wilderness permit is required to hike here and is available at the trailhead. A federal Northwest Forest pass is also required to park here. The cost is $5 for a day pass or $30 for an annual pass. You can buy a day pass at ranger stations, from private vendors, or through Nature of the Northwest Information Center.

Maps: For a map of Diamond Peak Wilderness and Willamette National Forest, contact Nature of the Northwest Information Center. For a topographic map, ask the USGS for Diamond Peak.

Directions: From Willamette Pass Highway/Highway 58, five miles west of Willamette Pass, turn south into the parking lot and trailhead for Salt Creek Falls.

Contact: Willamette National Forest, Middle Fork Ranger District, 46375 Highway 58, Westfir, OR 97492, 541/782-2283.

41 YORAN LAKE
10.6 mi/5.5 hrs

south of Highway 58 in the Diamond Peak Wilderness of Deschutes National Forest

Map 5.3, page 166

While many of the area's lakes are within an easy strolling distance of the trailhead, Yoran Lake plays hard to get, requiring a 5.3-mile walk. You won't mind a bit though, because for one it's not as crowded as other trails (although it does receive its fair share of visitors) and for two, it's a pleasant walk through spruce and fir forest, climbing steadily almost 1,150 feet. Yoran Lake sits with a front-and-center view of Diamond Peak, so it's worth the trip in. Keep in mind that this area's lakes have been plagued with blue-green algae blooms and may be closed to water use during August, so check ahead.

User groups: Hikers, dogs, and horses. No mountain bikes are allowed. No wheelchair access.

Permits: A free wilderness permit is required to hike here and is available at the trailhead. A federal Northwest Forest pass is also required to park here. The cost is $5 for a day pass or $30 for an annual pass. You can buy a day pass at ranger stations, from private vendors, or through Nature of the Northwest Information Center.

Maps: For a map of Diamond Peak Wilderness and Deschutes National Forest, contact Nature of the Northwest Information Center. For a topographic map, ask the USGS for Willamette Pass.

Directions: From Oakridge, drive southeast on Willamette Pass Highway/Highway 58 to Willamette Pass. Drive just beyond the summit to Forest Service Road 5810. Turn right (south) and drive around Odell Lake to the trailhead parking lot on the right side of the road.

Contact: Deschutes National Forest, Crescent Ranger District, 136471 Highway 97 North, P.O. Box 208, Crescent, OR 97733, 541/433-3200.

42 INDIGO LAKE/ SAWTOOTH MOUNTAIN
9.0 mi/5.5 hrs

southeast of Odell and Crescent Lakes in the Oregon Cascades Recreation Area of Willamette National Forest

Map 5.3, page 166

Check it out: Indigo Lake was named for its color. Intrigued? You should be. It's an easy two-mile walk through fir forest and mountain meadows to the lake itself, plus a mile-long loop around the shores. With Sawtooth Mountain as the backdrop, it's a perfect place to sit and enjoy the water (now would not be the time to try out your black-and-white film; you'll want to capture the intense blue of this pretty lake). But that's not all, folks. If you're up for a climb, pick up Indigo Extension Trail from the north shore, and make your way up for two miles to reach Windy Pass Trail, climbing a steep ridge and 1,400 feet to reach the summit. After getting a view and pictures of the vibrant lake from the top, return via Sawtooth Mountain Trail for a nine-mile loop.

User groups: Hikers, dogs, horses, and mountain bikes. No wheelchair access.

Permits: A federal Northwest Forest pass is required to park here. The cost is $5 for a day pass or $30 for an annual pass. You can buy a day pass at ranger stations, from private vendors, or through Nature of the Northwest Information Center.

Maps: For a map of Willamette National Forest, contact Nature of the Northwest Information Center. For a topographic map, ask the USGS for Cowhorn Mountain.

Directions: From Oakridge, drive southeast on Willamette Pass Highway/Highway 58 to Willamette Pass. Continue 1.2 miles east to Kitson Springs Road/Forest Service Road 23 at the sign for Hills Creek Reservoir. Turn right (south) and drive .5 mile to a fork, veering right onto Forest Service Road 21. Drive 32 miles to Forest Service Road 2154. Turn left and follow signs to Timpanogas Campground and the trailhead in the day-use parking area.

Contact: Willamette National Forest, Middle Fork Ranger District, 46375 Highway 58, Westfir, OR 97492, 541/782-2283.

43 UPPER ROGUE RIVER/ CRATER RIM VIEWPOINT
18.6 mi/1.0 day

parallel to Highway 230 in Rogue River National Forest

Map 5.3, page 166

Upper Rogue River Trail extends for 49 miles one-way past waterfalls, through the Rogue Gorge (see listing in this chapter), and past campgrounds, all the while sticking near the mighty, rushing river that is the Rogue. But let's be realistic here, are you really going to do 49 miles in one day, and then retrace your steps? Not. Here's an option that accesses the most scenic parts of the trail and gets you away from the campground crowds that tend to frequent the lower sections. Starting from the upper trailhead at the Crater Rim Viewpoint, you'll pass by the Boundary Springs trailhead (see listing in this chapter). Keep right at this junction to continue on Rogue River Trail for four scenic miles of clifftop viewpoints and waterfalls, then dip into the woods for the rest of the trip to Hamaker Campground. As always, you have your options here of retracing your steps or arranging for a personal chauffeur to whisk you from the trailhead in style. Of course, you can always continue on. And on. The trail ends near the Prospect Ranger Station, but it's incredibly difficult to find and not nearly as scenic as this upper half. (While you're there, though, stop in for their helpful advice and detailed trail descriptions.)

User groups: Hikers and dogs. No mountain bikes are allowed. Horses are allowed only on certain sections of the trail. No wheelchair access.

Permits: Permits are not required. Parking and access are free.

Maps: For a map of Rogue River National Forest, contact Nature of the Northwest Information Center. For a topographic map, ask the USGS for Pumice Desert West, Hamaker Butte, Union Creek, Prospect North, and Whetstone Point.

Directions: From Prospect, drive 12.2 miles north on Highway 62 to the junction with Highway 230. Stay to the left to drive on Highway 230 and continue 18.6 miles north to the Crater Rim Viewpoint and the trailhead on the right. The trail can also be accessed at the Hamaker Campground, Natural Bridge Campground, and River Bridge Campground, all conveniently lined up off of Highway 230.

Contact: Rogue River National Forest, Prospect Ranger District, 47201 Highway 62, Prospect, OR 97536, 541/560-3400.

44 MUIR CREEK
7.8 mi/3.5 hrs

north of Prospect in Rogue River National Forest

Map 5.3, page 166

A berry buffet of huckleberries, blackberries, and strawberries lines this easy path, as do plenty of picnic spots so you can munch on them. Maybe you'll have an unexpected lunch guest, too—deer and elk roam these parts, and you stand a good chance of bumping into one (just say "on your left" and they'll move right on over). Traveling through a fir and pine forest, the trail begins where the Rogue River and Muir Creek meet, and winds past mountain meadows filled with tiger lilies and scarlet gilia.

User groups: Hikers, dogs, and horses. No mountain bikes are allowed. No wheelchair access.

Permits: Permits are not required. Parking and access are free.

Maps: For a map of Rogue River National Forest, contact Nature of the Northwest Information Center. For a topographic map, ask the USGS for Hamaker Butte.

Directions: From Prospect, drive 12 miles north on Highway 62 to the junction with Highway 230. Stay left and continue 10.3 miles north on Highway 230. Turn left into the parking area before crossing Muir Creek Bridge. The trailhead is on the north side of the parking area, to the right as you're driving in.

Contact: Rogue River National Forest, Prospect Ranger District, 47201 Highway 62, Prospect, OR 97536, 541/560-3400.

45 MINNEHAHA
6.2 mi/3.0 hrs

north of Prospect in Rogue River National Forest

Map 5.3, page 166

If you hear that an OHV convention is planning to hit the Rogue River area, you'd be wise to steer clear of this trail, which is part of a network of OHV trails in the vicinity. It's also open to bikes, horses, dogs, scooters—just kidding about the last one, but you get the point: It's used by all, and you can see the tracks as evidence that someone was here. Still, it's a level, flat walk along Minnehaha Creek, an old route used in the 1860s by miners and stockmen on their way to the gold mines in the John Day Valley. It passes through a Douglas fir and pine forest and meadows before a climb overlooking the creek and waterfalls below. Check out the lava rock that still remains from the Mount Mazama ash that covered the area 6,800 years ago.

User groups: Hikers, dogs, horses, and mountain bikes. No wheelchair access.

Permits: Permits are not required. Parking and access are free.

Maps: For a map of Rogue River National Forest, contact Nature of the Northwest Information Center. For a topographic map, ask the USGS for Hamaker Butte.

Directions: From Prospect, drive 12 miles north on Highway 62 to the junction with Highway

230. Stay left and continue 12.2 miles north on Highway 230 to the junction with Forest Service Road 6530 at the sign for Hamaker Campground. Turn right and drive one mile (right after you cross a bridge), then turn right onto Forest Service Road 6530-800. Drive .1 mile to the parking area on the right. The trailhead is on your left, shortly before the parking area.

Contact: Rogue River National Forest, Prospect Ranger District, 47201 Highway 62, Prospect, OR 97536, 541/560-3400.

46 MIRROR LAKES
7.0 mi/3.5 hrs

west of Mount Bachelor in the Three Sisters Wilderness of Deschutes National Forest

Map 5.4, page 167

Passing through small streams and lava features, Mirror Lakes Trail gains just 600 feet in elevation along its 3.5-mile tour. It ends at the Pacific Crest Trail; just turn left to hit the lake, which sits at 5,950 feet elevation with a solitary view of South Sister. You ambitious types can continue another three miles to Nash Lake from the PCT, returning the way you came. It's a slightly lesser-used trail than others in the area, so you may have a little elbow room en route.

User groups: Hikers, dogs, and horses. No mountain bikes are allowed. No wheelchair access.

Permits: A free wilderness permit is required to hike here and is available at the trailhead. A federal Northwest Forest pass is also required to park here. The cost is $5 for a day pass or $30 for an annual pass. You can buy a day pass at ranger stations, from private vendors, or through Nature of the Northwest Information Center.

Maps: For a map of the Three Sisters Wilderness and Deschutes National Forest, contact Nature of the Northwest Information Center. For a topographic map, ask the USGS for South Sister.

Directions: From U.S. 97 in Bend, follow signs west to Mount Bachelor Ski Area, driving 27 miles on Cascade Lakes Highway/Highway 46.

Drive past Mount Bachelor to the Sisters Mirror trailhead on the right (west) side of the road, three miles past the Devil's Lake Campground.

Contact: Deschutes National Forest, Bend-Fort Rock Ranger District, 1230 Northeast 3rd Street, Suite A-262, Bend, OR 97701, 541/383-4000.

47 HORSE LAKE
8.0 mi/4.0 hrs

west of Mount Bachelor in the Three Sisters Wilderness of Deschutes National Forest

Map 5.4, page 167

Mosquito Lake is probably a better name for this lake, as they descend upon you, rubbing their little wings together in anticipation of some fresh blood. And since there aren't a whole lot of other hikers upon which to descend, you'll be a good target. Bring the bug juice, or avoid this place altogether in the buggy early-summer months. Gaining 700 feet in elevation, it's a gentle path to the lake through old-growth mountain hemlock forest. The trail also connects to the Pacific Crest Trail, and you know what that means: loops galore. Since some of the area's trails are not marked, if you try the loop back to the car via the PCT, bring a map along to make sure you're still on course. This route involves taking a left past Colt and Sunset Lakes for a little swap of scenery on the return trip. Otherwise, return the way you came for an easy eight-mile round-trip.

User groups: Hikers, dogs, and horses. No mountain bikes are allowed.

Permits: A free wilderness permit is required to hike here and is available at the trailhead. A federal Northwest Forest pass is also required to park here. The cost is $5 for a day pass or $30 for an annual pass. You can buy a day pass at ranger stations, from private vendors, or through Nature of the Northwest Information Center.

Maps: For a map of the Three Sisters Wilderness and Deschutes National Forest, contact Nature of the Northwest Information Center. For a topographic map, ask the USGS for Elk Lake.

Directions: From U.S. 97 in Bend, drive 32 miles west on Cascade Lakes Highway/Highway 46, following signs to Mount Bachelor Ski Area, to the Elk Lake trailhead on the left (west) side of the road across from Elk Lake Resort. **Contact:** Deschutes National Forest, Bend-Fort Rock Ranger District, 1230 Northeast 3rd Street, Suite A-262, Bend, OR 97701, 541/383-4000.

48 SIX LAKES
5.0 mi/2.5 hrs

southwest of Mount Bachelor in the Three Sisters Wilderness of Deschutes National Forest

Map 5.4, page 167

This is really the Land of Many Lakes, and Six Lakes Trail fits right in. You'll reach Blow Lake in just one mile, then Doris Lake after another easy 1.5-mile hike. Needless to say, it's a hit with families, because you can't beat the simple stroll to two lakes. If you feel ripped off by the trail name, don't worry, you can continue on to smaller lakes. Continue on for six miles total, where the trail ends and you can pick up the PCT (turning left) to reach the more remote Mink Lake. The total elevation gain along the trail is just under 1,000 feet.

User groups: Hikers, dogs, and horses. No mountain bikes are allowed.

Permits: A free wilderness permit is required to hike here and is available at the trailhead. A federal Northwest Forest pass is also required to park here. The cost is $5 for a day pass or $30 for an annual pass. You can buy a day pass at ranger stations, from private vendors, or through Nature of the Northwest Information Center.

Maps: For a map of the Three Sisters Wilderness and Deschutes National Forest, contact Nature of the Northwest Information Center. For a topographic map, ask the USGS for Elk Lake.

Directions: From U.S. 97 in Bend, drive 34.5 miles west on Cascade Lakes Highway/Highway 46, following signs to Mount Bachelor Ski Area, to the Six Lakes trailhead on the right (west) side of the highway.

Contact: Deschutes National Forest, Bend-Fort Rock Ranger District, 1230 Northeast 3rd Street, Suite A-262, Bend, OR 97701, 541/383-4000.

49 DESCHUTES RIVER/DILLON AND BENHAM FALLS
7.0 mi/3.5 hrs

southwest of Bend along the Deschutes River

Map 5.4, page 167

Deschutes River Trail is popular with mountain bikers, white-water rafters, horses, and, well, really just about anyone. So popular, in fact, that separate trails were created for each user (dogs don't get their own trail, though; they have to walk with you, leashed if you please). The riverside trail travels 9.1 miles one-way, passing through Big Eddy Rapids, Dillon Falls, and Benham Falls. You can take your pick, but the most popular sight is near Benham Falls, which has six degrees of separation from a lava flow. The lava spilled, a dam was created, the lake spilled over, and voilà, a scenic falls. In any case, it's a good place to start a walk down Deschutes River Trail, heading north to Dillon Falls for a seven-mile round-trip hike.

User groups: Hikers, dogs, horses, and mountain bikes. There is wheelchair access at Benham Falls.

Permits: A federal Northwest Forest pass is required to park here. The cost is $5 for a day pass or $30 for an annual pass. You can buy a day pass at ranger stations, from private vendors, or through Nature of the Northwest Information Center.

Maps: For a map of Deschutes National Forest, contact Nature of the Northwest Information Center. For a topographic map, ask the USGS for Benham Falls.

Directions: There are many places to access Deschutes River Trail. To reach the hike suggested above, drive 14.8 miles south from Bend on Highway 97. Turn right (west) onto Forest Service Road 9702 and drive four miles past the Lava Lands Visitor Center to the Benham Falls picnic area and trailhead.

Contact: Deschutes National Forest, Bend-Fort Rock Ranger District, 1230 Northeast 3rd Street, Suite A-262, Bend, OR 97701, 541/383-4000.

50 CULTUS LAKE
10.0 mi/5.0 hrs

southwest of Sunriver in the Three Sisters Wilderness of Deschutes National Forest

Map 5.4, page 167

Starting from the north shore of Cultus Lake, Winopee Trail extends 10 miles to reach the ever-present PCT. Along the way, you'll pass by Teddy Lakes (accessible on a side trail), Muskrat Lake, and the larger Winopee Lake. Day-trippers, pick your pleasure and head back when you can—a good stop is the small Muskrat Lake, where a shelter still stands, for a 10-mile round-trip. Or continue on to Winopee Lake, about three miles down the trail, to add six miles to your trip, which makes for a more remote experience than the popular Cultus Lake. Whatever you do, remember to bring bug juice because the lakes are also quite popular summer retreats for mosquitoes.

User groups: Hikers, dogs, and horses. No mountain bikes are allowed.

Permits: A free wilderness permit is required to hike here and is available at the trailhead. A federal Northwest Forest pass is also required to park here. The cost is $5 for a day pass or $30 for an annual pass. You can buy a day pass at ranger stations, from private vendors, or through Nature of the Northwest Information Center.

Maps: For a map of the Three Sisters Wilderness and Deschutes National Forest, contact Nature of the Northwest Information Center. For a topographic map, ask the USGS for Crane Prairie Reservoir, Irish Mountain, and Packsaddle Mountain.

Directions: From U.S. 97 in Bend, drive 44 miles west on Cascade Lakes Highway/High-

way 46, following signs for Mount Bachelor Ski Area, to the sign for Cultus Lake Resort. Turn right onto Forest Service Road 4635 and drive 1.8 miles, forking right toward the campground, then keep to the right again on a dead-end gravel road for .5 mile. The trailhead is on the left side of the road.

Contact: Deschutes National Forest, Bend-Fort Rock Ranger District, 1230 Northeast 3rd Street, Suite A-262, Bend, OR 97701, 541/383-4000.

51 PACIFIC CREST TRAIL TO ROSARY LAKES
6.0 mi/3.0 hrs

from Willamette Pass Ski Area to Rosary Lakes in Deschutes National Forest

Map 5.4, page 167

Accessing the Pacific Crest Trail from Willamette Pass, this easy hike travels 600 feet in elevation in three miles to Lower, Middle, and Upper Rosary Lakes. You'll hit Lower Rosary Lake first, the largest of three and a good place to stop for a picnic. Or continue up to the two smaller lakes and save your lunch for the trip back down. Either way, you'll be guaranteed a gentle walk, some views of Pulpit Rock and Maiden Peak on either side, and probably a few PCT hikers along the way, as Willamette Pass is a popular starting and ending point for long-distance hikers.

User groups: Hikers, dogs, horses, and mountain bikes. No wheelchair access.

Permits: A federal Northwest Forest pass is required to park here. The cost is $5 for a day pass or $30 for an annual pass. You can buy a day pass at ranger stations, from private vendors, or through Nature of the Northwest Information Center.

Maps: For a map of Deschutes National Forest, contact Nature of the Northwest Information Center. For a topographic map, ask the USGS for Willamette Pass and Odell Lake.

Directions: From Oakridge, drive southeast on Willamette Pass Highway/Highway 58 to Willamette Pass. The trailhead is on the left (north) side of the road just past the Willamette Pass Ski Area.

Contact: Deschutes National Forest, Crescent Ranger District, 136471 Highway 97 North, P.O. Box 208, Crescent, OR 97733, 541/433-3200.

52 FAWN LAKE
7.0 mi/3.5 hrs

south of Odell Lake in the Diamond Peak Wilderness of Deschutes National Forest

Map 5.4, page 167

This dusty trail shared by horses travels 750 feet up through fir and hemlock forest to reach Fawn Lake and the junction with Crater Butte Trail. You'll see views of the Redtop and Lakeview Mountains, a perfect setting to set up a picnic on the shores. It's a popular haunt in the Diamond Peak Wilderness, so try to hit this gem in the fall if you can (the trail is generally free of snow from June through November).

User groups: Hikers, dogs, and horses. No mountain bikes are allowed. No wheelchair access.

Permits: A federal Northwest Forest pass is required to park here. The cost is $5 for a day pass or $30 for an annual pass. You can buy a day pass at ranger stations, from private vendors, or through Nature of the Northwest Information Center.

Maps: For a map of Deschutes National Forest, contact Nature of the Northwest Information Center. For a topographic map, ask the USGS for Willamette Pass and Odell Lake.

Directions: From Bend, drive 50 miles south on Highway 97 to the junction with Highway 58. Turn right (west) and follow signs to Crescent Lake. Turn left onto Forest Service Road 60, and drive 2.2 miles to park in the boat ramp parking area. The trailhead starts from the Crescent Lake Campground.

Contact: Deschutes National Forest, Crescent Ranger District, 136471 Highway 97 North, P.O. Box 208, Crescent, OR 97733, 541/433-3200.

53 NO NAME
1.3 mi/0.5 hr

east of Cave Junction in the Oregon Caves National Monument area of Siskiyou National Forest

Map 5.5, page 168

You have to wonder what happened when the naming committee met with furrowed brows, trying to brainstorm a brilliant adjective to describe this gentle trail. The furrowing is understandable—it's a pretty nondescript trail, though pleasant. If you're already in the area visiting Oregon Caves National Monument, this is your best chance at ditching the crowds. Keep to the left at all junctions (to the right are a couple of dead-ends) along the peaceful path, which goes along a stream and through mixed forest. It's a one-way route, and you'll pop out at the Oregon Caves entrance and the paved road. Just mosey on down the road, back to the parking area, your car, and maybe your awaiting dog, who isn't allowed to take part in the action here (so avoid it on a sweltering day if you're with furry company).

User groups: Hikers only. No dogs, horses, or mountain bikes are allowed. No wheelchair access.

Permits: Permits are not required. Parking and access to the trails are free; the cave entrance fee is $7.50.

Maps: For a trail map, visit www.nps.gov/orca. For a topographic map, ask the USGS for Oregon Caves.

Directions: From Grants Pass, drive south on Highway 199 for 30 miles to Cave Junction. Turn left (east) onto Highway 46 and drive 19.3 miles to the end of the road at the Oregon Caves National Monument Visitor Center. The trailhead is to the right of the parking lot as you're driving in.

Contact: Siskiyou National Forest, Oregon Caves National Monument, 19000 Caves Highway, Cave Junction, OR 97523, 541/592-2100.

54 CLIFF NATURE INTERPRETIVE TRAIL
1.5 mi/1.0 hr

east of Cave Junction in the Oregon
Caves National Monument area of Siskiyou
National Forest

Map 5.5, page 168

For a little more of a challenge than No
Name, and a great viewpoint to boot, climb
350 feet up this interesting interpretive trail
that starts by looping around the cave wall.
Those who aced geology will love the little
plaques that line the route. Look for curious deer along the trail. As you climb, you
reach a bench on top for views of the Siskiyou mountain range below.

User groups: Hikers only. No dogs, horses, or
mountain bikes are allowed. No wheelchair
access.

Permits: Permits are not required. Parking and
access to the trails are free; the cave entrance
fee is $7.50.

Maps: For a trail map, visit www.nps.gov/orca.
For a topographic map, ask the USGS for Oregon Caves.

Directions: From Grants Pass, drive south on
Highway 199 for 30 miles to Cave Junction.
Turn left (east) onto Highway 46 and drive
19.3 miles to the end of the road at the Oregon Caves National Monument Visitor Center entrance. Walk through the visitors center
Cave Tour entrance and turn right on Big Tree
Trail to connect with Cliff Nature Trail near
the cave entrance.

Contact: Siskiyou National Forest, Oregon
Caves National Monument, 19000 Caves Highway, Cave Junction, OR 97523, 541/592-2100.

55 BIG TREE LOOP
3.3 mi/2.0 hrs

east of Cave Junction in the Oregon
Caves National Monument area of Siskiyou
National Forest

Map 5.5, page 168

It's a state of many Big Tree trails, but this guy
is one of the largest of the Douglas fir bunch.

You'll climb 1,120 feet up on this 3.3-mile loop,
traveling through mountain meadows and smaller trees. You'll be glad for the concession stand
in the nearby Chateau, because of all the hikes
in this area, this is by far the toughest—which
means you can lose the rush-hour traffic in
and out of the nearby caves.

User groups: Hikers only. No dogs, horses, or
mountain bikes are allowed. No wheelchair
access.

Permits: Permits are not required. Parking and
access to the trails are free; the cave entrance
fee is $7.50.

Maps: For a trail map, visit www.nps.gov/orca.
For a topographic map, ask the USGS for Oregon Caves.

Directions: From Grants Pass, drive south on
Highway 199 for 30 miles to Cave Junction.
Turn left (east) onto Highway 46 and drive
19.3 miles to the end of the road at the Oregon Caves National Monument Visitor Center entrance. Walk through the visitors center
Cave Tour entrance to the trailhead.

Contact: Siskiyou National Forest, Oregon
Caves National Monument, 19000 Caves Highway, Cave Junction, OR 97523, 541/592-2100.

56 DA-KU-BE-TE-DE
4.8 mi one-way/2.5 hrs

south of Applegate in Rogue River
National Forest

Map 5.5, page 168

Let the alarms sound, we have a winner for
coolest trail name, which gives a nod to the
small Indian tribe who used to live in Applegate Valley. It's an easy, if not the most peaceful, hike along the western shore of pretty
Applegate Lake. The trail itself isn't necessarily packed, but here's the rub: You end up
passing Hart-tish boat ramp in just .5 mile,
and that's when you hit the crowds. It can
get a touch confusing, because you have to
continue through the parking lot and along
a paved walkway on the lake, and then through
an open meadow to reach the trail again. (If
you get turned around, the helpful guy at the

boat-ramp store will steer you right.) The trail ends at Watkins Campground, so this is probably a good hike to do if you're camping there, having a friendly fellow camper drop you off at the trailhead, rather than doing an out-and-back. But you're the boss, so hike it as you wish.

User groups: Hikers, dogs, horses, and mountain bikes. No wheelchair access.

Permits: Permits are not required. Parking and access are free.

Maps: For a map of Rogue River National Forest, contact Nature of the Northwest Information Center. For a topographic map, ask the USGS for Carberry Creek and Squaw Lakes.

Directions: From Applegate, drive eight miles east on Highway 238 and turn right on Applegate Road. Drive 15 miles to Swayne Viewpoint. Turn into the viewpoint on the left to the parking area. The trailhead starts directly behind the restroom on the right side of the parking lot as you're looking at the lake. Note: Dogs are not allowed in Hart-tish Park, but you can continue through on the trail.

Contact: Rogue River National Forest, Applegate Ranger District, 6941 Upper Applegate Road, Jacksonville, OR 97530, 541/899-3800.

57 GROUSE LOOP
2.8 mi/1.5 hrs

south of Applegate in Rogue River National Forest

Map 5.5, page 168

If you're not up to the challenging Collings Mountain hike (see listing in this chapter) but want a quick quad stretch after sitting around the campground all day, try this short and sweet version. Reaching a fork, take either one (it's a loop, remember?). In the first mile, it gains 700 feet in elevation through old-growth fir and pine forest, to reach the ridgeline for a view of Red Butte and Applegate Lake before descending back to the Grouse Creek Valley and the trailhead.

User groups: Hikers, dogs, horses, and mountain bikes. No wheelchair access.

Permits: A federal Northwest Forest pass is required to park here. The cost is $5 for a day pass or $30 for an annual pass. You can buy a day pass at ranger stations, from private vendors, or through Nature of the Northwest Information Center.

Maps: For a map of Rogue River National Forest, contact Nature of the Northwest Information Center. For a topographic map, ask the USGS for Carberry Creek.

Directions: From Applegate, drive eight miles east on Highway 238 and turn right on Applegate Road. Drive 15.6 miles to Hart-tish Park, then turn left and park in the day-use area. The trailhead can be tricky to find: You have to walk back up to Applegate Road from the parking area and cross the street to the trailhead. Note: Dogs are not allowed in Hart-tish Park, but are allowed on the trail.

Contact: Rogue River National Forest, Applegate Ranger District, 6941 Upper Applegate Road, Jacksonville, OR 97530, 541/899-3800.

58 COLLINGS MOUNTAIN
14.0 mi/7.0 hrs

south of Applegate in Rogue River National Forest

Map 5.5, page 168

In case you were wondering, and even if you weren't, Collings Mountain was named for two brothers who mined here in the 1850s and '60s. After a gentle start along the Grouse Creek Valley, it's a steep climb up to the ridgetop, gaining 1,000 feet in elevation in the first mile, but then you get all that climbing stuff out of the way and let the views begin. Traveling along the ridge, you can check out the Siskiyou mountain range and Applegate Lake. The trail passes an abandoned miner's cabin, old tunnels, and even an inactive Bigfoot trap (!) along the way. Think it would be cool to saunter into an old mining tunnel? Think twice, because they can be dangerous and the Forest Service has asked us nicely to stay out of 'em. The trail ends at Watkins Campground, passing through the 1981 Watkins fire zone.

User groups: Hikers, dogs, horses, and mountain bikes. No wheelchair access.

Permits: A federal Northwest Forest pass is required to park here. The cost is $5 for a day pass or $30 for an annual pass. You can buy a day pass at ranger stations, from private vendors, or through Nature of the Northwest Information Center.

Maps: For a map of Rogue River National Forest, contact Nature of the Northwest Information Center. For a topographic map, ask the USGS for Carberry Creek.

Directions: From Applegate, drive eight miles east on Highway 238 and turn right on Applegate Road. Drive 15.6 miles to Hart-tish Park, then turn left and park in the day-use area. The trailhead can be tricky to find: You have to walk back up to Applegate Road from the parking area, cross the street, and turn left; the trailhead sign is on the right as you walk down the road a short distance. Note: Dogs are not allowed in Hart-tish Park, but are allowed on the trail.

Contact: Rogue River National Forest, Applegate Ranger District, 6941 Upper Applegate Road, Jacksonville, OR 97530, 541/899-3800.

59 PAYETTE TRAIL
9.2 mi one-way/5.0 hrs
south of Applegate in Rogue River National Forest

Map 5.5, page 168

If you're camping in the Applegate Lake area and want a longer hike without a lot of effort, you can't go wrong with Payette Trail. Beginning at the French Gulch Campground, the flat trail parallels the eastern shoreline of Applegate Lake for great views of the lake and nearby Collings Mountain. You can either camp overnight along the way in one of the walk-in campsites off the trail, or arrange for a friendly face to meet you on the other side at Manzanita trailhead; it's your choice. Look out for poison oak and ticks along the way.

User groups: Hikers, dogs, and mountain bikes. No horses are allowed. No wheelchair access.

Permits: Permits are not required. Parking and access are free.

Maps: For a map of Rogue River National Forest, contact Nature of the Northwest Information Center. For a topographic map, ask the USGS for Squaw Lakes.

Directions: From Applegate, drive eight miles east on Highway 238 and turn right on Applegate Road. Drive 12 miles and turn left on Squaw Creek Road over the dam. Drive one mile to the French Gulch parking area and the trailhead on the right. To reach the upper trailhead, continue six miles down Applegate Road from the Squaw Creek Road junction, and turn left at the T-junction onto Carberry Creek Road. Drive one mile to Manzanita Creek Road/Forest Service Road 1041. Turn left and drive two miles to the trailhead and parking area at the end of the cul-de-sac.

Contact: Rogue River National Forest, Applegate Ranger District, 6941 Upper Applegate Road, Jacksonville, OR 97530, 541/899-3800.

60 STEIN BUTTE
9.8 mi/5.0 hrs
south of Applegate in Rogue River National Forest

Map 5.5, page 168

Are you the type who likes to place one foot in one state and one in another? You'll get your chance on Stein Butte Trail, but you'll have to climb to do it (and there's no "Welcome to California" sign on the trail either, so you'll just have to go by feel). Named for one of the many gold prospectors who mined the area in the 1850s and 1860s, the trail takes a brief trip south of the border along the way, gaining 1,400 feet in elevation for 2.5 miles up to 4,400-foot Elliott Ridge. Along the ridge, you can look down at Applegate Lake and across to the Siskiyou mountain range. The trail ends at a junction with Elliott Ridge, where you can turn right to reach the Elliott Ridge trailhead, but you have to walk three miles back to your car along the road, so this is better as an out-and-back hike.

User groups: Hikers, dogs, mountain bikes, and horses. No wheelchair access.

Permits: Permits are not required. Parking and access are free.

Maps: For a map of Rogue River National Forest, contact Nature of the Northwest Information Center. For a topographic map, ask the USGS for Carberry Creek and Squaw Lakes.

Directions: From Applegate, drive eight miles east on Highway 238 and turn right on Applegate Road. Drive 18.9 miles down Applegate Road to a T-junction. Turn left onto Carberry Creek Road and drive .8 mile to the parking area on the left, across the street from the Seattle Bar sign. From your car, walk a short distance down the gravel road leading from the parking area; the trailhead is on your right. It can be easy to miss since it's hidden from the parking area, but it's well marked once you actually find it.

Contact: Rogue River National Forest, Applegate Ranger District, 6941 Upper Applegate Road, Jacksonville, OR 97530, 541/899-3800.

61 ANDERSON CAMP
1.5 mi/1.0 hr

north of Prospect in Rogue River National Forest

Map 5.6, page 169

If you're the type who likes to feel as if you're on an adventure, and you don't like or need everything mapped out for you, this is for you. But please bring a map along, because it's quite easy to get disoriented out here. The trail is slightly overgrown, which gives it a solitude bonus, and it almost seems to peter out when it hits a couple meadows, so be warned. Switchbacking up to just below the summit of Anderson Mountain (elevation gain on the trail is 1,100 feet), the trail ends at a junction with Rogue-Umpqua Divide Trail and Anderson Camp, a turn-of-the-century sheepherder's camp, where you'll be rewarded with amazing views of the Rogue and Umpqua valleys. You'll be glad you brought along your camera (you did bring one, right?). It's a good idea to memorize exactly which way you came up through the two mead-

ows, because it's easy to get lost. (Ahem.) Also, there's a tricky switchback on the way down that if you miss you'll continue straight into another meadow, creating even more confusion. On the way up, it's an obvious switchback with a sign on a tree pointing to Anderson Camp to the right. On the way down, though, you can easily continue straight without seeing the sign if you don't have your head up. All in all, though, this is a great place to bring a friend along and enjoy the peaceful scenery for a quick trip that will feel like an adventure.

User groups: Hikers, dogs, and horses. No mountain bikes are allowed. No wheelchair access.

Permits: Permits are not required. Parking and access are free.

Maps: For a map of Rogue River National Forest, contact Nature of the Northwest Information Center. For a topographic map, ask the USGS for Union Creek.

Directions: From Prospect, drive 6.1 miles north on Highway 62 to Forest Service Road 68. Turn left and drive 2.7 miles, then turn right onto Forest Service Road 6510 (gravel) for 5.8 miles to Forest Service Road 6515. Turn left and drive 6.3 miles to the trailhead on the left. There's no parking at the trailhead, but there are two small turnouts to the right, a short distance both before and after the trailhead.

Contact: Rogue River National Forest, Prospect Ranger District, 47201 Highway 62, Prospect, OR 97536, 541/560-3400.

62 GOLDEN STAIRS
8.6 mi/4.0 hrs

north of Prospect in Rogue River National Forest

Map 5.6, page 169

The name conjures up a "Stairway to Heaven" feeling, gliding up on an enchanted path to an enlightened and breathtaking view. Well, it does start in a stairlike fashion but quickly evens out, and it's decidedly run of the mill for such a fancy-schmancy name, which it got from an alleged gold mine in the area back in the 1860s.

Still, it is a good trail for solitude as it ventures into the fir forest and then switchbacks to 5,350 feet up the rocky southern ridge of Falcon Butte (total elevation gain is 1,600 feet). Views include Abbott Butte and Elephant Head, and, after another gentle uphill, the Crater Lake rim.

User groups: Hikers, dogs, and horses. No mountain bikes are allowed. No wheelchair access.

Permits: Permits are not required. Parking and access are free.

Maps: For a map of Rogue River National Forest, contact Nature of the Northwest Information Center. For a topographic map, ask the USGS for Abbott Butte.

Directions: From Prospect, drive 6.1 miles north on Highway 62 to Forest Service Road 68. Turn left and drive five miles, then turn right onto Forest Service Road 550 for 2.1 miles. Park in a small pullout to the left just past the trailhead marker, which is on the right side of the road.

Contact: Rogue River National Forest, Prospect Ranger District, 47201 Highway 62, Prospect, OR 97536, 541/560-3400.

63 UNION CREEK
8.8 mi/4.0 hrs

north of Prospect in Rogue River National Forest

Map 5.6, page 169

Union Creek is a pretty, flat creekside stroll, but as with many trails that are near campgrounds, it can get a little crowded. Traveling along Union Creek, the trail starts near the day-use area. A sign leads you to the amphitheater over a foot-bridge, but turn left instead to saunter down the path. It leads past Farewell Bend Campground and right on through Union Creek Campground before turning to leave the tent world behind. The best part of the trail is the upper portion, which is a more peaceful saunter through Douglas fir forest, because you can see Union Falls just .5 mile from the end of the trail.

User groups: Hikers and dogs. No horses or mountain bikes are allowed. No wheelchair access.

Permits: Permits are not required. Parking and access are free.

Maps: For a map of Rogue River National Forest, contact Nature of the Northwest Information Center. For a topographic map, ask the USGS for Union Creek.

Directions: From Prospect, drive 10.7 miles north on Highway 62 to Union Creek Campground. Turn left and park at the visitors center (there's no day-use parking at the Campground), to the right immediately after turning from the highway.

Contact: Rogue River National Forest, Prospect Ranger District, 47201 Highway 62, Prospect, OR 97536, 541/560-3400.

64 ROGUE GORGE
7.0 mi/3.5 hrs

north of Prospect in Rogue River National Forest

Map 5.6, page 169

The first part of this trail, traveling along the Rogue River, is nothing to write home about. It's sandy, crowded with people fishing and frolicking in the river, and passes right by and sometimes almost through campsites, so you feel as if you're invading someone's space. But the best things come to those who wait. Soon you'll lose the crowds and gain the view. It's 3.5 miles to Rogue Gorge, where the river rushes through a lava chute. After retracing your steps to the trailhead, take the short trail to Natural Bridge, which was formed by basaltic lava bubbling through the earth and moving through tubes, eventually to be replaced by a river of water. Indians and early settlers used the bridge to cross the river, but you can't. What you can do, though, is head up to a great viewpoint just a short distance up the popular trail, and this time, the view is worth the crowds.

User groups: Hikers and dogs. No horses or mountain bikes are allowed. No wheelchair access.

Permits: Permits are not required. Parking and access are free.

Maps: For a map of Rogue River National

Forest, contact Nature of the Northwest Information Center. For a topographic map, ask the USGS for Union Creek.

Directions: From Prospect, drive 9.7 miles north on Highway 62 to Natural Bridge Campground. Turn left and drive past the campground for .7 mile (turning left at the fork) to the end of the road and the parking area for Natural Bridge Viewpoint. The trailhead starts to the right as you're looking at the river.

Contact: Rogue River National Forest, Prospect Ranger District, 47201 Highway 62, Prospect, OR 97536, 541/560-3400.

65 PACIFIC CREST TRAIL TO BALD CRATER/BOUNDARY SPRINGS
18.0 mi/2.0 days

north of Fort Klamath in Crater Lake National Park

Map 5.6, page 169

It's possible to do this hike in one day, but you'll want to stick around longer because there are some great camp spots along the way. Starting on the Pacific Crest Trail, you'll walk for 3.2 miles to the junction with Boundary Springs (Red Cone Springs camping spot is a cozy area on a small spring just .5 mile past this junction). On your left you'll pass by the aptly named Red Cone, a red cinder-cone volcano, and see views of Mount Thielsen. Speaking of volcanoes, you'll definitely notice that you're walking on one, as the soft pumice has a way of creeping into your boots no matter how tightly laced they are. Continuing on the gentle downhill hike, you'll pass the small Bald Crater on your six-mile trek to the small, cold Boundary Springs. (If you're overnighting, you'll need to camp .25 mile from the springs.) You can also combine this trail with Spheghum Bog for a loop back to the PCT and your car. As with all the trails in this park, all junctions are clearly marked so it's nearly impossible to make a wrong turn.

User groups: Hikers only. No dogs, horses, or bikes are allowed. No wheelchair access.

Permits: There is a $10 entrance fee to the park.

A wilderness permit is also required for overnight visits as is available at the park entrance.

Maps: A trail map is available at the park entrance. For a map of Crater Lake National Park, contact Nature of the Northwest Information Center. For a topographic map, ask the USGS for Pumice Desert West and Crater Lake West.

Directions: From Fort Klamath, drive 15 miles north on Highway 62 to the West Crater Lake Park entrance. Turn right onto Munson Valley Road, and drive six miles east to Rim Village and the junction with Rim Drive. Turn left (north) onto Rim Drive and continue to North Entrance Road. Turn left and drive three miles north to the Pacific Crest trailhead on the left (west) side of the road. From the north entrance, it's 6.5 miles down the North Entrance Road for the trailhead on the right. Note: The park is usually open from June through November, depending on snow conditions.

Contact: Crater Lake National Park, P.O. Box 7, Crater Lake, OR 97604, 541/594-3100.

66 CLEETWOOD COVE/ WIZARD ISLAND
4.0 mi/1.5 hr

north of Fort Klamath in Crater Lake National Park

Map 5.6, page 169

Want to get a closer look at Crater Lake's clear, blue water? Cleetwood Cove Trail is the only way to do it. It's a short yet steep drop to the cove, losing 700 feet in elevation, but just remember that you have to climb back up at the end. Also keep in mind that the cove starts at 6,176 feet of elevation, so that combination of steep climb and altitude makes for a tough (but worth it) hike. If you want to get an even closer look at the lake, hop on a boat (the fee is $19.25 for adults) for a tour to Wizard Island, a 1.8-mile round-trip hike up 800 feet to the summit of the cinder-cone volcano, for a panoramic view of the caldera from a different perspective. The boat also cruises around the whole lake for a 1.75-hour guided tour, so you can glide along inside the caldera and see it from all angles. Note: As of this writing, they have added new, environmentally friendly boats, and so the price may be increasing. Also, the boats do not always run on a set schedule, so check before you go if you want to try this hike.

User groups: Hikers only. No dogs, horses, or bikes are allowed. No wheelchair access.

Permits: There is a $10 entrance fee to the park. A wilderness permit is also required for overnight visits and is available at the park entrance.

Maps: A trail map is available at the park entrance. For a map of Crater Lake National Park, contact Nature of the Northwest Information Center. For a topographic map, ask the USGS for Crater Lake East.

Directions: From Fort Klamath, drive 15 miles north on Highway 62 to the West Crater Lake Park entrance. Turn right onto Munson Valley Road and drive six miles east to Rim Village and the junction with Rim Drive. Turn left (north) onto Rim Drive and continue 4.5 miles past North Entrance Road, to the Cleetwood Cove trailhead, on the right. Note: The park is usually open from June through November, depending on snow conditions.

Contact: Crater Lake National Park, P.O. Box 7, Crater Lake, OR 97604, 541/594-3100.

67 WATCHMAN PEAK
1.4 mi/1.0 hr

north of Fort Klamath in Crater Lake National Park

Map 5.6, page 169

It would be a perfect 10 were it not for the large crowds streaming up the Watchman. But let them look, because the scenery is the best around, in a park packed with views. You'll start on the Rim Trail/PCT Bypass for .25 mile, then turn left and climb up 500 feet to a view from 8,025-foot Watchman Peak that takes in Wizard Island below—plus 360-degree vistas of the clear, blue lake and the omnipresent cinder cone peaks that seem to follow you around the park. It's worth battling the throngs to make it up to this one.

User groups: Hikers only. No dogs, horses, or bikes are allowed. No wheelchair access.

Permits: A $10 fee is collected at the park entrance. A wilderness permit is also required for overnight visits and is available at the park entrance.

Maps: A trail map is available at the park entrance. For a map of Crater Lake National Park, contact Nature of the Northwest Information Center. For a topographic map, ask the USGS for Crater Lake West.

Directions: From Fort Klamath, drive 15 miles north on Highway 62 to the West Crater Lake Park entrance. Turn right onto Munson Valley Road and drive six miles east to Rim Village and the junction with Rim Drive. Turn right onto Rim Drive and drive for three miles to the trailhead on the right. Note: The park is usually open from June through November, depending on snow conditions.

Contact: Crater Lake National Park, P.O. Box 7, Crater Lake, OR 97604, 541/594-3100.

68 PACIFIC CREST TRAIL BYPASS/RIM TRAIL
16.0 mi/8.0 hrs

north of Fort Klamath in Crater Lake National Park

Map 5.6, page 169

For viewpoints that the average car tourist who four-wheels it through Crater Lake will never see, check out the Rim Trail. You'll climb steeply up to the west rim of Crater Lake for a secluded view of the clear, blue lake, plus you'll get on a first-name basis with the Devil's Backbone and Hillman Peak along the way. But don't get carried away with the views, because there are truly ankle-twisting climbs and sandy spots. Walking and gawking at the same time can be hazardous to your health. The Pacific Crest Trail didn't pass through these parts until 1995, when the trail was rerouted so long-distance hikers could see the sights too (they'd earned it, after all). Starting from the trailhead, start up the Pacific Crest Trail a short distance to a junction. Turn right as the trail leaves the PCT (give it a wave) then quickly climbs up the crater of Mount Mazama. Enjoy your first viewpoint at Merrian Point, and then begin the seclusion part of the competition, as you continue the climb and leave those flatlanders behind. You can do the hike one-way or connect with any of the other trails in the northwest section of the park to create a big loop. The trail does meet the road at times, so hikers can also choose to access just part of the trail. At the entrance, you can get a handy trail map for all your options, because the list really does go on. The trails are incredibly well maintained and well marked, so you should never have problems finding your way. After a day of hiking, drop down to the Rim Village, where a burger and cold suds are tapping their toes waiting for you to get done already with this hiking business.

User groups: Hikers only. No dogs, horses, or bikes are allowed. No wheelchair access.

Permits: A $10 fee is collected at the park entrance. A wilderness permit is also required for overnight visits and is available at the park entrance.

Maps: A trail map is available at the park entrance. For a map of Crater Lake National Park, contact Nature of the Northwest Information Center. For a topographic map, ask the USGS for Crater Lake West.

Directions: From Fort Klamath, drive 15 miles north on Highway 62 to the West Crater Lake Park entrance. Turn right onto Munson Valley Road and drive six miles east to Rim Village and the junction with Rim Drive. Turn left on Rim Drive and continue to the Pacific Crest Trail parking lot on the left side of the road. The trail is on the right (east) side of the road. Note: The park is usually open from June through November, depending on snow conditions.

Contact: Crater Lake National Park, P.O. Box 7, Crater Lake, OR 97604, 541/594-3100.

69 LIGHTNING SPRING
8.0 mi/4.0 hr

north of Fort Klamath in Crater Lake National Park

Map 5.6, page 169

Crater Lake is one of the clearest lakes in the world. Scientists even came in and measured it with their clear-lake devices and discovered, on June 25, 1997, that they could see down to 142 feet. Whoa. It's also the deepest lake in the country and the seventh-deepest in the world—1,943 feet at its deepest point. It's also the bluest lake in the world. Okay, that last one isn't scientifically proven, but you will definitely think the same when you see it. Crater Lake is simply something you have to see. Now on to the hike: Starting near the rim of the lake, the well-marked Lightning Spring Trail leads four miles to the Pacific Crest Trail. After one mile, you'll hit Lightning Spring itself, which is a small cold spring with a backcountry camping spot. After passing the spring, the path travels down an easy hill along Lightning Spring Creek to the PCT. If you're just getting warmed up, you can turn right (north) on the PCT for a mile to Bybee Creek camping spot, a cozy site near a small cold stream. Continue on to connect with Spheghum Bog, Boundary Springs, and the Red Cone Springs Campground. Or just retrace your steps for some more lake views. The only reason this hike was not given a higher scenery rating is because it doesn't actually give you many views of the lake itself, except at the beginning. But it is good for accessing backcountry campsites, and the view at the start will make your camera start snapping shots by itself.

User groups: Hikers only. No dogs, horses, or bikes are allowed. No wheelchair access.

Permits: There is a $10 entrance fee to the park. A wilderness permit is also required for overnight visits and is available at the park entrance.

Maps: A trail map is available at the park entrance. For a map of Crater Lake National Park, contact Nature of the Northwest Information Center. For a topographic map, ask the USGS for Crater Lake West.

Directions: From Fort Klamath, drive 15 miles north on Highway 62 to the West Crater Lake entrance. Turn right onto Munson Valley Road and drive six miles east to Rim Village. The Lightning Spring trailhead is on the west end of the parking lot. Note: The park is usually open from June through November, depending on snow conditions.

Contact: Crater Lake National Park, P.O. Box 7, Crater Lake, OR 97604, 541/594-3100.

70 DISCOVERY POINT
2.6 mi/1.5 hrs

north of Fort Klamath in Crater Lake National Park

Map 5.6, page 169

Imagine walking along, lost in your own thoughts—maybe even having a conversation with yourself, anything's possible—when suddenly you come across a massive, clear-blue lake five miles in diameter and surrounded by steep 2,000-foot rock walls. Well, this is where it all happened, oh, about 150 years ago when 21-year-old John Wesley Hillman and his party were out mucking about, trying to find the Lost Gold Mine. Little did they realize they would happen upon a gold mine in a different form. Peering down at the lake, they declared it the bluest lake they'd ever seen. A hundred years later, it would also be declared one of the clearest lakes in the world. So check it all out up this path gaining just 100 feet in elevation to Discovery Point, where you can imagine discovering this amazing phenomenon.

User groups: Hikers only. No dogs, horses, or bikes are allowed. No wheelchair access.

Permits: There is a $10 entrance fee to the park. A wilderness permit is also required for overnight visits and is available at the park entrance.

Maps: A trail map is available at the park entrance. For a map of Crater Lake National Park, contact Nature of the Northwest Information Center. For a topographic map, ask the USGS for Crater Lake West.

Directions: From Fort Klamath, drive 15 miles north on Highway 62 to the West Crater Lake Park entrance. Turn right onto Munson Valley Road and drive six miles east to Rim Village. The Discovery Point trailhead is at the west end of the Rim Village parking lot. Note: The park is usually open from June through November, depending on snow conditions.

Contact: Crater Lake National Park, P.O. Box 7, Crater Lake, OR 97604, 541/594-3100.

71 DUTTON CREEK
4.8 mi/2.5 hrs

north of Fort Klamath in Crater Lake National Park

Map 5.6, page 169

Traveling from Crater Rim to the Pacific Crest Trail, this path isn't the best for views of the lake but is a good chance to check out the cool old-growth mountain hemlock and pine forest, and maybe even some Crater Lake natives, like black-tailed deer, red fox, coyotes, elk, and porcupines. The trail ends at the PCT junction and the Dutton Creek camp. The forest often gets overshadowed by the clear, blue lake, but it's scenic itself and worth checking out.

User groups: Hikers only. No dogs, horses, or bikes are allowed. No wheelchair access.

Permits: There is a $10 entrance fee to the park. A wilderness permit is also required for overnight visits and is available at the park entrance.

Maps: A trail map is available at the park entrance. For a map of Crater Lake National Park, contact Nature of the Northwest Information Center. For a topographic map, ask the USGS for Crater Lake West.

Directions: From Fort Klamath, drive 15 miles north on Highway 62 to the West Crater Lake Park entrance. Turn right onto Munson Valley Road and drive six miles east to Rim Village. The Dutton Creek trailhead is at the south end of Rim Village. Note: The park is usually open from June through November, depending on snow conditions.

Contact: Crater Lake National Park, P.O. Box 7, Crater Lake, OR 97604, 541/594-3100.

72 GARFIELD PEAK
3.4 mi/1.5 hrs

north of Fort Klamath in Crater Lake National Park

Map 5.6, page 169

Although it's a short trip, you do gain 1,000 feet in elevation, and when you're already starting at 7,000 feet, that can translate to high marks in the heavy-breathing department. The trail leads up to Garfield Peak for a panoramic view of the lake, and of Phantom Ship, a ship-shaped island that protrudes 169 feet above the water. As with all hikes in the Crater Lake area, you'll want to bring your camera along to capture the crystal-clear and deep-blue waters of this cool area.

User groups: Hikers only. No dogs, horses, or bikes are allowed. No wheelchair access.

Permits: There is a $10 entrance fee to the park. A wilderness permit is also required for overnight visits and is available at the park entrance.

Maps: A trail map is available at the park entrance. For a map of Crater Lake National Park, contact Nature of the Northwest Information Center. For a topographic map, ask the USGS for Crater Lake West and Crater Lake East.

Directions: From Fort Klamath, drive 15 miles north on Highway 62 to the West Crater Lake Park entrance. Turn right onto Munson Valley Road and drive six miles east to Rim Village. The Garfield Peak trailhead is on the east side of the Crater Lake Lodge. Note: The park is usually open from June through November, depending on snow conditions.

Contact: Crater Lake National Park, P.O. Box 7, Crater Lake, OR 97604, 541/594-3100.

73 MOUNT SCOTT
5.0 mi/2.5 hrs
north of Fort Klamath in Crater Lake National Park

Map 5.6, page 169

It seems that every hike in the Crater Lake area has a different claim to fame. Mount Scott, at 8,929 feet, holds the prize for the tallest peak

in the park and for the best views of the park's cinder cones, the lake below, and neighboring peaks (and the most strenuous climb to get there, gaining 1,500 feet in elevation). Keep in mind that you're starting at high elevation to begin with, so you may wheeze on this hike more than you would at sea level.

User groups: Hikers only. No dogs, horses, or bikes are allowed. No wheelchair access.

Permits: There is a $10 entrance fee to the park. A wilderness permit is also required for overnight visits and is available at the park entrance.

Maps: A trail map is available at the park entrance. For a map of Crater Lake National Park, contact Nature of the Northwest Information Center. For a topographic map, ask the USGS for Crater Lake East.

Directions: From Fort Klamath, drive 15 miles north on Highway 62 to the West Crater Lake Park entrance. Turn right onto Munson Valley Road and drive six miles east to Rim Village and the junction with Rim Drive. Turn right onto Rim Drive and drive for 14 miles around the east side of the crater to the Mount Scott trailhead on the right side of the road. Note: The park is usually open from June through November, depending on snow conditions.

Contact: Crater Lake National Park, P.O. Box 7, Crater Lake, OR 97604, 541/594-3100.

74 CASTLE CREST WILDFLOWER GARDEN
1.0 mi/0.5 hr

north of Fort Klamath in Crater Lake National Park

Map 5.6, page 169

If you're a fool for flowers, mark this one high on your list. Save it for July or August, and then tune in to the must-see meadows. The easy one-mile loop gains 500 feet in elevation to tour right through wildflower blooms. It's a perfect ending or warm-up for a day at Crater Lake, and since it's so short, you can combine it with several other trails in the park for a full day of hiking.

User groups: Hikers only. No dogs, horses, or bikes are allowed. No wheelchair access.

Permits: There is a $10 entrance fee to the park. A wilderness permit is also required for overnight visits and is available at the park entrance.

Maps: A trail map is available at the park entrance. For a map of Crater Lake National Park, contact Nature of the Northwest Information Center. For a topographic map, ask the USGS for Crater Lake West and Crater Lake East.

Directions: From Fort Klamath, drive 15 miles north on Highway 62 to the West Crater Lake Park entrance. Turn right onto Munson Valley Road and drive six miles east to Rim Village. The trailhead starts opposite the park headquarters. Note: The park is usually open from June through November, depending on snow conditions.

Contact: Crater Lake National Park, P.O. Box 7, Crater Lake, OR 97604, 541/594-3100.

75 CRATER PEAK
6.4 mi/3.5 hrs

north of Fort Klamath in Crater Lake National Park

Map 5.6, page 169

For views of Crater Lake itself, you'll need to hit the other viewpoints listed in this chapter. But for views of the surrounding cinder-cone volcanoes and peaks, not to mention the forest itself plus a 1,000-foot climb, take a walk up the crater itself to its 7,265-foot views of the southern crater rim—as well as surrounding peaks like Goose Nest and Union Peak. It's a tough haul, considering you're already starting out at 6,500 feet, so take it slow and take in the scenery on the way.

User groups: Hikers only. No dogs, horses, or bikes are allowed. No wheelchair access.

Permits: A $10 fee is collected at the park entrance. A wilderness permit is also required for overnight visits and is available at the park entrance.

Maps: A trail map is available at the park entrance. For a map of Crater Lake National Park, contact Nature of the Northwest Information Center. For a topographic map, ask the USGS for Crater Lake East and Maklaks Crater.

Directions: From Fort Klamath, drive 15 miles north on Highway 62 to the West Crater Lake Park entrance. Turn right onto Munson Valley Road and drive six miles east to Rim Village and the junction with Rim Drive. Turn right onto Rim Drive to the trailhead on the right side of the road. Note: The park is usually open from June through November, depending on snow conditions.

Contact: Crater Lake National Park, P.O. Box 7, Crater Lake, OR 97604, 541/594-3100.

76 COLD SPRINGS
5.2 mi/2.5 hrs

east of Prospect in Rogue River National Forest

Map 5.6, page 169

This is an incredibly simple trail to follow—thanks to the OHV tracks, it's wide enough to walk hand in hand with your hiking partner if that's what you feel like. At first you almost feel as if you're in a museum rather than a forest, because for once you can actually see what you're walking through, unlike other hikes, where you're so in the thick of things you have no perspective on the situation. Sure, some true wilderness folk may sniff at this trail because of its gentle course and OHV tracks, but it's surprisingly peaceful, and there's plenty to gawk at. After two miles, you'll come to a meadow clearing, with views across the valley to Bald Top. Wildflowers like Indian paintbrush, dwarf lupine, and larkspur are out in the early summer, and since the road in tends to be open in May, you'll have a good shot at seeing them. The trail ends at the unremarkable springs, so don't expect much there. The beauty is really just a walk down the peaceful path with wildflower meadows and a view you'll most likely have all to yourself. Word has it that Paul Bunyan's grave is also on this spot, but good luck finding it (and if you do, give me a call, because we searched for hours).

User groups: Hikers, dogs, mountain bikes and horses. No wheelchair access.

Permits: Permits are not required. Parking and access are free.

Maps: For a map of Rogue River National Forest, contact Nature of the Northwest Information Center. For a topographic map, ask the USGS for Red Blanket Mountain.

Directions: From Prospect, drive one mile east on Prospect-Butte Falls Highway and turn left on Red Blanket Road. Drive .3 mile and turn left onto gravel Forest Service Road 6205. Drive four miles and turn left onto Forest Service Road 6205-100. Continue 7.3 miles to the parking pullout on the left. The trailhead is on the right across the road.

Contact: Rogue River National Forest, Prospect Ranger District, 47201 Highway 62, Prospect, OR 97536, 541/560-3400.

77 VARMINT CAMP
6.2 mi/3.0 hrs

east of Prospect in Rogue River National Forest

Map 5.6, page 169

To beat the heat, head to Varmint Camp. It tours past Varmint Creek along a thick and shady forest of bigleaf maple and Shasta red fir. It crosses the creek, which doesn't have bridges, so if you really want to cool off, now's your chance (although it's best to steer clear when the water levels are high). The trail then passes along a mountain meadow filled with wildflowers and wild onion in the summer. When it hits the road at mile 3.1, hit the road back home, retracing your steps.

User groups: Hikers, dogs, mountain bikes, and horses. No wheelchair access.

Permits: Permits are not required. Parking and access are free.

Maps: For a map of Rogue River National Forest, contact Nature of the Northwest Information Center. For a topographic map, ask the USGS for Red Blanket Mountain.

Directions: From Prospect, drive one mile east on Prospect-Butte Falls Highway and turn left on Red Blanket Road. Drive .3 mile and turn left onto gravel Forest Service Road 6205. Drive 3.1 miles to Forest Service Road 830 and continue 10 miles to the trailhead on the left, parking at the side of the road.

Contact: Rogue River National Forest, Prospect Ranger District, 47201 Highway 62, Prospect, OR 97536, 541/560-3400.

78 SEVENMILE
3.5 mi/1.5 hrs

northwest of Klamath Falls in Winema National Forest

Map 5.6, page 169

Like the name suggests, the trail follows Sevenmile Creek. Unlike the name suggests, it's 1.75 miles one-way. Well, if you're really a stickler for numbers, you can tack on some miles when you access the Pacific Crest Trail. But that part comes later. The relatively flat trail gains less than 500 feet as it travels along the creek through lodgepole pine forest before leaving it behind to climb along the slopes of the Sevenmile Marsh. It ends at a junction with the Pacific Crest Trail, where you can turn left and continue three miles to Sevenmile Lakes Basin, part of the Sky Lakes Basin.

User groups: Hikers and dogs. No horses or mountain bikes are allowed. No wheelchair access.

Permits: No passes are required. Parking and access are free.

Maps: For a map of Winema National Forest, contact Nature of the Northwest Information Center. For a topographic map, ask the USGS for Devil's Peak.

Directions: From Klamath Falls, drive 25.3 miles west on Highway 140 and turn right on Westside Road. Drive 6.8 miles and turn left onto Forest Service Road 3330. Drive 2.9 miles on gravel Forest Service Road 3330, then turn left onto 3334. Go 5.5 miles to the end of road, the parking area, and the trailhead.

Contact: Winema National Forest, Klamath Ranger District, 1936 California Avenue, Klamath Falls, OR 97601, 541/885-3400.

79 NANNIE CREEK TRAIL TO SNOW LAKES

13.2 mi/6.5 hrs

northwest of Klamath Falls in the Sky Lakes
Wilderness of Winema National Forest

Map 5.6, page 169

Your heart will be racing the moment you
step out of the car, not only from the high
elevation (starting at 6,000 feet), but also
from the long switchbacks that begin as soon
as you set a hiking boot on this rocky trail.
Soon you'll enter the cool forest to refresh
you as your body temperature rises a couple degrees. Nannie Creek Trail travels up
the slope of Lather Mountain and then levels out to pass Puck Lake and to join up with
Snow Lakes Trail. This climbs past clear
alpine lakes and heads up steep rocky ridges
for viewpoints on both sides before gaining
nearly 1,000 feet in just under a mile to end
at the Pacific Crest Trail. Keep in mind that
trails are not always marked in this area, so
you should bring a map along if you want
to try this route.

User groups: Hikers and dogs. No horses or
mountain bikes are allowed. No wheelchair
access.

Permits: No passes are required. Parking and
access are free.

Maps: For a map of Winema National Forest,
contact Nature of the Northwest Information
Center. For a topographic map, ask the USGS
for Devil's Peak and Pelican Butte.

Directions: From Klamath Falls, drive 25.3
miles west on Highway 140 and turn right on
Westside Road. Drive 2.3 miles to gravel Forest Service Road 3484. Turn left and drive
5.3 miles to the road's end and the trailhead,
which starts just to the right of the trailhead
sign.

Contact: Winema National Forest, Klamath
Ranger District, 1936 California Avenue, Klamath Falls, OR 97601, 541/885-3400.

80 CHERRY CREEK TRAIL TO SKY LAKES BASIN

11.0 mi/5.5 hrs

northwest of Klamath Falls in the Sky Lakes
Wilderness of Winema National Forest

Map 5.6, page 169

You'll be greeted right off the bat by the sting
of pesky mosquitoes who have come to personally welcome you to Cherry Creek. (Bring
your bug juice.) Traveling through the Cherry
Creek Natural Research Area, which was carved
by glaciers, you'll also be greeted with a grad-
ual climb you'll barely notice at first, one of
those creeping-up-on-you climbs where you wonder why you're suddenly out of breath. Then
the real climb begins about three miles in before
popping out at the scenic Sky Lakes basin and
to Trapper Lake. Keep in mind that this trail
has some creek crossings, so save it for later in
the summer, when the water level is lower. The
total elevation gain on the hike is 1,400 feet.

User groups: Hikers and dogs. No horses or
mountain bikes are allowed. No wheelchair
access.

Permits: No passes are required. Parking and
access are free.

Maps: For a map of Winema National Forest,
contact Nature of the Northwest Information
Center. For a topographic map, ask the USGS
for Pelican Butte and Crystal Spring.

Directions: From Klamath Falls, drive 25.3
miles west on Highway 140 and turn right on
Westside Road. Drive one mile to gravel Forest Service Road 3450. Turn left and drive 1.8
miles to the road's end and the trailhead.

Contact: Winema National Forest, Klamath
Ranger District, 1936 California Avenue, Klamath Falls, OR 97601, 541/885-3400.

81 FISH LAKE

10.0 mi/5.0 hrs

northeast of Ashland in Rogue River
National Forest

Map 5.6, page 169

Traveling along the North Fork of Little Butte
Creek, you'll pass through old-growth forest

and small meadows. But the biggest hits on this trail are the lava features: About .5 mile from the trail's end at High Lakes Trail, the path crosses Cascade Canal, an 11-mile canal built in the 1900s to carry water from Fourmile Lake to Fish Lake. Water runs through the lava tube for one mile before ending at Fish Lake. You'll also get a glimpse of the Brown Mountain lava flows near the trail's end. And probably the best part about it, halfway up, is Fish Lake, which is a good place to grab some grub at the store there for a picnic. (As with any trail that leads through a campground, you'll have company for stretches of the trail.)

User groups: Hikers, dogs, and mountain bikes. No horses are allowed. No wheelchair access.

Permits: Permits are not required. Parking and access are free.

Maps: For a map of Rogue River National Forest, contact Nature of the Northwest Information Center. For a topographic map, ask the USGS for Mount McLoughlin.

Directions: From Ashland, drive two miles east to Dead Indian Memorial Highway. Turn left and drive for 21.8 miles, then turn left onto Highway 37. Continue 7.6 miles to the trailhead on the right, just before North Fork Campground.

Contact: Rogue River National Forest, Ashland Ranger District, 645 Washington Street, Ashland, OR 97520, 541/552-2900.

82 BROWN MOUNTAIN
10.6 mi/7.5 hrs

northeast of Ashland in Rogue River National Forest

Map 5.6, page 169

Huckleberry and wild-mushroom pickers get serious about searching through forests to find these sometimes-hidden treasures. They'll love this trail, which is lined with the little guys. Following the South Fork of Little Butte Creek, the path scoots around the edge of Brown Mountain, but you can't really get a glimpse of it until you hit about 3.5 miles. The trail gains 800 feet on the dot, ending at the Pacific Crest Trail.

User groups: Hikers, dogs, mountain bikes, and horses. No wheelchair access.

Permits: A federal Northwest Forest pass is required to park here. The cost is $5 for a day pass or $30 for an annual pass. You can buy a day pass at ranger stations, from private vendors, or through Nature of the Northwest Information Center.

Maps: For a map of Rogue River National Forest, contact Nature of the Northwest Information Center. For a topographic map, ask the USGS for Brown Mountain.

Directions: From Ashland, drive two miles east to Dead Indian Memorial Highway. Turn left and drive 21.8 miles to Forest Service Road 37. Turn left and drive six miles to Forest Service Road 3705 (a paved, one-lane road). Turn right and drive 3.2 miles to the trailhead and small parking turnout at the side of the road.

Contact: Rogue River National Forest, Ashland Ranger District, 645 Washington Street, Ashland, OR 97520, 541/522-2900.

83 BEAVER DAM
4.2 mi/2.0 hrs

northeast of Ashland in Rogue River National Forest

Map 5.6, page 169

A convention of creeks meets at Beaver Dam Trail: Beaver Dam itself is the ringleader of the operation, followed by Daley and Deadwood Creeks, which meet to travel through willows and beaver ponds. The path connects Beaver Dam and Daley Creek trails to form a partial loop through fir and pine forest. A particularly industrious plant that thrives in this area is the pacific yew, with red, peeling bark and short, dark-green needles (don't go gnawing at it, it's poisonous). Native Americans used it for archery bows and canoe paddles, and it has even come in handy in cancer research. Also look out for beaver-gnawed branches and woodpeckers along the peaceful path.

User groups: Hikers and dogs. No mountain bikes or horses are allowed. No wheelchair access.

Permits: Permits are not required. Parking and access are free.

Maps: For a map of Rogue River National Forest, contact Nature of the Northwest Information Center. For a topographic map, ask the USGS for Brown Mountain.

Directions: From Ashland, drive two miles east to Dead Indian Memorial Highway. Turn left and drive 21.8 miles to Forest Service Road 37. Turn left and drive 1.5 miles to the trailhead on the right, just before Daley Creek Campground.

Contact: Rogue River National Forest, Ashland Ranger District, 645 Washington Street, Ashland, OR 97520, 541/522-2900.

84 VARNEY CREEK TRAIL TO MOUNTAIN LAKES LOOP
17.0 mi/2.0 days
northwest of Klamath Falls in the Mountain Lakes Wilderness of Winema National Forest

Map 5.6, page 169

Crater Lake and Newberry Crater may get more attention because they're so easy to get to by car, but this unique caldera is reachable only by hiking in, which means you lose the crowds, gain the solitude. Eight peaks form the rim of the Mountain Lakes caldera, surrounding many smaller lakes that you can loop around on this 8.2-mile tour. Two backpacking musts: a camera and bug repellent, because it's thick with mosquitoes. Camp in this surreal setting for the night, but remember to set up tent away from water sources. Mountain Lakes Loop Trail is 4.5 miles down Varney Creek Trail, which is a peaceful path through dense forest and over footbridges across the creek. The trail is also accessible from Clover Creek Trail, which comes to the Mountain Lakes Loop junction at 3.3 miles.

User groups: Hikers, dogs, and horses. No mountain bikes are allowed. No wheelchair access.

Permits: Permits are not required. Parking and access are free.

Maps: For a map of Winema National Forest,

contact Nature of the Northwest Information Center. For a topographic map, ask the USGS for Pelican Bay and Aspen Lake.

Directions: From Klamath Falls, drive 21.2 miles west on Highway 140 and turn left on gravel Forest Service Road 3637. Drive 1.7 miles and turn left on Forest Service Road 3664. Continue two miles to the end of the road and the parking area. The trailhead is to the right as you're driving in. To reach Clover Creek Trail from Ashland, drive two miles east to Dead Indian Memorial Highway. Turn left and drive 28.8 miles, then turn right onto Clover Creek Road. Drive 5.8 miles and turn left onto gravel Forest Service Road 3852. Drive 3.2 miles and park in the pullout to the right. The trailhead is to the right as you walk down the road past the pullout.

Contact: Winema National Forest, Klamath Ranger District, 1936 California Avenue, Klamath Falls, OR 97601, 541/885-3400.

85 GRIZZLY PEAK
6.0 mi/3.0 hrs
northeast of Ashland and west of Dead Indian Memorial Highway

Map 5.6, page 169

Passing through mixed fir and pine forest, you'll start climbing right away, three miles up to the 5,922-foot summit of Grizzly Peak. Only about 10 miles north of Ashland, the peak is a popular trail for a view to see how things are faring a little south of the border. If you've ever wanted to be a fly on the wall and peer down at a city, you'll have a great vantage point of Ashland below, plus the Rogue River Valley, Mount McLoughlin, Diamond Peak, and Mount Shasta. Along the way, don't be surprised to see elk and deer (alas, no grizzlies). Note: In August 2003, this trail was closed due to the East Antelope fire; it's expected to open in May 2004. Check ahead before you set out.

User groups: Hikers, dogs, mountain bikes, and horses. No wheelchair access.

Permits: Permits are not required. Parking and access are free.

Maps: For a topographic map, ask the USGS for Grizzly Peak.

Directions: From Ashland, drive two miles east to Dead Indian Memorial Highway. Turn left and drive 6.7 miles to Shale City Road. Turn left onto Shale City Road and drive three miles, then turn left on unmarked road 38-2E-9.2 (there are signs to Grizzly Peak). Drive .8 mile, then fork left for .8 mile and drive up to the end of the road and the parking area. The trailhead starts just south of the parking area, up a short hill.

Contact: Bureau of Land Management, Medford District Office, 3040 Biddle Road, Medford, OR 97504, 541/618-2200.

© KEVIN FOREMAN

Chapter 6

Southeast Oregon

Chapter 6—Southeast Oregon

Take a gander at the surface area covered in the Southeast Oregon chapter map. Now count how many hikes are in this area. Get the point? There's not a lot by way of trails in the whole region. So if you crave solitude, if you crave the true wilderness experience, if you crave looking out on a vast expanse of desert and screaming at the top of your lungs, here's your chance.

Rewind . . . Desert? That's right. Although Oregon is probably (okay, *definitely)* known for the wet stuff, the state is actually mostly desert, most of which lies in the southeast region. This region includes Fremont-Winema National Forest, Gearhart Wilderness, and Steens Mountain, and also dips into the southeast portion of the Deschutes to bring Newberry Crater National Monument and Paulina Peak into the picture.

First off the bat, and right off the main drag of Highway 97, are the Newberry Lava Caves, which come courtesy of their neighbor to the south, Newberry Volcano. Four short and sweet walks are the perfect antidotes to the area's notoriously hot, dry summer days.

Just to the south, in the southeast corner of Deschutes National Forest, Newberry Crater National Monument and Paulina Peak offer short trips to Paulina Falls, a loop around Paulina Lake, and a steep climb up to 7,985-foot Paulina Peak. The Newberry Volcano erupted 1,300 years ago, resulting in lava—and lots of it. You can walk through it, including all 170 million cubic yards of the Obsidian Flow.

If it's solitude you're after, you can't find a better place in the state to be all by yourself than Gearhart Wilderness, in Fremont-Winema National Forest, located in the southwestern part of this region. Only three trails slice through this 22,823-acre wilderness area known as the "Oregon Outback." Over 300 species of fish and wildlife call the Fremont-Winema forest home, including mule deer, Rocky Mountain elk, and antelope.

And then there's the ever-expansive desert. Driving through this barren land, don't be surprised to see a tumbleweed cross your path (hey, they have to get to the other side, too). Steens Mountain is right in the heart of High Desert Country, in the southeastern corner of this region, and you don't have to climb far to see the sights. You can drive straight up the scenic road to just a quarter mile shy of the 9,733-foot summit itself, with viewpoints along the way of the deep green Kiger Gorge, the steep canyon and the desert valley below, and Wildhorse Lake, sitting pretty 1,000 feet below the summit.

Above all, what you'll notice driving through this area is the lack of people. Although the southeast region comprises roughly one-fourth of the state, it's remarkably unpopulated. The largest town is Burns, in the north-central part of the region, with a head count of just 3,064. Small towns dot the region, and they move at a different pace. Quick illustration of my point: While researching hikes in this area, I was buying trail food with my ATM card, and the lovely lady behind the desk just wrote down my number on a piece of paper, drew a long line underneath with an X, and handed me a pen carved out of wood to sign. I grasped the cumbersome pen and looked at her. "That's a new one," I laughed. "Honey, you're in the middle of nowhere," she replied. I couldn't have said it better myself. After all, with lava flows, caves, volcanoes, desert valleys, deep gorges, and remote wilderness, there's no room left for many people.

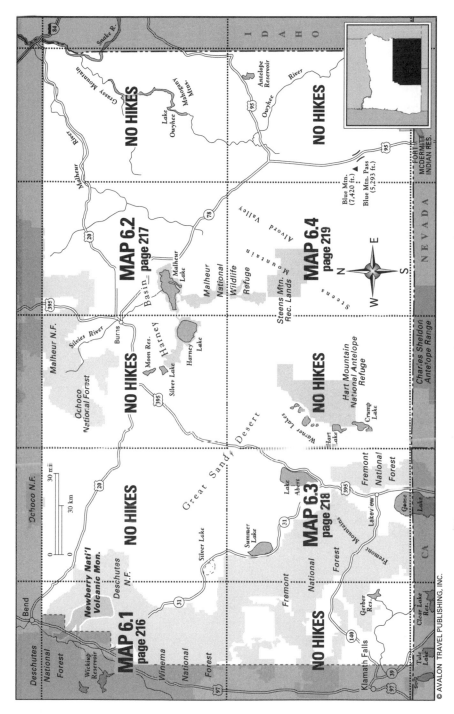

Map 6.1

Hikes 1–6
Pages 220–222

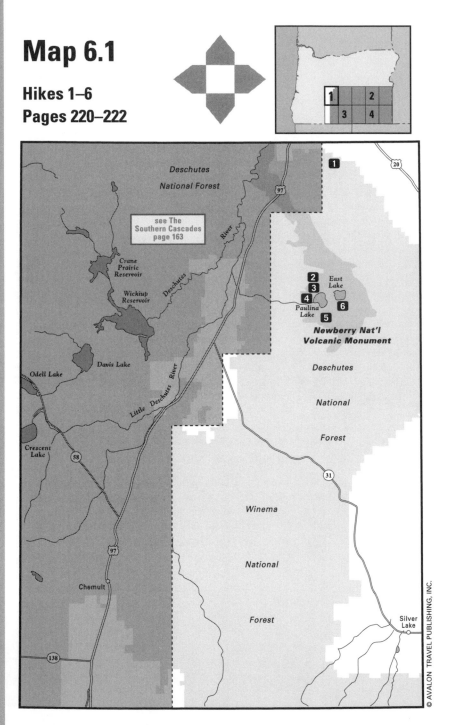

Map 6.2

Hike 7
Page 223

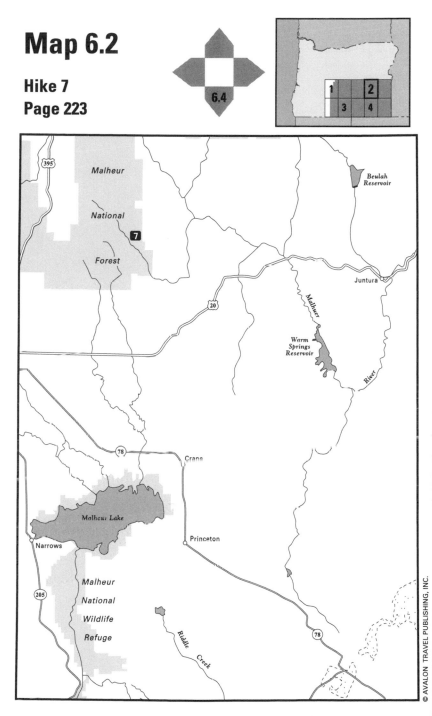

Map 6.3

Hikes 8–12
Pages 223–225

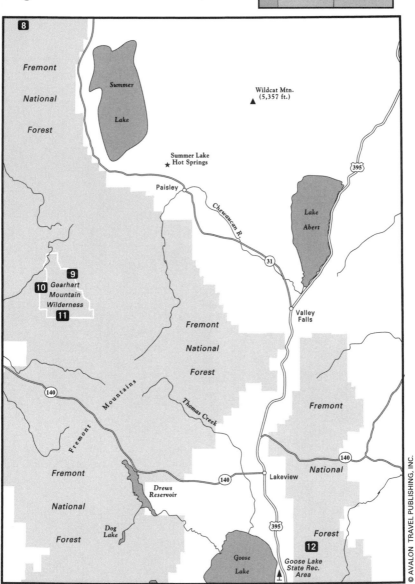

Map 6.4

Hike 13
Page 226

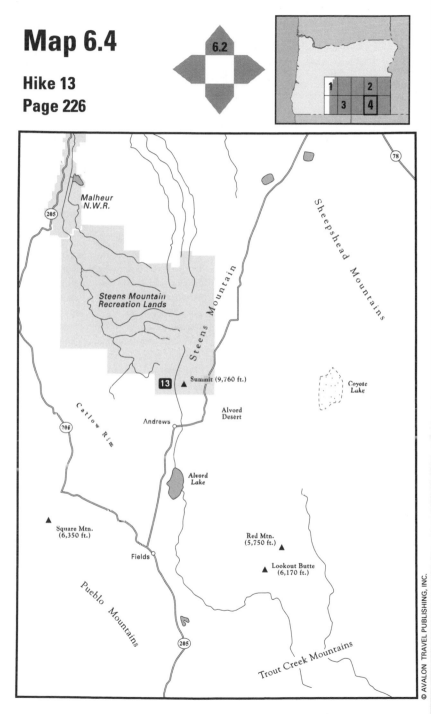

1 NEWBERRY LAVA CAVES
3.4 mi/1.5 hrs

south of Bend in Deschutes National Forest

Map 6.1, page 216

Who needs air conditioning when you can explore the icy depths of lava caves? Not to be confused with the Newberry Lava Monument to the south, these three super-short trails lead to caves right off the highway and are just the ticket to refreshment on one of the Bend area's infamous hot and dry days. The lava tubes were created courtesy of their neighbor to the south, volcano Mount Newberry, and the lava flows formed tunnels that you can explore. First stop: Boyd Cave, a .2-mile descent into the chilly cavern. Next up: Skeleton Cave, a .2-mile trip to two lava tunnels. Not to be left out in the um, dark, is the .5-mile journey down Wind Cave, which features a natural skylight. (Caution: It's hard to keep your footing on the huge rocky mess on the floor.) But those were just a warm-up for the main attraction: A 10-mile trip south on Highway 97 will bring you to Lava River Cave, which is the longest and spookiest of them all, extending one mile into the lava tube. Bring along warm clothes, gloves, a flashlight, and some rock-hopping shoes. Be warned, though: If you are claustrophobic, you may not enjoy these caves as much as the next person, so enter at your own risk. Lava River Cave and Wind Cave are closed between November 1 and April 15 to protect hibernating bats (not that you'd want to go there in the winter anyway; word has it that bears also slumber in these cozy caves).

User groups: Hikers, dogs, mountain bikes, and horses (no mountain bikes or horses allowed at Lava River Cave). No wheelchair access.

Permits: Permits are not required. Parking and access are free for Boyd, Wind, and Skeleton Caves; there is a $3 entrance fee for Lava River Cave.

Maps: For a map of Deschutes National Forest, contact Nature of the Northwest Information Center. For a topographic map, ask the USGS for Kelsey Butte and Lava Butte.

Directions: From Bend, drive four miles south on U.S. 97 to China Hat Road/Forest Service Road 18. Boyd Cave is nine miles down on the left side of the road; Skeleton Cave is .5 mile east of Boyd Cave; and Wind Cave is another two miles down Forest Service Road 18 from Skeleton Cave.

Contact: Deschutes National Forest, Bend-Fort Rock Ranger District, 1230 Northeast 3rd Street, Suite A-262, Bend, OR 97701, 541/383-4000.

2 NEWBERRY CRATER RIM
21.0 mi/2.0 days

between Bend and La Pine in Newberry Crater National Monument

Map 6.1, page 216

If you want to be a stickler about things, Newberry Crater is actually made of several overlapping calderas, so it should properly be called Newberry Caldera. But whatever you call it, you should check out this amazing sight. Sitting on the top of Newberry Volcano, the four-mile-diameter caldera was formed during a series of eruptions over a period of a half million years. The whole shebang is a 21-mile journey (backpackers should note that there's no water on the trail), but you can easily shorten the trip by taking one of the many access points, such as Paulina Peak Trail (see listing in this chapter).

User groups: Hikers, dogs, mountain bikes, and horse. No wheelchair access.

Permits: A federal Northwest Forest pass is required to park here. The cost is $5 for a day pass or $30 for an annual pass. You can buy a day pass at the trailhead, at ranger stations, from private vendors, or through Nature of the Northwest Information Center.

Maps: For a map of Deschutes National Forest, contact Nature of the Northwest Information Center. For a topographic map, ask the USGS for Paulina Peak and East Lake.

Directions: From Bend, drive 22 miles south on U.S. 97 to Forest Service Road 21, about seven miles north of La Pine. Turn left and drive 12 miles to park at Paulina Lake Lodge.

The trail is also accessible at Little Crater Campground on the south side of the park.

Contact: Deschutes National Forest, Bend-Fort Rock Ranger District, 1230 Northeast 3rd Street, Suite A-262, Bend, OR 97701, 541/383-4000.

❸ PAULINA LAKESHORE LOOP
7.0 mi/3.5 hrs

between Bend and La Pine in Newberry Crater National Monument

Map 6.1, page 216

Paulina Lake sits in Newberry Crater, which was created by a series of eruptions over a half-million year span. It's connected by an obsidian flow with sister lake East Lake, but bigger and grander Paulina hogs all the attention. Underground springs and snowmelt feed the lake, which can reach 250 feet in depth. Exploring the seven-mile rim of the lake, you'll come across lava, hidden beaches, hot springs, developed campgrounds, and even an old hand pump in Little Crater Campground that used to churn out 97-degree water (check out campsite 49 to see it). Nearby Paulina Peak looks out over the proceedings from its 7,985-foot summit.

User groups: Hikers and dogs. No horses or mountain bikes allowed. No wheelchair access.

Permits: A federal Northwest Forest pass is required to park here. The cost is $5 for a day pass or $30 for an annual pass. You can buy a day pass at the trailhead, at ranger stations, from private vendors, or through Nature of the Northwest Information Center.

Maps: For a map of Deschutes National Forest, contact Nature of the Northwest Information Center. For a topographic map, ask the USGS for Paulina Peak and East Lake.

Directions: From Bend, drive 22 miles south on U.S. 97 to Forest Service Road 21, about seven miles north of La Pine. Turn left and drive 12 miles to park at Paulina Lake Lodge. The trail is also accessible at Little Crater Campground on the south side of the park.

Contact: Deschutes National Forest, Bend-Fort Rock Ranger District, 1230 Northeast 3rd Street, Suite A-262, Bend, OR 97701, 541/383-4000.

❹ PAULINA CREEK/PAULINA FALLS
6 mi/3.0 hrs

between Bend and La Pine in Newberry Crater National Monument

Map 6.1, page 216

Are you an uphill or a downhill person? If you like a longer hike and don't mind a 2,000-foot gentle ascent, try the Peter Skene Ogden trailhead. Traveling along Paulina Creek, the trail hits several waterfalls along the way, but you'll have to walk nearly the whole distance to get to the big enchilada itself, the twin Paulina Falls. A better way to see the sights is to start from Paulina Lake Lodge, where you'll hit the falls after just .25 mile and continue another three miles along Paulina Creek to another falls, turning around for a six-mile round-trip. While you're there, explore Paulina Lake, Paulina Peak, and the Obsidian Flow (see listings in this chapter).

User groups: Hikers, dogs, and horses. Mountain bikes are allowed only on the uphill portion of the trail. No wheelchair access.

Permits: A federal Northwest Forest pass is required to park here. The cost is $5 for a day pass or $30 for an annual pass. You can buy a day pass at the trailhead, at ranger stations, from private vendors, or through Nature of the Northwest Information Center.

Maps: For a map of Deschutes National Forest, contact Nature of the Northwest Information Center. For a topographic map, ask the USGS for Finley Butte and Paulina Peak.

Directions: To the Peter Ogden trailhead: From Bend, drive 22 miles south on U.S. 97 to Forest Service Road 21, about seven miles north of La Pine. Turn left at the sign for Ogden Group Camp to the large parking area and the well-marked trailhead. To the Paulina Falls trailhead: From Bend, drive 22 miles south on U.S. 97 to Forest Service Road 21, about seven miles north of La Pine. Turn left and drive 12 miles, turning left to the Paulina Creek Falls picnic area, the parking area, and the well-marked trailhead.

Contact: Deschutes National Forest, Bend-Fort Rock Ranger District, 1230 Northeast 3rd Street, Suite A-262, Bend, OR 97701, 541/383-4000.

⑤ BIG OBSIDIAN FLOW TRAIL
0.8 mi/0.5 hr

between Bend and La Pine in Newberry
Crater National Monument

Map 6.1, page 216

It may be the youngest lava flow in Oregon, at a spring-chicken age of 1,300 years, but don't underestimate the power of the Obsidian Flow: Surgical knives made from obsidian are sharper than steel. An interpretive trail with eight signs point out the sights on this magical area, where the black-glass flow extends for 170 million cubic yards, enough rock to pave roads that circle the globe three times. The trail is close to the other Newberry Crater and Paulina Lake hikes, so you can use this as a worthwhile warm-up.

User groups: Hikers and dogs. Mountain bikes and horses are not allowed. No wheelchair access.

Permits: A federal Northwest Forest pass is required to park here. The cost is $5 for a day pass or $30 for an annual pass. You can buy a day pass at the trailhead, at ranger stations, from private vendors, or through Nature of the Northwest Information Center.

Maps: For a map of Deschutes National Forest, contact Nature of the Northwest Information Center. For a topographic map, ask the USGS for East Lake.

Directions: From Bend, drive 22 miles south on U.S. 97 to Forest Service Road 21, about seven miles north of La Pine. Turn left and drive 12 miles, past Paulina Lake Lodge to the south side of the lake. The trailhead and parking are on the right side of the road between Paulina and East Lakes.

Contact: Deschutes National Forest, Bend-Fort Rock Ranger District, 1230 Northeast 3rd Street, Suite A-262, Bend, OR 97701, 541/383-4000.

⑥ PAULINA PEAK
4.2 mi/2.5 hrs

between Bend and La Pine in Newberry
Crater National Monument

Map 6.1, page 216

The 7,985-foot summit of Paulina Peak (pro-

nounced paul-EYE-nah) is the highest point on Newberry Volcano, and you'll feel every step. It's an unrelenting two-mile climb to the summit (elevation gain is 1,500 feet), where on a clear day you can bear witness to more than eight peaks in three states—Mount Adams in Washington and Mount Shasta in California, along with the neighboring Cascade peaks. And since you'll be chugging water all the way up the steep ascent (or at least you should be), you'll be pleased to note there's a handy toilet up top, rumored to be the highest public toilet in Oregon. How's that for a claim to fame? It's because you can drive to the top, which means after all your effort, you'll arrive to find camera-toting visitors fresh from their cars. The trail also arrives at a junction with Crater Rim Trail, so you can extend your hike if you like. Best to start with the peak first to see if your legs can handle any more miles, though, because although it's not a long climb, it's tough.

User groups: Hikers, dogs, and horses. No mountain bikes allowed. No wheelchair access.

Permits: A federal Northwest Forest pass is required to park here. The cost is $5 for a day pass or $30 for an annual pass. You can buy a day pass at the trailhead, at ranger stations, from private vendors, or through Nature of the Northwest Information Center.

Maps: For a map of Deschutes National Forest, contact Nature of the Northwest Information Center. For a topographic map, ask the USGS for Paulina Peak.

Directions: From Bend, drive 22 miles south on U.S. 97 to Forest Service Road 21, about seven miles north of La Pine. Turn left and drive 12 miles to Paulina Lake Lodge. Follow signs to the Paulina Lake campground, and turn right on the gravel road. Continue .2 mile to the gravel turnout on the left side of road.

Contact: Deschutes National Forest, Bend-Fort Rock Ranger District, 1230 Northeast 3rd Street, Suite A-262, Bend, OR 97701, 541/383-4000.

7 CRAFT CABIN
15.2 mi/7.0 hrs

northeast of Burns in Malheur National Forest

Map 6.2, page 217

This trail wins the prize for the most mystifying name: No cabin is on this trail, although supposedly there used to be long ago. Craft Point is nearby, but you don't actually reach it. But hey, it's all just semantics, right? No matter its name, this is a pleasant creekside trail that everyone can enjoy—horses, mountain bikers, hikers, dogs, even cows. Especially cows, come to think of it. You'll most likely encounter plenty of these four-legged friends, or at least see evidence of them (watch your step!). Following Pine Creek, a slow-moving mere ribbon of water at the start of the trail, which widens out eventually, this is a peaceful stroll through steep canyon terrain. You'll have to cross the stream a couple times, but there are handy stepping stones to guide you. Now if only they could do something about the name. . . .

User groups: Hikers, dogs, mountain bikes, and horses. No wheelchair access.

Permits: Permits are not required. Parking and access are free.

Maps: For a map of Malheur National Forest, contact Nature of the Northwest Information Center. For a topographic map, ask the USGS for Craft Point.

Directions: From Burns, drive 12.3 miles east on U.S. 20 and turn left (north) onto Rattlesnake Road, which turns into Forest Service Road 28. Drive 12.1 miles and turn right onto Forest Service Road 2850. Travel 2.2 miles and turn right on Forest Service Road 2855. Drive 2.2 miles and turn left at a fork, drive another .9 mile, then turn right on Forest Service Road 125 for 1.1 miles to the end of the road and the trailhead parking area.

Contact: Malheur National Forest, Emigrant Creek Ranger District, 265 Highway 20 South, Hines, OR 97738, 541/573-4300.

8 FREMONT TRAIL TO HAGER MOUNTAIN
8.0 mi/4.0 hrs
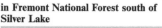

in Fremont National Forest south of Silver Lake

map 6.3, page 218

If you like to take pictures of majestic peaks to say, "Hey, I climbed that," you'll like this trail, because there are plenty of viewpoints of this lonesome lookout (which is available for rental). You'll start off in a dense forest for four miles up to the peak. It's a desolate area, so you're likely to have it to yourself, but don't be surprised if you have some company after hoofing it to the 7,200-foot summit, because visitors can also drive straight to the top. The pleasant, well-marked trail starts off flat to warm you up for the climb ahead. Once on top, you'll have views of the High Desert Country, the Cascades, and Mount Shasta.

User groups: Hikers, dogs, mountain bikes, and horses. No wheelchair access.

Permits: Permits are not required. Parking and access are free.

Maps: For a map of Fremont National Forest, contact Nature of the Northwest Information Center. For a topographic map, ask the USGS for Hager Mountain.

Directions: From La Pine, drive southeast on Highway 31 for 47.5 miles and turn right on East Bay Road/Highway 28. Continue 8.9 miles and turn into a small parking pullout and the trailhead on the left.

Contact: Fremont National Forest, Silver Lake Ranger District, Highway 31, P.O. Box 129, Silver Lake, OR 97638, 541/576-2107.

9 BLUE LAKE
6.0 mi/3.0 hrs

north of Bly in the Gearhart Mountain Wilderness within Fremont National Forest

Map 6.3, page 218

Meandering through the remote Gearhart Wilderness (which sees only about 500 visitors each year, during the summer), this trail travels on Gearhart Mountain Trail for three scenic miles to 7,031-foot Blue Lake. Before hitting the lake, you'll pass through wildflower meadows and forests of lodgepole pine and white fir, with vistas of Gearhart Mountain in the distance. A .5-mile loop surrounds the lake, or you can simply rest here and return the way you came. This trail continues another 10 miles over the Gearhart Mountain summit, and can also be done as a shuttle hike for 13.5 miles total (see Gearhart Mountain listing for directions for shuttle parking).

User groups: Hikers, dogs, and horses. No mountain bikes are allowed. No wheelchair access.

Permits: Permits are not required. Parking and access are free.

Maps: For a map of Fremont National Forest, contact Nature of the Northwest Information Center. For a topographic map, ask the USGS for Lee Thomas Crossing.

Directions: From Bly, drive 1.2 miles east on Highway 140 and turn left on Campbell Road. Go .4 mile and turn right onto paved Forest Service Road 34. Drive 18.9 miles and turn left onto gravel Forest Service Road 3372. Drive 8.2 miles and turn left onto gravel Forest Service Road 015, and continue 1.2 miles to the road's end and the trailhead.

Contact: Fremont National Forest, Bly Ranger District, Highway 140, P.O. Box 25, Bly, OR 97622, 541/353-2427.

🔟 DEMING CREEK TO BOULDER SPRINGS
13.5 mi/7.0 hrs
north of Bly in the Gearhart Mountain Wilderness within Fremont National Forest

Map 6.3, page 218

It used to be a whole lot easier to access this part of the Gearhart Wilderness, but the bulltrout in Deming Creek didn't care for the old access road—apparently, the silt erosion was threatening their precious little gills. "Let them walk, that's what they have feet for!" sniffed the head bulltrout, and the Forest Service heeded the advice: In 1999, the old access road to

this trail was done away with, lengthening the trail by six miles. Today, trout and trekkers happily exist side by side. Well, not exactly side by side, because while you can hear the creek while you walk, it's a tease on a hot day, because you never really come up to it. Instead, it ventures along a wide trail at first, with views of Gearhart Mountain, before climbing steadily (total elevation gain is 2,500 feet), entering 3.2 miles later into the Gearhart Wilderness. You'll pass through wildflower-dotted Boulder Meadow and pass Boulder Creek before the trail ends at the junction with Gearhart Trail. Look out for wildlife like cougars and deer.

User groups: Hikers, dogs, and horses. No mountain bikes are allowed. No wheelchair access.

Permits: Permits are not required. Parking and access are free.

Maps: For a map of the Fremont National Forest, contact Nature of the Northwest Information Center. For a topographic map, ask the USGS for Campbell Reservoir and Gearhart Mountain.

Directions: From Bly, drive 1.2 miles east on Highway 140 and turn left on Campbell Road. Drive .4 mile and turn right onto paved Forest Service Road 34. Continue 3.9 miles and turn left onto dirt Forest Service Road 335. Go 1.3 miles and turn right onto dirt Forest Service Road 018. Continue 2.8 miles to the end of the road and the trailhead straight ahead as you drive in.

Contact: Fremont National Forest, Bly Ranger District, Highway 140, P.O. Box 25, Bly, OR 97622, 541/353-2427.

🔢 GEARHART MOUNTAIN
12.0 mi/7.0 hrs
north of Bly in the Gearhart Mountain Wilderness within Fremont National Forest

Map 6.3, page 218

The word "remote" was created in the 22,823-acre Gearhart Wilderness. There are only two trails (which are categorized as three hikes in this book) that slice through this area, and there's plenty to witness along the way. Have a hankering for some rocks? Check it out: Only .75 mile in from the trailhead, you'll come across the Palisades, a 10-acre display of interesting rock formations and walls. Continue on a couple miles to witness the Dome, a 300-foot bare rock plunked down in the middle of the forest. Then climb farther to amazing views and The Notch, a ridgeline pass of the 8,120-foot Gearhart Mountain summit. The trail continues from here for seven more miles, passing Blue Lake along the way (see Blue Lake listing for trailhead access if you want to arrange a shuttle hike). You can either camp there for the night (adding another eight miles total to your journey) or return once you reach the summit for a 12-mile round-trip day hike.

User groups: Hikers, dogs, and horses. No mountain bikes are allowed. No wheelchair access.

Permits: Permits are not required. Parking and access are free.

Maps: For a map of Fremont National Forest, contact Nature of the Northwest Information Center. For a topographic map, ask the USGS for Gearhart Mountain.

Directions: From Bly, drive 1.2 miles east on Highway 140 and turn left on Campbell Road. Go .4 mile and turn right onto paved Forest Service Road 34. Drive 14.7 miles and turn left onto Forest Service Road 34-012 (a rocky road) for 1.4 miles to the road's end, past the Corral Creek Campground. Trailhead is to the left beside the welcome sign. (Note: The trailhead on the Forest Service map is referred to as the Lookout Rock Trailhead, although the trail itself is named Gearhart Mountain Trail. Don't ask.)

Contact: Fremont National Forest, Bly Ranger District, Highway 140, P.O. Box 25, Bly, OR 97622, 541/353-2427.

12 CRANE MOUNTAIN
16.0 mi/1.0 day

east of Lakeview in Fremont National Forest

Map 6.3, page 218

Jeep owners, this one is calling your name. If you don't mind a bumpy ride to the trail, you can drive directly to the top of Crane Mountain without passing Go, and start from the summit itself. (Those of us who prefer to pass on having our brains jangled around in our heads while driving would be wise to walk the final two miles up the road to reach the summit and trailhead.) Whether you arrive by wheel or foot, you're definitely in for a great view: Crane Mountain stands at 8,357 feet, and from here hikers can take a peek into California and the surrounding vistas and peaks. Crane Mountain National Recreation Trail is actually 36 miles in length total, and from this trailhead it travels eight miles to the California border, so it's up to you and how much muscle power you have in your legs. One option is simply to hike up to the actual trailhead (if you're one of the aforementioned non-four-wheel drivers), take in the view, and head back down to your car, because the actual beauty of it is the summit itself. Another option is to access the trail at Rogger Meadow trailhead, which reaches Crane Mountain in eight miles for a 16-mile round-trip (see driving directions below). Whatever your pleasure, you're guaranteed some solitude and scenery. Since it starts at such high elevation, the trail can be snowbound through July.

User groups: Hikers, dogs, mountain bikes, and horses. No wheelchair access.

Permits: Permits are not required. Parking and access are free.

Maps: For a map of the Fremont National Forest, contact Nature of the Northwest Information Center. For a topographic map, ask the USGS for Crane Mountain.

Directions: From Lakeview, drive 4.6 miles north on U.S. 395 to Highway 140. Turn right (east) onto Highway 140 and drive 8.1 miles to Warner Road/Forest Service Road 3915.

Turn right and drive 12.2 miles (first 6.7 miles are paved, then it turns to gravel) to Forest Service Road 4011. Turn right and go 3.6 miles to the end of 4011. The road now turns into Forest Service Road 015 for 2.5 bumpy miles, so park at the side of the road and walk up here if you wish. To get to Rogger Meadow trailhead, follow directions above to get to Forest Service Road 3915, then drive 5.6 miles on 3915; the trailhead and parking area are on your right.

Contact: Fremont National Forest, Lakeview Ranger District, HC-64, Box 60, Lakeview, OR 97630, 541/947-3334.

13 WILDHORSE LAKE
3.0 mi/2.0 hrs

southeast of Burns in the Steens Mountain Wilderness area

Map 6.4, page 219

You don't even need to get out of your car to witness the beauty of 9,700-foot Steens Mountain, because the long and winding road up the mountain gives you glimpses into the deep gorges and desert below. But you'll definitely want to hop out and see Wildhorse Lake, perched 1,000 feet below the summit. It's a steep and rocky descent to this alpine lake, but it's well worth the trip, as it sits surrounded by wildflowers, with a view of the summit. Steens Mountain paintbrush and thistle are loyal little plants, and they choose to reside only on this mountain. Animals also love to roam this vast expanse, including deer, elk, and bighorn sheep. As you drive up Steens Mountain Loop Road, viewpoints beckon you to hop out to snap a shot or two, such as Kiger Gorge viewpoint, East Rim viewpoint, and the summit itself (which you can climb .5 mile to). Remember, you're already starting at 9,500 feet of elevation, so don't be surprised if you feel like you're moving in slow motion—it's better that way anyway, because then you have more time to take in the views. The best time of year to visit is late July and on, because it's usually snowbound before then; check ahead on road conditions. Also, even if it's a warm day, it can get chilly here, so bring warm clothes.

User groups: Hikers and dogs. No mountain bikes or horses are allowed. No wheelchair access.

Permits: Permits are not required. Parking and access are free.

Maps: For a map of Steens Mountain, contact Bureau of Land Management, Burns District Office, 541/573-4400. For a topographic map, ask the USGS for Wildhorse Lake.

Directions: From Frenchglen (60 miles south of Burns on Highway 205), drive east on gravel Steens Mountain Loop Road. Drive 2.9 miles to a T-intersection, and turn left. Keep right at all junctions, and continue 24.2 miles to the end of the road and the trailhead. Park at the side of the road.

Contact: Bureau of Land Management, Burns District Office, 28910 Highway 20 West, Hines, OR 97738, 541/573-4400.

© MEGAN McMORRIS

Resources

Resource Guide

National and State Forests

Deschutes National Forest, Bend-Fort Rock
Ranger District
1230 Northeast 3rd Street, Suite A-262
Bend, OR 97701
541/383-4000

Deschutes National Forest, Crescent
Ranger District
136471 Highway 97 North
P.O. Box 208
Crescent, OR 97733
541/433-3200

Deschutes National Forest, Sisters
Ranger District
Highway 20/Pine Street
P.O. Box 249
Sisters, OR 97759
541/549-7700

Fremont National Forest, Bly
Ranger District
Highway 140
P.O. Box 25
Bly, OR 97622
541/353-2427

Fremont National Forest, Lakeview
Ranger District
HC-64
Box 60
Lakeview, OR 97630
541/947-3334

Fremont National Forest, Silver Lake
Ranger District
Highway 31
P.O. Box 129
Silver Lake, OR 97638
541/576-2107

Malheur National Forest, Blue Mountain
Ranger District
431 Patterson Bridge Road
P.O. Box 909
John Day, OR 97845
541/575-3000

Malheur National Forest, Emigrant Creek
Ranger District
265 Highway 20 South
Hines, OR 97738
541/573-4300

Malheur National Forest, Prairie City
Ranger District
P.O. Box 337
Prairie City, OR 97869
541/820-3311

Mount Hood National Forest
Information Center
65000 East Highway 26
Welches, OR 97067
503/622-7674

Mount Hood National Forest, Barlow
Ranger District
Dufur Ranger Station
780 Northeast Court Street
Dufur, OR 97021
541/467-2291

Mount Hood National Forest, Clackamas
River Ranger District
Estacada Ranger Station
595 Northwest Industrial Way
Estacada, OR 97023
503/630-6861

**Mount Hood National Forest, Hood River
Ranger District**
6780 Highway 35
Mount Hood-Parkdale, OR 97041
541/352-6002

**Mount Hood National Forest, Zigzag
Ranger District**
70220 East Highway 26
Zigzag, OR 97049
503/622-3191

**Ochoco National Forest, Lookout Mountain
Ranger District**
P.O. Box 490
Prineville, OR 97754
541/416-6500

**Ochoco National Forest, Paulina
Ranger District**
7803 Beaver Creek Road
Paulina, OR 97751
541/477-6900

Oregon Dunes National Recreation Area
855 Highway 101
Reedsport, OR 97467
541/271-3611

**Rogue River National Forest, Applegate
Ranger District**
6941 Upper Applegate Road
Jacksonville, OR 97530
541/899-3800

**Rogue River National Forest, Ashland
Ranger District**
645 Washington Street
Ashland, OR 97520
541/552-2900

**Rogue River National Forest, Prospect
Ranger District**
47201 Highway 62
Prospect, OR 97536
541/560-3400

**Siskiyou National Forest, Chetco
Ranger District**
P.O. Box 4580
539 Chetco Avenue
Brookings, OR 97415
541/412-6000

**Siskiyou National Forest, Galice
Ranger District**
200 Northeast Greenfield Road
P.O. Box 440
Grants Pass, OR 97526
541/471-6500

**Siskiyou National Forest, Illinois Valley
Ranger District**
26568 Redwood Highway
Cave Junction, OR 97523
541/592-2166

**Siskiyou National Forest, Powers
Ranger District**
42861 Highway 242
Powers, OR 97466
541/439-3011

**Siuslaw National Forest, Hebo
Ranger District**
31525 Highway 22
Hebo, OR 97122
503/392-3161

**Siuslaw National Forest, Mapleton
Ranger District**
4480 Highway 101, Building G
Florence, OR 97439
541/902-8526

**Siuslaw National Forest, Waldport
Ranger District**
1094 Southwest Pacific Highway
Waldport, OR 97394
541/563-3211

Tillamook State Forest, Forest Grove
  District Office
801 Gales Creek Road
Forest Grove, OR 97116
503/357-2191

Umatilla National Forest, Heppner
  Ranger District
P.O. Box 7
Heppner, OR 97836
541/676-9187

Umatilla National Forest, North Fork John
  Day Ranger District
P.O. Box 158
Ukiah, OR 97880
541/427-3231

Umatilla National Forest, Walla Walla
  Ranger District
1415 West Rose Street
Walla Walla, WA 99362
509/522-6290

Umpqua National Forest, Cottage Grove
  Ranger District
78405 Cedar Parks Road
Cottage Grove, OR 97424
541/942-5591

Wallowa Mountains Visitor Center, Eagle
  Cap Ranger District
88401 Highway 82
Enterprise, OR 97828
541/426-5546

Wallowa-Whitman National Forest, Baker
  City Ranger District
3165 10th Street
Baker City, OR 97814
541/523-4476

Wallowa-Whitman National Forest, Wallowa
  Valley Ranger District
88401 Highway 82
Enterprise, OR 97828
541/426-4978

Willamette National Forest, Detroit
  Ranger District
HC 73
Mill City, OR 97360
503/854-3366

Willamette National Forest, McKenzie River
  Ranger District
57600 McKenzie Highway
McKenzie Bridge, OR 97413
541/822-3381

Willamette National Forest, Middle Fork
  Ranger District
Lowell Office
60 South Pioneer Street
Lowell, OR 97452
541/937-2129

Willamette National Forest, Sweet Home
  Ranger District
3225 Highway 20
Sweet Home, OR 97386
541/367-5168

Winema National Forest, Klamath
  Ranger District
1936 California Avenue
Klamath Falls, OR 97601
541/885-3400

Parks, Recreation Areas, and Other Resources

Bend Metro Park and Recreation Department
200 Northwest Pacific Park Lane
Bend, OR 97701
541/389-7275

Bureau of Land Management, Burns
  District Office
28910 Highway 20 West
Hines, OR 97738
541/573-4400

Bureau of Land Management, Salem
  District Office
1717 Fabry Road Southeast
Salem, OR 97306
503/375-5646

Bureau of Land Management, Medford
  District Office
3040 Biddle Road
Medford, OR 97504
541/618-2200

City of Eugene Parks and Open Space
Recreation Services Division
99 West 10th Avenue, Suite 340
Eugene, OR 97401
541/682-5333

Columbia River Gorge National Scenic Area
902 Wasco Avenue, Suite 200
Hood River, OR 97031
541/386-2333

Crater Lake National Park
P.O. Box 7
Crater Lake, OR 97604
541/594-3100

Hells Canyon National Recreation Center
88401 Highway 82
Enterprise, OR 97828
541/426-5546

John Day Fossil Beds National Monument
32651 Highway 19
Kimberly, OR 97848
541/987-2333

Lane County Parks Division,
  Armitage Park
90064 Coburg Road
Eugene, OR 97408
541/682-2000

National Historic Oregon Trail
  Interpretive Center
22267 Oregon Highway 86
P.O. Box 987
Baker City, OR 97814
541/523-1843

The Nature Conservancy of Oregon
821 Southeast 14th Avenue
Portland, OR 97214
503/230-1221

Nature of the Northwest Information Center
800 Northeast Oregon Street, Suite 177
Portland, OR 97232
800/270-7504 for Northwest Forest permits
503/872-2750 for maps and other products
www.naturenw.org

Oregon Caves National Monument
19000 Caves Highway
Cave Junction, OR 97523
541/592-2100

Oregon Parks and Recreation Department
1115 Commercial Street Northeast
Salem, OR 97301
800/551-6949
www.oregonstateparks.org

Oregon State University, College of Forestry
8692 Peavy Auditorium Road
Corvallis, OR 97330
www.cof.orts.edu

Tryon Creek State Natural Area
11321 Southwest Terwilliger Boulevard
Portland, OR 97219
503/636-9886

Portland Parks and Recreation
1120 Southwest 5th Avenue, Suite 1302
Portland, OR 97204
503/823-PLAY (503/823-7529)

Map Resources

Green Trails, Inc.
P.O. Box 77734
Seattle, WA 98177
206/546-MAPS (206/546-6277)
www.greentrails.com

USGS
Oregon Office
10615 Southeast Cherry Blossom Drive
Portland, OR 97216
503/251-3200
www.usgs.gov

Nature of the Northwest Information Center
800 Northeast Oregon Street, Suite 177
Portland, OR 97232
503/872-2750 (800/270-7504 for Northwest
    Forest permits only)
www.naturenw.org

Hiking Clubs and Groups

Chemeketans Outdoor Club
www.chemeketans.org

Oregon Trails Club
www.trailsclub.org

Mazamas
909 Northwest 19th Avenue
Portland, OR 97209
503/227-2345
www.mazamas.org

Acknowledgments

Who's kidding who here. You think I did all this myself? Not by a long shot. While I was zipping across the state, others were right there with me, researching trails, giving their two-cents' worth, and adding valuable details. Here's a shout out to everyone who helped and supported me throughout this entire project.

First and foremost, I want to thank Kevin Foreman. Your extensive research helped me add in some cool "insider" tips and scope out the best routes. Your love of researching fun facts on the Internet helped me fill in tidbits. Your cool ideas and our brainstorming summits rounded out the book. And that's only the half of it. Reminding me to fill my car's tires, searching for me in the middle of the night when there was a "miscommunication" about when I was supposed to arrive home (oops!), and showing me how to use your camp stove so it wouldn't blow up kept me safe. Finally, your endless patience and support (not to mention the endless trips to the store for Pepsi One and chocolate!) toward the end of this project—when I suddenly turned into an unrecognizable, mumbling form of myself—kept me sane. Thanks for everything.

Secondly, a hearty high-five to my research team: Kevin "DJ Master Flash Kevie Kev" Dickson and Anne Marie "Queen o' Puns" Moss. Dudes, thanks for your enthusiasm, time, and efforts. Kevin, thanks in particular for becoming the proud owner of Roxie the Jeep, who tirelessly went on back roads through Mount Hood and Umatilla National Forest. One would think that after you got Roxie stuck in the mud, encountered rattlesnakes, searched endlessly for nonexistent trails, and got hopelessly lost, you would have called it quits. But thanks to your insane love of adventure, you were always ready for more—with humor. Thanks to both of you for taking this project and running with it, for your adventurous spirits, and most of all, for never failing to make me double over with laughter.

Also, thanks to my mom, Penny, for keeping me fed with homemade trail mix (and tuna wraps as we drove!) and entertained with talking books, and for braving the elements with me on two weekend hiking trips. I'm officially on a first-name basis with the UPS man because of your many care packages! And to my dad, Fred, thanks for keeping me safe and oriented on the road with your many gifts of Sue the trusty Subaru, maps, and emergency kits (and don't worry, I do have health insurance). Let the Amazon.com wars begin with the McMorris books!

To the countless forest and park service workers and others I met with, called, and emailed, thanks for filling in details and encouraging my many questions without making me feel like a pest. A special nod to wilderness whiz Rene Casteran, of the Chetco Ranger District of the Siskiyou National Forest, for your thorough details on trails in the Kalmiopsis Wilderness. Also thanks to friends Jacki, Ryan, and Heather for personal insights and tips on several trails.

Thanks to my sister Erin and my McBuddies Diane, Heather, and Andy for their support and understanding that I was going to cancel trips and not return emails or phone calls for a while, and for still being on a speaking basis with me when all was said and done.

Of course, thanks to Avalon Travel Publishing for their already stellar Foghorn Outdoors series and for letting me come on board; thanks especially to my ever-enthusiastic editor, Marisa Solís.

Last but certainly not least, thanks to my Hiking Paw-Dah in Crime, Corvus the Dog. Corvie, what can I say? You were always eager to go every weekend, never complained when the drive was bumpy or when we got lost, and painstakingly researched interesting wildlife and plants along the trail. You kept me safe from a bear, let me use your moonlit white tail as a beacon when we got stuck in the dark, kept an ear open for strange sounds outside our tent, and most of all just kept me sane with your sweet company. This one is for you, little buddy.

Index

About the Author

© KEVIN FOREMAN

On a postcollege road trip in 1992, Ohio native **Megan McMorris** and her childhood buddy, Andy, fell in love with Oregon, prompting them to write a "cool things about Oregon" list as they drove along U.S. 101. (Included on the list: friendly, waving highway workers and Portland businessmen in suits who play Hacky Sack on their lunch breaks.) But alas, the real world beckoned: The Indiana University graduate's goal of becoming a freelance magazine writer led her to New York City instead. She spent eight years in cramped cubicles writing about the outdoors (most recently as the outdoors editor at *Fitness* magazine) before finally moving to Portland to write full time. Having run 11 marathons, she decided to enter an orienteering race shortly after moving to her new state, where she quickly learned that she was somewhat navigationally challenged. Nonetheless, she swapped her road-running shoes for trail shoes and has never looked back. Now she lives and works in a barn in Hood River and a loft in Portland where she hikes, runs, mountain bikes, snowboards, and snowshoes, followed by a cold pint or two of the local microbrew.

While covering every inch of Oregon to research this book, Megan and her husky dog, Corvus, got a crash course on the outdoors—including hail, rain, snow, lightning, a bear sighting, and plenty of off-road car adventures—and she has proudly emerged unscathed as an expert on the trails; how to drive on bumpy, snowy Forest Service roads without getting stuck; how to set up a tent in two minutes flat; and yes, even navigation. Her articles have appeared in *Fitness, Self, Shape, Sports Illustrated Women, Parents, Glamour, Marie Claire, Adventure Sports,* and *Hooked on the Outdoors,* among others.

Notes

Notes

Notes

Notes

Notes

Notes

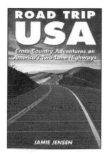